Mennonites in Canada, 1786-1920

Mennonites in Canada, 1786-1920

The History of a Separate People

Frank H. Epp

Illustrations by Douglas Ratchford

Macmillan of Canada
Toronto

Library of Congress Catalogue Card No. 74-10297
ISBN 0-7705-1229-1

The publishers gratefully acknowledge the assistance of Mennonite Central Committee (Canada) and the Joint Committee of Mennonite Historical Societies in making the publication possible.

Printed in Canada for
The Macmillan Company of Canada Limited

Reprinted 1975

Contents

v

List of Illustrations

List of Maps and Charts

ix

List of Tables

Table

Author's Acknowledgements

MENNONITES IN CANADA became possible through the efforts of several agencies and many people. The research and writing was sponsored by the Joint Committee of provincial Mennonite historical societies. The Joint Committee in turn was assisted by various other Mennonite agencies and individuals. Generous grants from the Canada Council facilitated the completion of this work. The source materials provided by various libraries and archives (see list in the bibliography) were indispensable to this undertaking.

Among those to whom I would like to give special recognition are the following: my wife Helen, research assistant and stenographer since *Mennonite Exodus*; she gave painstaking attention to every detail of the manuscript; our daughters Marianne, Esther and Marlene, who were part of the research team for several summers; various other research assistants, especially Edward Dahl, Ernie Dick, Adolf and Anna Ens, Bob and Linda Janzen, William Janzen, and Ernie Regehr; the officers of the Joint Committee—J. Winfield Fretz, chairman; T. E. Friesen, secretary;

Herbert Enns and Alson Weber, treasurers; John W. Snyder, business agent; others who carried Committee responsibilities during all or part of the period — Lorna Bergey, Henry Dueck, Gerhard Ens, Henry H. Epp, Orland Gingerich, Newton Gingrich, Wilson Hunsberger, Gerhard Lohrenz, Vernon Ratzlaff, P. J. B. Reimer, Gerald Schwartzentruber, Don Snyder and A. P. Unger; in addition to the above Committee members a group of advisors and readers including Eddie Bearinger, Richard Coryer, Leo Driedger, Virgil Duff, Leonard Freeman, Walter Klaassen, Lawrence Klippenstein, Harry Loewen, Noah Martin, T. D. Regehr, Rodney Sawatzky and J. A. Toews. Last but not least I must recognize A. E. Hildebrand, cartographer, and Douglas Ratchford, artist. W. Rempel and A. G. Janzen helped with the mapping of the Saskatchewan reserves. Maps of the Manitoba reserves are based on E. K. Francis.

To all who were partners in this production, I express my deepest gratitude. However, the responsibility for the form and content of this history is mine alone.

Frank H. Epp
Conrad Grebel College
University of Waterloo
Ontario, Canada
July 1, 1974

Foreword

CANADIAN IMMIGRANTS were seldom a very fashionable-looking crowd. On arrival in their country of adoption peoples in search of better economic opportunities or refugees from political, religious, or social harassment often appeared as less than desirable citizens. If the new arrivals had obvious peculiarities or idiosyncrasies their arrival could lead to protests and deputations urging their immediate return to the country of origin. They were, at least initially, a separate people in a new country.

Some immigrants tried hard to fit themselves into the Canadian style of life. They learned the language and imitated the habits and culture of their adopted country as quickly as possible. Others came because they wanted to preserve a distinctive way of life, and saw the isolation of the rural Canadian frontier as an ideal setting in which to do this. If such people were prepared to render important pioneering work on the unsettled and underdeveloped agricultural frontiers of British North America most Canadians and their governments were happy to see them come and quite willing to tolerate a harmless, if sometimes rather peculiar, way of life.

Among the many somewhat strange and separate immigrants who came to Canada there were many Mennonites. They were descendants of a radical wing of the reformation, believing in the complete separation of church and state, and in the heinousness of all war, killing, and any other actions not based on an ethic of love and respect for human life. Bitter persecution had also taught them the value of a simplistic, unobtrusive, abstemious, and often prosperous way of life, separated and isolated as much as possible from modern secular society.

The historical roots of these people lay in Europe. Their experiences and the insights and habits of life derived from those experiences conditioned and influenced their response to the Canadian frontier experience. A history of the Mennonites in Canada must therefore begin with an identification and explanation of the European background of these people. The attempt to create a separate community and way of life has been identified by the author of this book as one of the dominant themes in that background, and also in the Canadian Mennonite experience.

A separate life style is not easy to maintain. It is constantly threatened by a wide range of assimilationist pressures from the larger surrounding society, and undermined by internal pressures and fragmentation. For the Mennonite people very serious internal difficulties often developed as the basic purposes of their separatist aspirations were questioned from within and without. The founders of the movement had generally been motivated by radical and reformist attitudes, and these attitudes and insights gave the movement much of its vitality. Yet later generations often fastened on very specific forms and details of the early movement and insisted that these be preserved as an integral part of a distinctive Mennonite way of life. The result was severe internal fragmentation as disputes raged between those intent on preserving the forms of a tradition which had been radical centuries earlier, and those who demanded a continuing radicalism and reform. These disputes tended to drive some factions further into isolation, while others succumbed to assimilation.

The continuing attempts of many Mennonites to maintain a separate identity and, to a lesser extent, a separate way of life have much in common with the experiences of other Canadian minority groups. Despite the problems of external assimilationist pressures and internal fragmentation, however, there remains a deep conviction that the faith and culture of these various distinctive groups are worthy of preservation in Canada. Recently the Canadian government has established a ministry and a program of multiculturalism. The objective is to encourage Canadians of different ethno-cultural traditions to preserve and share their ancestral heritage for the benefit and enrichment of all. "Canada," according to a recent government announcement, "is a nation of many cultures. Our citizens come from almost every country in the world, bringing with them the cultures of almost every major world civilization. This cultural diversity offers all Canadians a great variety of human experience . . . the opportunity to share other ideas, understand various philosophies, to appreciate new art and literary forms." This book was written with the hope that all interested Canadians might benefit from and be enriched by a better understanding of the Mennonite culture, faith, and history.

For the Mennonite people of Canada this book has additional significance. It marks a departure from the old isolationism and an acceptance of the invitation to share with other Canadians the philosophy and history of Mennonite life in Canada. To many this may appear to be merely a further stage in the process of assimilation. It would be more correct, however, to view this book as a contribution to a true Canadian multiculturalism and a true religious pluralism.

The book also marks a significant advance in inter-Mennonite cooperation and understanding. It was written in part to commemorate the 450th anniversary of the movement itself, the approaching bicentennial of the arrival of Mennonite pioneers in Ontario, the sesquicentennial of the coming of the Amish, the centennial of the first immigration from Russia, and the 50th and 25th anniversaries of the other two major migrations of Mennonites from Europe to Canada. It tells the story of all the Canadian Mennonites and has received broad support from most of various Mennonite groups. It draws together the experiences of a people often separated not only from the larger Canadian society, but also from one another. It is not, however, written from a narrow or parochial point of view. National, provincial, and Mennonite archives have been searched for relevant documentary materials. The objective has been to tell the Canadian Mennonite story accurately, within its European, North American, and Canadian contexts.

This history tells us much about a particular Canadian minority group, defined by religion, and about the place and problems of minorities generally. It also tells us about Canada as a nation in search of its own identity, which it appears is gradually emerging as a tolerant federation of other identities, all in some way unique.

T. D. Regehr
University of Saskatchewan
Saskatoon

Prologue

THIS HISTORY of the Mennonite minority was begun in 1967, the year of the Canadian centennial. It was developed at a time when separatisms of one kind or another were rife, and it was completed just when multiculturalism, as a federal policy, was coming into its own. This was an unusually opportune time to reconstruct the history of a people whose character and experiences had been shaped so much by intolerance, by the crushing of dissent, and by the deliberate attempt of various national societies in which Mennonites found themselves to create cultural homogeneities. It was a time when the thematic framing of this history was helped along by the contemporary language. Concepts like counter-culture, minority groups and separation appeared rather easily in the literature of the day. Thus, without forcing them upon the material, they became readily usable for the shaping of a story which illustrates those ideas over a long period of time.

Mennonitism originated in Europe as an Anabaptist counter-culture, separatist in nature. The religious ideas which sparked it led to an ecclesiastical separation. Like the Protestant Reformation everywhere, the rise of Anabaptism inevitably involved and affected European politics. In the case of the Anabaptists or Mennonites, their separatist, value-oriented theological ideas produced a reaction and backlash so intense that they reaped for themselves not a respectable, ecclesiastically identifiable sector in Europe, as did the Lutherans, but rather a bloody sociological separation in the form of the most bitter persecutions. Heretics they were called, and heretics they were. Their ideas were unconventional and dangerous, not necessarily because they were wrong, but quite possibly because they were right, at least partly so.

The theological separation and the sociological ostracism, involuntary for the most part, were followed in due course by a voluntary geographic isolation and by a rather willing cultural separation. As time went on, the separated Mennonite way of life acquired a separatist psychology as well as separate institutions for its constant undergirding. These in turn required a philosophical justification, which a latter-day theology of withdrawal from the world could provide. Thus the cycle of separation was completed as cause and effect followed each other. An inevitabe by-product of the Mennonite experience was not only a sharp delineation between church and state, between sect and society, but also some equally sharp divisions within Mennonitism itself. These rather frequent internal fragmentations were multiplied by the rather frequent uprootings and migrations.

Yet, somehow a general Mennonite identity evolved and a Mennonite contribution to society was recorded. As so many separate seeds falling into the ground, the separate Mennonite peoples sprouted in the soils of various national societies and produced for those cultures some rather unique additives. In spite of separation, or perhaps because of it, the Mennonites became an unavoidable sector of the multicultural Canadian mosaic and an essential patch in the multi-coloured quilt of the Christian tradition.

The Crushing of Dissent

1. The Most Separated Brethren

Anabaptism was a socio-religious movement that was neither Catholic nor Protestant. It was a Christian movement of the most radical sort in that it questioned virtually all the assumptions upon which sixteenth century society, culture, and church rested—WALTER KLAASSEN[1]

THE MENNONITES, first known as Anabaptists, emerged in history about 450 years ago as the most "separated brethren" of the Protestant Reformation.[2] They were separated not only from the Catholics but also from the Protestants, and sometimes from each other. Most pronounced and problematic of all was their withdrawal from the surrounding society and from the state. The resulting tensions, often persecutions, had the effect of dispersing them over all of Europe and overseas. Eventually they were found in over 40 countries, including Canada, where their number is approaching 175,000.

The origin of the Anabaptists as separatists in the above sense is crucial to the later development of the Mennonites in Canada and to their continuing self-understanding. It becomes necessary, therefore, to travel back into history and to take a closer look at the times in which they arose and the dynamics which gave them their unusual, often paradoxical, character for centuries to come.

Anabaptism was only one of several major and numerous minor fragmentations which characterized the era of reform and

23

counter-reform. In some ways the divisions of sixteenth-century Europe were inevitable. The unity of the Middle Ages was eroding on all fronts. As the new era dawned, it became impossible to hold the united world of the Holy Roman Empire together, though both pope and emperor tried their best. Newness and change were evident everywhere.

The imperial and papal authorities had difficulty understanding the ferment. The unified European world of church, state and society had been developed with great diligence and a deep conviction that this represented an unfolding of the kingdom of God. After all, the holy Roman world had brought the civilizing influence of Christianity to a barbaric Europe and was now protecting that same Europe from a universally feared external invader — the Ottoman Turks. At the beginning of the 1500s the Turks were, so it seemed, threatening the entire continent with an alien culture and imperial domination.

However, for many people there were more immediate concerns; to some the greatest threat to truth and to their welfare and security lay much closer to home. Whatever enemy might be pushing from the East, he could not be as great a problem as Rome itself. It was Rome that was exacting the heavy taxes and tithes which did not bring the promised forgiveness of sins. It was Rome that was drawing young men into mercenary armies from throughout the continent. It was Rome that assigned luxury to some and poverty to others, in the name of religion. And it was Rome that suppressed the truth by persecuting its proponents and by insisting on a single authority — its own. As good as a single kingdom and a unified world might be, this one had not been put together correctly. To the dissenters, the Roman world with its concentration of religious truth, political power and material wealth represented an unacceptable synthesis.

Although the frustrations of Europe were focused in Rome, there was among the dissenters no commonly advocated solution or even a commonly felt motivation. Some people wanted more truth, others more power and still others more wealth; some, as in the case of the peasants, simply wanted less poverty. There was, therefore, no common identification of the total enemy and, consequently, no easy coalition against that single foe. The resulting multitude of responses to the problems of the day produced not so much a shattering reformation as they did a great separation.

For instance, the kings of England rebelled against the papacy. By his Parliament's Act of Supremacy, King Henry VIII was declared to be the Supreme Head of the Church of England. The act was called a religious reformation, but it was little more than an institutional separation. The assumptions underlying the new Church of England varied little, if at all, from those supporting the Church of Rome.

The king of France, on the other hand, could fulfil his ambitions for power without excluding himself from Rome. In 1516 Francis I negotiated the power to appoint his own bishops and abbots, thus freeing France to act separately from Rome without departing from it completely. Spain also benefited from a continuing, more intimate relationship with Rome. In 1519 the link between the Spanish church and crown was made more secure than ever; Charles, the Spanish king whose family was tied to the House of Hapsburg, was elected Emperor. Committed to the Church of Rome, he now served as the secular power of the Holy Roman Empire. Both the secular and the sacred embraced each other in the face of the common enemy, the Ottoman Turks.

The unity, however, could not be complete since various small Germanic entities in central Europe had doubts about both the religion of Rome and the power of the Hapsburgs. Most concerned about the power arrangements were the princes in states such as Saxony, Brandenburg and Bavaria. Sharing their anxieties were the imperial free cities, about 50 of them, all commercial and financial centres beginning to enjoy the gold that was flowing from the new world. There were also the thousands of lesser knights and nobles who controlled small territories and manors, paid taxes, and provided men for the Emperor. Why, they all asked, should so many taxes and so many mercenaries go for the protection of Hapsburg power and Roman institutions?

Even more powerless, however, was the bottom socio-economic layer of society, those hundreds of thousands of peasants whose tears, sweat and blood benefited the noblemen, knights, princes, kings and emperors, as well as the abbots, bishops and popes. A peasants' revolt, sparked in the Black Forest, quickly spread throughout the Holy Roman Empire, only to be extinguished in May of 1525 when the radical leader and priest, Thomas Muentzer, was captured and promptly executed.

The peasants' main grievances were directed at their immediate overlords, whose major complaints in turn were laid before emperor and pope. These, in turn, thought that all of western Europe should unite with them against the Turks. It was a mixed-up situation. The confusion resulting from this manifold struggle for power and wealth was compounded by an equally intense search for truth and by the strange alliances arising from this likewise multi-dimensional encounter.

The new paths to truth had been pioneered by Renaissance philosophers such as Leonardo da Vinci, who found insight and enlightenment, not only in the documents of religion, but also in nature and in the great human classics. For some, these wider sources of reality had a secularizing effect while others became better equipped, thereby, to revitalize religion. Included in this latter category was the foremost representative of the Renaissance in northern Europe, Erasmus of Rotterdam. An ordained priest, Erasmus studied at Oxford and lectured at Cambridge, where he produced a new Greek text of the New Testament. Published in 1516, the new Bible not only showed Christendom some of the fallibilities of the Latin Vulgate Bible, thus undermining traditional authority, but also laid the foundation for Martin Luther's German popularization of the Bible. For this reason it was already said at that time that "Erasmus laid the egg that Luther hatched."

Luther, however, became the leader and central figure of the religious-political revolution which challenged the church of Rome and the authority of its pope, a challenge very much to the liking of rebellious German nobles. In the end he was threatened with excommunication by the Pope and banishment by the Emperor. The elector of Saxony and other north German princes, however, were themselves sufficiently independent by this time to grant protection to Luther. Slowly but surely his movement for religious reform and their political revolt made a common cause. The new alliance went to war against the Emperor and when it ended with the Peace of Augsburg a new principle of religious and political organization had triumphed. "Whose region, his religion" indicated that the princes could decide which religion would dominate in their own areas.

The result was a reorganization of Europe. Lutheranism was the choice of most of the northern German states and of a few in the south. The Baltic states and all of Scandinavia became Lutheran and, like England, integrated church and state. Lutheranism for the princes meant Lutheranism for all their subjects as well, and dissenters often had as little freedom in Lutheran areas as they did in the Catholic states. In both situations, entrance to both church and state was gained by baptism which was required of all newborn babies. In these and other ways the German

Reformation, like the English one, was little more than an institutional division that resulted in political realignment.

Meanwhile, a Swiss contemporary of Martin Luther was attempting a similar reform in cooperation with the civil authorities in Zurich. He was Ulrich Zwingli whose studies in Vienna had introduced him to Erasmus, to his humanism, and to his Greek Testament, of which he became very fond by the time he was appointed priest at the Grossmuenster in Zurich. Like Luther, he preached against the system of indulgences, and clerical celibacy, as well as against mercenary armies which had drawn so many Swiss youths into unwanted wars and early deaths.

The civic leaders of the Canton of Zurich were generally in agreement with reforms proposed to keep men and money at home. They soon persuaded the cantons of Berne, Basel and Constance to join with them in an evangelical federation known as the Christian Civic League. Twice the League went to war against the Catholic regions, and in 1531 Zwingli himself was killed in the decisive battle at Kappel which permanently divided Switzerland into Protestant and Catholic territories.

Thus in Switzerland too there was a separation and, to some degree, a reformation. Zwingli was genuinely interested in a renewed society in which God's word was proclaimed and properly applied. In his scheme, the prophet of God and the magistrate of the city cooperated for the benefit of all. Like other men of the Middle Ages, he thought of society as a single Christian body. In that corpus Christianum the pastor and the magistrate worked together to achieve the rule of God on earth, the civil order being the external framework for the church. Zwingli envisioned a community pervaded by divine teaching which would transform the entire society. The Christian man became a good citizen, and the Christian city was the Christian church.[3]

As time passed, some of Zwingli's own disciples, more radical than himself, had difficulty accepting his approach to reformation, and that difference led to the greatest separation of all. They agreed with him on "the abolition of the mass, the rejection of celibacy, the dissolution of monasteries and convents, and the use of the vernacular instead of the Latin in baptism."[4] On the other hand, they quarrelled with his tolerance of images and pictures. Most of all, however, they challenged the assumptions that an entire community could adequately represent Christianity and that civic authority should be decisive in matters of religion.

The preacher of Grossmuenster looked to his city council as a theological court of appeal. The resolution of differences between himself and the radicals, which he willingly debated in public, was assigned to the council. But the submission of theological and moral issues to civic authorities was precisely what the dissenters were not ready to do. In the words of Simon Stumpf, their spokesman at a public debate in 1523:

> "Master Ulrich, you have no right to refer this question to the Council; the matter is already settled, the Spirit of God has decided."[5]

Zwingli, however, continued to refer matters to the Council, as he proceeded to form a non-Catholic reformed state church in which, as in Lutheranism, the entire society in a given geographic region was enrolled. The dissenters turned elsewhere for their authority and discovered in the New Testament a church different not only from Catholicism, but also from Lutheranism and Zwinglianism.[6] Meeting frequently in private homes for the study of the Bible, they concluded that true reformation could not proceed from the entire society but rather from a dedicated nucleus of true believers who lived their faith. True believers were people who, at a mature age, voluntarily became disciples. They were not those who as infants and without conscious decision were baptized into the church.

The group of dissenters whose Bible studies were resulting in such conclusions was small at first, consisting mostly of ecclesiastics and academics. Debater Stumpf, for instance, was a pastor. Balthasar Hubmaier was a theologian and former university rector and was one of the first to preach against infant baptism. Wilhelm Reublin, the first of the Zurich priests to take a wife, insisted on carrying the Bible in public processions, instead of the relics of the church. A monk, George Blaurock, became known as "Strong George" for the vigour with which he took up the cause of the dissenters. The distinctive blue coat which he insisted on wearing gave him the name of Blaurock. He was not the last of the radicals to insist on non-conformist dress.

Two of the youngest men associated with the group were Felix Manz and Conrad Grebel, both well educated and from prominent families. Manz was the son of the canon of the Cathedral Church, and Grebel was the son of a Zurich councilman. Both had been recommended by Zwingli for teaching positions in Hebrew and Greek at a theological school he proposed to found in Zurich.

Educated at the universities of Basel, Vienna and Paris, and probably influenced by the humanism and pacifism of Erasmus, Grebel was attracted to Zwingli for his integration of classical antiquity and biblical Christianity.[7] And until they discovered the variance in their respective positions Zwingli was attracted to Grebel. That difference focused on infant baptism, both as a test of where authority lay and as a point of dispute regarding the nature of the church.[8] Some priests had already persuaded many parents in their parishes to withhold baptism from their infants, and Hubmaier and Zwingli debated the issue publicly. On January 17, 1525, Zwingli and the Zurich council staged a public debate to settle the matter and to silence the opposition once and for all. The following day, council ordered baptism within eight days of all unbaptized children, the end of special Bible study meetings, and the banishment from the city of non-resident radicals.

The opposition would not be silenced that easily, however. Within a few days and while the brethren were together for study and prayer, George Blaurock asked Conrad Grebel to baptize him with "the true baptism" on the basis of voluntary faith. Grebel complied with the request, and Manz, Reublin and Grebel were then baptized by Blaurock.[9] In the context of city council policy, the event could not help but draw public attention. It had a two-fold effect. It made the Council more determined than ever to suppress the new movement, and, at the same time, became more attractive to certain of the masses. New laws calling for punishment of dissenters were written into the statute books. Parents not permitting the baptism of their infants were fined one silver mark for a first refusal and threatened with exile if they repeated the offence. The preachers against infant baptism, as well as the rebaptizers (*Wiedertaeufer* or Anabaptists, as the Zwinglians called them) faced imprisonment. Grebel, Manz and Blaurock soon found themselves incarcerated and sentenced to remain so "until they rot," though all escaped with the help of sympathetic jailers.

More drastic measures followed against the brethren. Felix Manz, the first martyr of the Anabaptist cause, was forcibly drowned in the Limmat River on January 5, 1527, when he refused to recant. Had Grebel not died of the plague, he would probably have met the same fate. George Blaurock was stripped, whipped out of town and, two years later, executed. Hubmaier escaped Zurich only to be burned at the stake in Vienna.

City councils, princes and kings, as well as bishops and popes,

saw the movement for what it was — a non-recognition of civil
and ecclesiastical authority in matters of conscience and faith. To
them the Anabaptist invalidation of infant baptism was much
more than liturgical or even theological deviance. For them, and
they probably assessed the situation correctly, the new baptism
was an anarchical threat to the maintenance of a united, homogeneous, obedient and serene society. Infant baptism, it must be
remembered, was not only the channel into the church but also
into the state. The ecclesiastic and civic authorities, faced by
such a fundamental threat to the social system by which they
controlled and "saved" the masses, saw no alternative but to
have it rooted out. In this they were supported by the imperial
diet which, in 1529, outlawed Anabaptism throughout the empire.

The banishment of Anabaptism, however, was no easy task
because its very threat to authority made it attractive to the
masses, who were rebelling for their own reasons against the
authorities and systems of the day. The movement advanced
rapidly in Southern Germany, Tyrol, Austria and Moravia, as
well as into regions of the Upper Danube, the Rhine Valley and
all the way down to the Netherlands. Not all historians agree on
the magnitude of the movement. Perhaps the truth lies somewhere between the claim of one chronicler that "their teaching
soon covered the whole land" and another's insistence that it was
only "a minor episode in the history of sixteenth century German
society."[10]

The attractions of the movement were several. For those seeking truth and a genuinely reformed church, the Anabaptist movement clearly offered an alternative to Lutheranism and Zwinglianism, which had disappointed many of those who had tasted
humanist and biblical enlightenment. It also appealed to those
who were rebelling against the estabishment for economic reasons.
It is no coincidence that Anabaptism began in the year of the
Peasants' Revolt, that historians subsequently identified Anabaptism with Muentzer, and that so many of the weak, the poor and
seekers-after-truth were attracted to those who dared to stand up
to the powerful Zwinglian, Lutheran and Catholic coalitions.

The simple life-style advocated by the Anabaptists and so
radically exemplified by the leaders and preachers of the movement was also attractive. They went about their work in Pauline
fashion, requiring little to live, asking little of their followers, and
ready to endure any deprivation for the sake of the Gospel. The
fundamentals of the Anabaptist faith itself were first systematic-

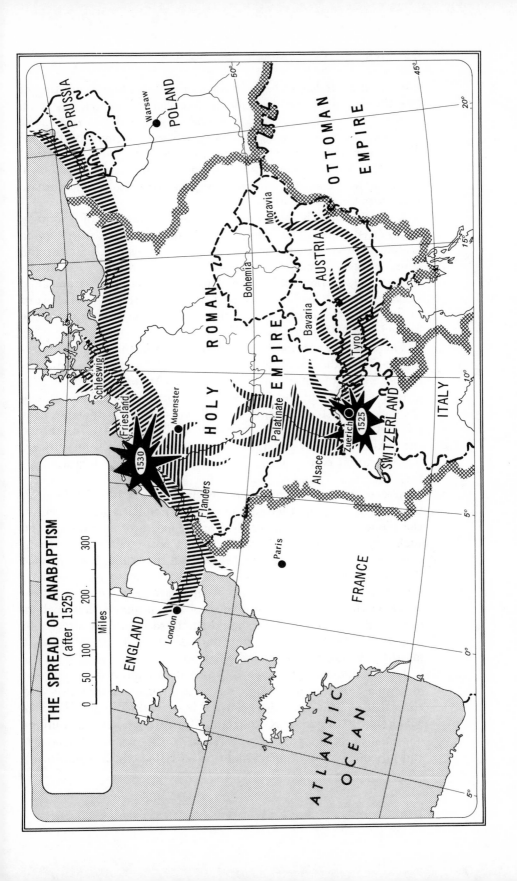

THE SPREAD OF ANABAPTISM
(after 1525)

Miles
0   50   100   200   300

PRUSSIA

Warsaw ●
POLAND

OTTOMAN
EMPIRE

Bohemia

Moravia

AUSTRIA

Schleswig

HOLY

Muenster ●

Friesland

1530

ROMAN

Bavaria

Tyrol

EMPIRE

Palatinate

Zuerich ○ 1525

SWITZERLAND

ITALY

Flanders

Alsace

London ●

ENGLAND

Paris ●

FRANCE

ATLANTIC

OCEAN

ally outlined at Schleitheim in Switzerland in 1527. A meeting of "brethren" under the direction of Michael Sattler, an ex-monk, resulted in what they called the *Bruederliche Vereinigung*, the confession of faith for the Swiss and South German brethren.[11] The confession dealt with baptism, the ban or excommunication, breaking of bread, separation, worldly abominations, pastors in the church, the sword, and the oath, meaning the act of ultimate loyalty to kings and rulers.

In August of the same year another conference of about 60 Anabaptist leaders was held at Augsburg in Bavaria. Although no statement was issued, doctrine and practice were discussed, and those present committed themselves to be faithful even in the face of persecution and death. Most of them were later called upon to honour that commitment, as they were put to the sword or burned at the stake. For this reason, the meeting became known as the Martyrs' Synod.[12]

The early agreement on the fundamentals of the faith — believers' baptism, the life of discipleship, nonresistance, etc. — did not mean complete uniformity among the Anabaptists. The geographic isolation of the groups, the frequent loss of their leaders, the lack of a tested tradition, as well as independent thought, contributed to extensive diversity. Besides, everywhere in Europe the reforms, revolts and renewals were characterized initially by disintegration of the old rather than by a unified integration of the new.[13]

In Moravia, where hundreds of Anabaptists found refuge on the estates of sympathetic nobles, much emphasis was placed on the proper economic organization of the new brotherhood. On one such estate, Jacob Hutter organized an entire community along communistic lines. Although he died at the stake, his influence remained, and after him this wing of the Anabaptists became known as Hutterites. Like other Anabaptists, the Hutterites were strict on the non-use of the sword, although one of their leaders once made allowance for it, should the Lord request it directly to help the Turks bring in the millennium, a period of righteousness in which Christ would rule the earth.[14]

The confluence in these early stages of Anabaptism of a strong millennial expectation, elements of economic communism and allowance to bear arms also occurred in central Germany. Thomas Muentzer of Peasants' Revolt fame, for instance, opposed infant baptism and the two state churches (Lutheran and Catholic), and advanced revolutionary political doctrine which would bring in the new age. Hans Hut, another prominent Anabaptist, shared Muentzer's belief in an early millennium. If necessary, the new age would come by "the little company of true Christians" using force, if perchance "the Turks fail to destroy the princes, monks, priests, nobles, and knights."[15]

Much more precise in his millennial beliefs was Melchior Hoffman, a former preacher at the court of Denmark. He calculated that the Turks would bring about the cataclysm which could usher in the new Jerusalem at Strassburg in 1533. He also predicted that he would be imprisoned for six months if his calculation became a reality. Hoffman was only partly right. He was imprisoned, not for six months but for life. And 1533 marked the beginning of a cataclysm, not at Strassburg but at Muenster, a city of Westphalia, which at first was Catholic, then Lutheran, and finally almost Anabaptist. It happened when Jan Matthys, who accepted Hoffman's millennarianism but not his nonresistance, undertook by force to set up the new Jerusalem at Muenster.

In the annals of reformation history, Muenster the city, like Muentzer the man, became the symbol of a violent, revolutionary, and chiliastic Anabaptism. Enemies of the Anabaptist movement forever identified Muenster as its centre; friends of the movement forever tried to disown the city. The Reformation, like other great social upheavals in history, produced a spectrum of human responses, few of them completely right, none of them completely wrong. Anabaptism, like Protestantism, was and remains such a spectrum. Some historians identified as many as 40 Anabaptist groups known by such names as Muentzerites, Muensterites, Staebler, Free Brethren, Silent Brethren, Holy Brethren, Bare-footed Brethren, Hoffmanites and Hutterites.[16] There were even some Anabaptist nudists and polygamists!

Eventually, considerable organizational and theological unity was achieved in one wing of the Anabaptist movement by Menno Simons (c. 1496–1561), from whom the followers derived their more permanent name. A Dutch Catholic priest, Simons was embracing the Anabaptist faith just as the Muenster episode was running its course. Ironically, it was Muenster and a similar incident at Bolsward, where 300 died, including his brother, that contributed to his conversion. He renounced the Catholic priesthood in 1536, the same year in which John Calvin, another of the great reformers, was publishing the *Institutes*. Menno accepted rebaptism and ordination as an Anabaptist elder; he also married, though his family life was constantly disrupted. Menno became a hunted man after 1542, when Charles V issued an imperial edict offering 100 guilders, a priest's annual salary, for the apprehension of the Anabaptist fugitive.[17]

Menno Simons spent much of the next two decades hiding from his persecutors, studying the scriptures, and writing treatises and letters for friend and foe alike. Two of his most important books, written in 1539 and 1541, were *Foundations of Christian Doctrine* and *True Christian Faith*; both portrayed the church as a disciplined community of the redeemed.[18] During the same time he visited the small groups of Anabaptists, counselled their leaders, baptized, and otherwise built up the congregations, first in Holland and later in other areas of northern Europe. Occasionally he entered into debates with Lutheran and Calvinist ministers.

Menno Simons turned the northern Anabaptists in the direction of passiveness and civil obedience, but this did not erase their revolutionary image or lessen their threat to the authorities. Not even the new name, Menists, which was first used in 1544 in the Dutch province of East Friesland, to distinguish the peaceful Anabaptists from the Muensterites, deflected the wrath of the imperial and ecclesiastical hierarchies. The consequence of their relentless hostility was a sustained and bloody persecution which all but wiped out the faithful, although Menno himself died a natural death in 1561. In northern Europe, as in the south, many survived only because they hid or moved about, eventually finding it most secure farther east and in the distant west.

The Anabaptist threat to the establishments of the day was both imagined and real. In the minds of the rulers, all Anabaptists were linked to the Peasants' Revolt and to the violent attempt at Muenster to establish a new kingdom. The followers of the movement as it had been re-fashioned by Menno Simons, however, were totally peaceful, shunning the sword even in self-defence. They were generally obedient to their overlords, holding back only when an oath or other acts of ultimate loyalty were demanded. Menno's followers had no intention of overthrowing any government, and he himself firmly believed that the righteous reign of God which had to come on earth could not come about through unrighteous means. In that context, the rulers were fearing a nonexistent threat to their authority.

In another sense, however, the Anabaptists, and especially the peaceful Menists, had unleashed an ideological force that frightened the establishment. By creating a new, though small, society under the discipline of Christ (i.e., the church), they judged as un-Christian the old societies, which would not easily be persuaded of their own errors. By naming every believer a priest, they started European humanity on the road to democracy. By their egalitarian teachings and brotherhood structures, they undermined established totalitarian authority. By their rejection of infant baptism, they destroyed conventional social control. With their life-style they exposed hypocrites and unsettled the rich. Through their nonresistance they confounded their enemies, and by their exemplary obedience short of an oath they thoroughly frustrated magistrates and monarchs.

One of those monarchs was Emperor Philip who, like his father Charles V, was determined to prevent further erosion of the empire. The territorial losses suffered by the Peace of Augsburg in 1555 represented defeat already too bitter. Philip, therefore, forbade all laymen to teach the scriptures under threat of execution. For women who taught the forbidden, he decreed death by burial while still alive. Burnings at the stake were ordered for both men and women if they persisted in their witness.[19]

In this bitter attack the emperor was supported by the Catholic Inquisition which crushed Anabaptism completely in the province of Flanders by the end of the century. The Dutch martyrologist van Braght, whose famous record of 1500 Anabaptist executions was published 100 years after Menno's death, counted at least 400 from Flanders alone. The frightful manner in which many of them met their death is illustrated by one of the accounts from this *Martyrs' Mirror*:

> Also sentenced to death with him was a woman named
> Levina with six children. Arriving on the scaffold, David
> attempted to pray but they were immediately driven to the
> stakes. A little bag of gunpowder was tied to each of them,
> whereupon they were strangled and burned. David was still
> seen to move his head. The executioner thrust a fork three
> times into his bowels and bound him to the stake with a
> chain and broke his neck.[20]

These bitter persecutions from 1531 to 1597, when the first and last Dutch executions occurred, sent a continuous flow of Anabaptist refugees from the lowlands into areas of greater safety. Although they fled in all directions, including across the North Sea to England, their main route led eastward to the fringes of the Holy Roman Empire. Thus, in the same way that southern Anabaptists found refuge to the north and east in Bohemia, Moravia and beyond, so the northern Anabaptists found security in the eastern territories, and for a time in Tudor England. Most of the congregations which later appeared in northern Germany, Prussia, Poland, and Russia arose directly or indirectly from these northern refugee movements.

This eastern Anabaptist thrust played such a prominent part in Canadian Mennonite history that it must be given more than just a passing reference. The competing Catholic, Lutheran and Reformed landlords soon discovered that the value of Anabaptist virtues far exceeded the danger of their so-called heresies. At first the refugees were serfs and labourers only; later they were granted leases as managers, and eventually they came into full possession of their own lands in the vicinity of Danzig, Elbing and Koenigsberg. By 1608 a Lutheran bishop was compaining that the whole delta was overrun with Mennonites.

The complaint was virtually useless, however, since the landlords were mainly interested in the economics of their settlement policies. Although at first a derogatory epithet — a name born in derision and oppression — the Mennonite label had become proper and respectable and was proving its usefulness. They were Mennonites, not Muensterites, a most helpful introduction to anxious noblemen. Wherever the name guaranteed a certain open reception and above all escape from persecution, they learned to accept it, cherish it, and defend it.

Not all of the Anabaptists in the lowland provinces had fled, however. Those who stayed and survived increased their numbers and improved their status, especially after 1576 when the noblemen of the various provinces united under William of Orange to drive out Philip II and the Spanish imperial influence. Several important changes resulted. Calvinism replaced Catholicism as the dominant religion, and the Netherlands became a national entity.

The greater tolerance for the Dutch Anabaptists or *Doopsgezinde*, as they preferred to be called, arose not so much from the official change of religion as from the political need of the Dutch to recognize the exceptionally large religious minorities, including the Catholics, in their midst. This also meant tolerance for small minorities. All were invited to participate in the building of a new national life. This Dutch nationalism soon developed a commercial focus beyond the seas with the founding of the Dutch

East India Company in 1602, and overseas colonies such as New York in 1612. Amsterdam became the commercial and financial centre of Europe. The economic opportunities that arose and the growth of political tolerance had real significance for the Doopsgezinde. Before long they were participating fully in the cultural, economic, and political life of the Netherlands. From their ranks emerged leading Dutch poets, painters, businessmen, bankers, and civic leaders, including mayors of large cities, governors of the Dutch West Indies and, by 1795, cabinet ministers.

The enthusiastic participation in the national life and commercial activities had the effect of diluting Anabaptist theology; but it also led to an effective intercession on behalf of persecuted Anabaptists elsewhere. During the early centuries this influence benefited mostly the Anabaptists of England and Switzerland, but generous works of relief, especially on behalf of their brethren, has remained characteristic of the Dutch throughout their history.[21]

In their intercessions, the Doopsgezinde were often joined by their national leaders. One Dutch statesman, William of Orange, on becoming King of England in 1689, also became the first of the English monarchs to side with dissenters when he pleaded the Mennonite cause in 1694.

The close relationship between the Netherlands and England was, of course, partly determined by geography. Anabaptists by the hundreds had found their way to England, their movements being joined to a steady stream of Dutch immigrants who were attracted there for a variety of reasons. Henry VIII tolerated the dissenters, but only until he discovered that their protest affected him as much as it affected Rome. When, in 1534, he became aware of the presence of Anabaptists among the other immigrants, he and his successors (until William III) ordered them exiled or imprisoned and executed. Thirteen were burned in different parts of England in 1534 alone. The English bishops, loyal to the Crown and objecting to Anabaptist views on the oath and baptism, cooperated in their exclusion or punishment.[22]

Thus, in Anglican England, as in Catholic Flanders, the Anabaptists disappeared from the scene, though not without planting the seeds of separation and nonconformity. Their presence led directly to the founding of the Baptist Church in England which, like the Anabaptists, insisted on a "voluntary, democratic church, composed of newborn men and women, entirely free from the state, granting to all freedom of conscience in matters of religion."[23] The two groups maintained some fellowship in Amsterdam, but union was out of the question since the Baptists held different doctrinal views on the oath, government, war, and baptism.[24]

The influence of Anabaptist separation was later acknowledged by the Congregationalists, but with no other group did the Anabaptists have as much in common as with the Quaker dissenters who emerged in England in the 1640s. Quite early the Quakers, followers of George Fox, established contact with Anabaptists on the continent and a mutual helpfulness resulted.

In southern Europe the struggle to reverse or advance the political results of the Reformation continued a whole century after the Peace of Augsburg had supposedly settled the matter. The Swiss brethren did not achieve complete toleration and full citizenship until the Congress of Vienna in 1815. Their struggle for liberty had lasted 300 years, less 10.[25]

In southern as well as in northern Europe, the persecution of the Anabaptists became the basis of a rich literary and musical heritage for the church. As the northern executions had inspired the *Martyrs' Mirror*, so the southern imprisonments produced a group of hymns which became the foundation of the well-known *Ausbund* hymnal. Both resources accompanied the descendants of these groups of persecuted Anabaptists through many generations of spiritual pilgrimage from one country to another.[26]

In times of severe persecution in Switzerland, the Dutch Mennonites interceded on behalf of their brethren, sending delegations to the Swiss councils and to the prisoners, at first to no avail. The Swiss responded in 1671 with the expulsion of 700 men, women and children, of whom 100 ended up in Alsace and the rest in the Palatinate. In addition to the Lutheran nobles of the Vistula, the Calvinist counts of the Palatinate and the Alsace recognized the Anabaptists as builders and, in this case, the right kind to build up a countryside almost totally devastated by the war.

The ultimate sociological destiny of the majority of the Swiss as well as Dutch Anabaptists was affected, however, not only by the migrations but also by internal divisions. Because of its prevalence among the Anabaptists, this tendency to fragmentation was called the *Taeuferkrankheit* (the Anabaptist sickness). Menno Simons had once identified the essentials of the Anabaptist movement but, for his followers, the nonessentials had a way of moving to higher priorities.

For reasons other than differences in language, dress and other customs, the Flemish Anabaptist refugees, after Menno's death, could not be integrated with the Frisian Anabaptists. The Flemish were less rigid in the use of the ban and less autocratic in their ministerial elections and practices. The Frisian-Flemish divisions were carried into Prussia and later to Russia, and separate congregations were maintained for nearly 200 years.

Although all groups held similar views on baptism, the oath, and war, even more liberal in their ministerial practices than the Flemish were the Waterlanders. Between the Waterlanders and the Flemish stood the Upper Germans, and these divisions were sub-divided, not so much from basic theological differences as from varying approaches to congregational discipline and liturgical practices:

> The Flemish and Frisian . . . each developed left and right
> wings. Thus, the former party sprouted an "Old Flemish"
> offshoot, and this offshoot was later subdivided into
> "Groniger" Old Flemish and "Danzig" Old Flemish wings.
> The Frisians in turn expanded into a "Hard" and a "Loose"
> or "Young" Frisian party.[27]

The reasons for this original and continuing atomization among the Anabaptists — the old ones were carried with the migrations and many new ones appeared along the way — are not hard to find. To begin with, the geographic, economic and cultural divisions of Europe at the time of the Reformation were more pronounced than Rome or the Empire had ever been prepared to acknowledge. Besides, the time of reformation and revolution was itself a process of atomization, as indeed such times have always been in the experience of man. A society which discards en masse an old way of putting the world together normally produces a wide range of responses before a new one is synthesized.

Among the Anabaptists the variety of responses and the resulting bifurcations were almost endless. Two paradoxical principles to which they adhered contributed to the divisions. On the one hand, they recognized no external religious authority such as was enjoyed by the Catholics, Lutherans and Calvinists. They had no popes or princes. The new authority of the Anabaptists was the Christ of the Bible, but since they all were priests, at least in theory, there tended to be as many interpretations of the Bible as there were Anabaptists or Anabaptist leaders with strong opinions and leadership.

Secondly, they also insisted on a pure church. Reacting to the undisciplined state churches, they exercised rigorous discipline, frequently carrying to extremes their concern for correctness in liturgical, cultural and moral practices. Having rejected the normal flesh-and-blood battlegrounds of the state churches, the Anabaptists often found their contest with the evil one within the Anabaptist kingdom itself.

Fortunately for their own sake, the Anabaptists also recognized this tendency toward internal fragmentation as one of their main problems. The southern gatherings for doctrinal unity, as at Schleitheim and Augsburg in 1527, had their early-sixteenth-century parallels in the north. Numerous confessional statements were drafted to bring about a measure of internal unity to protect against unwanted foreign influences and to explain the Anabaptist position to outsiders. The most lasting of these were the eighteen articles of a confession drawn up at a "peace convention" in Dordrecht in 1632.[28] For a while this statement became normative, not only for some Dutch Mennonites but also for the Swiss who had moved up into Alsace, the Palatinate, and the Lower Rhine where they received Dutch help and came under their influence.

While Dordrecht contributed to unity, its doctrine of excommunication, or the ban, became a source of contention before the end of the seventeenth century. The controversy began when two Swiss leaders, Hans Reist and Jacob Ammann, expressed different views on such matters as foot-washing and the ban. Being the stricter of the two, Ammann insisted on two foot-washings a year and the extension of the ban to all social intercourse. Reist thought the ban could and should effectively be limited to eating and drinking at communion.[29]

According to Ammann, a total social discipline was necessary to guard against the encroachment of new social customs and re-absorption into society. Such re-entry into the world was sure to follow the attendance of funerals in the state church and the adoption of new fashions such as fancy clothes, a clean-shaven face, and long hair. After all, shaving the beard, and perhaps, wearing a moustache instead, meant erasing the distinction between themselves, the Christian community, and the culture, particularly military culture, surrounding them. Ammann travelled extensively in Switzerland and elsewhere, advocating this point of view. While the Reist view prevailed among the majority in Switzerland and in the Palatinate, Ammann's viewpoint of ecclesiastical strictness and cultural conservatism was adopted by the congregations throughout the Alsace.

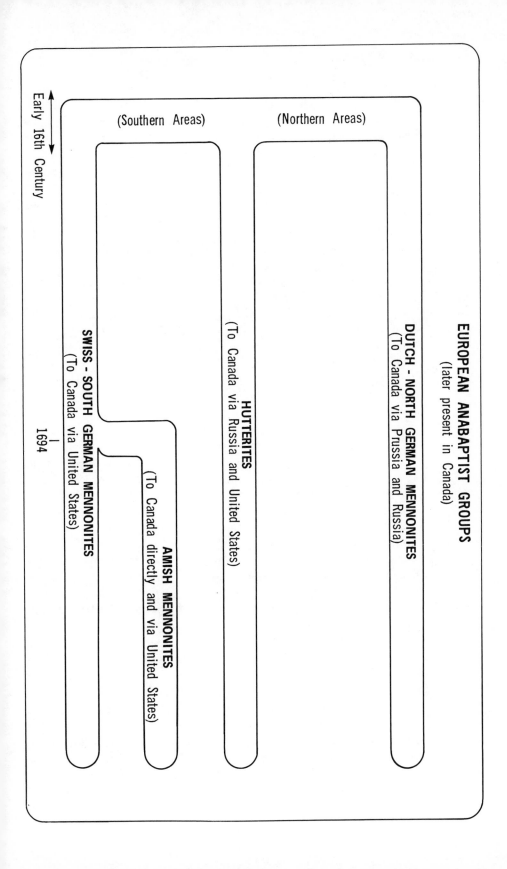

EUROPEAN ANABAPTIST GROUPS
(later present in Canada)

Early 16th Century

(Southern Areas)

(Northern Areas)

SWISS - SOUTH GERMAN MENNONITES
(To Canada via United States)

AMISH MENNONITES
(To Canada directly and via United States)

HUTTERITES
(To Canada via Russia and United States)

DUTCH - NORTH GERMAN MENNONITES
(To Canada via Prussia and Russia)

1694

In 1694, those whom Ammann could not persuade to his point of view were placed by him under the ban. Under the leadership of Reist, the "excommunicated" community returned the compliment and, although reconciliation attempts were made by both sides for nearly two decades, the division remained. The differences on the ban could not be overcome in Europe for two centuries, and in North America they remained even longer.

The Alsace concentration of the Amish, as Ammann's followers came to be known, was disrupted by a 1712 expulsion order issued by Louis XV. The result was that the Amish were on the move throughout the eighteenth century, establishing congregations in southern Germany, France, Holland, in the Austrian provinces of Volhynia and Galicia and in North America.

In the greatest separation of all — the migration away from the European continent and westward across the ocean — the Amish had been preceded by other Dutch and Swiss Mennonites. Anabaptists first appeared on the North American continent in 1643 as Dutch traders to New Netherlands, later known as New York. Their appearance in Manhattan, Long Island, the Delaware shores and perhaps in the Maritimes was not of permanent duration, however.

The first permanent Mennonite settlement in North America was founded in 1683 at Germantown, later a part of Philadelphia. At that time the Quaker, William Penn, was setting up his "holy experiment" in the lands which he had received from Charles II in 1681 in lieu of debts which the monarch had owed Penn's father, an admiral of distinction in the English navy. A man of wealth and aristocratic sophistication, and yet a devout, William Penn was anxious to apply his talents and resources to a religious cause. The land which he had inherited was to become a place of righteous government among men and a place of civil liberty for the oppressed. As his first citizens he selected the persecuted Quakers of England, and other troubled nonconformists, such as the Mennonites on the continent.[30]

News of the tolerant state and abundant land spread to Europe and soon thousands of immigrants were hoping to make their homes anew in the Colony of Penn. They included hundreds of German religious dissenters and, among them, Swiss Mennonites and Amish, whose migrations to Pennsylvania extended, with some interruptions, over two centuries (see Table 1).[31] Between 1710 and 1756, over 3000 Mennonites settled in the regions of Bricks, Chester, Montgomery, and Lancaster counties. The

Amish, about 300 in that initial immigration, also chose the Lancaster area, though farther north and west than the Mennonites.

TABLE 1

MIGRATIONS OF SWISS MENNONITES(M) AND AMISH(A) TO AMERICA

	DATE	NUMBER	ORIGIN	DESTINATION
1.	1683–1705	100*M*	Lower Rhine	Germantown
2.	1707–1756	3-5000*M*	Palatinate and Switzerland	Franconia and Lancaster
3.	1815–1880	3000*A*	Alsace, Bavaria, and Hesse	Ohio, Ontario, Indiana, Illinois
4.	1830–1860	500*M*	Switzerland	Ohio, Indiana
5.	1861–1865	300*M*	Palatinate	Ohio, Indiana, Illinois

Thus began a benevolent and promising era for the Swiss Mennonites. As agriculturists they now had an abundance of land in the "paradise of Pennsylvania." As nonconformists they enjoyed the tolerance of a Quaker state which, like them, was opposed to fighting and swearing. Like their Quaker hosts, they were exempted from the judicial oath. As German-speaking peoples, the new immigrants were not immediately threatened by absorption into an English world. By 1776, they were among about 100,000 Germans, which comprised one third of the entire Pennsylvania population, and with whom they eventually shared a Pennsylvania *Deutsch* culture.

Behind all of these aspects of immigration to Pennsylvania was the British Crown which, though not agreeing with the religious dissenters, had come to tolerate and accept them after they were identified as assets to the British Empire. In Pennsylvania, as in faraway Prussia, the minorities were welcomed because they were useful. The new British tolerance for dissent made such a deep impression on the Mennonites on both sides of the Atlantic that they would seek refuge under its wide umbrella again and again — eventually in Canada — in the years to come.

FOOTNOTES

1. Walter Klaassen, "The Nature of the Anabaptist Protest," *Mennonite Quarterly Review*, XLV (October 1971), p. 311.
2. Term used by Pope John XXIII (1958–1963) to identify Protestants as he initiated a new relationship with them. See Whelan's *Separated Brethren*.
3. Robert C. Walton, *Zwingli's Theocracy* (Toronto: University of Toronto Press, 1967), p. 218.
4. C. Henry Smith, *The Story of the Mennonites*, 3rd ed. (Newton, Kans.: Mennonite Publication Office, 1950), p. 4.
5. John H. Yoder, *Taeufertum und Reformation in der Schweiz* (Karlsruhe, Germany: Mennonitischer Geschichtsverein, 1962), p. 20. Translation by Smith, *op. cit.*
6. Walter Klaassen, *Anabaptism: Neither Catholic Nor Protestant* (Waterloo, Ont.: Conrad Press, 1973).
7. Harold S. Bender, *Conrad Grebel 1498–1526: Founder of the Swiss Brethren* (Goshen, Ind.: Mennonite Historical Society, 1950), p. 73.
8. On the nature of the theological dispute see: Bender, *op. cit.*; John H. Yoder, *Taeufertum und Reformation im Gespraech* (Zurich: EUV-Verlag, 1968); and Franklin H. Littell, *The Origins of Sectarian Protestantism: A Study of the Anabaptist View of the Church* (New York: Macmillan Company, 1964).
9. For a delightful account of this story see: Fritz Blanke, *Brothers in Christ* (Scottdale, Pa.: Herald Press, 1961).
10. Claus-Peter Clasen, *Anabaptism: A Social History, 1525-1618* (Ithaca: Cornell University Press, 1972), p. 428.
11. John C. Wenger, "The Schleitheim Confession of Faith," *Mennonite Quarterly Review*, XIX (October 1945), pp. 247–53 (translation).
12. Regarding Anabaptist martyrdom, see: T. J. van Braght, *Martyrs' Mirror* (Scottdale, Pa.: Herald Press, 1950). English translation 1964.
13. See the concluding chapter in George H. Williams, *The Radical Reformation* (Philadelphia: Westminster Press, 1962).
14. For an introduction to the Hutterites see: Victor Peters, *All Things Common: The Hutterian Way of Life* (Minneapolis: University of Minnesota Press, 1965).
15. Smith, *op. cit.*, p. 40; James M. Stayer, *Anabaptists and the Sword* (Lawrence, Kans.: Coronado Press, 1972).
16. Smith, *op. cit.*, pp. 79–80; Claus-Peter Clasen, "Anabaptist Sects in the Sixteenth Century: A Research Project," *Mennonite Quarterly Review*, XLVI (July 1972), pp. 256–79.
17. Ernst Behrends, *Der Ketzerbischof* (Basel, Switzerland: Agape-Verlag, 1966), pp. 61–5.

18. J. C. Wenger, ed., *The Complete Writings of Menno Simons* (Scottdale, Pa.: Mennonite Publishing House, 1956), p. 670.
19. See extract of 1556 decree in T. J. van Braght, *Martyrs' Mirror*, pp. 552–53.
20. *Ibid.*, p. 549.
21. Nanne van der Zijpp, "The Dutch Aid the Swiss Mennonites," in C. J. Dyck, ed., *A Legacy of Faith* (Newton, Kans.: Faith and Life Press, 1962), pp. 136–58.
22. Irvin B. Horst, *Anabaptism and the English Reformation to 1558* (Nieuwkoop , Netherlands: B. de Graaf, 1966); Fred J. Zerger, "Dutch Anabaptism in Elizabethan England," *Mennonite Life* (January 1971), pp. 19–23.
23. Smith, *op. cit.*, pp. 196–97.
24. For an introduction to the controverted issue of Anabaptist-Baptist relationships see: William R. Estep, *The Anabaptist Story* (Nashville, Tenn.: Broadman Press, 1963), Chap. XI.
25. Delbert L. Gratz, *Bernese Anabaptists* (Scottdale, Pa.: Herald Press, 1953).
26. Rudolf Wolkan, *Die Lieder der Wiedertaeufer* (Nieuwkoop, Netherlands: B. de Graaf, 1965); Paul M. Yoder, *et al., Four Hundred Years with the Ausbund* (Scottdale, Pa.: Herald Press, 1964).
27. Smith, *op. cit.*, p. 174.
28. van Braght, *op. cit.*, pp. 38–44.
29. John A. Hostetler, *Amish Society* (Baltimore: Johns Hopkins University Press, 1963).
30. Edwin B. Bonner, *William Penn's "Holy Experiment": The Founding of Pennsylvania, 1681–1701* (New York: Temple University Publications, 1962), pp. 1–23.
31. H. S. Bender, "Migrations of Mennonites," *M.E.*, III, pp. 684–87.

Trek to Upper Canada

2. On to Russia and Canada

*The movement of the Mennonites into Canada from the
United States . . . coincided with that of the United Empire
Loyalists, yet theirs was a deeper purpose, a religious loyalty
which wavers not nor fails because of changing sentiments of
political impact only*—s. f. coffman[1]

As the 1700s drew to a close, thousands of Mennonites in
Pennsylvania and Prussia were on the move, once again
seeking a new homeland which might offer them a greater measure
of liberty, security and prosperity. This search on each side of the
Atlantic led in an opposite geographic direction, although the
new migrations and settlement experiences produced some remarkable parallels. Unknown to the Dutch-German Mennonites
in Prussia migrating east and south and to the Swiss-German
Mennonites in Pennsylvania moving west and north, their common search predestined the joining of their respective eastern
and western histories less than 100 years later.

The historic circumstances and political developments leading
up to the two migrations were similar; in both situations, national
ambitions and revolutionary ferment produced much uncertainty
and insecurity for the Mennonites. However, in both settings
the discomfort was not so great or so complete that they were
forced to move on. If, at the time of their rising anxieties, they
had not been confronted with settlement offers from the Russian

47

Tsar and the British King, the Mennonites could have remained a while longer in their old homes without too much distress. Indeed, the majority of them did. This fact alone makes the sorting out of motives and causes for resettlement somewhat problematical.

Long-term considerations, however, were crucial. In the distant and even near future, the Mennonites could see themselves increasingly crowded in the sense of both geographic opportunity and religious liberty. In Prussia the two factors were intimately related. The military reign of Frederick the Great (1740–1786) had produced many concessions for the Mennonites. As respectable and appreciative citizens, they presented their best gifts to him — on one occasion their two best oxen, 400 pounds of butter and 20 cakes of cheese. Nevertheless, they remained a problem for an ambitious monarch who could not easily allow so many large families with so many non-military sons to expand into farm after farm in the kingdom he was enlarging and consolidating.

The reign of his father, Frederick I (1688–1740), the first king of Prussia, had already produced a strong army which Frederick II (the Great) now intended to improve and expand. Believing that might made right, he renamed his tax collectors war commissars and his cabinet members war ministers, as he insisted on authority and discipline from top to bottom. Then he seized Silesia from Austria and, in the reversal of European alliances that followed, Prussia found herself confronting, and being confronted by, France, Austria, Russia, Saxony and Sweden. Only Britain, which was fighting France in the Seven Years War (1756–1763), remained friendly.

Even with a powerful ally, however, Frederick's continental enemies could be overwhelming and so the militarization of his regime continued. In this policy he was loyally supported by the Lutheran state clergy. Thus, once more, church and state stood out against the Mennonites. By 1774 the industrious nonconformists were being limited in their land acquisitions, and by 1780 they were being taxed 5,000 thaler annually for the support of military schools. The impact of these impositions was ameliorated by Frederick's basic goodwill toward his enterprising citizens, whose own internal discipline he could appreciate.

The time after Frederick's death in 1786, therefore, became an ominous one for the Mennonites. In the same year they dispatched a delegation to the new eastern land of promise from which the Tsarina, Catherine the Great, had sent a special emissary inviting western and central European agriculturists to settle in her lands. Such invitations had been extended prior to her time and not only by the Russian tsars. The Hapsburgs of Austria, for instance, were similarly settling their province of Galicia, and here also Mennonites were involved. Thousands of colonists from some of the small German states were leading pioneers in the Middle Volga region. This time there was a special invitation from Russia for the Mennonites in Prussia. Having just been seized from the Turks, the particular lands to be domesticated (to ensure long-term Russian control) were known as new Russia, north of the Black Sea.[2]

Two years later, in 1788, 228 families — most of them poor and already landless — set out to found the Colony of Chortitza east of the Dnieper River and near the present city of Zaparozhe. They were delayed en route by renewed fighting between the Russians and the Turks and forced to endure a most oppressive winter in temporary camps. Yet, in spite of these troubles and a switch in settlement plans due to Turkish intervention in the areas originally chosen, as well as other seemingly endless hardships, the decision appeared to be a good one. They arrived at the revised destination in July 1789, the same year the Prussian land-purchase restrictions were completed.

In the face of such militarism, the eastern solution seemed to be right for the nearly 10,000 Prussian Mennonites who migrated to Russia over a period of 60 years and more. In 1803 they founded the Molotschna Colony, about 100 miles across the Dnieper River, east of Chortitza. And later, when the new Prussian constitution failed to provide for military exemption on religious grounds, two additional colonies were established east of the Volga River in the Saratov region, also known as the Middle Volga area. Indeed, the eastern movements had not yet run their course when the sons of the pioneer immigrants to Russia were looking westward for an even better destiny.

In British North America, the Swiss-German Mennonites were slowly though unwittingly preparing and being prepared to receive the Dutch-German Mennonites from Russia. To begin with, they were steadily pushing forward the frontiers of economic opportunity and religious liberty, both essential elements of that preparation. In southeastern Pennsylvania the good land had been rapidly bought up, and already in the middle of the 1700s there was movement to new and cheaper lands, offering ample room for expansion. These were found in Virginia to the south; in

western Pennsylvania and Ohio to the west; ultimately in Indiana, Illinois, and Iowa; and beyond the Mississippi to regions
almost unknown then. Most important for our story was the
discovery of Ontario or Upper Canada.

Although the first permanent Mennonite settlements in Canada
were founded as a direct result of the American Revolution, the
possibility that Anabaptists were present in the Maritimes in the
mid-eighteenth century must not be overlooked. The same movements which produced the larger German and Quaker colonies
in Pennsylvania brought Germans from the Rhineland and the
Palatinate, Quakers and Baptists from England, and Anabaptist
groups to New England and the Maritimes.[3] In 1754 an Anglican
rector in Lunenburg, Nova Scotia, made specific mention of
Anabaptists in his area, and these were subsequently linked to the
Anabaptists of the Reformation.[4] It does appear that such small
groups, if they were indeed Anabaptists, were quickly absorbed
either by the Quakers or by the Baptists. Anabaptists have also
been identified in New Brunswick, but here too they were so
"closely aligned dogmatically with the Society of Friends or
Quakers that, for religious purposes, they joined forces."[5]

Some Anabaptists apparently came to the Maritimes as part of
the post-revolution loyalist movements. At St. John's River in
Nova Scotia, for instance, there appeared in 1783, alongside a
Quaker Company of 102 persons, an "Anabaptist Company of
47 persons of which 20 were adult men, 11 women, and 16 children."[6] But again, no subsequent record of a continuing separate
identity has been discovered, so that a disintegration or absorption into the community can be assumed in this case.

The movements that endured were those to Upper Canada,
aided and abetted by the thirteen American colonies' declaring
themselves independent from the British in 1776. Their revolution against the king resulted in the creation of a republican state,
the United States of America. Like the nationalist kingdoms of
Europe, the U.S.A. had expansive ambitions of its own. Within
its first generation the new republic would reach out for more
British-American land in the north precisely at the time when
her ally, France, was reaching eastward as far as possible. In
Prussia, as in Pennsylvania, the Mennonites had difficulty forgetting the benefits of monarchical friendships. Political promises,
in addition to the abundance of land to which the British government was inviting them, led about 2,000 to migrate to Upper

Canada beginning in 1786, the very year the Prussian delegation was entering Russia.

Catching the Mennonites in the middle, the troubles between Britain and her colonies had been brewing for many years. The more George III restricted the aspirations of the colonies, the more the Americans rebelled, especially when confronted by what they called "intolerable acts." One of these was the 1774 Quebec Act by which the British sought to make peace with their newly-won province of French Quebec by recognizing not only the boundaries of that province but also the legitimate presence of the French people in all the territory north of the Ohio River. The British, for their own reasons, were finding ways of accommodating non-Anglican minorities — but not without benefit to such migrating peoples as the Mennonites.

The American rebellion against the British presented the Mennonites of Pennsylvania with a real dilemma. On the one hand, they owed much of their freedom to the British. The concessions on the oath that had been made to the Quakers had gradually, with Quaker help, extended to the Mennonites and to the Amish. The Militia Act of 1757 provided for Quaker, Mennonite, and Moravian exemption from the bearing of arms. This exemption, however, required service in other capacities such as extinguishing fires, suppressing the insurrections of slaves, caring for the wounded, and transporting food and information.

Also favouring the British, at least for a time, was Mennonite respect for authority and government. While their nonresistance doctrine demanded non-participation in British wars, it also did not allow for participation in political revolution, least of all against the British.[7] Moreover, a pro-American stance would mean siding with those people in Pennsylvania who through the 1700s had agitated against Quaker-Mennonite peace principles and against the Quakers and Mennonites themselves. It was difficult for the Mennonites to be pro-American, at least as long as the super-patriots harassed them, confiscated their properties, imprisoned them and on occasion threatened their lives.[8] A message passed on to "the highest authorities" from Mennonites and German Baptists (or Dunkards, later known as the Church of the Brethren) in Lancaster County expressed well the pro-British view:

> The Mennonists and German Baptists (Brethren) . . . in the different parts of Pennsylvania have long wished to know

from Authority how to conduct themelves during the present
Rebellion, that they might not give offence to His Majesty
or His Representative in America ... some of the Ministers
and leading men of those two Societies, drew up an Address
and Petition to the King in behalf of those two Societies ...
setting forth their Happiness while under His Government,
their desire to be reinstated in the enjoyment of their former
Blessings, and their Readiness to part with Goods and
Chattles to bring about so desirable an Event, and praying
that a general Line of Conduct might be pointed out to
them, to conduct themselves by, and whether their sowing
Grain, planting Corn was not in some measure considered as
aiding and abetting the Rebellion, and whether they would
be suffered to enjoy their religious principle as heretofore.[9]

On the other hand, the Americans also took actions favourable
to dissenters. The Continental Congress of 1775, for instance,
assured people "who from religious principles cannot bear arms
in any case" that it intended no violence against their consciences,
even while it ordered the colonies to form militia companies. The
Pennsylvania Assembly on November 7, 1775, having heard a
joint petition from the Societies of Mennonists and German
Baptists, likewise recognized "the good people ... conscientiously
scrupulous of bearing arms"and asked all pacifists to "spend their
time and substance in the public service."[10]

In addition to the Quakers, Mennonites, and Dunkards, another
group of evangelical pacifists emerged in Pennsylvania at this
time. They were the River Brethren or Tunkers (not to be confused with Dunkards); later they were also known as Brethren
in Christ. A revivalistic group, partly of Mennonite origin, the
Tunkers shared many Mennonite emphases. Both being immersed
in the ambivalent mood of the times, they would later share a
common destiny — emigration.

Following the Continental Congress of 1776, there was further
cause for pro-American feelings. The defenders of the revolution
seemed to express truths which the Anabaptists had defended
with their lives 250 years before. After all, the colonial revolution
represented no less than the cause of liberty for all mankind. In
that sense the revolutionaries were not really rebels, but like the
Anabaptists before them, they insisted on higher rights and committed themselves to a stricter obedience than could be represented or demanded by a usurping British king. Quite clearly,
the Declaration of Independence contained self-evident truths to
which Anabaptists might readily be able to assent.

There were obstacles, however, to Mennonite acceptance of the situation. The declared right of a people to abolish government presented problems to the civilly obedient pacifists. The revolution might mean liberation for the majority of Americans, but what could it mean for the minorities, religious or otherwise? The Germans had already been harassed — not to mention the Indians and the Negroes. The same Thomas Jefferson who had drafted the declaration about equally created men had at least 100 slaves on his own plantation. Thus the ambivalent elements of virtue and vice became quite confused in the revolutionary struggle. It wasn't always clear who was fighting hardest for a free humanity — the British, the Americans, or perhaps the so-called non-associators, that is, the non-participants in the militia.

To the non-associators, the American cause tended to lose its legitimacy whenever the super-patriots took the law into their own hands as when, in 1777, the Pennsylvania Assembly called for a new oath of allegiance, allowing no exemptions. In the establishment of a new sovereignty and a new nationalism, the oath, of course, was essential for America. But for the Mennonites the oath was also paramount. More than a simple linguistic exercise or a political liturgy which might be forgotten immediately after the swearing, the oath for them was a statement of ultimate loyalty which, since 1525, had belonged only to God.

On the matter of taxes, also, the authorities were not so considerate, and it was this issue which precipitated a debate and tested the loyalties in the Mennonite community, soon leading to another division in the Church. In 1776 Preacher Christian Funk of the Franconia Conference stood out against the other eight ministers in insisting that a special congressional war tax be paid. As far as he was concerned, the new state constitution was as favourable as the old charter from Penn. "Were Christ here," said Funk, "he would say to give Congress that which belongs to Congress, and to God, that which is God's."[11] Besides, he said, the Congressional paper money with which the tax was to be paid was already in current use.

As it turned out, Funk's opinion was a minority position. The 1775 Mennonite-Dunkard petition which said that "we are willing to pay taxes" to Caesar apparently did not necessarily have reference to the new American caesars. The other eight ministers equated the payment of three pounds and ten shillings with a personal involvement in war. They objected not only to paying taxes but also to the impressment by the militia of some of their horses, wheat, and provender. In addition, their objection was conditioned by the uncertainty of the outcome; some were still predicting that the king would win. The end of the debate came in 1778 when Christian Funk was silenced and separated from the Church in a splinter movement which eventually died out. The majority of the Mennonites paid fines or went to jail rather than submit to the oath of allegiance or to the payment of war taxes.

The 1783 Peace of Versailles confirmed the sovereignty of the American nation. Those fighting with the British accepted the invitation to live elsewhere in the British realm, mostly in Canada, where they became known as United Empire Loyalists. The non-associators needed more time to make up their minds, and in the end the vast majority accepted the new sovereignty. Their leanings toward the British, however, were not forgotten very easily, and in the end those leanings made the abundance of land in Upper Canada that much more attractive.

The prospects of a more congenial political climate and favourable cultural environment may also have influenced their decision. The possible role of German culture in the northward movement has, heretofore, been overlooked, but it must not be forgotten that Mennonites were still quite German in their cultural expression. Their religious activity was carried on in the High German of the Luther Bible, and their social communications were in the Pennsylvania *Deutsch* dialect. In the Pennsylvania environment the Mennonites had learned to integrate their religion with British politics, German culture, and colonial land as a total formula for the good life. That good life had now begun to break apart. German culture had felt the fires of the American melting pot before 1756. After 1776 the revolution not only dissolved the British Crown but it also hastened the dissolution of the German cultural commonwealth.

It was soon apparent that the British environment in Upper Canada offered not only British privileges, freedom for Mennonite religion, and an abundance of good land, but also the easier continuance of the German culture. After all, George III was tied to the German House of Hanover, and the four districts of Upper Canada had been given German names — Lunenburg, Mecklenburg, Nassau, and Hesse — in order to flatter the Hanoverian king. Besides, the princes of Hesse had supplied German troops for the British struggle against the American rebels. These troops and one thousand other German loyalist families from New York placed the Germans second in line after the English among the early loyalists. Indeed, many of these Germans were nicknamed Hessians after their mercenary prototypes. It should not be surprising, therefore, to discover that German-speaking minorities looked to British North America not only because it was British but also because it could very well be German and, for migrating Mennonites at least, German considerations were strong. They formed the German Land Company to mediate the buying and selling of their land, and their most important centre later became known as Berlin (the present-day Kitchener).

The first requirement for settlement, however, was land, and it is safe to assume that without its easy availability there would have been no migration. In Pennsylvania as in Prussia there was no great urgency to depart since there was no persecution that seriously imperilled life, faith or prosperity. The only urgency lay in the cultural, political and geographic limitations which appeared on the horizon.

In Upper Canada the frontier was just being opened up by government "purchases" of lands from the Indians, the first of which was made in 1766. Each deal or treaty involved some cash, instalment payments as "eternal rent," and guarantees of security for the Indians. The instalments, though, were sometimes forgotten and so were the guarantees of security for the Indians. Piece by piece the Indian surrendered his land on the assumption that each new treaty would halt the white man's advance. Less than a century later only the so-called Indian reservations were left for him.

Agricultural settlement in Upper Canada began with farm operations around military outposts, the first at Fort Niagara around 1780. This policy in turn led to land grants to soldiers and others loyal to the king, of which 40 per cent were Germans by 1784. That same year three million acres of land were "purchased" from the Indians along the St. Lawrence, as hundreds of loyalists, mostly officials, teachers, businessmen, real estate men, officers and soldiers were attracted by the British promise of free land, free settlement provisions and compensation for losses sustained in support of the British cause. By 1791, when Upper Canada became a separate province, it boasted a settlement population of 25,000, of which 20,000 were loyalists. By that time, the Crown had freely granted over 12 million acres of land, of which more than 11 million had gone to generals, officers, militiamen and other loyalists. Government officials, barristers, clergymen and surveyors got most of the rest, although some land was set aside for schools. The Constitutional Act of 1791 further reserved one-seventh of all land (seven lots in every 48) for the Crown and another one-seventh for the church.

Not all of the newcomers were serious settlers or even serious loyalists. Among those who had left the thirteen colonies voluntarily were many land speculators and exploiters. And among those who took up land, there were also many soldiers and bureaucrats who knew nothing about agriculture; their weaknesses became advantages for the Mennonites, who did not qualify for free land since most of them were not true loyalists. The Mennonites were serious settlers and, in their own way, pro-British. Among the so-called late loyalists, the Mennonites were the last, both in a chronological sense and in emotional-political terms.[12] One of their descendants made loyalism a cause sufficient for himself to become president of the Dominion Council of the United Empire Loyalist Association.[13] As good agriculturists, Mennonites and Tunkers became buyer-prospects for those lands which loyalists were anxious to sell. At the turn of the century such sales had been made or were in progress in four communities, or counties as they were later known: Lincoln, Welland, Waterloo and York.

The first migration leading to permanent Mennonite community in Canada occurred in 1786 and coincided with main loyalist movements, suggesting a strong association with the loyalist cause. That first group seems to have consisted of "fringe" Mennonites. (In Russia the first emigrants also came without preachers to lead them). None of the five who constituted that first prospecting party — three brothers, John, Thielman (or Tilman) and Stoffel (or Christopher) Kolb, and Franklin Albrecht (Albright) and Frederich Hahn — were ever found registered in any church books in Upper Canada.[14] In spite of their loyalist tendencies they did not qualify — nor did they choose to qualify — for free land grants.

The "prospectors" took up land at the Twenty, i.e., along a creek 20 miles from the Niagara River, in the fertile lowlands between the Niagara escarpment and Lake Ontario. What price they paid is not known, but thirteen years later their relatives and friends bought 1,100 acres in the area with a deposit of $40.00, paying $2.50 per acre for a portion lying near the Indian Trail that later became highway number eight, and $1.50 per acre for the portion nearer the lake.[15] By 1802, 33 families from Bucks County had found their new frontier in Lincoln County, more particularly between Vineland and Beamsville at sites which later became known as Jordan and Campden.

Meanwhile, other enterprising individuals, apparently fringe Mennonites, were establishing themselves in other areas. In 1788 Jacob Sevits became the forerunner of groups of Mennonite, Quaker and Tunker families, in the Sherkston area of Welland County, fifteen miles to the west of Fort Erie.[16] In 1789 John Troyer took up an offer for a land grant at Long Point Bay with authority later to build a dock. A year later Jacob Burkholder from Lancaster took up land near what was to become the city of Hamilton.

As in the Maritimes, not all of these settlements led to permanent Mennonite communities. The Sherkston group was eventually absorbed by the Tunkers and partly by the Quakers. The Burkholders became the foundation of a Methodist church which was named after them. Troyer was an overactive loyalist — he claimed to have "suffered much by the rebellious Americans" and was too far removed from other Mennonites to remain one himself. He was a pacifist, however, unwilling to bear arms, though he had "no objection to employ his team in any service of government either civil or military."[17]

The Waterloo settlement had its beginnings in 1800 with settlers from Franklin County in Pennsylvania. The Joseph Schoerg (Sherk) and Samuel Betzner families had travelled to the Twenty in the fall of 1799 and wintered there; in the spring they moved on via the Indian trail to Brantford and up the shores of the Grand River to land known as Block No. 2 or the Beasley Tract. Within a year they were joined by six families from Lancaster County; among them was Samuel Betzner, Sr. In 1801 seven families also arrived from Montgomery County. In 1802 the arrivals, which included Joseph Bechtel, a minister, and John and Sam Bricker, brought the total to 25 families, with a sound promise of others to follow.

By 1803, however, there were problems to be overcome. The legal title to the land the Mennonites thought they had purchased was not clear. The lands for six miles on either side of the Grand River had been granted, on vaguely defined terms, to a particular and unusual group of loyalists — the Six Nations Confederacy of the Iroquois.[18] The ancestral home of the Iroquois was the Finger Lakes region of up-state New York. During the Revolutionary Wars these Indians, particularly the Mohawk tribe, had remained loyal to the British cause. Consequently they were driven from

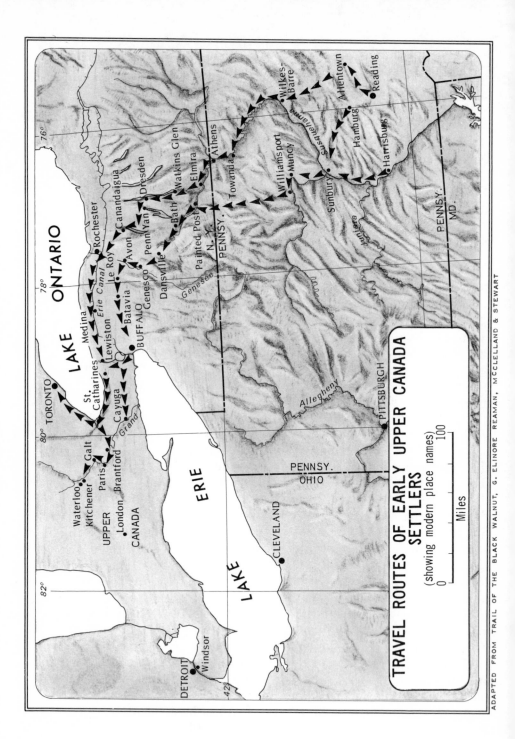

TRAVEL ROUTES OF EARLY UPPER CANADA
SETTLERS

(showing modern place names)

0   100

Miles

ADAPTED FROM TRAIL OF THE BLACK WALNUT, G. ELINORE REAMAN, McCLELLAND & STEWART

their homes when the Americans prevailed in that conflict.[19] The British then agreed to provide new lands for their native allies. Under the leadership of Joseph Brant, the Six Nations were granted 576,000 acres of choice lands along the Grand River. Approximately 2,000 Indians, the majority of them Mohawks, followed Brant to Canada to settle on these lands. At the time much of this land was occupied by the Mississauga Indians with whom the British negotiated a treaty without difficulty.[20] The Huron tribes which had long occupied the area had been dispersed in earlier wars with the Iroquois.

Joseph Brant had always been the subject of much controversy. At times he acted as though he hoped to establish an independent Indian state within British territory. At other times he seemed very eager to sell as much land as possible. He soon found several persons interested in purchasing large tracts of Grand River lands and made private arrangements with them, justifying the proposed sales by suggesting that successful farmers would teach the Indians agriculture.[21] His people were also in great need of funds which the land sales would provide. Therefore Brant, without any reference to the government and only limited consultation with his own sachems, "sold" large tracts of land to private land speculators and "jobbers."[22]

Serious disputes quickly developed. There were charges that Brant personally pocketed much of the money he received for the lands. Certainly most of his followers remained in poverty. Furthermore, the government was unwilling to recognize these sales for two reasons. First, the sales had not been properly processed, approved and registered at York. Second, the authorities had grave doubts about alienating large tracts of Indian lands, fearing serious problems if the Indians sold the lands, spent the money and then found themselves destitute. The government insisted that any funds accruing from land sales be placed in trust funds administered by government trustees. Private and possibly corrupt arrangements between Brant and the buyers were entirely unacceptable and, for several years, the government refused to grant any legal titles to the land.

Brant was greatly irritated by the British attempt to block his land sales and threatened hostile action. The Lieutenant-Governor at the weakly defended capital of York thought the threats of Indian hostilities most serious, especially after the outbreak of the Napoleonic Wars, when renewed French and Spanish campaigns might be expected. The situation was made much worse by the fact that, in 1794, the British finally, and much to the disgust of the western Indians, met one of the terms of the 1783 Peace Treaty and surrendered the strategic western posts of Niagara, Detroit, and Michilimackinac. In this troubled situation the authorities at York decided to placate Brant and his Confederacy and, in 1798, the land transactions between the Six Nations and the white men who wished to purchase lands were approved.[23]

Six large blocks of land were quickly sold. The government insisted that the funds be paid to trustees, but Brant had himself named as a special agent of the Six Nations and continued to make private arrangements. The land of interest to the Mennonites was in Block No. 2. That block consisted of 94,012 acres and was sold for £8,887 to Richard Beasley, James Wilson and St. Jean Baptiste Rousseau; it was payable on or before the first day of April "which will be in the year of our Lord Two thousand seven hundred and ninety eight," in other words a thousand years later.[24] Interest was at six per cent annually payable by April 1. The terms of sale were justified as providing a permanent income to the Indians, but they allowed for a convenient forgetting of the principal and some of the buyers also forgot to pay, or misdirected their payments of, interest. Thus it was with Beasley and company. The two interest payments that were made after 1798 went directly to Brant rather than to the government trustees.[25]

It is difficult to believe that Beasley, who acted in business affairs on behalf of the three land speculators, did not know what he was doing, although his numerous private and public involvements could have produced forgetfulness and carelessness. As an early and youthful loyalist, Beasley had entered the ground floor of economic and political development in Upper Canada and subsequently made the most of it. At sixteen he had already fought with a British ranger corps, been captured, and then released on account of his youth. He became an early trader, later a miller, and in the 1780s a land speculator. At the same time he was named a justice of the peace, then a magistrate, and finally he became a legislator.

In his search for buyers of his land he responded eagerly to the Mennonite interests. Being partly of Dutch descent, he moved easily in Germanic circles. One of his sons married a Hesse, and a daughter wed one of the Hamilton Burkholders. With the help of an Indian guide, Richard Beasley introduced Sherk and Betzner to the land. Both declared it much better than they had expected to find and immediately bought sites near an abundant supply of water. Joseph Sherk took 261 acres opposite Doon, paying for them with the sale of a horse, and Samuel Betzner purchased 200 acres on the west bank of the Grand River at Blair. Thereafter, John Biehn and George Bechtel registered the purchase of over 3,000 acres each, including the sites of Doon, New Aberdeen and German Mills, and reaching within little more than a mile of what later became the city of Kitchener. These purchases aroused a good deal of excitement in the homeland and it appeared that a considerable movement was beginning to take shape.[26]

Then, early in 1803, the Executive Council of Upper Canada discovered that Beasley had not paid either interest or principal on the mortgage, and that he had never informed the Mennonites that there was a mortgage on the lands they had purchased. Beasley, when challenged, readily admitted the problem, producing great consternation both at York and in the Mennonite settlements. The situation was not improved when it was revealed that some interest had in fact been paid directly to Brant without the knowledge of the trustees. Eventually an arrangement was worked out between Beasley, the government, and the Mennonites whereby the latter agreed to buy a 60,000-acre block from Beasley for £10,000. Beasley received credit for the money he had paid directly to Brant and agreed to pay off the entire mortgage, this time to the government-appointed trustees.[27]

These negotiations took time, of course, and some settlers gave up their holdings and looked elsewhere; for a time, abandonment of the entire settlement was considered. New settlers refused to go to the Waterloo area before the land ownership question was settled. Indeed, some families already en route to Waterloo in 1803 were redirected at the Twenty to York County. Among the new Mennonite settlers to go to this area were two ministers, Henry Wideman and Peter Musselman, both from Montgomery County. They were followed a year later by the Christian Reesor family (the parents and four married children) as well as by Casper Sherk who had intended to join his pioneer brother at Waterloo. A slow but steady trickle of settlers increased the colony to about 30 families by 1825.

Meanwhile the Bricker brothers, John and Samuel, of Waterloo, had gone back to Lancaster County in Pennsylvania to obtain help in raising the £10,000 needed to purchase the 60,000 acres from Richard Beasley. After some discouragements and setbacks, they found 23 farmers ready to join them in the formation of the German Land Company. Among them were John Bricker's sister-in-law and three Erb brothers, John, Jacob and Abraham, and a cousin Daniel Erb, all of them having plenty of pioneer spirit. The formation of the land company made financial sense, at least later on, but at the time the event was also a triumph for the religious principle of helping brothers in need.

The German Land Company completed the land transaction with Beasley and the government, with Daniel Erb and Samuel Bricker concluding the deal at Niagara on November 28, 1803.[28] Nearly all the purchase amount, which had been brought in silver dollars by horseback from Pennsylvania, constituted the down payment. The balance, including 6 per cent interest, and having also been brought in silver coin from the homeland, was paid on May 23, 1805. In the words of a Kitchener historian:

> The second bulk of silver was placed in a keg on a pleasure wagon, driven by Samuel Bricker, while John Bricker, Daniel, John, and Jacob Erb, mounted on horseback, acted as guards, and delivered the specie at Niagara. Afterward the wagon was presented to Samuel Bricker for his praiseworthy services.[29]

The government saw to it, so the white man's story goes, that the Indians got their share, and the German Land Company gained clear title to the land. The same story reads differently, as does all North American history, when it is remembered that this land belonged originally to the Indians. Their views of land and ownership were foreign to European understanding; land negotiations following the system of the colonizers were strange at best. In this light the red man's story, only now being recorded, saw few blessings in the best of deals.[30] The idea of selling, the method of measuring, the nature of the contract, the setting of the price, and the lawyers, all emerged from the white man's society, which handled the whole deal and pocketed the profits, while the Indian was crowded into the corners of what had once been unlimited space.

The land block itself was subdivided into 128 lots of 488 acres and 32 lots of 83 acres each. Although lots were cast to ensure equitable access to the various parcels of land, there was no limit to the number any one party could buy, and some, like Jacob Wisler, bought as many as 21.[31] In a few years the 60,000 acres had been spoken for, and in 1807 the German Company was buying an additional 45,195 acres in Woolwich Township, this time from William Wallace of Niagara. The Abraham Weber party, which on June 22 of the same year delivered a half-barrel of gold and silver coin to pay for the Wallace tract, included the people who cleared the lands on which later the city of Kitchener was to stand. They arrived in four wagons, or Conestogas, drawn by two- and four-horse teams.[32]

Among them was one man destined to play a role more significant than any other in the development of the community — Benjamin Eby, the founder of Ebytown. Before entering more fully into the story of his leadership in the Waterloo County community, in the Ebytown congregation, and in the Mennonite Conference of Ontario, it is well to survey the agricultural and legal pioneering in which he shared.

FOOTNOTES

1. S. F. Coffman, "The Adventure of Faith," *Waterloo Historical Society,* XIV (1926), p. 232.
2. David G. Rempel, "The Mennonite Migration to New Russia, 1788–1870," *Mennonite Quarterly Review,* IX (April 1935), pp. 71–91, and IX (July 1935), pp. 109–28; "The Mennonite Colonies in New Russia . . ." (Ph.D. dissertation, Stanford University, 1935); P. M. Friesen, *Die Alt-Evangelische Mennonitische Bruderschaft in Russland, 1789–1910* (Halbstadt, Russia: Raduga, 1911).
3. Ian F. Mackinnon, *Settlements and Churches in Nova Scotia, 1749–1776* (Montreal: Walker, 1930), pp. 12–15; W. O. Raymond, "Alexander McNutt and the Pre-Loyalist Settlements of Nova Scotia," *Transactions of the Royal Society of Canada,* 3rd Ser., Vols. IV, V, VI (1910–12), pp. 83–9, 105–7; George Edward Levy, *The Baptists of the Maritime Provinces, 1753–1946* (Saint John: Barnes-Hopkins, 1946), pp. 1–5; Edward M. Saunders, *History of the Baptists in the Maritime Provinces* (Halifax: John Burgoyne, 1902), pp. 61–2; Esther Clark Wright, *The Loyalists of New Brunswick* (Fredericton: published by the author, 1955), pp. 92, 158–91, 202–37.
4. L. Richter, "Germans in Nova Scotia," *Dalhousie Review,* XV (January 1936), pp. 425–34. See also a contradiction of Richter by William P. Bell, *"The Foreign Protestants" and the Settlement of Nova Scotia: A History of a Piece of Arrested British Colonial Policy in the Eighteenth Century* (Toronto: University of Toronto Press, 1961), pp. 102–3.

5. Donald Warden, New Brunswick Provincial Archives, letter to Edward Dahl, July 22, 1969 (CGC).
6. Wright, *op. cit.*, p. 244.
7. Wilbur J. Bender, "Pacifism Among the Mennonites, Amish Mennonites, and Schwenkfelders of Pennsylvania to 1783," *Mennonite Quarterly Review*, I (July 1927), pp. 23–40; 1 (October 1927), pp. 21–47.
8. Glenn Weaver, "Benjamin Franklin and the Pennsylvania Germans," in Leonard Dinnerstein and Frederic C. Jaher, eds., *The Aliens: A History of Ethnic Minorities in America* (New York: Appleton-Century-Crofts, 1970), pp. 47–64.
9. Donald F. Durnbaugh, "Relationships of the Brethren with the Mennonites and Quakers, 1708–1865," *Church History*, XXXV (March 1966), pp. 35–59.
10. Smith, *Immigration*, pp. 283–7.
11. Christel Funk, *Ein Spiegel fur Alle Menschen* (Reading, Pa.: Johann Ritter & Company, 1813), p. 54.
12. Marcus Lee Hansen, *The Mingling of the Canadian and American Peoples* (Toronto: The Ryerson Press, 1940), Vol. 1, Chap. IV, "The Followers of the Loyalists, 1785–1812."
13. Letter from H. S. Honsberger to Frank H. Epp (CGC Archives). See also H. Stanley Honsberger, Q.C., "A Message from the President to the Dominion Council United Empire Loyalists Association of Canada," *The Loyalist Gazette*, April 1963, p. 1. Also *The Loyalist Gazette*, November 1964.
14. CGC Archives, "The One Hundred and Fiftieth Anniversary of the Founding of the Mennonite Church at Vineland, Ontario" (unpublished manuscript, n.d.), 111-24.
15. L. J. Burkholder, *A Brief History of the Mennonites in Ontario* (Markham, Ont.: Mennonite Conference of Ontario, 1935), p. 31.
16. *Ibid.*
17. *Ibid.*, p. 38. See also: *Ontario Historical Society Papers and Records*, Vol. 24, p. 142; and *Ontario Historical Society, Ontario History*, XXXIX, pp. 18–20.
18. The Confederacy originally included five nations: the Oneidas, Onondagas, Senecas, Cayugas and the Mohawks. At the beginning of the nineteenth century they were joined by the Tuscaroras, whose ancestral home was in the Carolinas but who had also remained loyal to the British cause. Throughout the period under consideration the Confederacy was referred to as either Five Nations or Six Nations. Most of the Indians who actually came to Canada were Mohawks. Many members of the other tribes remained or returned to the United States after 1783.
19. G. F. G. Stanley, "The Six Nations and the American Revolution," *Ontario History*, LVI (1964), pp. 217–34.
20. PAC, Record Group 10, Vol. 26, Folder for 1801–1802. Memor-

andum from Joseph Brant regarding land surrendered by the Mississauga, dated 3 April, 1802.

21. C. M. Johnston, ed., *The Valley of the Six Nations: A Collection of Documents on the Indian Lands of the Grand River* (Toronto: The Champlain Society, 1964).

22. PAC, Record Group 1, E3, Vol. 7, No. 12, pp. 31–64. Trusteeship of Funds of Five Nations lands. Also File No. 20, pp. 79–83 (1897). Funds arising from the sale of Grand River lands. Also Vol. 68, File No. 35, pp. 206–18 (1803). Report on Six Nations Grand River lands. Also Vol. 27, Folder for 1806–1807. Speeches by Captain Brant on 3 September and 9 November, 1806.

23. C. M. Johnston, "Joseph Brant, the Grand River Lands and the Northwest Crisis," *Ontario History*, LV (1903), pp. 267–82.

24. PAC, Record Group 10, Vol. 26, Folder for 1798. Declaration by Richard Beasley, James Wilson and St. John Baptiste Rousseau, regarding terms on the acquired Grand River lands 1 April, 1798.

25. PAC, Record Group 10, Vol. 26, Folder for 1803–1804.

26. A. B. Sherk, "The Pennsylvania Germans in Waterloo County," *Ontario Historical Society Papers and Records*, VII (1906); C. M. Johnston, "An Outline of Early Settlement in Grand River Valley," *Ontario History*, LVI (1962), pp. 43–67.

27. PAC, Record Group 10, Vol. 26, Folder for 1803–1804. Articles of Agreement between Richard Beasley, Daniel Erb and Samuel Bricker, 28 November, 1803. Also Claus's Receipt for Funds paid by the German Land Company, 21 May, 1804.

28. *Ibid.*

29. W. V. Uttley, *The History of Kitchener, Ontario* (Kitchener: The Chronicle Press, 1937), p. 10.

30. See, for example, Harold Cardinal, *The Unjust Society: The Tragedy of Canada's Indians* (Edmonton: M. G. Hurtig, Ltd., 1969); Peter A. Cumming and Neil H. Mickinberg, eds., *Native Rights in Canada*, 2nd ed. (Toronto: The Indian-Eskimo Association of Canada in association with General Publishing Ltd., 1972).

31. Irwin C. Bricker, "The Trek of the Pennsylvanians to Canada in the year 1805," *Waterloo Historical Society*, XXII (1934), pp. 123–31.

32. The Conestoga wagon of Abraham Weber is on display at Doon Pioneer Village, Kitchener, Ontario.

First Schoolhouse in Waterloo

3. Pioneers in a New Land

The Mennonites were among the pioneers of Central Ontario
and have always been noted for their excellent farms,
exemplary conduct, and orderly cooperation with the general
community, in spite of their unique marks of separation
from the secular world—DOUGLAS J. WILSON[1]

THE PIONEER Mennonite immigrants entering the Province of Upper Canada had the advantages, and the disadvantages, of building their new homes in a land which itself was fresh and unstructured. Like their contemporary co-religionists migrating to Russia and their fathers arriving in Pennsylvania a century earlier, they were entering an environment which was primeval in many of its essential features. This new geography was only partly sympathetic to the development of sectarian communities, notwithstanding the Lieutenant-Governor's direct invitation to Mennonites, Quakers, and Tunkers to settle in Upper Canada.

The first Mennonite colonists in each of the three major settlements and those in the numerous minor ones which developed faced a difficult period of back-breaking work in the new province. But all qualified for their task by a heritage of ancestral pioneering and by their own conquest of the 400-mile trail from Pennsylvania to Upper Canada. Some came on foot, some on horseback, and some with the famous Conestoga wagons drawn by four- and six-horse teams. The heroism of the migrants was later immortalized by Mabel Dunham in her novel *The Trail of the Conestoga*.

These covered Conestoga wagons were the best available for the transport of freight, family belongings, and the families themselves. They had been named after the Conestoga River Valley, in which they first appeared around 1736. Created by the Mennonites, the Conestogas reflected the talent and skills for innovation so necessary in a new frontier. The boat-shaped body of the Conestogas prevented loads from easily shifting on the slopes. Their wide wheels reduced or slowed the sinking in soft road beds, and their wide axles prevented easy upsets. A high and wide frame allowed large loads, and a white canvas cover protected the precious cargo from chilling winds, soaking rains and burning sun.

Most often these sturdy wagons decreased, though sometimes they increased, the perils of the heroic journey that wound through forests, over mountains, across rivers, through swamps and marshlands. The typical journey must briefly be recalled not only because of its intensity but also because of its longevity. These treks remained an inevitable part of the pioneer encounter, as prospectors returned to Pennsylvania to get their families, as bachelor settlers rode back to find wives, as young couples set out, though only rarely, to visit their aging parents, and as prospectors, homesick relatives and church bishops travelled northward to attend to their respective interests.

The earliest journeys were, of course, the most difficult, but during the entire period of the migration they were never easy. For most of the immigrants, the 400 or more miles covered included the crossing of the Susquehanna, the mighty Niagara, and other great rivers, as well as the Allegheny Mountains. Some trails could be trod only after they were widened with scythe and axe. Some mountains could be ascended only if the wagons were unloaded and some narrow passes crossed only after the wagons were disassembled. Rivers were bridged with rafts or with floating corduroy hastily put together, or by converting tightly sealed wagons into boats. Many times the passengers, including women and children, walked for long stretches because the loads were too heavy and the roads too muddy. Burkholder has written:

> They required as much as seven weeks to make the whole journey. The part that came to The Twenty in 1800 consisted of 11 four-horse teams, and there were 60 persons in the company. One evening as they camped for the night a tree fell and killed three horses. Sometimes the wagons upset into the mud.[2]

One of the greatest obstacles of all, at least for the Waterloo people, was the Beverly Swamp; this one crossing could take more than a week. Recalling the adventures of one family, Mabel Dunham described this most difficult part of the Conestoga trail:

> On three different occasions the men had to take their
> Conestogas apart and carry the pieces and their baggage upon
> their backs for long distances to more solid ground. They
> were in constant danger of losing their way. The vegetation
> was so luxurious that it hid the path in many places, and on
> every hand there were yawning death-traps half-concealed
> by shrubbery, where insects and reptiles grew and multiplied.
> Even the trees entered into the dark conspiracy, intertwining
> their heavy branches to exclude the light.[3]

At the end of the trail, however, nature and the natives for the most part smiled upon the newcomers, offering them a life of abundance in return for their hard work. The settlers assumed that the conquest of nature would be their greatest challenge while building their new communities, but they soon found that human nature and government policies could also pose obstacles to the achievement of their utopia.

The Upper Canadian province had been set up as an administration separate from Lower Canada as recently as 1791, after the first wave of loyalist immigration had already run its course. The provincial apparatus, being largely responsible to the imperial government of London, was, therefore, quite distant from the people and only partially representative of them. To be sure, an average of three persons from each of the eight districts of Upper Canada were elected to the legislative assemblies of the successive provincial parliaments. The assembly's decisions, however, were easily ignored and often overruled by the legislative and executive councils, both of which were appointed by the lieutenant-governor, who himself had veto power. Even more powerful were the governor, the Crown's direct representative in Quebec, and, of course, His Majesty in London.

Each level of this government hierarchy had as its fundamental goal the preservation and advancement of British North America. But with only French Canadians already resident and immigrants arriving from the continent and overseas as the human elements, the authorities quite understandably guarded carefully the direction of the new society. Too much control could once more lead to a colonial secession, but too little direction would also be meaningless in terms of the British intention. The policies of Upper Canada in its first half-century vacillated between the two alternatives and rebellion in 1837 changed the direction only temporarily.

In that autocratic context, it was clear that Upper Canada's early political and religious hospitality, compared to that of frontier Pennsylvania, was spelled out in limited, if not mostly negative, terms. Whereas Pennsylvania's holy experiment had been set up primarily with sectarians in mind, the loyalist experiment was assumed to benefit primarily British interests; more specifically, British aristocracy and the Church of England. Both of these could flourish only in an expanding society, and that is where the agricultural settlers fitted in.

In a society where land and other natural resources were abundant and cheap, an increasing population was the most important indication of wealth and strength. New York already had one million people, one third of them added in one decade, and Upper Canada was believed to have a similar potential. To facilitate such an increase, a second land grant program was instituted after the first phase of free loyalist land grants had come to an end.

His Majesty gave up to 200 acres of land in return for the payment of certain fees, usually $37, for the clearing of five acres (including road allowances) and for the erection of a dwelling. As long as a settler was not an anti-British revolutionary and otherwise fitted into the British settlement patterns, he could qualify for one of these grants.

In the new province many sectarian settlers hoped for plots adjacent to each other, but that possibility had been prevented by Crown and clergy land reserves. In a township of 66,000 acres, for instance, there were scattered no less than 96 reserved lots of 200 acres each. Not only did these lots separate the settlers but they placed on those adjoining a reserve the full burden of fencing and ditching. Although the Mennonites took advantage of it, a newly introduced system of leasing the reserves at low rates only partly alleviated these problems.[4] Absentee loyalists further contributed to immigrant settlement problems. Mennonites in Lincoln County, particularly, felt themselves handicapped, and they petitioned the Lieutenant-Governor to remove the obstacles to adjoining settlement as follows:

> Your petitioners are desirous of keeping up as much as
> possible among them [young persons seeking land], those

sentiments of morality and religion which it has been their
case to instill into their minds . . . to prevent these fearful
evils, your petitioners humbly beg your Excellency will
consider, how highly advantageous it would be to them and
to the Province in general, were one half, or even any portion
of one of the Townships now about to be surveyed . . . to be
located by the Mennonists only . . .[5]

Their petition failed because of the feeling at the time "that in
future no lands be granted to persons who will not enroll themselves in the Militia and bear Arms in the defence of the Province."[6] Thus there was no easy way for the settlers to achieve
the remarkable compactness that had been negotiated in Russia
and which would at a later time be transferred to Canada. In that
country the Mennonites were virtually forming little states and
worlds within the larger state and world of tsarist Russia. The
original four settlements (see Table 1) had complete autonomy

TABLE 1

SUMMARY OF ORIGINAL FOUR SETTLEMENTS IN RUSSIA

NAME OF SETTLEMENT	PROVINCE	FOUNDING	ACREAGE	VILLAGES
Chortitza	Ekaterinoslav	1789f	102,163	18
Molotschna	Taurida	1804f	324,000	57
Trakt (Koeppental)	Samara	1853	37,800	10
Old Samara (Alexandertal)	Samara	1861	37,800	10

within their respective areas in the Ukraine and Middle Volga
regions, totalling over 500,000 acres and 95 villages.[7] They built
their own roads, established their own taxing system, their own
discipline, their own schools and welfare institutions, albeit with
some guidance and the approval, if not ratification, of the Russian
government.

The Russian Mennonite villages and the land belonging to
them were laid out in such a way as to make its people next-door
neighbours. They lived on small plots on both sides of the street
with equal access to roads, the common pasture, and individually
assigned lands, both the good and not so good, farther away from
the village. This homogeneous and self-sufficient system was so
conducive to the separatist development of sectarian community

that one sociologist referred to it as "the Mennonite commonwealth."[8]

The Russian experience represented the pinnacle of the long
transition from a prophetic protest movement to a withdrawn,
peaceful, largely rural culture, and then to a full-fledged ethnic
entity. Not only did these Mennonites in Russia develop a common language, culture, and familial relationships, but they also
controlled their own government affairs. Church and state once
again became closely allied as almost everyone within the Mennonite territory was a baptized Mennonite.[9]

Although they were "ethnic Mennonites" in the sense that they
shared with their European counterparts a unique culture and
geneological heritage, the Mennonites of Ontario were in no
position to develop any Russian-type commonwealth. Geographically the settlers and settlements were too separated and scattered. By 1841, one of the earliest years producing a reasonably
complete census, they could be found in no fewer than 30 townships in 7 of the 17 census districts. In 23 of these townships
the Mennonite population was less than 50 and in only 7 were
there more than 200 (see Table 2).[10] No township had a
majority of Mennonites and even in the "heavily Mennonite"
township of Waterloo they barely exceeded 10 per cent of the
population. In Woolwich they approached 30 per cent, but only
because the non-Mennonite population was so small. The largest
number of Mennonites in any one district was 3,022 in the Niagara
area; this was more than half the provincial total of 5,379. But
the Niagara people were scattered over 13 townships in which
there were some 20,000 other people, so that Mennonites had
difficulty maintaining a separate identity. Before too long a high
degree of integration would obliterate some of the scattered islands
of Mennonitism.

Where the Mennonites approached compactness of settlement,
as in Woolwich and Waterloo, they did not necessarily form homogeneous communities. The immigrants to Waterloo County originated in at least half a dozen counties in Pennsylvania. They
included the poor and the wealthy, those who migrated because
they would never be able to pay $100 per acre in Pennsylvania
and those who could afford very substantial investments of land.

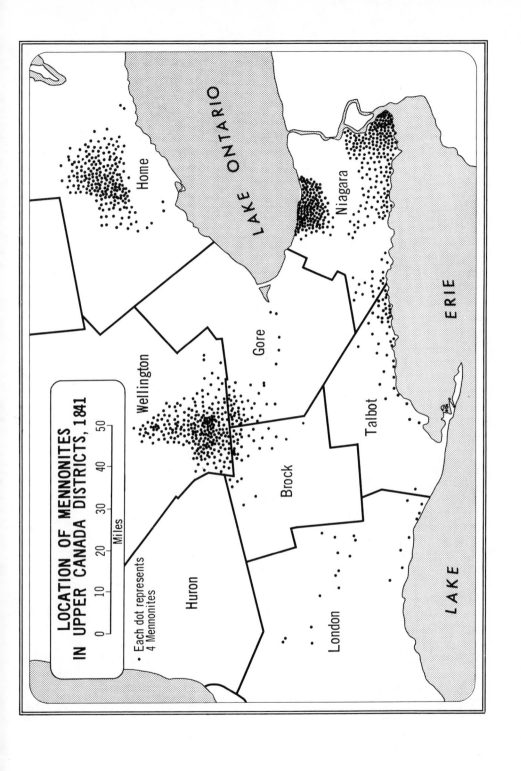

LOCATION OF MENNONITES
IN UPPER CANADA DISTRICTS, 1841

Miles
0   10   20   30   40   50

• Each dot represents
  4 Mennonites

LAKE ONTARIO

LAKE ERIE

Home

Niagara

Gore

Wellington

Brock

Talbot

Huron

London

TABLE 2

MENNONITES AND TUNKERS
IN UPPER CANADA TOWNSHIPS IN 1841*

DISTRICT AND TOWNSHIP	MENNONITES	TUNKERS	TOTAL
LONDON			
Bayham	17	—	2,196
Colborne	15	—	437
Dorchester	23	—	620
Ellice	—	4	200
Lobo	18	—	1,169
Malahide	9	—	2,187
Westminster	17	—	2,680
Yarmouth	7	21	3,762
Others (27)	—	—	19,006
Total	106	25	32,257
TALBOT			
Woodhouse	31	10	1,694
Charlotteville	12	—	1,974
Townsend	—	11	2,512
Houghton	2	3	277
Others (3)	—	—	3,169
Total	45	24	9,626
BROCK			
East Oxford	—	7	1,185
Zorra	24	—	2,768
Burford	10	—	1,986
Blenheim	100	21	1,689
Others (6)	—	—	7,993
Total	134	28	15,621
WELLINGTON			
Woolwich	271	—	1,009
Wilmot	259	57	2,220
Waterloo	463	78	4,424
Others (7)	—	—	6,198
Total	993	135	13,851
GORE			
Nelson	—	12	3,060
Puslinch	23	14	1,709
Beverly	—	159	2,684
Dumfries	180	70	6,129
Barton	—	9	1,434

DISTRICT AND TOWNSHIP	MENNONITES	TUNKERS	TOTAL
Ancaster	20	—	2,930
Others (10)	—	—	24,631
Total	223	264	42,577
NIAGARA			
Bertie	349	108	2,318
Caistor	—	8	599
Clinton	377	18	2,122
Crowland	43	—	973
Gainsborough	13	27	1,598
Grimsby	7	11	1,784
Humberstone	133	—	1,376
Louth	211	28	1,392
Pelham	—	33	1,522
Thorold	—	17	2,284
Wainfleet	158	—	1,147
Willoughby	120	—	895
Cayuga	57	—	837
Dunn	19	—	345
Rainham	83	4	716
Walpole	41	—	831
Others (8)	—	—	42,716
Total	3,022	504	63,455
HOME			
York	7	—	538
Pickering	22	—	502
Markham	455	188	4,636
Vaughan	198	110	3,421
Whitchurch	169	37	2,718
Etobicoke	7	—	1,794
Uxbridge	1	1	99
Chinguacousy	—	10	3,970
Others (31)	—	—	46,723
Total	859†	346†	64,401
10 Other Districts with 132 Townships‡	—	—	197,957
GRAND TOTALS	5,382	1,326	439,745

* Compared to total population.
† 1839 figures.
‡ No figures for Johnstown; two districts based on 1840 figures.

There were other factors militating against community development. Culturally, the Ontario Mennonite settlers were not as clearly differentiated from the total population as were the Mennonites in Russia. Governmentally they were not autonomous, although in many ways community development depended on their own initiative. Religiously they were not sufficiently united and uniformly motivated to successfully counteract all the cultural forces surrounding them. Not all of these factors were disadvantages, however, for the British society which was hoping to shape the sectarians was itself largely unstructured. Its ultimate character depended greatly on the initiative of the people. In the area of religion, Upper Canada was officially Church-of-England territory, but this strength was offset sheerly by the non-Anglican population and their much more zealous clergy (see Table 3).[11]

In the final analysis the cultural realities of Upper Canada leant toward the background of the people who lived on and cultivated the land, and who developed their own institutions. And where land and people met, the Mennonites found assets favourable to the solid development of their communities. Above all, they came equipped with a deep love for the soil and with the skills, developed through generations of experience in agriculture, to manage it.

In Europe the Swiss and Swiss-Palatine Mennonites had been the first to introduce such practices as crop rotation, use of animal manure and lime for fertilizers, and legumes to enrich the soil. In Pennsylvania they had been credited with the "first intensive agriculture in America."[12] One of the signers of the Declaration of Independence, Benjamin Rush, a Philadelphia physician, wrote about Mennonites and other Germans:

> ... taken as a body especially as farmers [they] are not only
> industrious and frugal but skillful cultivators of the earth.
> They are noted for their good fences, the extent of their
> orchards, the fertility of the soil, the productiveness of the
> fields, and the luxuriance of their meadows.[13]

Their way of life required the marriage of the people to the soil and to agriculture, which they recognized as the foundation of civilization. More than just a way of making a living, agriculture was for them a way of life. Clearing of the land was therefore not so much a burden as it was an exciting challenge and adventure without which life would be incomplete. Years later a

TABLE 3

RELIGIOUS CENSUS OF UPPER CANADA BY DISTRICTS*
IN SELECTED CATEGORIES IN 1841

DISTRICTS	DENOMINATION OR CHURCH BODY								
	ENG-LAND	SCOT-LAND	ROME	METHO-DIST	MENNO.	TUNK-ER	QUAK-ER	OTHERS†	TOTAL
Western	—	—	3,464	4,357	—	—	89	15,116	23,026
London	7,322	3,744	1,144	5,422	103	25	364	14,133	32,257
Talbot	800	190	131	2,325	45	24	54	6,057	9,626
Brock	2,655	2,042	415	3,921	134	28	873	5,553	15,621
Wellington	2,108	1,648	1,426	925	993	135	38	6,578	13,851
Gore	9,683	6,599	2,514	2,340	223	264	181	20,773	42,577
Niagara	—	71	1,800	6,498	3,022	504	1,069	50,491	63,455
Toronto	6,754	1,503	2,401	1,698	—	—	5	1,888	14,249
Home‡	15,825	12,468	3,709	8,395	859	346	1,097	21,702	64,401
Newcastle	12,397	—	5,726	7,293	—	1	606	15,929	41,952
Victoria	1,852	962	1,709	3,591	—	—	113	4,472	12,699§
Midland	2,383	1,004	1,689	2,370	—	—	58	24,704	32,208
Prince Edward	2,581	542	1,314	5,342	—	—	882	4,000	14,661
Bathurst	?	?	?	?	?	?	?	24,674	24,674§
Johnstown	?	?	?	?	?	?	?	?	?
Ottawa	1,703	2,459	3,723	956	—	—	—	483	9,324
Eastern	4,519	11,820	9,246	2,356	—	—	—	2,338	30,279
Total	70,582	45,052	49,411	57,789	5,379	1,327	5,429	218,891	444,860

* From southwest Upper Canada to northeast.
† Including Episcopalians, Wesleyans, British Connexions, Congregationalists, Presbyterians, Universalists, Restorationers, Mormons, Lutherans, Baptists, Jews, Apostolic Church, Unitarians, Disciples, Irvinites, Church of God, Cameronians.
‡ 1839 figures.
§ 1840 figures.

London Free Press reporter, visiting the Mennonites for the first time, described them precisely in this way:

> ... a hospitable, kindly folk, who, in the face of tremendous
> odds pushed into Western Ontario ... and laid the
> foundations of an agricultural development unparallelled
> anywhere else in the province.[14]

A people responding kindly to the beauty and bounty of nature found that nature responded likewise to them, revealing its abundance and potential: unpolluted streams bubbling with fish, woods abounding with live venison, trees in creek beds thick with plums and berries, bee-trees filled with tubfuls of honey, and maple trees dripping with gallons of syrup. Pigeons often darkened the skies by the tens of thousands, and early Mennonite folklore had it that a young farmer named Shantz at one shooting downed 84 of the birds as they rose from the wheat stooks. One writer described this relationship between the benignity of nature and these enterprising people:

> The timber was of mammoth growth and diversity. Stately
> pines, whose trunks were six feet in diameter waved their
> topmost branches more than 200 feet above the ground ...
> The first table used in the county was in the dwelling of
> Joseph Sherk and consisted of a huge pine stump, five feet in
> diameter over which the house had been erected.[15]

The Indians, too, were part of that generous environment; they were friendly to the extent that the settlers were friendly to them. As the Indians led them down the trails to the choicest lands, to the best hunting grounds and fishing waters, the Mennonites shared their bread and milk and frequently the huge fireplaces which were incorporated into even the earliest homes. Indian women gladly and reliably watched over Mennonite babies and young Mennonite lads learned the skills of surviving in the woods from their Indian teachers.

The cordiality and mutual helpfulness did not remain, however. As the settlers, among them Mennonites, established distilleries, and as liquor became one of the ingredients of social relationships and trade, acute problems developed. In 1808 the Legislative Assembly heard a petition which stated that one Abraham Stauffer, a Mennonite of Waterloo Township, had been shot by a drunken Indian and was in danger of his life. Request was made that trading with spirits be stopped by law lest settlers be endangered and Indian children, unprovided for by drunken parents, be forced to go begging.[16] The petition to that effect entered by John Shoop, Joseph Bearinger, and 25 others said in part:

> Several of our township inhabitors take kegs and barrels full
> of spirits from the distillers and trade with the Indians,
> which causes them to get drunk and lie about and not follow
> their hunting, and their young ones starving for hunger,
> going about begging and hallowing for victuals before our
> doors like beasts, and at the same time often the old ones
> coming along and being drunk, scaring ourselves, and our
> families by their bad behaviour.[17]

Rarely did the Indians become farm help for the settlers. The settlers in Upper Canada, however, were not without some cheap labour brought along from the States. Although the importation of slaves to Canada was abolished in 1793, existing master-slave relationships were still respected, "voluntary contracts" of nine years' duration were permitted, and children born of slaves after 1793 were allowed to go free only at the age of 25. Slavery was not quickly abolished in practice; slaves were bought and sold in Toronto as late as 1806. Whether or not Isaac Jones, who was brought into Canada by Abraham Erb, was such a slave or perhaps a runaway who had found security with Erb cannot be ascertained definitely.[18] In Pennsylvania slavery had been rejected by most Quakers and Mennonites, but some had accepted it. Mennonite history is not as explicit as Quaker history on this question, but at the time of the civil war Mennonites in at least one area were praised for their loyalty to the constitution and the government "which protects the slave holders as well as themselves."[19]

Apart from slave-holding, common labour itself was cheap. A day's wages amounted to one dollar, the equivalent in value of five pounds of butter or cheese. If salaried by the year the labourer would be worth $100, enough to buy a horse with saddle and perhaps a cow.

Whatever the settlers owed the Indians and other cheap labour, the actual agricultural skills required for settlement were theirs. It was not uncommon for a Mennonite to be handy in all manner of wood, brick, iron, and leather work. He did not have to be told how to build a log cabin, how to make a clearing in the woods, how to construct a fireplace, or how to repair his harness. As time went on, of course, specializations developed among blacksmiths, masons, and carpenters. The farmer's basic knowledge, however, was sufficient, as long as there were relatives and neighbours to help him and to assist with the tasks too heavy for one family.

Relatives, it seems, made up for much that was otherwise lacking due to the scattered nature of the Canadian Mennonite communities. In small as well as large settlements it was common for a number of brothers and brothers-in-law to settle together. Frequently parents with large families would uproot themselves in Pennsylvania and move to frontier areas where each member of the family would some day have his own parcel of land. Ezra Eby's biographical history gives some examples:

> David Gingerich travelled from Lancaster . . . in company with his wife, his father Abraham Gingerich and wife, and eight children . . .[20]

> In 1819 Peter Martin and family, which numbered only nine sons and eight daughters, came to Waterloo . . .[21]

> In 1820 David Martin and family of twelve children . . .[22]

> In 1826 came Henry Moyer and family, Jacob Clemens and family . . . Jacob Kolb and family, Solomon Gehman and family, Henry Clemmer and family, Charles Mohr and family, Martin Schiedel and family . . . Abraham Thoman and family . . .[23]

The 1820s brought numerous immigrant families to Upper Canada from Pennsylvania, especially after 1825 when times became unusually bad there. A harvest day's wage for labourers working from sunrise to sunset, for instance, was less than 40 cents. This period of depression, though temporary, marked a turning point for many, including the Amish, who now also set their sights on Upper Canada and who became closely tied to the Mennonite communities.

The Amish movement began in 1822 when Christian Nafziger, a peasant farmer from Bavaria, arrived in Waterloo County. He had hitch-hiked to Amsterdam where he had boarded a freighter to New Orleans. After travelling overland on foot to Pennsylvania, he came to Canada by horse. The Mennonite leaders in Waterloo directed him westward to the township later called Wilmot, a

Crown reserve untouched except for three road lines running into it. Nafziger conferred with Governor Maitland, who reserved the land for Nafziger's people, naming it the German Block. Mindful of the Beasley affair, Nafziger wasn't satisfied with his deal until he had seen the King himself. In London, George IV, being himself of German descent and sympathetic, confirmed the governor's offer and even assisted Nafziger financially.

On his way back to Germany, Nafziger told the good news in the Palatinate whence it quickly spread to Amish settlements in Alsace and even America. Nafziger himself did not emigrate until 1826, three years after Amish settlers had actually begun to arrive, first from Pennsylvania and then from Europe. With the help of a Mennonite settlement committee from Waterloo County they settled in 200-acre plots along the township roads in the German block. The Amish migrants trickled into the country for about fifty years, during which time there was also considerable movement to the United States and back again.[24]

Sociologically speaking, the Amish had at least two things in common with the Mennonites: a love for land and for large families. The sons all became farmers like their fathers. The girls all learned to milk cows, to plant vegetable gardens, to weave wool, to spin flax, and to sew their own clothes. Every home had its loom, its apple cider barrels, and its vegetable cellars, and some, especially the Amish, had their wineries, striking another similarity with the Rhineland.

Not all the requirements of pioneer life and community building could be met in the context of the family, no matter how large. Besides, some families were small and there were also bachelors homesteading there. But for everyone help and fellowship, and indeed fun, could be found in the working parties or "bees" that were formed. Through these bees entire communities of men and women would do together what could not otherwise be accomplished. Often this was the way roads were built, barns raised, and sheep fleeced. The working bees were necessary, dictated by circumstances, for all the pioneers; but for the Mennonites they were an outgrowth of their religion of sharing and the practice of intimate community dating from the Anabaptist beginnings. Believing mutual aid and other self-help programs to be a Christian obligation, they resisted insurance policies promoted so vigorously by the world outside. Their special kind of teamwork became best known to the public through their communal barn raisings.[25] Mutual aid eventually expressed itself in the formal establishment of both Amish and Mennonite insurance

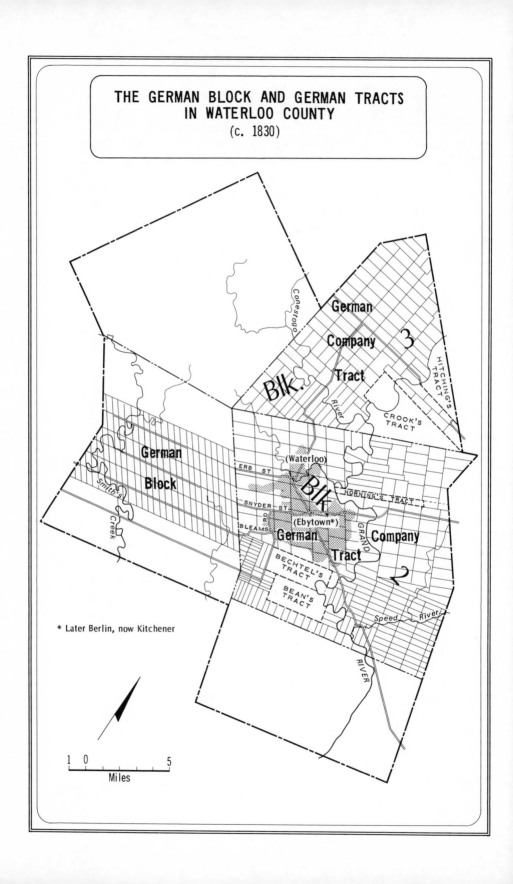

THE GERMAN BLOCK AND GERMAN TRACTS IN WATERLOO COUNTY
(c. 1830)

Conestogo

German Company Tract

3

HITCHING'S TRACT

Blk.

CROOK'S TRACT

River

German Block

(Waterloo)

ERB ST

Blk.

HOENING'S TRACT

SNYDER ST

Smith's Creek

BLEAMS

(Ebytown*)

Company

German Tract

GRAND

2

BECHTEL'S TRACT

BEAN'S TRACT

Speed River

* Later Berlin, now Kitchener

RIVER

1 0   5
Miles

TYPICAL FLOOR PLAN OF ONTARIO MENNONITE HOME

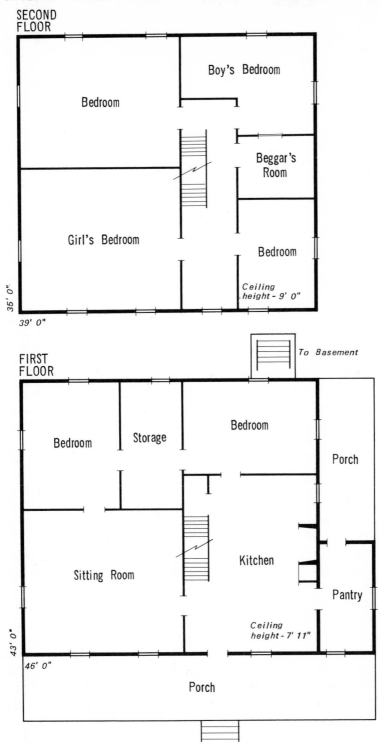

SECOND FLOOR

Boy's Bedroom

Bedroom

Beggar's Room

Girl's Bedroom

Bedroom

Ceiling height - 9' 0"

35' 0"

39' 0"

To Basement

FIRST FLOOR

Bedroom

Storage

Bedroom

Porch

Sitting Room

Kitchen

Pantry

Ceiling height - 7' 11"

43' 0"

46' 0"

Porch

organizations, designed to replace fire and storm damage. The Ontario Mennonite Aid Union, the first in North America, was officially organized in 1866.

While a substitute for commercial insurance, Mennonite mutual aid was more than a business venture. It had deep religious roots and was an effort to restore the community which had been exemplified by the Apostolic Church as well as by the Anabaptists. The acts of brotherhood also included hospitality to strangers. Scores of transients obtained food and night lodging in Mennonite homes, sometimes in exchange for such chores as splitting wood. Permanent homes built by the settlers between 1820 and 1870 included a beggar's room, especially for transients.

One common community task requiring a maximum of co-operation concerned the building of good roads, especially since not much help was forthcoming from York (Toronto).[26] The provincial government was concerned primarily with building trunk roads to meet the requirements of defence before the needs of settlement. This fact, of course, was not entirely a disadvantage, since military garrisons provided the first ready markets for the produce of the agricultural pioneers. The settlement roads themselves evolved from trails through the woods. At first the swamps were bridged with tree trunks up to two feet thick. Eventually they were covered with earth or gravel, generally a thin layer, leaving them very rough and bumpy. The commonest, easiest, and quickest mode of travel was by horseback, and every farmer had two or three saddles, which were particularly useful in the spring when roads were almost impassable for vehicles.

Another common task concerned the building of schools. For many years the settlers in Upper Canada who wanted schools for their children had to establish them through their own initiative with the resources available in the neighbourhood. Attempts were made in the Legislative Assembly to establish public schools as early as 1804 but the bills failed to pass. And although eight grammar schools, one in each of the districts, were established with $400 annual subsidy in 1807, public education as it was later known did not arrive until the passing of the Common Schools Act in 1842.[27]

The Mennonites were not particularly worried about the lack of government support for education. To many of them, government intervention in education was an intrusion into their value system and was not particularly welcome. Indeed, the time would come when they would fight government-funded education to the ex-

tent of founding their own schools, thereby submitting themselves
to double taxation. On the frontier, however, the Mennonites took
strong initiative in founding community schools. In Waterloo
County four schools were established before 1830. In that year
Abraham Erb deeded $2000 of his estate, or the interest thereof,
for educational purposes, especially for the poor and the orphaned.
That legacy was administered for 60 years by trustees of the
Mennonite Society and the Waterloo school portion was eventually transferred to the Waterloo County Board of Education.[28]

In Mennonite areas the school instruction was generally in the
German language and included such subjects as reading, writing,
arithmetic and religion. The neighbourhood schools were usually
located in private homes, abandoned dwellings, unused shops or
meeting houses; sometimes they were in the open air or under any
available and convenient shelter. Later log schoolhouses were built
and funded by private subscriptions. Schools were kept open during the winter months only, and the teachers were preachers or
people who had no special professional qualifications and were
engaged in other occupations the rest of the year.

The community aspect of the schools established in Mennonite
and Amish areas cannot be overemphasized, inasmuch as it represented yet another difference from the Mennonites in Russia. The
common dialect among German Mennonites, Catholics and
Lutherans contributed, of course, to the easier mixing of the
people. Be that as it may, a spirit of openness and tolerance
toward non-Mennonites became characteristic of some Mennonite
communities to a greater degree than could be observed elsewhere
in North America. Common burial grounds were another expression of neighbourliness, and some Mennonite meeting-houses
were freely used by other denominations for their services.

Frontier settlement on the whole served well the purpose of
bringing diverse peoples together and of melting down traditional
enmities, including those already indicated between Mennonites
and Catholics, dating back to the Reformation. Mennonite-Amish
and Catholic sources both speak of warm relationships between
the two groups and mutual helpfulness in settlement. The words
of one Catholic chronicler are worth noting:

> The newcomers from Europe, having scanty means and
> being quite inexperienced in bush-life, obtained valuable
> advice, employment, and credit from their better-situated
> Mennonite neighbors. These were uniformly kind, neighborly
> and hospitable to a degree. In fact, without this helpful

disposition of the Mennonites, the European settlers could
scarcely have remained in the wilderness. Almost every one
of them could tell of many instances of getting help in
distress and great need.[29]

The manner of farming was primitive in the early nineteenth
century; implements were simple, many of them hand-made.
Ploughs were usually wooden and the first harvests were cut with
sickle and scythe. Threshing, done with the flail, took all winter.
The grain drills, the reapers, and the threshers did not make their
appearance until the 1840s and 1850s. Team threshing was to
become common only after 1860, and the twine-binder wasn't
perfected until near the end of the century.

The installation of small industrial units, however, did not have
to await complete agricultural mechanization. As the Mennonite
settlers sowed and harvested their first wheat in the small clear-
ings and among the stumps they began to establish corporate
grist mills. The Erb brothers, John in Preston and Abraham in
Waterloo, became prominent grist mill owners. As the farmers
cleared the land they became lumbermen and established saw-
mills; then wood-working establishments and later pulp and
paper mills were begun. As game was taken from the forests for
food, the skins were dried and tanneries were developed. The
weaving of wool from many sheep led to the creation of woollen
mills.

As agriculture expanded and barley was introduced, breweries
were added to the grist mills; both flour and alcoholic beverages
were considered essential to the social economy of the day.[30] By
mid-century 150 distilleries and breweries in Upper Canada were
producing 1.17 million gallons annually, most of it being consumed by a population of less than one million. Social drinking
patterns soon became an issue of religious controversy which the
Mennonites, too, could not escape. In the words of Gourlay, an
Upper Canada statistician:

> To this fault the early settlers here were peculiarly exposed,
> from the manner of life they had followed several years in
> the army, their want of cider, that common drink in which
> they had been accustomed before the revolution, and the
> facility with which distilled liquors could be procured as a
> substitute.[31]

The Canadian pioneers were gifted not only in extracting spirits
and wine from the domesticated and wild fruits, but also in pro-

ducing from plants medicines and home remedies of many kinds. Among the healing powers derived from the natural environment, those of the elderberry bush rated particularly high. The juice of the root cooked in water could induce vomiting and urination. The flowers and the bark of the elderberry likewise contained laxative powers. A tea-like drink from the flowers had the effect of inducing perspiration in cases of influenza, smallpox and measles. The elderberry was also used for reducing inflamed swellings, for muscular pains, and for checking ulcers and contagious diseases. Last, but not least, the elderberry bushes yielded pleasant elder wine.

Bitter sage or mint tea and a little bit of charming seemed to cure many diseases. Charming, or prayer incantations, was sometimes also called "powwowing" or "Braucherei."[32] One formula for the cure of goitre, preserved with others for posterity in the Jordan Village Museum at the Twenty, is as follows:

> At the beginning of each new moon,
> Look at the moon,
> Rub the goiter,
> and say the following words:
> "I see something that grows,
> I rub something that goes,
> In the name of Jesus."[33]

Like other social and practical problems, medical problems were abated by genuine neighbourliness and community spirit. Every cluster of neighbours boasted a midwife and a bone-setter ready, willing, and able to attend to those medical needs which tea could not cure. As the 1820s approached there still were no "medical practitioners" in any of the communities where Mennonites lived. A limited census of 1817 indicates shortages of other public servants, such as preachers and teachers. Otherwise there were signs of material progress, seen partly in the tripling and quadrupling of land prices in about two decades.

The general experience of early self-sufficiency and prosperity in the Mennonite community did not mean the absence of adversity. On the contrary, the pioneers were confronted by many problems, including the vicissitudes of natural and man-made disasters. In 1806, for instance, raging forest fires destroyed a large number of houses, barns, fences, pastures, and animals in the Blair, Preston and Berlin areas. One Abraham Bechtel lost his barn, house and all the provisions he had stocked up to receive friends from Pennsylvania. To give another example of pioneer misfortune, the year 1816 brought frost every single month, including seven heavy frosts in the months of June and July alone. On June 1 the ice was thick enough to bear the weight of wagons on small ponds and heavy snow fell as late as June 26. Provisions for the people and food for the animals were in extremely short supply. The only available hay was the wild growth in marshes of heavier meadows. Wheat that had been selling as low as 50 cents a bushel increased in price six times; the same price rise also affected other essentials.

Perhaps the most difficult and continuous hardship was the separation from families and friends in Pennsylvania. Visits to and fro were rare and letters went slowly and only as frequently as riders or stage coach drivers would take them. Perhaps the women who left parents, brothers and sisters behind to join their young husbands on the frontier deserve the greatest credit of all in the pioneer venture.

In all their loneliness, pioneering and community building, the settlers enjoyed a resource which so far has hardly been mentioned. The reference is to the congregational sector and its leaders who nurtured the spirits of the settlers. Indeed, so significant was the religious impulse in building and dividing the communities that special attention will be given to this phase of the settlement experience in Chapter 5. But first, in the next chapter, there must be a review of how Mennonitism related to the law of the land, especially with reference to the militia of Upper Canada.

FOOTNOTES

1.   Douglas J. Wilson, *The Church Grows in Canada* (Toronto: Canadian Council of Churches, 1966), p. 75.

2.   L. J. Burkholder, *Mennonites of Ontario* (Markham, Ont.: Mennonite Conference of Ontario, 1935), p. 25.

3.   Mabel Dunham, *Trail of the Conestoga* (Toronto: McClelland & Stewart, 1924), pp. 124–25.

4.   Gerald M. Craig, *Upper Canada: The Formative Years 1784–1841* (Toronto: McClelland & Stewart, 1963), pp. 50, 131. See also Gourlay, *Statistical Account of Upper Canada* (London: Simpkin & Marshall, 1822), Vol. I, p. 321.

5. PAC, *Upper Canada Land Petitions*, R. G. 1, L3, Vol. 340, "M" Bundle 12, #83. Petition of the Mennonites (or harmless Christians) of the District of Niagara, Jacob Meyer—Minister, April 7, 1819.

6. *Ibid.*

7. "Russia," *Mennonite Encyclopedia*, IV, p. 383.

8. E. K. Francis, "Mennonite Commonwealth in Russia, 1789–1914: A Sociological Interpretation," *Mennonite Quarterly Review*, XXV (1951), pp. 173–82, 200.

9. E. K. Francis, "Mennonite Commonwealth in Russia," *op. cit.*; "The Nature of the Ethnic Group," *American Journal of Sociology*, LII (March 1947), pp. 393–400; "The Russian Mennonites: From Religious to Ethnic Group," *American Journal of Sociology*, LIV (September 1948), pp. 101–7; Robert Kreider, "The Anabaptist Conception of the Church in the Russian Mennonite Environment 1789–1870," *Mennonite Quarterly Review*, XXV (January 1951), pp. 17–33.

10. Canadian Government Census of Canada, Population Returns for the Year 1841.

11. *Ibid.*

12. Ira D. Landis, "Mennonite Agriculture in Colonial Lancaster County, Pennsylvania," *Mennonite Quarterly Review*, XIX (October 1945), p. 254ff.

13. *Ibid.*

14. W. G. Trestain, "Mennonites Hospitable, Kindly; Stick Closely to Their Faith," *London Free Press*, September 9, 1938.

15. *Hundred Years Progress in Waterloo County: Semi-Centennial Souvenir, 1856–1906* (Waterloo, Ont.: The Chronicle Telegraph), pp. 6–18.

16. Province of Upper Canada, *Journal of Legislative Assembly*, February 18, 1808.

17. *Ibid.*

18. Miriam H. Snyder, *Hannes Schneider and his Wife Catherine Haus Schneider: Their Descendants and Times, 1534–1939* (Kitchener, Ont.: published by the author, 1937), p. 188. For the detailed story of slavery in Canada see Robin W. Winks, *The Blacks in Canada* (Montreal: McGill-Queen's University Press, 1971).

19. Samuel Horst, *Mennonites in the Confederacy* (Scottdale, Pa.: Herald Press, 1967), p. 26.

20. Ezra E. Eby, *A Biographical History of Waterloo Township: A History of the Early Settlers and Their Descendants* (Berlin, Ont.: published by the author, 1895), p. 168.

21. Snyder, *op. cit.*, p. 21.
22. *Ibid.*, p. 21.
23. *Ibid.*, p. 22.
24. Orland Gingerich, *The Amish of Canada* (Waterloo, Ont.: Conrad Press, 1972), p. 27ff.
25. Edwin Guillet, *The Pioneer Farmer and Backwoodsman* (Toronto: University of Toronto Press, 1963), pp. 160–61.
26. Petition: complaint about state of roads between Waterloo and lake ports. November 9, 1828. Mennonites included. (CGC Archives)
27. Thomas Pearce, "School History, Waterloo County, and Berlin," in Snyder, p. 211.
28. M. A. Johnston, "A Brief History of Elementary Education in the City of Waterloo," *Waterloo Historical Society*, LIII (1965), pp. 56–66.
29. Eby, *op. cit.*, p. 52. See also *Waterloo Historical Society*, XVI (1928), pp. 26–30.
30. Theobold Spetz, "The Catholic Church in Waterloo County," in *ibid.*, p. 269.
31. Robert C. Gourlay, *Statistical Accounts of Upper Canada* (London: Simpkin & Marshall, 1822), Vol. 1, p. 252.
32. "Medicine," *Mennonite Encyclopedia*, III, p. 208; "Powwowing," *ME*, IV, pp. 550–52.
33. Jordan Village Museum Scrapbook, Jordan, Ont.

Retreat from the Thames

4. The Nonresistors and the Militia

These two beliefs [against killing and swearing] required
special consideration in view of the provincial statutory
requirement for universal manhood service in the militia and
the need for oaths of office and sworn testimony in the
courts—JOHN S. MOIR.[1]

UPPER CANADA had provided an abundance of good land
for the new Mennonite and Tunker immigrants, but
without an equal measure of legal latitude the wide horizons did
not hold the promise of the coveted freedom. The bitter experience of their persecuted ancestors had taught the Anabaptists
that restrictive laws could make a prison out of an otherwise
liberal territory. In the great land of the loyalists the liberty-
conscious settlers soon discovered that, in spite of all their acreage,
they had no legal right thereon to build their churches or even to
lay out cemeteries for their dead. They could not solemnize their
own marriages, not to speak of immediately and fully enjoying
those liberties which to them were most important of all: freedom
from the oath (the swearing of ultimate loyalty to the Crown) and
exemption from military service.

There was, therefore, pioneering to be done not only on the land
but also with respect to the law of the land. It has been argued
that economic factors, especially the availability of cheap arable
land, accounted for the Mennonites' coming to Canada. The eco-

93

nomic interpretation of immigration movements is not without its valid application in Mennonite history, and it cannot be dismissed entirely here. But it would be incorrect to assume that land was all that these immigrants required for their fulfilment.

The evidence is strong that the thousands of Mennonites on the move around 1800 in both the eastern and western hemispheres were looking for a special kind of liberty as well as a special kind of land. The negotiated agreement for settlement in Russia, for instance, included not only generous parcels of land but also equally generous legal concessions. Among the settlement promises, patiently negotiated with several tsars, was the permanent exemption from military service.

A similar condition of settlement held true in Canada. A degree of military exemption was sought and achieved early in the immigration, even before the main movements got underway, before the land along the Grand River had been selected, before any ministers had been ordained, and before any churches had been built. It is true, of course, that Upper Canada was anxious for good settlers and ready to make certain allowances to minority groups who otherwise served the British. But considering the difficulty with which even the smallest concessions were made, it seems fair to conclude that the immigrant Quakers, Mennonites, and Tunkers were a fairly determined band.

As noted before, a clear-cut position on nonresistance, a term used by Mennonites more often than pacifism, was both fundamental and central to the Anabaptist faith.[2] The Schleitheim Confession of 1527 had identified weapons of force, "such as the sword, armour and the like," as un-Christian.[3] And Menno Simons, one of the foremost champions of nonresistance, had said without equivocation:

> The regenerated do not go to war, nor engage in strife. They are the children of peace who have beaten their swords into plowshares and their spears into pruning hooks, and know of no war.[4]

The nonresistant teaching and tradition had been adopted and strengthened in Pennsylvania. In William Penn's land of the holy experiment, pacifist sectarianism had flourished with the official encouragement of Quaker assemblymen and remained strong even after their fall from power in 1756. The *Ausbund* hymnal, the *Martyrs' Mirror*, and the Dordrecht Confession of Faith had been the chief instruments of the perpetuation of the pacifist conscience and the doctrine of nonresistance.[5] That the Confession remained important to the Upper Canada immigrants is seen in the fact that it became the very first document printed by them. Printed at Niagara-on-the-Lake in 1811 and in English, it was undoubtedly a testimony to and a defence of their faith.[6]

At the heart of the problem in Canada was the fact that the new society had not yet adjusted to religious pluralism beyond the acceptance of the Roman Catholic Church as predominant in Lower Canada and the Church of England as normative for Upper Canada. The old idea of the Roman Empire, that an ordered society required one law and only one recognized church in a given state, had survived long after the Protestant Reformation. Indeed, as mentioned before, the principle that the religion of the ruler is the religion of the people had been reinforced by the Reformation and its sometimes exclusionistic Calvinist establishments, its comfortably allied Lutheran princes and priests, and its rebelling English monarchs who became the "popes" of a national church. And, paradoxically, the Mennonite commonwealth in Russia, later to be transplanted to Canada, also combined a single religion with a given territory.

Nevertheless, such notions of all the people belonging to the same territorial or national church were no longer absolute doctrine in England. And political allegiance was no longer necessarily equated with adherence to the official religion. But since the idea of a single state with a single official church was reborn in Upper Canada, the dissenters felt obliged to challenge it all over again.

The Constitutional Act of 1791 granted to the Church of England certain statutory rights which made her the preeminent religious institution. Among the strongest and most problematic of her rights was the free possession of one-seventh of the land, the so-called clergy reserves, set aside for the support of the clergy and church institutions. Such patronage of religion and endowments for the church were, of course, not entirely a new policy. In New France the Catholic Church had been granted immense land holdings in return for certain social services, and even in America, where the separation of church and state was most championed, land was set aside for the purposes of religion, both before and after the revolution. In all cases the land grants were made on the assumption that religion had a useful, if not indispensable, service to perform in the social order. In the mind of one British colonial secretary the support of religion was justified by its contribution to "the internal peace of society."[7] Upper Canada's first Lieutenant-Governor, John Graves Simcoe, put the argument thus:

> A regular Episcopal establishment, subordinate to the
> primacy of Great Britain, is absolutely necessary in any
> extensive colony which this country means to preserve ...
> due support to that church establishment, which I consider
> as necessary to promote the national religion ... and to
> maintain the true and venerable constitution of my country.[8]

In Upper Canada, however, official religious authority did not ensure internal peace. On the contrary, the non-Anglican loyalists, who turned out to be the majority of the population, were in no mood to accept, join or tolerate a privileged and powerful state-endowed church. The height of that intolerance was reached when that church allied itself with conservative ruling groups to become a "family compact," reluctant to share its power with the people.

All of the non-establishment religious groups had their reasons for seeking "relief" from discriminatory laws, but the followers of the Church of Scotland and the Methodists took up the struggle for religious equality with greatest vigour. The former wanted to share the land being granted to the Church of England. The latter insisted that clergy lands should benefit all the people and that clergy rights (i.e. marriage) should be enjoyed by all denominations. The Methodists introduced marriage bills no less than twelve times between 1802 and 1829 and, though all were lost in the legislature, the marriage cause triumphed in 1831 when royal assent was finally given to a law that had been passed two years before.[9] That law, providing for "the future solemnization of matrimony in this province," defined "clergyman or minister" rather narrowly but within that narrow context solemnization rights were granted to:

> ... any Clergyman or Minister or any Church, Society,
> Congregation, or Religious Community of Persons professing
> to be Members of the Church of Scotland, Lutherans,
> Presbyterians, Congregationalists, Baptists, Independents,
> Methodists, Mennonists, Tunkers, or Moravians ...[10]

There were other similar legal battles. The land question itself did not come near to resolution until the 1840s, after the fiery Methodist leader, Egerton Ryerson, had proved himself a political match for the Anglican bishop, John Strachan.[11]

The law on marriage indicated that the Mennonites and Tunk-ers were benefactors of the general religious rights struggle, but it must not be thought that they were only hangers-on. On the contrary, the Mennonites, along with the Tunkers and Quakers, achieved fundamental and particular religious recognition more than a generation before the Methodist triumph. Indeed, their exemption from military service preceded Methodist participa-tion in marriage by 38 years. Perhaps the Mennonites could get favourable treatment sooner because their numerical minority did not suggest the threat to the establishment which was posed by the Methodists, who were soon the largest Protestant de-nomination in the province. Besides, the Mennonites established no indigenous organization, no provincially-oriented power group, as did the Methodists, whose break with the United States after 1812 extended into the sphere of religion. As congregationalists, the Mennonites were not interested in provincial organization and, as continentalists, they continued to look to Pennsylvania as much as to York (Toronto). Provincial political weight was not a matter to which they gave much attention. The immigrant Mennonites can, therefore, take some credit for the expansion of religious privileges in Upper Canada.

The Mennonites in turn were heavily indebted to the English Quakers, who advanced their own liberty with the help of the Dutch Doopsgezinde. In opposing the oath and warfare, the Quakers had opened the door to freedom not only in Penn-sylvania; before that they had achieved in British imperial law the recognition of religious scruples and a nonconformist Christian conscience. In other words, the Militia Act of 1793, which ex-empted Quakers, Mennonites and Tunkers from personal militia duties, had the benefit of English legal precedents which recog-nized as non-criminal certain forms of religious dissent. Consider-ing the importance of British law in the Canadian Mennonite experience, let us review those precedents and the evolution of the law which led to the full recognition of these conscientious objectors.

The significant precedents were set only slowly and with great difficulty. When Henry VIII broke away from Rome and, as monarch, made himself the "pope" of England, it became a crime to have other allegiances. Identification with the Church of England was a test of loyalty to the Crown. At first the dissenters in England were all assumed to be papists, who constituted a real and continuing threat to the Crown, not least of all because the papal doctrine sanctioned the murder of monarchs, like the Henrys, who opposed the popes. As dissenters born on English soil, the Quakers experienced the full brunt of persecution and restriction in the days when all dissenters were on a par with the papists. As Crown-blessed colonizers, i.e. William Penn, they also knew first hand the benefits of a liberalizing British law at a time when much of Europe was still restricting religious nonconformists.

The precedents of tolerance in British law of greatest importance to the Mennonites came under William and Mary in 1688, five years after the Germantown settlement got underway. Anxious to unite in peaceful co-existence all the "Protestant subjects who had scruples of conscience,"[12] the Church of England exempted certain dissenters from the penalties of certain crimes. Anabaptists, for instance, were no longer penalized for not baptizing infants,[13] and other dissenters who objected to taking an oath could satisfy the Crown by making a declaration of fidelity. Such a declaration required the denial of submission to any princes as well as refutation of the "damnable doctrine that princes excommunicated by the pope could be deposed or murdered by their subjects." Positively the declaration required that:

> I do sincerely promise and solemnly declare before God and the World that I will be true and faithful to King William and Queen Mary . . .[14]

These provisions of 1688 represented progress, but the Quakers could not be satisfied with a negative statute, chiefly because their imprisonment and the seizure of their properties continued. They therefore sought and obtained an act which stipulated "that the Solemn Affirmation and Declaration of the People called Quakers, shall be accepted instead of an Oath in the usual Forme."[15] Among the evidence supporting the petitioning of the Quakers were abstracts of the "placates" in favour of the Dutch Doopsgezinde. These indicated that royalty in the person of the Prince of Orange had already accepted a word of affirmation instead of the oath a hundred years before.[16]

However, the desired legislation thus obtained still specified certain limitations. The obligations of citizenship could not be lessened and the qualities of allegiance could not be modified, even if the milder "oath," which was a solemn declaration, might suggest such moderation. Church tithes had to be paid, and no one making a solemn declaration only was considered qualified to give evidence in court or to serve on juries. The Act was also limited to a time period of seven years. But once the precedent had been set a law could with less difficulty be renewed and its liberal clauses expanded. After the English kings had discovered that not all dissenters were necessarily on the side of the pope, they even began to realize that the fair treatment of dissenters could be advantageous in strengthening the English Crown and in expanding the empire. Queen Anne was most explicit on the imperial value of treating dissent with tolerance. A bill to that effect began with the following preamble:

> ... the increase of people is a means of advancing the
> wealth and strength of a nation and whereas many strangers
> of the Protestant or Reformed religion out of due
> consideration of the happy constitution of the government of
> this realm would be induced to transport themselves and
> their estates into this kingdom if they might be made
> partakers of the advantages and privileges which the natural
> born subjects thereof do enjoy ...[17]

This tolerance of dissenters, otherwise useful to British purposes, permitted the Quaker state of Pennsylvania to build, without interference from the Crown, a rather tolerant legal base — a base which could not be erased even after the Quaker fall from power and the British loss of the thirteen colonies. In Britain itself exemption from militia service and the provision of a substitute was first provided for in 1761, the second year of George III's reign.[18]

The principles of religious dissension and military exemption as recognized in British law and applied on the American frontier now needed to be introduced into Upper Canada. Apparently there was some readiness for this and the authorities had their own reasons for acting, quite apart from any initiatives which Quakers, Mennonites or Tunkers may have taken. After the first wave of loyalist immigration had nearly come to an end, the most desirable immigrant prospects appeared to be those who, though they had not fought for the British, had at least not joined the American side. As Lieutenant-Governor Simcoe wrote to the British Secretary of State:

> There is every prospect of very great migrations taking
> place out of the United States into His Majesty's Dominions,

and I have not hesitated to promise to the Quakers and the
other sects the similar exemptions from militia duties which
they have always met with under the British government.[19]

It was not that Simcoe was particularly enthusiastic about
sectarians, especially if they were pacifists — he, above all,
wanted a strong militia and an unchallenged regular religious
establishment. But he also wanted to preserve British North
America, a difficult task without more people in its domains. In
any event, it could not be done with only an official religion and
a loyal militia. His invitation to Quakers and other sects must,
therefore, be seen as an imperial attempt not so much to benefit
sectarians as it was to benefit the empire and, if need be, with
their help.

The British establishment was not altogether sure of the benefits, and the Lieutenant-Governor's promises immediately ran into
the kind of opposition which made him and his successors somewhat more cautious. No less an authority than the British colonial
secretary, the Rt. Hon. Henry Dundas, discouraged the pre-
ferential exempting of any groups from the normal obligations of
citizenship and in particular from taxation and submission to the
oath.[20] This probably explains why the earliest provision of
military exemption required substitute taxation and specified
other limitations, and why the obligations of the oath were not
removed until later.

One Simcoe promise, exemption from militia duties for Quakers,
Mennonites and Tunkers under certain conditions, obtained the
strength of a public statute at the second session of the first
Upper Canada parliament held at Niagara. The conditions specified by the Militia Act of 1793 included the payment of special
annual fines in time of war (5 pounds or 20 dollars) and a
lesser amount (20 shillings or 4 dollars per annum) in time of
peace by all male inhabitants from age 16 to 50. The provisions
read in part:

> And it be further enacted, that the persons called Quakers,
> Mennonists, and Tunkers, who from certain scruples of
> conscience, decline bearing arms, shall not be compelled to
> serve in the said Militia, but every person professing that he
> is one of the people called Quakers, Mennonists, or Tunkers,
> and producing a certificate of his being a Quaker, Mennonist,
> or Tunker, signed by any three or more of the people (who
> are or shall be by them authorized to grant certificates for

this or any other purpose of which a pastor, minister, or preacher shall be one) shall be excused and exempted from serving in the said Militia, and instead of such service, all and every such person and persons, that shall or may be of the people called Quakers, Mennonists, or Tunkers, shall pay to the lieutenant of the county or riding, or in his absence to the deputy lieutenant, the sum of 20 shillings per annum in time of peace, and five pounds per annum in time of actual invasion or insurrection.[21]

The Militia Act of a year later increased the exemption age to 60.[22] Non-payment of imposed fines could mean the "distress and sale of the offender's goods and chattels," sufficient to cover the fines and the expenses of collecting the same. Flour, wheat, hogs, watches, books, cheese, blankets and furniture all were items that qualified for collection as payment of the military exemption tax.

Most of the Quakers did not readily consent to the payment of the yearly fees since the proceeds went directly to the support of the militia. Quakers who paid the taxes or hired substitutes were disciplined by their brothers as severely as those who actually joined the militia. Non-compliance with the law, on the other hand, also had its consequences. The Yonge Street Monthly Meeting of the growing town of York, for instance, had over $1,000 worth of goods confiscated in 1810 and eight of their members hauled off to jail for one month.[23] While for Quakers it was an exception to the rule if they voluntarily paid the tax, the Mennonites tended to accept the payment of fines, objecting, if they did, for financial rather than moral reasons. For Mennonites not to pay the tax was the exception, according to precedents that had been set in Pennsylvania and Prussia, and in the Alsace where Napoleon did the collecting.

There were exceptions, however, and a reported court action of 1814 confirms their occurrence. The action led to a forced collection of "the exempt money" or its equivalent.[24] Another record a year later strongly suggests that Mennonites themselves went to court to plead their case,[25] a possibility allowed by the Militia Act in the event of treatment felt to be too harsh. The Mennonites, however, did not only object to a strict interpretation under the law, but they undertook to change the law in their favour. Indeed, one of the most active lobbies in the half-century of Upper Canada appears to have been that of the Quakers, Tunkers and Mennonites, acting individually or collectively.

The reference to lobby is not an exaggerated description of

how laws came to be changed. It was the necessary custom of those times for groups of all kinds to approach the Crown, governor, councils, and/or the assemblies for privileges, relief, indulgences, and rights, or however the requested concessions were described. British imperial law, American colonial law, and Upper Canada law arose largely from petitions directly presented by civic groups, business interests, and individuals, as well as religious groups and their leaders. This becomes clear from a reading of the *Journal of the Legislative Assembly*, and the petitions of the Methodists on the marriage problem alone have already been referred to.

For the Mennonites the separation of church and state did not mean that they had nothing to say to, or ask of, the state, but rather that the state could not ask everything of them. Their ancestors had learned to petition in Europe, continuing to petition in Pennsylvania, and the immigrants began their life in Canada with petitions.[26] To what extent their entry into Canada was directly related to or preceded by or followed by petitioning cannot be determined in any comprehensive way, but Quaker[27] and Tunker[28] history have their examples. Petitioning among the Mennonites, especially after 1800, is reported below.

The most objectionable feature of the Militia Act for both Mennonites and Tunkers who obeyed it and for Quakers who did not obey it were the fines. The Mennonites felt that they were altogether too heavy for pioneering farm folk. The full burden of the special militia tax was felt after 1809, when the law provided for jail sentences lasting until the fines were paid.[29] Another objection related to the fact that the militia exempted only those Mennonites who possessed a certified membership. This meant that the young men of 16 were not likely to be covered, since baptism and church membership tended to coincide with the marrying age and consequently did not normally occur until about age 21.

To bring about the desired changes in the law, the Mennonites and Tunkers, as has already been indicated, followed the normal petitioning procedure of the time — they sent their delegates armed with signed petitions to make the desired requests. While it cannot be documented, it may be assumed that the favourable clauses in the 1793 Militia Act were inspired precisely by the kind of Mennonite petitioning frequently referred to in the first 50 years of the *Journal of the Legislative Assembly* of Upper Canada.

The first recorded petitioning, according to available records, appears to have been made in June of 1801 when a bill granting indulgences to Quakers, Mennonites and Tunkers was introduced and passed by the Legislative Assembly only to be stalled at other levels. Apparently the first successful petitioning occurred in 1809 when the Mennonites and Tunkers were granted the same right as the Quakers to make "affirmation or declaration" instead of taking an oath where such was required. The same Act that granted this privilege, however, also disqualified Mennonites and Tunkers from giving evidence in criminal cases, from serving on juries, or from holding any office or place in the government.[30]

In 1810 two petitions were delivered, signed in the first instance by "two preachers, two elders, and 35 members of the Society of Mennonists and Tunkers," and in the second instance by 34 members. The petitions were of similar tenor and began by expressing appreciation for "favourable law and liberty of conscience" and the "God and the Government under which we live." The petitions admitted that "Our sons now under age and incapable of judging in matters of conscience" were not considered church members and hence unable to produce the necessary certificates. Thus they asked for "the relief of minors" and also for the relief from money payments:

> ... we therefore humbly pray the same indulgence may be
> extended to them that is granted to ourselves, their parents,
> that is that they may be exempted from serving in the
> Militia by paying the commutation money until they arrive
> at the age of twenty-one, or until they be admitted as
> Church Members.
> ... And Your Petitioners further pray that your Honourable
> Body will take into consideration the many difficulties which
> poor people, with large families have to labour under in new
> settlements, and if you in your wisdom should deem meet to
> lessen the burden of our commutation money, Your
> Petitioners, as in duty bound, shall ever pray.[31]

The first petition was granted in "An Act for the Relief of Minors of the Society of Mennonists and Tunkers."[32] But the second petition remained unattended, and the matter was apparently laid to rest until 1827 and the years immediately following. In the meantime, the pacifists were confronted not only by the militia but by actual warfare. Perhaps it was the war experience itself that persuaded the Mennonites that the exemption of their men, even in return for payment of fines, was a high enough privilege and in recognition of this they refrained for a time from seeking relief from fines.

The War of 1812–14 saw the United States allied with France against Great Britain. British interference with American shipping was the reason for the United States to invade Canada in hope of obtaining more of the coveted territory. While the attack from Detroit was repulsed and the city captured by the British in 1812, the Americans retook the city in October of 1813 and pursued the British up to the Thames River.

In that retreat or evacuation the Mennonites who were settled along the Grand River also became involved in the war. According to a statute of 1809, the King had the power to "impress such horses, carriages, and oxen" as might be required "in case of emergency, by actual invasion or otherwise."[33] A noted Waterloo County biographer summarized the meaning of the impressment in that area as follows:

> A number of the Waterloo people were up at the battle on the Thames. These Waterloo boys acting as teamsters, had taken shelter in a swamp nearby while the battle was being fought. An officer of the British army, seeing that all was lost, gave them warning, said, "Boys, all is lost, clear out and make the best you can," upon which some ran, while others unhitched their horses and rode off for their lives. Christian Schneider, Jr., who carried the money-safe on his wagon, cleared out on his horses, leaving the wagon with all its contents behind. In this defeat old Adam Shoupe was taken prisoner by the Americans. He was taken before General Harrison who, perceiving his innocent and harmless appearance, dismissed him and granted him permission to return to his Canadian home.[34]

Just how many Mennonites had their teams and equipment impressed is not known, but when it was all over at least 22 farmers lawfully claimed loss or damage for two horses, 14 wagons, 17 harnesses, one coat, five blankets, 54 bags, 13 chains, two yokes, and four singletrees. This particular claim amounted to about $5,000. The heaviest loss was encountered by Henry Wanner who claimed $500 for horses, wagon, harness, and bags.[35]

It can be concluded that the Mennonites served with great reluctance, though their opposition to participation was not as intense as that of the Quakers (the latter accepted fines and jail

TABLE 1

STATEMENT OF MILITIA TAXES PAID
BY MENNONITES, QUAKERS AND TUNKERS (1813–1826)

DISTRICT	PERIOD	AMOUNT PAID*
Home (including York and Waterloo)	1813–26	$20,100
Niagara	1815–26	4,684
Midlands	1813–16	1,288
London	1813–18, 1822–26	1,356
Newcastle	1813–19	676
Johnstown	1813–20	1,128
Western	1813–19	76
Eastern	1813–19	92
Bathurst	—	—
Ottawa	—	—
Gore	1827	40

* Collected in pounds, shillings, and pence, and here converted into approximate dollar equivalents.

terms rather than involvement in military affairs). For the Mennonites this type of passive war service was not an isolated example. In Russia, where Napoleon marched on Moscow the same year that America tried to seize Canada, the Mennonites of Molotschna assisted the tsar in similar ways.[36] And when the Crimean War came a half-century later the Mennonites in that country likewise would provide horses, transport carriages and drivers.[37]

For most of the loyalists, the War of 1812 confirmed the wisdom of their exodus from the States and many cut all their remaining ties. To give one example, the Methodists soon thereafter saw no alternative to the organizing of their own Canadian conference. For the Mennonites, however, the blood and faith ties south of the border remained strong. After the peace treaty was ratified in 1815, the visiting to and fro and the international marriages, as well as the migration itself, were resumed. Allegiance to the British Crown did not require of them, as it did of the other true loyalists, enmity with the United States and its people. Indeed, this continuous fraternity with the Americans

helped to shape the Canadian Mennonite destiny for decades to
come.

For one and a half decades after the war, apparently very little
effort was made to reduce or eliminate the militia fines. This may
have been partly due to easier collection, indicating gratitude
that the war was over, and partly to what appears to have been
an inconsistency in the collection of the militia taxes in the various
districts. In 1829 the Lieutenant-Governor was curious about
amounts received "from Mennonists, Quakers and Tunkers from
military service, during the last 16 years" but none of the district
reports, with one exception, covered the full 16 years. The absence
of given years, as seen in Table 1, suggests neglect in collection
or in reporting, or both.[38]

At the end of the 1820s the effort to eliminate the militia tax
altogether was taken up again. In 1829 notice to amend the
militia laws was given but, according to the *Journal* record, no bill
was presented.[39] However, the matter was brought up frequently
until the efforts were crowned with success 20 years later. The
chronology of that sustained lobby was as follows:[40]

1829   January 14 — Notice was given but no bill was
       introduced.[41]

1830   February 10 — Isaac Robb and 18 other Mennonites
       from Niagara district asked for relief from military
       fines.[42]

1830   February 17 — Jacob Erb from Gore and 70 other
       Mennonites and Tunkers asked that fines be reduced
       and paid in form of work on the roads.[43]

1830   March 1 — A bill disposing of fines in peacetime was
       passed by the Assembly but stalled in the Council.[44]

1832   December 31 — S. Bowman from Waterloo County
       and 240 others, Mennonites and Tunkers, asked
       reduction of fines in time of peace and their collection
       as part of regular taxes.[45]

1833   November 30 — Jacob Fry, again supported by
       others, made a request for removal of all militia
       fines.[46]

1834   January 4 — A petition against severity of fines was
       presented by James Johnson, Esq., and 110 others
       from the Niagara district.[47]

1834   February 18 — A bill calling for removal except in
       time of actual invasion, failed to pass.[48]

1835   April 14 — Another Assembly bill, designed to
       eliminate militia exemption fees in time of peace, was

lost in Council and repeated efforts to gain acceptance
failed.[49]

1836 January 30 — Yet another bill to cancel fines in time
of peace was passed by Assembly and lost in
Council.[50]

1837 January 18 — Repetition of the above; Militia Act of
that year reduced yearly fines in time of peace to ten
shillings.[51]

1841 June 15 — Mennonite ministers Jacob Gross and
Jacob High asked for reconsideration of militia fines,
but without result.[52]

1846 April 3 — A petition similar to the above was
submitted.[53]

1847 July 1 — Petitions on behalf of Mennonites and
Tunkers by Municipal Council of Niagara. The
Assembly passed a favourable bill which again fell
through in Council.[54]

1849 May 30 — Royal assent was given to a bill which
rejected the principle of fines as a substitute for
militia service.[55]

By 1849, it must be remembered, the administration of the
provinces had undergone change with the effect that Upper and
Lower Canada were united on July 1, 1841, into the Province of
Canada.[56] But the new Militia Law of that year left the exemption with the traditional limitations unaltered. With the removal
of the fines in 1849 the legal status of pacifists in respect to military service at the century's halfway mark stood as follows: no
compulsion for militia service or payment of fines for Quakers,
Mennonists and Tunkers aged 16 to 60, provided they produce
certificates of belonging, signed by the meeting or society, and
presented to the assessors of the locality every year before the first
of February.[57]

The unusual privileges achieved by the pacifist groups in over
50 years of effort were reaffirmed by subsequent Acts, before and
after Confederation.[58] But opposition to the privileges remained
sufficiently strong to keep Mennonites constantly alert. When
civil war broke out in America, Mennonite leaders in Canada
once again made sure that their rights were properly secured.[59]
To what extent the Canadian people as a whole really approved of
the special privileges could only be tested in wartime, for which
the twentieth century was to provide ample opportunity.

The Mennonite preoccupation with exemption from the militia,
as reported above, should not be allowed to imply that the non-

resistors took their civic responsibilities lightly. On the contrary, in the building of roads, in the founding of schools, and in the maintenance of community life they became exemplary. And here and there, lay Mennonite leaders also entered the political arena. Among the families establishing a most remarkable record were the Reesors of Markham, who held seats on the Council of the County of York during 37 of the first 50 years. Sometimes more than one of the Reesor family connections were involved so that 53 years of service were recorded in that half-century.

This service began with David Reesor (1823–1903), third son of Abraham Reesor, an immigrant settler from Pennsylvania. At the age of 27 David was elected to the first Council in 1850 when the Municipal Act came into force, and was re-elected five times thereafter. During the course of his civic career he held positions as Reeve of Markham, Warden of York County, Member of Provincial Legislative Council (Senate) for Kings Division.

Among his projects were the establishment of a grammar school, a newspaper, the *Markham Economist*, a cheese factory, a bank, an agricultural society, and a telegraph company of which he became president. Apparently, all of these involvements were not possible without total respectability in the community, and so David Reesor also became a colonel in the Sedentary Militia.[60]

Ironically, at that very time in the middle of the eighteenth century when the Mennonites were achieving respectability and legality within Canadian society, they were beginning to lose their internal serenity, their congregations being shaken by various dissensions and strife. That story, however, should not be told before the life of those congregations and the role of their leaders is more fully described, as it is in the next chapter. After all, the petitioning pertaining to the law represented only a small fraction of the total Mennonite effort in developing the congregations and in advancing the cause of God's greater kingdom, as they perceived it.

FOOTNOTES

1. John S. Moir, ed., *Church and State in Canada 1627–1867: Basic Documents* (Toronto: McClelland & Stewart, 1967), p. 153.
2. H. S. Bender, "The Pacifism of the Sixteenth Century Anabaptists," *Mennonite Quarterly Review*, XXX (January 1956), pp. 5–18.

3. John Horsch, "A Historical Survey of the Position of the Mennonite Church on Nonresistance," *Mennonite Quarterly Review*, I (July 1927), p. 10.
4. *Ibid.*
5. J. Wilbur Bender, "Pacifism Among the Mennonites of Pennsylvania," *Mennonite Quarterly Review*, I (July 1927), pp. 23–40.
6. At Niagara-on-the-Lake in 1811. Copy of original printing available in Niagara Historical Society Library.
7. Alan Wilson, *The Clergy Reserves of Upper Canada*, Booklet No. 23 (Ottawa: Canadian Historical Association, 1969), p. 5.
8. *Ibid.*, p. 6.
9. Ramsay Cook, *Canada: A Modern Study* (Toronto: Clarke, Irwin & Company, Ltd., 1963), pp. 43–5.
10. 1 William IV, c. 1 (1829).
11. Cook, *op. cit.*, pp. 43–5.
12. 1 William and Mary, c. 18 (1688).
13. *Ibid.*, Sec. 7.
14. *Ibid.*, Sec. 10.
15. 7 and 8 William III, c. 34 (1695–6).
16. William C. Braithwaite, *The Second Period of Quakerism* (Cambridge: Cambridge University Press, 1961), p. 183.
17. 7 Anne, c. 5 (1708).
18. 2 George III, c. 20, s. 42 (1761).
19. W. A. Cruikshank, *The Simcoe Papers* (Toronto: Ontario Historical Society, 1923).
20. Arthur Dorland, *The Quakers in Canada* (Toronto: Ryerson Press, 1968), pp. 53–5.
21. 33 George III, c. 1 (1793).
22. 33 George III, c. 7 (1794).
23. Arthur Dorland, *A History of the Society of Friends (Quakers) in Canada* (Toronto: Macmillan, 1927), pp. 311–13. See also: "Quakers Opposed War Preparation in Upper Canada" (Extracts from the *Minute Book of Yonge Street Preparative and Monthly Meeting*, 1804–1818), *The Canadian Friend*, LXIX (February–March 1973), pp. 10–11.
24. Alexander Fraser, *Twenty-Second Report of the Department of Public Records and Archives of Ontario* (Toronto: Herbert H. Ball, 1934), p. 133. See also: A. B. Sherk, "Early Militia Matters in Upper Canada, 1808–1842," *Ontario Historical Society Papers and Records*, XIII, pp. 67–73.
25. Fraser, *ibid.*, p. 144.
26. C. Henry Smith, *The Mennonite Migration to Pennsylvania in the Eighteenth Century* (Norristown, Pa.: Norristown Press, 1929), pp. 278–302.
27. Arthur Dorland, *op. cit.*, pp. 53–5. See also: "The Petition of

John Troyer," *Ontario Historical Society Papers and Records*, XXIV, pp. 142–43.

28. E. Morris Sider, "History of the Brethren in Christ (Tunker) Church in Canada," M.A. thesis, University of Western Ontario, 1955.

29. 48 George III, c. 1, s. 27 (1808).

30. 49 George III, c. 6 (1809).

31. Alexander Fraser, *Eighth Report of the Bureau of Archives* (Toronto: King's Printer, 1911), dealing with Legislative Assembly of February 10, 1810.

32. 50 George III, c. 11 (1810).

33. 49 George III, c. 2 (1809).

34. Ezra Eby, *op. cit.*, p. 43.

35. H. S. Bender, "New Data for Ontario Mennonite History," *Mennonite Quarterly Review*, III (January 29), pp. 42–6.

36. Henry J. Gerbrandt, *Adventure in Faith* (Altona, Man.: D. W. Friesen & Sons, 1970), p. 19.

37. Frank H. Epp, *Mennonite Exodus: The Rescue and Resettlement of the Russian Mennonites Since the Communist Revolution* (Altona, Man.: D. W. Friesen & Sons, 1962), p. 26.

38. See *Journal of Legislative Assembly*, January 8 to March 20, 1829, and "Statement of Amount of Money Received from Mennonists, Quakers, and Tunkers for Exemption from Militia Service for Last 16 Years," March 19, 1829, PAC, *Upper Canada Sundries*, Record Group 5, A1, Vol. 93, p. 51604.

39. Province of Upper Canada, *Journal of Legislative Assembly*.

40. E. Morris Sider, "Nonresistance in the Early Mennonite Brethren in Christ Church in Ontario," *Mennonite Quarterly Review*, XXXI (October 1957), pp. 282–86.

41. *Journal of Legislative Assembly*, January 14, 1829.

42. *Ibid.*, February 10, 1830.

43. *Ibid.*, February 17, 1830.

44. *Ibid.*, March 1, 1830.

45. *Ibid.*, December 31, 1832.

46. *Ibid.*, November 30, 1833.

47. *Ibid.*, January 4, 1834.

48. *Ibid.*, February 18, 1834.

49. *Ibid.*, April 14, 1835.

50. *Ibid.*, January 30, 1836.

51. *Ibid.*, February 14, 1837. See also 1 Victoria, c. 8, s. 50.

52. *Ibid.*, June 15, 1841.

53. *Ibid.*, April 3, 1846.

54. *Ibid.*, July 1, 1847.

55. *Ibid.*, May 25, 1849.

56. 4 Victoria, c. 1 (1841); 4 Victoria, c. 2 (1841).

57. An Act to Amend the Militia Law, August 17, 1841.

58. See, for example, 8 Victoria, c. 77, s. 71; 31 Victoria, c. 4, s. 17; *Revised Statutes of Canada*, c. 1, s. 26 (1886).

59. Orland Gingerich, *Amish*, pp. 230–47.

60. See L. J. Burkholder, "The Reesors in Canada," an address given at Reesor Reunion, Locust Hill, June 30, 1928 (CGC); also, *The Markham Economist*, August 8, 1901.

The Bishop on Horseback

5. The Congregations and their Leaders

*Many such so-called lay preachers became effective teachers
and respected pastors of their congregations. Since there
were no members with more than a common education, the
lay preacher was able to serve without handicap* — J. C.
WENGER.[1]

THE IMPORTANCE of the clergyman and the church congregation as keepers of the peace and shapers of public
morality on the frontiers of Upper Canada has already been
inferred. The Mennonite communities were no exception to that
rule. The role of their farmer-preachers varied, however, in some
ways from that of the state-salaried Anglican priests as well as
from the Methodist missioners. Often, the Mennonite ministers
fulfilled the functions of both of these opposite varieties of ministry, though without pay.

The most obvious difference between the state clergy and the
sectarian ministers lay in the official role of the former. They were
considered "highly useful in a political as well as a religious" sense,
and this usefulness was rewarded, as we have seen, with clergy
land reserves and pay. The "political contribution" of the Mennonite leaders, on the other hand, was not by official support of
state norms but by occasional dissent from them. In their smaller
world of the congregational community, however, the denominational bishops represented functions similar to those of the Ang-

licans and the Methodists. On the one hand, they symbolized all that was respectable, moral and official. On the other hand, they also reached out to all those scattered members of the flock on the fringes of the ordered community and shared with them their humanity. Theirs was a politics not so much for undergirding the British imperium as for the building up of the kingdom of God, as they saw it. This often brought them into conflict with public opinion and the law of the land, not because they were disrespectful of that law, but because they represented a higher law. In the Pelham township, for instance, one Tunker preacher, with a "beard long down to his breast and hair over his shoulders,"[2] was accused by the schoolteacher of encouraging lawlessness simply because he opposed capital punishment.[3]

Thus, apart from the petitions regarding the oath and militia taxes, most of the "politics" of the Mennonite preacher was local. Since the days of persecution the Mennonite message had been mainly directed inward for nurturing the faithful and developing congregational community. It must be remembered that the congregation, the local body of believers, was for the Mennonites the essential and maximum expression of the kingdom of God. They still feared the state-wide church against which their fathers had once rebelled, and besides, for them the fundamental features of God's kingdom could only be expressed in a living and localized community. To the development of such communities, the preachers gave their greatest attention. Among the widely scattered settlements of Upper Canada this task was quite sufficient in magnitude, especially when the leaders had their own woodlands to clear, their own crops to sow and harvest, and their own large families to feed.

The clergy of most other denominations could not work in the Mennonite style. The German Evangelical Protestants, for instance, appealed for help to the Lieutenant-Governor of Upper Canada. Addressing him as being of the Prussian Military Order of Merit, they recognized his "zeal and exertions in propagating the invaluable blessing of religious instruction among his majesty's subjects." Then the petitioners asked him to supplement the £50 ($200) that they were paying the minister and which they could raise "only with great irregularity."[4] Their goal was the allowance of the priests of the Church of England who were receiving £100 annually from the public purse.

Among Mennonites, material support for the ministers, approved at Schleitheim in 1527, had become completely unthinkable in the long decades of persecution and deprivation. It was not revived again until the congregations began to demand better-educated ministers and, for the most part, that did not occur until the twentieth century. But, even in that eventuality, support could never have come from the state purse — that part of the Anabaptist revolt against Catholicism, Lutheranism and Zwinglianism was never forgotten. But this lack of support for the Mennonite clergy was not without ill effect. The heavy loss of membership through the absorption of Mennonites into other denominations and their communal disintegration, later to be reported, can be attributed at least in part to an unpaid and untrained clergy, too busy with their own affairs to attend to all the needs of their flock.

Be that as it may, no Canadian Mennonite community was complete without at least one minister and, if possible, a bishop who preferably resided among them or at least occasionally visited them. Among the Anabaptists it had been that way from the beginning. In one sense everyone was a priest but, for the sake of order and according to the example of the New Testament, certain persons had to be chosen for certain functions or offices. There was the deacon who served, the minister who preached, and the elder or bishop who officiated. The word "bishop" was at first avoided because of its Catholic associations, but as time went on the designation became quite appropriate to the leader's role and image. Eighteenth-century Pennsylvania and nineteenth-century Ontario knew no other term for their religious authority.

These Mennonite offices were so important to the welfare of the congregation that they could not be left solely to the wishes and machinations of men. The church members could nominate certain members for the positions of deacon and minister, and certain ministers for the office of bishop. But if more candidates were nominated than there were positions to be filled, and all of them qualified, then it was only logical to leave the final decision to God, lest human choice lead to competition and division among candidates and their supporters. That, in the providence of God, was believed to be the intention of the lot. As it was written, "The lot is cast into the lap; but the whole disposing thereof is of the Lord."[5] Further scriptural support for the lot was found in at least one reported instance of its use, namely the selection of Matthias to complete the ranks of the apostles after the defection and death of Judas.[6]

The lot was used by Mennonites in the following manner, with variations in detail from time to time and from district to district. After the nomination of candidates by individuals or by congregational vote, the bishop(s), resident and/or visiting, would lay a thoroughly shuffled set of hymnbooks or Bibles, equal to the number of candidates, on a table in full view of the congregation. One of the books contained "the lot," a slip of paper with Proverbs 16:33 on it. The candidate selecting the book with the lot would be accepted as the one having been selected by God, and he was then immediately ordained. Persons selected for holy office by lot rarely refused, because the decision to "follow the Lord" in this manner had been made not only at the time of nomination but prior to that — at the time of baptism. For the young men who might some day be preachers and for the young women who might some day be their wives, the baptismal vows included such eventualities. Sometimes the candidates for baptism were asked very directly concerning their willingness to be ministers or ministers' wives, and, at such times, there was only one satisfactory answer.

This method of selection, however, occasionally led to the ordination of rather poorly endowed preachers, whose weakness was compounded by lack of education and, if they were farmers, by lack of time. Nomination of such persons could arise from the desire of friends or family cliques to be represented on the councils of the church. Not surprisingly, therefore, the temptation became strong from time to time, if not to discard the lot, then certainly to give God as much help as possible in its proper use. Indeed, some bishops felt it was their responsibility to protect God from foolish nominations and undesirable candidates, which occasionally they knew how to do, one way or another. In some areas it became customary for nominations to be made only in the privacy of a bishops' meeting, where nominators could sometimes be persuaded to withdraw the nomination of "undesired candidates."

Deviations from the established practices of choosing leaders in both Canada and Russia could and did occur. As previously indicated, the first Mennonite immigrants arrived without ministers, but in both countries the concern for congregational fellowship and leadership became evident soon after the settlers had selected land. The families who had located 15 miles west of Fort Erie by 1793, for instance, established three centres of worship immediately, though little is known from the historical records of how they went about it.[7]

More is known about the congregation at the Twenty, which

eventually became the locus or bishop's seat for all the congregations in the Niagara peninsula region. The second group of immigrants had barely arrived at the Twenty in 1799, set up their
log cabins, and cleared some land, when they voiced desire for a
congregation with a properly chosen leadership. No minister had
arrived with the first 24 families, and so early in 1800 Samuel
Moyer wrote on their behalf to the parent group in Bucks County
for advice and help. The bishop and ministers at Bedminster in
the County advised that they should, by themselves, choose their
leader without the assistance of a visiting bishop. While the presence of a senior leader was viewed as desirable, this was not considered necessary since "human assistance and arrangement are
also from God" and without him "no calling is sufficient . . . even
if every minister were to place his hands upon him." Thinking
that such words were not sufficiently clear or precise, Bedminster
Bishop Jacob Gross added a personal note to the above instruction, which was then counter-signed by his five colleagues and
confirmed by an assembly of ministers in both Bucks and Lancaster counties. The postcript was intended to leave no doubt as
to the course of action to be taken. It said:

> You will likely have understood that you among yourselves
> can acquire, with prayer and fear of God, by votes and lots,
> ministers and elders to teach, keep, and maintain the same
> rules as we.[8]

The group at the Twenty proceeded according to instructions
and John Fretz, age 71, was chosen deacon and Valentine Kratz,
age 41, was chosen minister. Neither of the two men was formally
ordained. A year later Jacob Moyer was selected as minister and
in 1805, as bishop. It is not known when, where, or by whom
he was ordained, but in all probability a visiting bishop from
Pennsylvania officiated.

The Mennonites going to Russia began in a similar way. The
first immigrants from Prussia also started on their pilgrimage
without ministers. Apart from the lot, which was used among the
Dutch-German Mennonites only on rare occasions to break a tie,
the process of ministerial selection was very similar, as was that of
deacons, ministers, and bishops. En route they selected from their
number several men to read the Sunday morning sermons, but a
real minister had to be found or "made" when about a dozen
couples announced their engagements and impatiently waited to
get married. The Prussians would not send one out but recom-

mended instead that the emigrants nominate candidates. From the twelve names submitted to Prussia, four were approved for the ministry and one was later "ordained" as elder (bishop) by letter.

One of the established roles of a bishop in North America, as well as in Europe, was to make himself available to other congregations or groups of congregations (districts) until they could choose their own leader. In such instances he was said to have "the bishop oversight." Otherwise he officiated at nominations, elections, ordinations, marriages, funerals, baptisms, communions and meetings of the ministers and congregations. As a leader chosen and appointed by God he was greatly respected and hence carried much authority, especially if a winsome personality, strong character, sound preaching, dedicated leadership and personal piety were part of his contribution to the office. Not infrequently the stature of the man would grow beyond his own and the people's expectations as he exercised his leadership role.

The normal origin of a congregational community in Canada was in the form of house meetings, sometimes held in barns, sheds or in the open air. The next step was to erect a small community building, usually of logs, which served the dual function of week-day school and Sunday worship. Finally a wooden church building was erected for use by the congregation and sometimes for community meetings. Brick buildings appeared about the middle of the nineteenth century. At the Twenty the third step came in 1824 when a wooden meeting-house was erected for a cost of $245, including materials and some labour but not including the stove. The details of its costs are given in Table 1.[9]

When a settlement expanded and distances increased, new places of worship were established. This was often followed by the election of additional ministers and the erection of more meeting places, though not necessarily by the formation of other autonomous congregations or the election of additional bishops. Whether or not a congregation or groups of congregations became independent enough to select their own bishop would depend on a variety of factors: size, distance and the initiative (or lack of it) of members or ministers. Such initiative, in turn, might depend on whether or not the present bishop was satisfactory or whether or not there was any challenge to his leadership.

As it happened, the Niagara area became a single district, for the most part served by a single bishop who was, however, not always resident at the Twenty, as can be seen from Table 2.[10]

TABLE 1

SUMMARY OF MOYER'S MEETING-HOUSE COSTS IN 1824

ITEMS	COST
Johannes Schmidt: 14 bushels of lime, timber hewed, hauled, and trimmed, one gallon dram (strong drink), gable end closed and covered, shingles, nails–27 pounds, boards–684, beams, rafters, window facing, boards–2,713 feet.	$112.00
Jim Braun: for hewing, hauling timber, one day shingling, one gallon dram, shingles, nails and hinges, painting one day.	34.00
Johannes Puterbach: for six days hewing timber.	6.00
Jacob Schunk: for one day shingling.	1.00
Miscellaneous labour.	2.00
Miscellaneous (latches, nuts, bolts, nails, screws, glass).	90.00
Total	$245.00

During some periods there were several bishops. The New York congregations, for instance, had their own bishop until they became firmly incorporated into the Niagara district. Occasionally the bishop from across the border was invited to serve certain congregations in Upper Canada.

Similarly, Jacob Moyer served outside of his immediate area. In his early years he travelled to Waterloo and possibly to York. In due course, both areas became separate bishop districts. York became independent in 1808 when Abraham Grove came to Markham from Pennsylvania, having been charged with the bishop's office for that area before his departure. The initiative for that action had come in the form of a request from Markham, where the pioneer settler, Henry Wideman, had given ministerial leadership since 1803.

Waterloo district gained its own bishop with the ordination of Benjamin Eby in 1812. He was the third bishop in the province. Mennonites did not have archbishops, but in actual fact Benjamin Eby became one by virtue of the growth of his own district, the longevity of his service, his manifold abilities and creative leadership, his "bishop oversight" roles in other districts, and the ordination of bishops in Niagara and York districts. More versatile, visionary and gifted than any of his contemporaries, Eby

TABLE 2

EARLY BISHOPS AND BISHOP DISTRICTS IN UPPER CANADA

DATE	NAME	LOCATION
	I. NIAGARA DISTRICT	
	A. *Upper Canada*	
1805–1833	Jacob Moyer*	The Twenty
1834–1849	Jacob Gross*	" "
1850–1873	Dilman Moyer†	" "
1875–1889§	Christian Gayman	Cayuga
	B. *New York*	
1839–1860	Jacob Krehbiel	Clarence Centre
1860–1878	John Lapp	" "
	II. MARKHAM DISTRICT	
1808–1836	Abraham Grove	Markham
1837–1863	Jacob Grove†	" "
1867–1889§	Christian Reesor	" "
	III. WATERLOO DISTRICT(S)‡	
	A. *Waterloo*	
1812–1853	Benjamin Eby	Berlin
1852–1876	Joseph Hagey	Breslau
1879–1909	Elias E. Weber	" "
	B. *Wilmot*	
1842–1877	Henry Shantz	Wilmot
1875–1909	Amos Cressman	Wilmot
	C. *Woolwich*	
1867–1889§	Abraham Martin	Woolwich

* After the death of a bishop and until a new one was chosen, the bishop from another district, in this case Waterloo, would have the "bishop oversight."
† Ordained by Benjamin Eby.
‡ Three bishop districts in Waterloo became official after 1879, but as the above indicates a de facto situation existed before then.
§ The year 1889 does not mark the date of termination for these bishops but rather their separation from the main Mennonite Conference. See Chapter 11.

was not only a farmer-businessman like Erb, and not only a farmer-preacher like the Moyers and the Widemans, but also a schoolteacher, a writer of school texts and teaching resources, a publisher, and a church statesman of a quality and stature the Ontario Mennonites did not see again in that century.[11]

Eby was born at Hammer Creek in Lancaster County, on the old family homestead established by his great-grandfather, Theodore Eby, an immigrant from Switzerland via the Palatinate in 1715. The eleventh child of Christian and Catherine Eby, Benjamin married Mary Brubacher in the winter of 1807 and they had eleven children. Indeed, it was his engagement to Mary that prevented Benjamin from staying in Waterloo in 1806 after he rode up from Pennsylvania and claimed Lot #2 of the Beasley Tract as his own; he did not suspect that some day his land would comprise a large part of the eastern ward of a modern city named Kitchener. Its earliest name was Ebytown after Benjamin Eby; thereafter it was called Berlin.

A small Mennonite community of about 40 families on the Grand River had already been meeting with their minister Joseph Bechtel since 1802. But due to the Beasley episode the community had not grown until 1805–7, when more than 35 additional families arrived. Young Benjamin Eby, 22 years old at the time, and his young bride were in that group. After two years in the community he was elected minister and, three years later, bishop. In both instances, his brother Peter, 20 years his senior and already a "venerable bishop," came up from Lancaster by horseback to perform the ordinations.[12]

If the lot was used according to the rules in the selection of Benjamin, then its usefulness needed little further defence. In this case it had resulted in the election of a man very much needed, and very well qualified to serve the community. It is true, of course, that not all ministerial selections were left directly to God and/or chance as it sometimes seemed. His brother Peter, to give one example, personally selected the man who would become his assistant and successor, and ordained him.[13] In the case of Benjamin, it is also probable that he was the only candidate nominated, thus essentially eliminating the lot in his selection.

As it was, Benjamin Eby the farmer-bishop left his mark not only on Berlin but also on Waterloo County and the entire Ontario Conference which emerged during his time. Though small (5′ 6″) and slight (150 pounds) — one tradition says he was frail[14] — he overcame all the physical obstacles of the frontier and handled the equivalent of several jobs in addition to normal agricultural pioneering.

Immediately after his ordination as bishop Eby had a modest log structure erected to serve the congregation of some 150 members, which had hitherto been worshipping in private homes and barns, in buildings erected for school purposes, and in the open air. A half-acre of land for a church building had previously been reserved by Joseph Eby. Another acre was added in 1816 at the cost of $10 — the value of some land had already increased ten-fold since the date of original purchase[15] — and in that same year Benjamin Eby donated three-fourths of an acre, to make a total of two and one-fourth acres. All this was for the purpose of "a meeting house, a public school house, and graveyard."[16] the latter being used for Mennonites and non-Mennonites alike.

Although the Mennonite meeting-house served primarily as a worship centre, it was also used for public assemblies of all kinds, including funerals, since there was no other facility. Weddings for the most part were at the home of the bride's parents, until the turn of the century when "real churches," in distinction from meeting-houses, were built.

The typical Mennonite worship service, about two hours in duration, consisted of several hymns led by a chorister and an introductory or "opening" sermon by a junior minister, followed by silent prayer with all the congregation on their knees facing the backs of their own benches. Then came the main sermon by the bishop or another senior minister. This was "preached quietly, with few gestures if any, with dignity and sincerity, sometimes with tears, but never with a loud voice or with exuberance — that would have been considered poor taste."[17] Other ministers then testified to the soundness of the message, sometimes adding thoughts of their own. The preaching minister would then, as the congregation knelt, conclude the service with an audible prayer, then the Lord's prayer. A closing hymn and the benediction ended the service.

Eby soon realized that the traditional liturgy administered by uneducated farmer-preachers, sincere and dedicated though they might be, could sometimes become quite sterile. He set about compiling aids for a more vital experience. One of his first projects was to improve the congregational singing by shortening the songs, quickening their pace a little, and adding tunes learned from other sects in Pennsylvania. By 1836 he had published his first collection of hymns for use in Ontario churches. *Die Gemein-*

schaftliche Liedersammlung became the accepted hymnbook in the churches until the end of the century and was reprinted five times in Ontario and twice in Pennsylvania.[18]

With his compilation of hymns Eby reinforced a strong Anabaptist emphasis on hymnology, concluded in part from the fact that 130 Anabaptist hymn writers have been identified by name. Hymns were used for private devotional reading, family worship and congregational singing. For a long time the chief source of hymns was the *Ausbund*. This was a collection of hymns on the martyred heroes of the faith, and was brought to America and used for over two centuries by those congregations whose cultural and theological conservatism linked them most easily with the past. For some, the new world required a hymnody at least a little different. Both Franconia and Lancaster conferences had by 1804 produced their own hymn collections; Benjamin Eby's collection represented a synthesis of the two. His chief innovation was a further reduction in the number of stanzas. All hymns were sung in unison, four-part singing being considered too worldly.

At the same time Eby searched for adequate materials for the religious instruction of youth. This led him, in the space of 15 years, to publish two catechisms. One was borrowed in 1824 from Prussia and was first used in America. Subsequently it went through eight German and five English printings.[19] The second catechism was known as *Christliches Gemuetsgespraech* (Christian Soul-Talk or Heart-to-Heart Conversations), which had originated in Hamburg. Containing 148 questions, this catechism was reprinted five times in Germany and went through 20 editions in America, including six in English.[20] Eby himself arranged for the first English edition, which appeared shortly before his death. He may even have done the translating himself, a full generation before the language issue really troubled the churches.[21]

The catechisms were outlines of Christian doctrine, presented in question-and-answer form. Used as an instrument of instruction in early Christian times, the catechism had been rediscovered by the Reformers, including the Dutch Anabaptists among whom the catechism was most used in Prussia and Russia. It was the Elbing, Prussia, version of the catechism, first printed in 1773, which found entry among the Amish and Swiss Mennonites and which Eby promoted for use in North American churches. Used in both school and church, the catechism served the purposes of both education and evangelism. Through it the young people were taught and brought to a public confession of faith. This confession was followed by baptism. Although the baptismal age tended to be close to the marriage age, some church leaders insisted that baptism was related to faith alone:

> We do not look on the age of a person. We endeavour to preach the Word as plainly, and with as much unction in our meetings as the Lord enables us to do; we seek to declare to them from the Scriptures the will of God; we keep nothing back from them but announce to them repentance toward God and faith in Christ, and, as soon as they become willing to submit to the Word of Life and desire to be baptized, we then proceed to impart to them further special instructions in the principles of non-resistance, for which purpose we use here in Canada the eighteen articles drawn up in Dordrecht, Holland; and as soon as they are sufficiently instructed and convinced that the doctrine of non-resistance is taught by the apostles and prophets, Jesus Christ being the chief cornerstone, and are willing to live in accordance with the same; and to aid in building up the church, they are then baptized in the three holy names and received into the church, whether they have been brought up in the church or otherwise.[22]

Under Eby's leadership the congregation grew. In one year more than 50 persons were baptized into the Eby church, 40 of them being of Mennonite descent and between the ages of 17 and 24, and the others of Lutheran or Reformed descent. Non-Mennonites were constantly being attracted by Eby and received into the church after instruction and rebaptism upon confession of faith. Soon additional congregational groups were being formed under his supervision in the Waterloo County area. By mid-century, when the Mennonite population in Upper Canada had reached about 6,600, about half of which lived in Waterloo, 12 congregations had already built their first meeting-houses (see Table 3).[23] In Ebytown a frame annex with a movable partition was added soon after the first church was built in 1813. This annex accommodated additional hearers at worship on Sunday and, beginning in the winter of 1818–19, weekday classes for children.

Eby was himself the teacher, a profession decided on for him by his relatives. Observing his frail form as a youth, they had predicted that "Aus 'em Bennie gebts ka Bauer, er muss Schulmester Werre" (Bennie will never make a farmer, he must become a schoolteacher).[24] The curriculum was limited to reading, writing,

TABLE 3

MENNONITE POPULATION, CONGREGATIONS, AND MEETING-HOUSES IN
UPPER CANADA COUNTIES AROUND MIDDLE OF NINETEENTH CENTURY

COUNTY	POPULATION*	CONGREGATION	DATE OF FIRST MEETING-HOUSE BUILT
Brant	26	—	—
Bruce	7	—	—
Carleton	5	—	—
Elgin	106	Port Elgin	1861
Grey	3	—	—
Haldimand	213	Rainham	1830
		Cayuga	1840
Halton	34	—	—
Huron	94	—	—
Kent	7	—	—
Lambton	51	—	—
Lincoln	713	Moyer	1810
		Mountain	1850
		Jordan	c. 1845
Middlesex	7	—	—
Norfolk	37	—	—
Ontario	182	—	—
Oxford	447	Blenheim	1849
Peel	4	—	—
Perth	116	—	—
Simcoe	27	—	—
Victoria	1	—	—
Waterloo	3,620	Berlin	1813
		Hagey	1814
		Snyder	1817
		Dettweiler	1830
		Cressman	1838
		Latschar	1839
		Conestoga	1842
		Geiger	1842
		Weber	1842
		Shantz	1849
		Waterloo	1853
		Wanner	1853
Wellington	74	Glen Allan	—
Welland	1,171	Bertie	1810
		Black Creek	1828
Wentworth	192	—	—

COUNTY	POPULATION*	CONGREGATION	DATE OF FIRST MEETING-HOUSE BUILT
York	1,033	Wideman	1817
		Schmitt	1824
		Altona	1852
		Almira	1860
		Risser	1857
		Cedar Grove	1861
Total	8,230		

* 1851-52 Census of Mennonites includes Tunkers. The latter represented about 20 per cent of the total, if the the 1841 census, when Mennonites and Tunkers were kept separate, can be considered as a guide.

spelling and arithmetic, and in Eby's school most of this was done in German. In due course Eby produced his own German spelling-reading books, *Neues Buchstabier und Lesebuch* (New Speller and Reader) and *Fibel* (Primer). For Eby the education of the young was not complete, however, without theology and church history. The lessons he prepared for this purpose, supplemental to the catechism, were published as a *Kurzgefasste Kirchengeschichte und Glaubenslehre der Taufgesinnten Christen oder Mennoniten* (Brief Church History and Doctrine of Anabaptist Christians or Mennonites).[25] With some interruptions, he taught until the 1840s, assisted when he was busiest by wandering unattached men, old soldiers as well as masons and carpenters without work in the winter months.

As the week-day schools became more public, i.e. less parochial, the need to preserve the values of the frontier educational program became a crucial issue for certain Mennonite communities. In that context the first Mennonite Sunday schools in North America arose in Upper Canada. The very first one was begun jointly in 1840 by the Wanner congregation near Hespeler and the Hagey congregation at Preston. It was conducted on alternate Sundays and in its second year boasted an attendance of 75.[26] Though not permanent — it gave way to community-wide union Sunday schools for periods of time — it anticipated the time 50 years later when Sunday schools would become a strong movement throughout the church.

Benjamin Eby's writing activities led him to pioneer in another venture — printing and publishing — beginning in 1835. He had already involved himself in various business ventures, including the establishment of a furniture factory, although the credit for Ebytown's first industry goes to Joseph Schneider, who erected a saw-mill in 1816.[27] But Eby anticipated the development of a town and, recognizing that farming was not his first love, he became, in 1814, the first settler to sell land (56 acres) to incoming townsmen. He thereafter divided the remainder of his land among his children.[28]

The first printing press in Ebytown was established in 1835 by H. W. Peterson, an 1832 German Lutheran immigrant from Virginia who, in all probability, worshipped at Benjamin Eby's meeting-house. The bishop was one of Peterson's "oft-proved friends."[29] As one of the shareholders in both the printing press and the newspaper, *Das Kanadische Museum,* which first appeared on August 27, 1835, and which "catered particularly to the Mennonite group,"[30] Eby may very well have been the first Mennonite printer in North America.[31] One of the items in an early issue of the *Canadian Museum,* apparently placed there by Benjamin Eby, announced that a stray pig had entered the church premises and could be claimed from him upon payment of entailed expenses. Before the coming of the newspaper such announcements were made from the pulpit on Sunday morning or at other public assemblies.[32] By 1840 the Eby interests in printing were being carried on by Benjamin's son, Henry, who proceeded to publish some of his father's works. He also replaced the *Museum* with *Der Deutsche Kanadier.*

The church also served the function of community discipline until the provincial government extended its own legal arms to the frontier. If a wrong was committed, complaint was laid with the elders of the church. The offender, if found guilty, would either have to make proper amends or forfeit the privilege of church membership, the latter being a dreaded alternative.[33] One such disciplinary action involved a member whose bushel measure for purchasing purposes was larger than standard. This would give him an unfair advantage when buying commodities from his neighbours. One of the disadvantaged was a non-church member who entered his complaint with church officials, who then investigated the matter and had the wrong redressed.[34]

In Waterloo, as the number of congregations and ministers expanded, it became necessary for the bishop and his colleagues to meet on a regular basis to discuss their problems, regulate their affairs, and arrange for preaching appointments. Within a bishop's district all the preachers essentially belonged to all the worship centres and they would circulate within practical limitations. Not all the centres, especially the small and outlying ones, could be serviced every Sunday, but efforts were made "to bring the word" to them at least once a month, if not every two weeks. So that all members might know where services were being held on a given Sunday, beginning about 1835 the "appointments" were published in advance in booklet form.

At the same time the bishops of the various districts consulted together. Before long their meetings involved the ministers and deacons. Together they formed the Canada Conference district which met annually, alternating between each of the three main areas — Niagara, Markham, and Waterloo. Thus, about 100 years after the founding of the Franconia and Lancaster conferences, the Canada district followed their example. The three conferences themselves, however, were not related except through the very rare consultations of the bishops. Similar conferences began in Virginia in 1835, Ohio in 1843, and Indiana-Michigan in 1864. The Upper Canada conferences, held in October before 1840 and afterward in May, were known as *Die grosze Zusammenkunft* (The Big Gathering).[35] In addition the separate bishop districts held semi-annual conferences.

The formation of general conferences, embracing all the Mennonite congregations and districts in North America, as well as the involvement of unordained laymen in policy decisions at any level, had to await an unknown future. Militating against the wider fellowship was not only the problem of distance but also questions of principle and practice. The primacy of the local community and congregational autonomy and the independent role of the bishop made large-scale conferring somewhat difficult even when the problem of distance was overlooked.

Most separated of all were the new Amish-Mennonite congregations that were emerging in counties west of Waterloo (see Table 4).[36] Some day in the next century they too would relate to the *grosze Zusammenkunft*, but for the time being they remained an island unto themselves. Indeed, they were often islands *among* themselves.

Some recognized the long-term survival of isolated Mennonite communities as a serious problem. Apparently Benjamin Eby and some of his colleagues recognized it on the international scale. He tried to find all those islands and to relate to them. The publication of Eby's church history and "Letters to the Mennonite Community in Upper Canada" in 1840 revealed that he, as well as

TABLE 4

SUMMARY OF ORIGINAL AMISH SETTLEMENT-CONGREGATIONS

NAME*	DATE	ORIGIN	BISHOPS
Wilmot	1824	Pennsylvania	Peter Nafziger (1825–1831)
Waterloo County		Europe	John Oesch (1831–1848)
East Zorra	1837	Europe	
Oxford County		Wilmot	Joseph Ruby (1853–1897)
also Perth			
Hay	1848	Wilmot	John Oesch (1818–1850)
Huron County		East Zorra	
Wellesley	1859	Europe	John Jantzi (1859–1881)
Waterloo County		Wilmot	
Mornington	1874	Wilmot	Joseph Gerber (1875–1893)
Perth County		Europe	
		East Zorra	

* Name indicates location, since congregational settlements were un-known by the townships.

Jacob Moyer, had been in touch with the community of Mennonites in Europe. Eby surveyed for himself the extent of that community — about 260 congregations in 16 European states or regions — entered into a relationship with its leaders, and shared with them their problems. Eby's hopes of an international Mennonite fellowship, implicit in his activities, could not be considered, let alone fulfilled, for at least another 100 years.

There were other elements of internationalism and universalism in Eby's view of the church. The purpose of his church history, among other things, was to demonstrate that the Mennonites were not descended from the Muensterites but rather that they were spiritually related to the apostles. Accordingly, he traced the Anabaptist history to like-minded nonresisting Christians, including the Waldensians of Italy and numerous churches in the region of Thessalonica, which dated back to the first century and which, he said, had established contact and served communion with sixteenth-century Anabaptists both in Moravia and in the Netherlands. His universalism also made him optimistic about the church's future. He expressed the confidence that in times to come all Christians would recognize that *Kriegfuehren, Eidschwoeren, und Ehescheidung* (war, oaths, and divorce) were unacceptable to the kingdom of God, indeed that they were evil, and that the governments of the world would then also become willing to uphold the teachings of Jesus.[37]

For most Mennonites, the main issue of the times was not a redeemed world but simply a satisfactory community. Far from speculating about the universe and hoping for international community, common congregationalists were preoccupied with their particular and local affairs and, in that preoccupation, increasingly restless. Somehow the new beginnings on virgin lands were not resulting in a kingdom of God as pure and true as the people had expected. The result was that new migrations were set in motion, not so much physical migrations as spiritual migrations into new movements of one sort or another. Some movements reached back into history for their models; others began to imitate the Protestant environment around them.

FOOTNOTES

1. J. C. Wenger, *The Mennonite Church in America* (Scottdale, Pa.: Herald Press, 1966), p. 79.
2. PAC, *Upper Canada Sundries*, Record Group 5, A1, Vol. 74, pp. 39259–39262, James Linsey to Lieutenant-Governor Maitland concerning a sect called "Dunkers," September 14, 1825.
3. *Ibid.*
4. PAC, *Upper Canada Sundries*, Record Group 5, A1, Vol. 173, pp. 94612–94615, Rev. F. W. Bindman to Sir Francis Bond Head, December 8, 1836.
5. Proverbs 16:33.
6. Acts 1:23–26.
7. Oscar Burkholder, "Bishop Benjamin Eby (1785–1853)," *Gospel Herald*, XXIX, April 19, 1929, pp. 61–2.
8. Letter from Jacob Gross, Bucks County, to Samuel Moyer, September 4, 1801 (CGC).
9. Hist. Mss. 1–10.1 (AMC).
10. Burkholder, *op. cit.*, pp. 146–51.
11. J. Boyd Cressman, "Eby, Benjamin," *Mennonite Encyclopedia*, II, pp. 138–9; "Historical Plaque . . ." issued by the Department of Travel and Publicity; Burkholder, *op. cit.*, pp. 61–2; M. E. Gingerich, "Mennonite Leaders of North America: Benjamin Eby (1785–1853)," *Gospel Herald*, March 2, 1965, p. 178; J. Boyd Cressman, "Bishop Benjamin Eby," *Waterloo Historical Society*, XXIX (1941), pp. 152–58.
12. Ira D. Landis, "Bishop Peter Eby of Pequea," *Mennonite Quarterly Review*, XIV (1940), pp. 41–51.
13. Landis, *op. cit.*, and Martin C. Eby, "Peter Eby," *Mennonite Encyclopedia*, II, pp. 139–40.

14. Cressman, "Eby, Benjamin," *op. cit.*, p. 138.
15. Cressman, "First Mennonite Church, Kitchener," *Mennonite Quarterly Review*, XIII (July 1939), pp. 172–3.
16. Cressman, *ibid.*, p. 172.
17. Wenger, *op. cit.*, p. 77. Among the Old Order this service has changed hardly at all, with the exception that some English words have crept into the German and Pennsylvania Dutch usages.
18. Burkholder, *op. cit.*, p. 62.
19. *Ibid.*
20. *Mennonite Encyclopedia*, I, pp. 529–30.
21. Burkholder, *op. cit.*, p. 62.
22. Based on correspondence between David Sherrick, Preston, Ontario, and Baden ministers Christian Schmutz, Ulrich Hege, and Heinrich Landis (1859–1862), in CGC Archives, translated in Leslie D. Witmer, *Pioneer of Christendom of Waterloo County 1800–1967: History of the Hagey-Preston Mennonite Church* (n.p.: 1967 (?)), pp. 33–5.
23. Compiled from Census of the Canadas for 1851–52 from J. S. Hartzler and Daniel Kaufman, *Mennonite Church History* (Scottdale, Pa.: Mennonite Book and Tract Society, 1905), pp. 247–49, and from Burkholder, *op. cit.*
24. *Mennonite Encyclopedia*, I, pp. 128–39.
25. Benjamin Eby, *Kurzgefasste Kirchen-Geschichte* (Berlin, Ont.: published by the author, 1841).
26. Mrs. O. A. Snyder, "The First Mennonite Sunday School," *Waterloo Historical Society*, LI (1963), pp. 27–28.
27. Uttley, *op. cit.*, pp. 16–18.
28. *Ibid.*, pp. 21–22.
29. Cressman, *Mennonite Quarterly Review*, *op cit.*, p. 176.
30. Herbert K. Kalbfleisch, *The History of the Pioneer German Language Press of Ontario 1835–1918* (Toronto: University of Toronto Press, 1968), p. 24.
31. According to John A. Hostetler, "the first Mennonite printing house in America" was established by Joseph Funk in 1847. See John A. Hostetler, "Joseph Funk: Founder of Mennonite Publication Work 1847," *Gospel Herald*, XXXIII (December 23, 1941), pp. 830–31.
32. "Interesting Highlights . . ." (n/d. c.1950), unidentified newspaper article (CGC).
33. Miriam H. Snyder, *Hannes Schneider and His Wife Catharine Haus Schneider: Their Descendants and Times, 1534–1939* (Kitchener: published by the author, 1937), p. 246a.
34. "Interesting Highlights . . . ," *op. cit.*
35. "The Mennonite Conference of Ontario" (CGC II: 5–7).
36. Gingerich, *The Amish of Canada*, p. 39.
37. Benjamin Eby, *Kurzgefasste Kirchen-Geschichte*, p. 140.

Open-air Revival Meetings

6. Mid-Century Renewal Movements

Had the Mennonites not entered upon this disastrous course
[ruinous factionalism], but few schisms would have occurred
and they might rank among the leading denominations of
this country — H. P. KREHBIEL.[1]

THE SOLIDARITY of the Mennonite congregations and the
influence of their dedicated leaders was to be sorely
tested in the middle of the 1800s. Internal as well as external
change confronted the rather independent bishops, the relatively
autonomous congregations and the loose organization of the conference with problems they could not competently handle or
peacefully resolve. Occasionally, the leaders themselves were the
problem; they were often caught unprepared by the engulfing
trends of the time and by the undercurrents in their congregations. These long-ignored rumblings eventually erupted.

As new ideas, ways, and movements challenged the old, and as
the established order reacted against the new threats, the Mennonite community once again fell prey to the *Taeuferkrankheit*.[2]
Again, the Anabaptist sickness brought psychological injuries so
deep and left organizational scars so lasting that for the most part
they could not easily be healed. Indeed, the century of division, as
this phase of the Mennonite experience in the 1800s may properly
be called, extended into the 1900s, in spite of the ecumenical

movements which cropped up subsequent to almost every division.

The Canadian experience of fragmentation was not an isolated phenomenon. The internal divisions in Ontario were not only duplicated, but at several junctures actually conditioned, by developments in the United States. In spite of the revolution, the migrations, and the War of 1812, the destiny of the Mennonites was still very much felt in continental terms. And what was happening among the Swiss-German Mennonites in North America again had its remarkable parallelisms among the Dutch-German Mennonites in Russia. The two Mennonite families were not aware of each other's factionalisms, but their common tendency to divide led to a later western meeting of some of the Dutch and Swiss factions.

Nor was the Mennonite experience unique in the ideological sense. It was duplicated, often preceded, and at all times certainly influenced by the surrounding religious environment from which even Mennonite separatism had not been able to escape. As a people whose worldview was uniquely religious, they could not avoid responding in some fashion to the religious movements about them. The second great awakening in the United States[3] and the great revival in Canada,[4] both of which sought in the early nineteenth century to evangelize North America by revivalistic means in the tradition of Methodism, were a strong influence on Mennonites. Some protested the new emphases; others proceeded toward imitation. The latter was especially true among those groups that liked to think of themselves as progressives or as new Mennonites. Whatever the response, the Mennonites joined with their fellow North Americans in fragmenting into many new groupings to be known as denominations.[5]

The renewal theme, to be explored here mainly in its mid-century manifestations, had some earlier antecedents which must not be overlooked. The most important for Upper Canada was the Lancaster movement founded by John Herr (1782–1850) in 1812. Herr's father, Francis Herr, had been expelled from the church in 1800, giving as the reason his demand for reform; according to others excommunication was due to a dishonest horse deal. Whatever the reason, the entire family had subsequently remained aloof and unbaptized, though they carried out their own religious services.

John Herr took over when his father died. Much like the earliest Swiss brethren, he had himself baptized by a member of

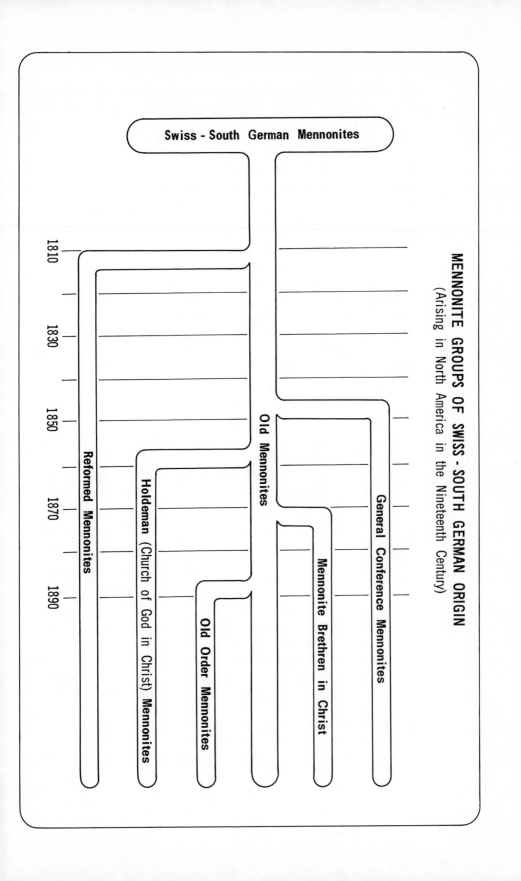

MENNONITE GROUPS OF SWISS - SOUTH GERMAN ORIGIN
(Arising in North America in the Nineteenth Century)

Swiss - South German Mennonites

1810
1830
1850
1870
1890

Reformed Mennonites

Holdeman (Church of God in Christ) Mennonites

Old Order Mennonites

Old Mennonites

Mennonite Brethren in Christ

General Conference Mennonites

the group selected for that purpose. After being chosen minister and elder, again without an officiating bishop from the established church, he baptized all the rest and immediately proceeded to advance the thesis that the church had strayed far from the Bible and the writings of Menno Simons and that it was the duty of reform-minded Mennonites to bring about a renewal of the true church. He wrote six small pamphlets and books and went on many preaching tours, including some to Upper Canada where he died in 1850.

Wherever he went he found others disillusioned with the conventional Mennonite church, its permissiveness in elections, political campaigns, attendance at county fairs and horse races, and drinking. The dissenters, a total of 2,500 by the time of his death, were gathered into the "true" Mennonite church, once again to practise consistent foot-washing, the kiss of peace, and the discipline of erring members. The old church referred to them as Herrites. They themselves preferred to be called Orthodox or Reformed Mennonites, the latter name eventually becoming official.[6]

TABLE 1

REFORMED MENNONITE CONGREGATIONS IN CANADA

NAME	YEAR OF FOUNDING	LOCATION
Humberstone	1825	Welland County
Rainham	1825	Haldimand County
Stevensville	1835	Welland County
Hostetler's	1844	Waterloo County
Kingwood	1850	Waterloo County
Amulree	1850	Perth County

The assumption of the Herr group was that renewal of the true church could be found only by returning to the fundamentals of the faith and the old customs. By contrast, the renewal groups that arose at mid-century, with one or two exceptions, sought renewal in new experiences and new organizations, although their looking to the past was never completely absent. The main body of the church stood somewhere in between the Herrites and the new Mennonites.

These new Mennonite groups, having started in local congregations, each with its own dissenting leader, were quite numerous in their North American beginnings around the middle of the nineteenth century. Eventually they coalesced into several minor groups and two major ones: the General Conference Mennonite Churches in North America and the Mennonite Brethren in Christ Church. The Mennonites in the United States were affected primarily by the former group, while the church in Canada was most affected by the schisms resulting from the emergence of the latter group.

The founding father of the General Conference Mennonites was John H. Oberholtzer (1809–95), although he was by no means alone in advocating change. A number of Oberholtzer's ministerial colleagues, including his own bishop, John Hunsicker, deplored what they thought was an intolerable spiritual sterility, ecclesiastical standstill, and social separatism. Their quarrel was not so much with old theology as with old methods and the opposition to all new trends. English preaching, Sunday schools, extra meetings for prayer and evangelism, better relations with other denominations, involvement in community affairs, changes in clothing styles — none would be sactioned by the established leadership.

That leadership consisted of five bishops, 40 ministers, and 25 deacons in 22 congregations in eastern Pennsylvania. Loosely organized as the Franconia Conference, they met as a council semi-annually to agree on preaching appointments for the coming months and otherwise to regulate the affairs of the churches. Such regulation proceeded not so much as a process of discussion, clarification and negotiation, but literally as regulation, the reinforcement of those rules and practices which had been made sacred by custom and tradition.

Yet, the utility and validity of many of those practices were being questioned, as outside influences arising from education, commerce and increased mobility made themselves felt. There was no easy way to resolve the resulting differences, because both the attitude and the mechanism necessary for such resolution were missing. The majority of Mennonites and their bishops had not yet learned, perhaps had no intention of learning, the process of resolving differences and conflict through discussion, negotiation and compromise. The only way known to deal with new influences was to reaffirm the old laws. Sometimes such action brought peace, but most often only temporarily, since the inner revolt of the dissidents was thereby intensified. The results were endless grumblings, bickerings, and personality clashes. In the words of H. P. Krehbiel, one of the earliest historians of the period, the situation was one of war and no peace:

> Peace, peace! that was the watchword; but there was no peace. Instead of fraternally cooperating, many churches, animated by intolerant prejudices, came actually to antagonize each other with great bitterness.[7]

The differences between conservatives and progressives had begun to surface first on the school issue, after the issuance in 1834 of a new law which strengthened the public role in education. Some Mennonites opposed this growing influence of the American society on themselves and tried to shut it off wherever they could. Others saw much good in interaction and no harm in some of the changes. The more tolerant and accommodating ones not only approved of public education but also attended county fairs, political conventions and even courts of law. They adopted the new oil-cloth covers for their wagons and shed the plain coats for newer styles of dress. In their social life they allowed marriage with non-Mennonites and in their liturgy they favoured open communion.

Those who were proponents of change did not necessarily agree among themselves. Some, like the Abraham Hunsickers, definitely wanted more secular involvement. Others, like the Johnsons, wanted modernness without discarding some of the sacred traditions. Still others, like the Gehmans, saw rejuvenation in evangelical excitement and emotionalism. In the middle stood the Oberholtzers, who insisted that they simply wanted healthy religious progress. None wanted basic changes in historic Mennonite doctrine, such as voluntary baptism, discipleship, and nonresistance. However, once the doors of change were opened on minor matters, the major or fundamental matters rarely remained unaffected. The bishops probably felt this instinctively and therefore holding the line became for them the imperative of holy office, the essence of their divine calling, the only reasonable response to the confused calls for change.

Caught in the middle of the argumentation was Oberholtzer, who aggressively pursued newness and his idea of progress. Once a teacher, then a locksmith and printer, he became at the age of 33 a minister in the Swamps Mennonite Church. His oratorical talent, leadership ability, and general stance on nonconformity soon got him into trouble with the bishops. Their sole way of dealing with a novelty was to ignore it, to avoid it or to oppress it. Oberholtzer, on the other hand, was not given to patience. In and out of season, he preached renewal of both content and form in the church. He started children's Bible classes, introduced new materials of instruction, and began to advocate more formal ministerial training, as well as missionary endeavours.

Perhaps Oberholtzer's greatest "offences" were his excursions outside of the Mennonite denomination, and his change of ministerial attire, first when he went out and later also at home. The styles for men's clothing were changing as mid-nineteenth century approached, and Oberholtzer soon found himself exchanging the plain coat, the ministerial long-tail, straight-collar, no-lapel uniform, sanctioned by use since colonial days, for a more modern style. His coats had no tails, fewer buttons at the top, and the high collar turned over to form a lapel, thus exposing the shirt, which would soon be begging for the decorative tie.

Going out to preach the gospel was one thing; bringing back new and unacceptable ideas was quite another. One of those ideas was a new constitution which, in his opinion, would clarify the internal decision-making process and strengthen the ties between the congregations. He wanted rules of procedure adopted and minutes kept of council meetings. Above all, he wanted to guarantee a hearing for the dissenting minority, including himself, which was so often arbitrarily overruled by the conservative bishops.

While Oberholtzer's advancement of the new ideas and the rejection of the plain coat had set the stage for the ensuing clash, it was the preparation of a constitution which brought on the real crisis. Having been denied the vote at ministerial meetings in 1844, Oberholtzer had returned to wearing the plain coat in 1847 in order to give his ideas on the constitution a better chance. He had also recruited some support. Not only was his own bishop encouraging him, but 13 ministers and deacons were supporting the presentation of the constitution to council. The ministerial council, however, refused to allow its reading and forbade also its printing and circulation in advance of the fall meeting. The dissenters, led by Hunsicker and Oberholtzer, printed and circulated the document anyway. When the fall came they had 16 ministerial supporters. All of them were expelled from the meeting for subscribing to the document. Reinstatement, the bishops ruled, could only happen if proper confession of error were made.

The dissenters, being equally uncompromising, believed too

much in the rightness of their cause to repent. On October 28, 1847, they formed the East Pennsylvania District of Mennonites, with Abraham (brother to John) Hunsicker as chairman and Oberholtzer as secretary, taking one-third of the Franconia membership with them. This included the majority in six congregations, where the rest were left to erect new meeting-houses. In other places the new Mennonite minorities erected their own meeting-houses, and in still others the two groups worshipped in the same place, though on alternate Sundays.

Meanwhile, Oberholtzer had taken full advantage of the new freedom to advance his ideas. Beginning in 1847, he gathered the young people around himself on Sunday afternoons for religious instruction and thus founded the first Mennonite Sunday school in the United States, which achieved formal organizational status by 1853. He helped introduce organ and other instrumental music into worship services. In 1852 he founded the *Religioeser Botschafter* (Religious Messenger), the first American Mennonite periodical, through which he stirred missionary interest leading to the formation of missionary societies.

Most of all, he was concerned with organizational questions both within and among the congregations. The constitution, or *Ordnung* as he termed it, was made an all-important document of proper governance and discipline. It provided for a *Hohe Rath* (High Council or Executive Committee) which had some of the authority formerly held by the bishops, perhaps even more so, but whose membership was subject to election, whose discussions were open, and whose decisions were public. Indeed, the *Verhandlungen des Hohen Rathes der Mennoniten Gemeinschaft* (the Proceedings of the High Council of the Mennonite Society) became the "broadsides" which the pamphleteering and crusading Oberholtzer spread throughout the populace.

Sometimes these broadsides were directed at the new Mennonite society itself, because there were many differences of opinion within the group. Whenever the new Mennonites contrasted themselves with what was old, these differences were overcome, but whenever they tried to agree on what should be new, they became disunited. An attempt to compromise was made, however, and for this reason the society remained flexible; indeed, it vacillated on issues quite important to the old society. In the first decade the society completely changed its position on prayer meetings from approval to disapproval, on foot-washing from encouragement to declaring it unnecessary, and on members of secret societies attending communion from forbidding the practice to allowing it. To help resolve the internal conflict the Hohe Rath on one occasion formulated a ten-point decision at the heart of which stood the following sentence addressed to the new society:

> We ask all ministers and all members to have patience with each other . . . every minister should consider it his duty, if the church requests it, to submit himself for the sake of peace.[8]

Discipline within the church also became a matter not to be taken too seriously because of its disruptive effect. One historian claims that this was one of the greatest points of real difference (a position probably somewhat exaggerated) between the new Mennonites and their opposites, those who came to be known as old Mennonites.[9]

In spite of the reduced discipline, reflecting greater tolerance, the new Mennonites experienced further divisions in their first decade. For some the Oberholtzer views were too conservative, and one faction, wanting even more community and political involvement, separated under the leadership of Abraham Hunsicker, the presiding chairman at the 1847 founding. For Henry G. Johnson, the Oberholtzer tendency to make foot-washing optional was much too liberal, and his people bowed out to form another independent organization that would retain some of the sacred traditions while pursuing some of the new ideas. William Gehman saw the substance of renewal in private meetings attended only by the inner circle. By 1858, the year in which the Johnsons withdrew, the Eastern District Conference was sufficiently disturbed by the manifestations of emotionalism and super-piety that Gehman and 22 others were dismissed. The result was another denominational grouping known as Evangelical Mennonites, which will enter our story again at a later time.

These splinter groups were small, however, and as much as they hurt the Oberholtzer cause they did not deter his external purpose of bringing together in a general conference all dissenting groups that shared the ideas of the progressive Eastern Pennsylvania group. Some of these factions could be found on the western frontier, particularly in Ohio and Iowa and beyond. In Ontario also there were members and leaders who were drawn to the new Mennonite movement.

The diverse character and views of the Oberholtzer following were an asset as well as a liability in this task. Although the secularists, the traditionalists and the emotionalists had as groups been separated from the middle-of-the-road Oberholtzers, their views remained represented in the emerging General Conference. This helped to attract a diversity of other groups, but it also meant that complete internal unity in that General Conference would always be less than perfect. Very soon the slogan appeared "In fundamentals unity, in secondary matters diversity, in all things charity." The formula was simple enough, but with differences of viewpoint arising precisely on which matters were primary and which were secondary, charity, forever in great need, would somehow always be in short supply.

Among those in the distance who eyed the Oberholtzer movement with favour were people of the Twenty, where the gathering of fringe Mennonites and other divergent elements into a unified congregation had never been completely successful. It was in the Niagara peninsula area more than at Markham or Waterloo that outside influences were felt first and most, and where external absorption of the Mennonites had been evident from the beginning. The reasons for this may lie in part in its closer proximity to Pennsylvania and to the direct line of United States–Canada traffic. The Niagara settlements lacked compactness compared to Waterloo, but in the end compactness did not spare Waterloo and Markham.

Openness to outside influences was also conditioned in part by the Mennonite churches and their leaders. Benjamin Eby, for instance, had in his own way been progressive, in many of his emphases anticipating the work of John H. Oberholtzer. But preoccupation with internal economic and ecclesiastical affairs sapped their energy and prevented them from doing all they might, or would like to, have done. The *Diener* (ministers and deacons) wrestled intensely with some of their problems, but their responses to the spiritual and moral problems of the times were considered quite inadequate by some people and their spokesmen.

One of these problems was alcoholism, and some Christian groups, notably the Methodists, organized temperance societies to combat the evil. The Mennonite leaders, however, discouraged membership in the temperance society, partly no doubt because of an old aversion to membership in outside societies of any sort, be they secret or public, religious or secular. In their opinion, membership in the Christian congregation was fundamental and should be all-inclusive. Other memberships, even the good ones, could only harm the Christian community. Their strongest words, therefore, expressed in a 1842 resolution, were temperance and moderation. They may very well have been the most helpful words for a time which knew mostly only excesses and extremes.[10]

An examination of the resolution reveals a compromising spirit and the attempt to reconcile divergent views. "Young brethren" who had already joined the temperance association were not asked to remove themselves but rather only to stay away from meetings and otherwise not to agitate because "temperance is already sufficiently commanded to us as Christians." In making this request, the ministerial council expressed the traditional Mennonite attitude to outside societies, which was that they were probably evil, but if not evil then surely unnecessary. Those opposed to membership, on the other hand, should not "take offence" at those who were members. Both should "bear with one another in love." Further, it was considered "not good" for "additional brethren and sisters to join so that further misunderstanding may be avoided."

On drinking itself, the three bishops, 15 preachers, and 14 deacons also advocated temperance, rather than abstinence, and tolerance. It was generally recommended to "avoid use of strong drinks as much as possible." On the occasion of social visits, the hosts, in order to avoid abuse, should "not be so much concerned to set the same before visitors." At auction sales likewise, strong drink should be kept away in order to avoid disorder. Also at large gatherings of workers "all abuse shall be prevented" so that our light "may shine before others who are not in our churches."

The ministerial conference did not take an abstinence stance, as one writer has concluded.[11] That same 1842 meeting took strong action on "shows," ruling that "it is forbidden every member to go to such places and to give money to see a show." Repeated transgressions without repentance would be followed by discipline and excommunication. By contrast, the action on drink represented no such ruling. Strong drink, but not all drink, was discouraged at social events and larger public gatherings, but not in private. In other words, a position of moderation and not total abstinence had been advanced.[12]

A similar moderating stance was taken when the issue of prayer meetings came up several years later. In 1849 it was ruled that "prayer meetings for all true worshippers" were permitted "as long as it is done in an evangelical order, especially with the weak and sick who cannot attend the regular church service." But the evangelical order above all required that those who believed or did not believe in such meetings bear each other with "love, meekness, and patience." No minister should be required "to act contrary to his feeling, or his view of the Word." The scriptural order was that all things should be done "in charity."[13]

To the renewal-minded, the Conference positions and proceedings were not sufficiently positive, clear-cut and determined. To them, the Methodists with their abstinence crusades, tent meetings, and efficient organization were more impressive and by their definition much more spiritual. Methodist models of theology, strategy, and organization were later adopted by the dissenters. Some families joined the Methodists and large numbers tried to emulate them, especially those Methodists who most perturbed the Episcopalians and other established orders. "Ignorant enthusiasts" the Anglican bishop of Quebec called the revivalists, characterizing them:

> The Methodist uses all kinds of techniques. His approach
> was often highly emotional. He threatened his listeners with
> the torches of everlasting hell-fire. He painted glorious
> pictures of salvation. He did not believe that the devil
> should have all the good times.[14]

This outside influence was also not wanting in the Markham area, and especially at the Moyer Mennonite Church in Vineland. In the 1840s its disruptive effect was reinforced at Moyer's by misunderstandings and rivalries among three ministerial personalities, one of them a bishop, two others likely candidates for that office. It was thought that Jacob Moyer, Jr., ordained to the ministry in 1824, might eventually succeed his father as bishop. But Jacob, Jr., died in 1831, two years before his father. Ordained in 1831, Daniel Hoch, a very able preacher and energetic leader, was not considered by some to be the right man to succeed the senior Moyer as bishop in 1833 because of his impulsiveness and occasional stubborn streaks. Thus the election of a bishop was delayed, while Benjamin Eby exercised the "bishop oversight" until at least one more minister could be ordained. The result was that Jacob Gross was elected minister in 1833 and bishop in 1834, both times under the supervision of Eby.

Both Gross and Hoch were open to outside influences and by the early 1840s definitely tended in evangelical directions. Both became interested in the prayer meeting movement, though Gross was more interested in the example of the Methodists than was

Hoch. Gross was particularly fascinated by their temperance movement, baptism and communion. However, since the majority of his congregation would not support him, he and his followers left the church in 1849 and formed or joined what was known as the Evangelical Church Association. It was still under Methodist influence when the man who would be Gross's successor reported in September of that year:

> Their evening meetings and prayer meetings became louder and louder and more often. They have had already for a time in order to help them, a daughter of the Methodist preacher, William Hippel. And two others were baptized by the Methodists three times backwards under the water. Daniel Hoch thus far will not have anything to do with Methodists, as a part of the others also. Last Sunday the most of them went to the Methodists to communion. They had a big meeting which lasted 10 days about 10 miles from here.[15]

With Bishop Gross gone, Daniel Hoch could once again have been in line for the succession to the bishop's office, except that in 1842 two of the late Bishop Moyer's other sons had been ordained to the ministry. Abraham, the older, known as "Big Abe," was ruled out because of illness.[16] Dilman Moyer, however, like all the Moyers before him, stood solidly in the main traditions of the Moyer Church, which, in spite of the withdrawal of Gross, still struggled with its various factions.

Daniel Hoch and his followers, designated by himself as the prayer-minded group, stood out against the *gebetslose Teil der Gemeinde* or the non-praying group.[17] The non-praying group, however, saw it the other way around. After all, Daniel Hoch had already voiced non-support for the prayer veil, the traditional head-covering of worshipping Mennonite women, by supporting his wife, who had already discarded it. Holding themselves to these sacred traditional symbols and the conference prayer resolution of 1847, the followers of Dilman Moyer saw themselves on surer ground as far as prayer was concerned than the impulsive though extremely able and aggressive Hoch. Attempting to reconcile the two factions once again was Benjamin Eby, who in his later years had once again assumed the "bishop oversight." Three times in 1849, and at three levels, unity was sought and to an extent achieved: on May 25 within the congregation, on August 18 between Eby and Hoch, and on September 15 at the provincial conference with 28 out of 30 ministers, deacons, and bishops in attendance. But every time relationships broke down again, with Hoch, Moyer, and their followers blaming each other.[18]

Hoch, however, would not be easily discouraged or silenced. Not only did he immediately establish relationships with Oberholtzer and Hunsicker of Pennsylvania as they entered Ontario in 1850, but he travelled extensively himself, especially in the small congregations and isolated districts where internal Mennonite neglect and outside Methodist influences prepared for him a ready audience. In 1853 all those interested in his work promised him sufficient financial support if he would become an itinerant minister in the churches. Two years later he organized the Conference Council of the United Mennonite Community of Canada West and Ohio for the purposes of home missions and evangelism.

Supporting Hoch were dissident groups in Waterloo, Lincoln, and York counties in Ontario and a newly organized congregation at Wadsworth, Ohio, led by Ephraim Hunsberger, whose members were Oberholtzer immigrant families from the east. Before the end of the 1850s, Hoch had established a fully organized "Home and Missionary Society of the Mennonites." Moreover, Hoch, Hunsberger, and Oberholtzer were sufficiently united to make even greater plans. They had come to the conclusion that reconciliation of the dissident groups with the mother church was not a likely possibility and so they proceeded to organize the General Conference of the Mennonite Churches of North America at West Point, Iowa, on May 28, 1860. Only three congregations were represented at that meeting but, with Oberholtzer as chairman, a plan of union was worked out, and on that basis eight congregations attended the second meeting at Wadsworth, Ohio, a year later.

It was an auspicious beginning, but there were problems ahead. One of the obstacles to a wide and solid union was once again fundamental disagreement on what constituted renewal. The newness represented by the General Conference was not quite what Hoch and others had in mind. The result was their later defection and the gradual formation of a second new Mennonite alliance. But some defections also benefited the new General Conference, namely dissident individuals and groups separating from the old Mennonites. With more immigrants arriving from Switzerland, Poland, Prussia and Russia, the Conference soon showed signs of becoming the second largest Mennonite grouping in North America (see Table 2).[19]

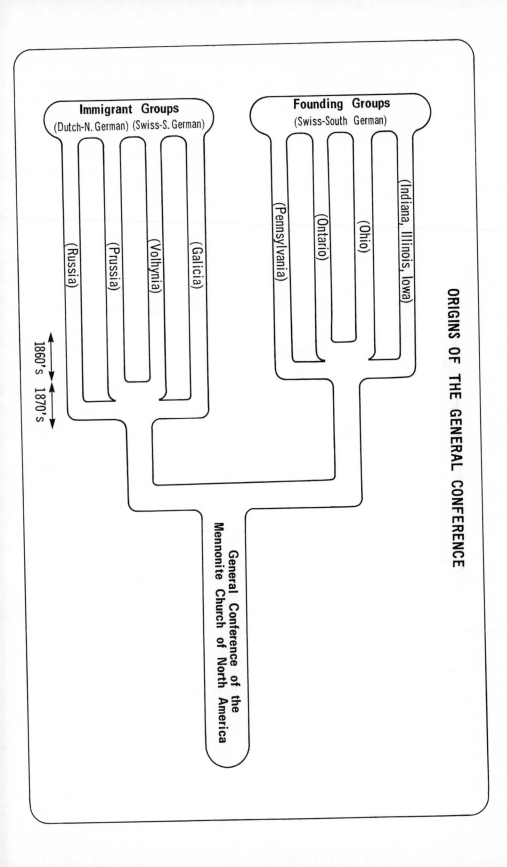

ORIGINS OF THE GENERAL CONFERENCE

Immigrant Groups
(Dutch-N. German) (Swiss-S. German)

Founding Groups
(Swiss-South German)

(Russia)
(Prussia)
(Volhynia)
(Galicia)

(Pennsylvania)
(Ontario)
(Ohio)
(Indiana, Illinois, Iowa)

1860's
1870's

General Conference of the
Mennonite Church of North America

TABLE 2

SUMMARY OF GENERAL CONFERENCE
OF MENNONITE CHURCHES OF NORTH AMERICA IN 1884

LOCATION	NO. OF CONGREGATIONS	MEMBERSHIP*
Ontario	1	30
Pennsylvania	15	1,290
Ohio	1	60
New York	2	60
Missouri	5	150
Kansas	9	1,620
Iowa	2	210
Indiana	1	180
Illinois	1	150
South Dakota	1	150
Total	38	3,900

* Based on votes at Tenth General Conference in 1884. The number of members in a church which could be represented by one vote was multiplied by 30.

The General Conference might very well have become the largest formation in North America except for several other forces at work. A minor factor was the presence of other schismatics. In Ohio, for instance, John Holdeman in 1859 began preaching the return to the true church, meaning the fundamental doctrines, the experience of the new birth, church discipline, and social separation. Very much in the tradition of John Herr of the Reformed Mennonites, he also formed a separate dominational group, which became known popularly as the Holdeman Church, although he named it the Church of God in Christ Mennonite.[20] In two decades Holdeman's influence was to extend to Canada, as will later be seen.

A second factor limiting the growth of the General Conference was the "awakening" which took place among the old Mennonites themselves. That story must be told later, but already in the 1860s the man who became "the outstanding leader of the [old] Mennonite Church in the nineteenth century" made his influence felt.[21] He was John F. Funk (1835–1930) of Elkhart, Indiana, whose ideas and initiatives had much in common with John

Oberholtzer. But, unlike Oberholtzer, Funk determined to stay with his brethren, and to bring "progress" to them no faster than they could bear it. Funk attributed many of his Oberholtzer-type ideas on Sunday school, evangelism and religious publication to D. L. Moody, a renowned American evangelist with whom he became associated in Chicago. Like Oberholtzer, Funk exerted much of his influence through a monthly periodical, which he started in 1864, but he did Oberholtzer one better by publishing his *Herald of Truth* in both English and German.

So great was the ferment of the time, however, that neither Oberholtzer, Holdeman nor Funk could together contain or direct all the stirrings in the church. As the General Conference brought together the groups dissenting from the old church and the old world, another new Mennonite alliance gathered up those renewal groups which, because of distance, leadership or differing point of view, did not readily relate to the General Conference. This grouping of new Mennonites arose in various places in Ontario and under several leaders between 1850 and 1860. All had common complaints — the church was too rigid and sterile, too formal in its worship, too reserved in its religious expression, and not sufficiently explicit in preaching the new birth. The dissenters also seemed to advocate a similar formula for renewing the church — more prayer meetings, more services in the evangelistic style, more preaching for a decisive verdict, a climactic conversion experience which in the imitation of the Methodist tradition meant more fire and brimstone, and, above all, better direction and organization.

The first locus of this new Mennonite movement, as has already been indicated, was at the Twenty in the 1840s with Daniel Hoch and his followers, though, as we have seen, Hoch chose to go the way of the General Conference, at least at first. In the 1850s a new centre arose at Markham where two men, despite their lack of ordination, felt the call to preach subsequent to their conversion. The followers of these two men, Abraham Raymer and Christian Troyer, gathered around them and in 1863 built the first church of the movement at Markham. In the Waterloo area small congregations of new Mennonites arose at Blair, New Dundee and Breslau. The adherents met, with or without ministers, mostly in homes to "sing, pray, and testify as the Holy Spirit would direct."[22]

This new Mennonite movement in Ontario remained one of the most isolated groups throughout the 1860s. But the "conversion" of Solomon Eby, a preacher in the old Mennonite Church at Port Elgin in Bruce County for 11 years, both increased the number of supporters and added direction. Soon his whole congregation followed him in the new ways. The Mennonites in Waterloo County, who had heard rumours of the whole church in Port Elgin going Methodist, sent a delegation to investigate. Their favourable report reinforced similar tendencies in Waterloo County.

Bishop Joseph Hagey, who had succeeded Benjamin Eby upon his death in 1853, was not ready, however, to incorporate all the "new things." He refused, along with the majority of the church, to baptize some of the candidates instructed by Preacher Daniel Wismer who, like Solomon Eby, was a revivalist. After a year of special conferences and much haggling, the dissenters called Bishop John Lapp of Clarence Centre, New York, to come up and baptize those unacceptable to Hagey, and in 1871 Lapp consented to do so, wrongly assuming that the converts would none the less be incorporated into the old church.

Meanwhile, a similar struggle between the old and the new had surfaced in Northern Indiana, where Daniel Brenneman (1834–1889) was attempting to renew the church after the style and manner of Solomon Eby in Bruce County, Ontario. Brenneman, however, was even more able, eloquent, and aggressive, and at the same time popular. He was known as the preacher who spoke in English and who sang bass. Both the English sermon and four-part singing were progressive signs of the times. The aggressive and popular evangelist soon clashed, not only with "exceedingly conservative" people, but also with other, perhaps more moderate, progressives. The former were led by Bishop Jacob Wisler of the Yellow Creek congregation, where Brenneman was minister. Jacob Wisler, like John F. Funk, will re-enter our story as part of a later nineteenth-century theme.

The moderate progressives, who clashed with both the Wisler and Brenneman types, were led by Funk, the publisher-minister who had come to Elkhart from Chicago in 1867, hoping to renew the entire church. In 1872 Funk and Brenneman had shared the platform in what was called "the first revival compaign held in the Mennonite Church in the United States."[23] These two able men could, however, easily become rivals in the reform movement, which is precisely what happened. Funk chose to renew the old church from within; Brenneman ended up attempting to renew the church from without, though not entirely by his own choice. He was strengthened in his position by Solomon Eby, with whom he conferred first when Eby visited Indiana and later when Brenneman was travelling in Ontario.

By 1873 both Eby and Brenneman were in trouble with their respective conferences, which disagreed not only with their revivalism and emotional Christianity but also with their independent methods of operating. Their cases and the issues they represented came up at respective meetings of the Ontario and Indiana conferences, with the result that in 1874 both were declared not to be conference members because of the dissension and disorder that resulted from their activities.

Immediately thereafter, on May 15, 1874, at a conference held in Berlin, Ontario, Eby and Brenneman organized their followers into the Reformed Mennonites, being similar in name though not in outlook to the Herrite group. The organization provided for Indiana and Ontario districts under the leadership of Brenneman and Eby respectively. The size of the separate group was approximately 500 adult members, including four ministers and three deacons in Ontario and two ministers in Indiana. A year later, at a Union Conference held at Bloomingdale during March 23 and 24, 1875, the new Mennonites, officially so called, of the Markham area joined with the Reformed Mennonites to form the United Mennonites.

That three-day conference based the union on "the Word of God as contained in the Old and New Testaments, and a synopsis of the Word of God" as contained in the 1632 Dordrecht Confession. In addition it spelled out its emphasis on revival meetings, the acceptance only of those who had experienced conversion, the missionary cause, prayer and fellowship meetings, Sunday schools, house visitations and family worship. Negatively, the union conference spoke out on membership in secret organizations, the manufacture, sale and use of spirituous liquors, the use of tobacco, unbecoming modes of dress, foolish talking and jesting and attendance at wordly amusements.

The separation from the old church and the formation of the new movement was not without blame cast in both directions.[24] The new Mennonites insisted that Brenneman and Eby had been excommunicated without good reason, there having been no immoral conduct. They were guilty only of having progressive ideas, being a generation ahead of their time, and being zealous in missions and evangelism. The old Mennonites, on the other hand, remembered that English preaching, Sunday schools, prayer meet-

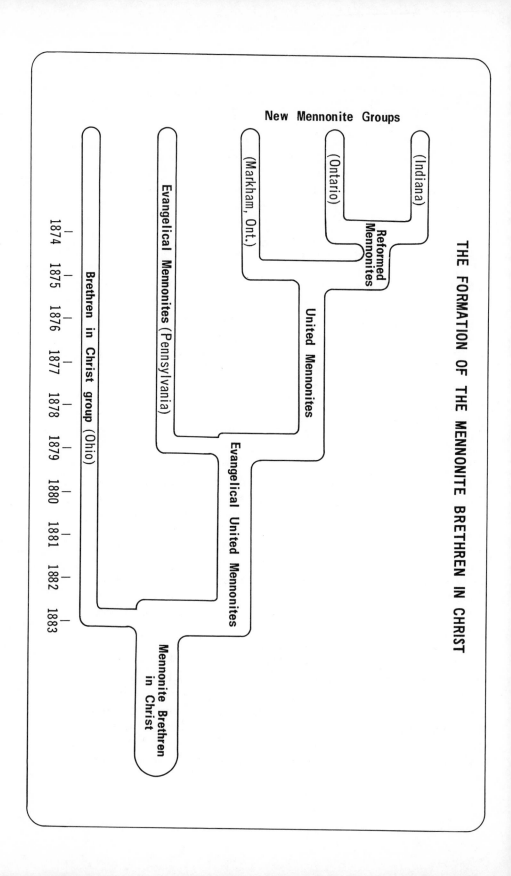

ings and spiritual awakenings had all happened and been tolerated before the new Mennonites had come along. According to them the cleavage was caused not so much by "particular activities" but by "the spirit in which they were undertaken and the disposition behind them." Two historians of the respective groups agreed on one thing:

> Had a little more tolerance and patience been exercised on both sides at the time, the division might perhaps have been avoided.[25]

In 1879 the United Mennonites, meeting at Blair, incorporated the Evangelical Mennonites of Pennsylvania (the Gehman group), the resulting union being called the Evangelical United Mennonites. In 1883 an Ohio faction of the Brethren in Christ (Tunker) group, which had also been fragmenting in similar ways, joined the group and the more permanent name of Mennonite Brethren in Christ was adopted. At that point the new denomination had about 1647 members (see Table 3).[26]

TABLE 3

SUMMARY OF MENNONITE BRETHREN IN CHRIST IN 1883

DISTRICT	APPOINTMENTS*	MEMBERS
Ontario	43	909
Indiana-Ohio-Michigan	22	452
Pennsylvania	14	286
Total	79	1,647

* Congregations and mission points

The membership of the Mennonite Brethren in Christ was increasing rapidly, not only because of defection from the old Church but also because of new converts. The ministers of the new group went about preaching with great zeal. Open-air "field" and "bush" meetings were common, and the results were immediately consolidated in the formation of congregations under the supervision of strong, centrally organized conferences whose Methodist-type superintendents wielded an oversight and direction stronger than any of the Mennonite bishops.

Why didn't the two new Mennonite movements, the General Conference and the Mennonite Brethren in Christ, join their forces in a common organization? They had much in common — emphasis on evangelism, missions, publications, organization, trained ministry, education and vigorous opposition to secret societies. It should be noted that there was some fellowship between the two groups in the early stages, until Daniel Hoch and his followers withdrew from the General Conference. The parting and permanent separation seem to have been for several reasons. The new Mennonite movement represented by the General Conference occurred earlier and reached an ecumenical peak at least 20 years before that of the Mennonite Brethren in Christ. Besides, the main locus of the former movement was in the United States while that of the latter was in Canada.

There were also, however, real differences in emphasis and direction, as real as the differences between Oberholtzer and those like Gehman in Pennsylvania and Solomon Eby, who later left the Mennonite Brethren in Christ to join the Pentecostals in Ontario. Most important, the General Conference movement sought very consciously to temper its reform activity with a strong emphasis on maintaining the Mennonite tradition.[27] The Mennonite Brethren in Christ, by contrast, would with time largely abandon that tradition, including the pacifist position. These differences in orientation gave direction to future Mennonite developments and identities. Accordingly, in the next century the General Conference and the old Mennonites would come closer together once again to become champions of the Mennonite heritage, while the Mennonite Brethren in Christ, by their own choice, would not only drop their name but would move outside the Mennonite family altogether.

FOOTNOTES

1. H. P. Krehbiel, *History of the Mennonite General Conference*, Vol. I (Canton, Ohio: published by the author, 1898), p. 8.
2. See p. 38.
3. Bernard A. Weisberger, *They Gathered at the River* (Boston, 1958). On the revivalist movement which especially influenced Upper Canada see: Whitney R. Cross, *The Burnt-Over District: The Social and Intellectual History of Enthusiastic Religion in Western New York, 1800–1850* (New York: Harper & Row, 1950).

4. A general survey is provided in: S. D. Clark, *Church and Sect in Canada* (Toronto: University of Toronto Press, 1948).

5. On the American concept of denomination see especially: Sidney E. Mead, *The Lively Experiment: The Shaping of Christianity in America* (New York: Harper & Row, 1963). For comments on the use of the term "denomination" in Canada see: H. H. Walsh, "The Challenge of Canadian Church History of its Historians," *Canadian Journal of Theology*, V (1959); and his "A Canadian Christian Tradition," in J. W. Grant, ed., *The Churches and the Canadian Experience* (Toronto: Ryerson Press, 1963); cf. John W. Grant, "Asking Questions of the Canadian Past," *Canadian Journal of Theology*, I (1955).

6. "Reformed Mennonite Church," *Mennonite Encyclopedia*, IV, p. 268. Interpretations of this schism have by no means been uniform but tend to correspond to denominational commitments. For example, see: Leland Harder, *op. cit.*; H. P. Krehbiel, *op. cit.*; Robert Friedmann, *op. cit.*; J. C. Wenger, *op. cit.*, and his *History of the Mennonites of Franconia Conference, op. cit.*; Edmund G. Kaufman, *The Development of the Missionary and Philanthropic Interest Among Mennonites of North America* (Berne, Ind.: Mennonite Book Concern, 1931); F. Pannabecker, "The Development of the General Conference of the Mennonite Church of North America in the American Environment," (Ph.D. dissertation, Yale University, 1944); "Oberholtzer Division Issue," *Mennonite Quarterly Review*, XLVI (October 1972). See also: Wilmer J. Eshelman, "History of the Reformed Mennonite Church," *Lancaster County Historical Society*, XLIX (1945), pp. 85–116.

7. Krehbiel, *op. cit.*, p. 9.

8. "An das Publikum . . . ," *Oberholtzer Papers*, May 1, 1851 (MSHL).

9. J. C. Wenger, *Franconia Conference, op. cit.*, p. 359.

10. J. Boyd Cressman, "First Mennonite Church, Kitchener," *Mennonite Quarterly Review*, XIII (July 1939), pp. 159–86.

11. Cressman, *op. cit.*

12. Conference Resolutions in Waterloo at Benjamin Eby's Meeting House, May 28, 1842 (CGC and AMC).

13. Conference Resolutions, Ontario Mennonite Conference, 1847–1928 (CGC and AMC).

14. Craig, *op. cit.*, p. 165.

15. Letter from Dilman Moyer to Jacob Gross, Stouffville, P.O., September 6, 1849 (CGC).

16. Burkholder, *op. cit.*, p. 301.

17. Daniel Hoch, "Wichtige Begebenheitem . . . in Bezug der Trennung unserer Gemeinden," September 30, 1868 (CGC).

18. *Ibid.* See also: "Die Scheidewand" in the *Daniel Hoch Papers* in the CGC Archives. Also see: L. J. Burkholder postscript to letter

from Dilman Moyer to Jacob Gross, *op. cit.* Also, L. J. Burkholder, *op. cit.*, pp. 142ff.

19. Krehbiel, *op. cit.*, pp. 380–81.

20. John Holdeman, *A History of the Church of God as it Existed from the Beginning, Whereby it May be Known, and How it was Propagated Until the Present Time* (Lancaster, Pa.: John Baer's Sons, 1876); Clarence Hiebert, *The Holdeman People: The Church of God in Christ Mennonite, 1859–1969* (South Pasadena, Calif.: William Carey Library, 1973).

21. Quote from "John Fretz Funk," *Mennonite Encyclopedia*, II, pp. 421–23.

22. Everek R. Storms, *History of the United Missionary Church* (Elkhart, Ind.: Bethel Publishing Company, 1958), p. 34.

23. *Ibid.*, p. 41.

24. *Ibid.*, pp. 46–7; Burkholder, *op. cit.*, pp. 191–93.

25. Burkholder, *op. cit.*, p. 192; Jasper Abraham Huffman, ed., *History of the Mennonite Brethren in Christ Church* (New Carlisle, Ont.: Bethel Publishing Company, 1958), p. 37.

26. *Mennonite Encyclopedia*, III, p. 603.

27. Harder, *op. cit.*

Village Scene in Russia

7. Revitalization and Separation in Russia

*The formation of a separate body within the brotherhood
was necessary and to a certain extent salutary for the whole
of Mennonitism* — P. M. FRIESEN.[1]

MENNONITES HAD first entered into Canada and Russia
in 1786 and since then their parallel developments became manifest — especially their attempts to revitalize the
the brotherhood. In Russia as in Canada the migration to virgin
agricultural frontiers had by itself not produced the desired
utopia. There arose a conviction that the salvation of a people
could not come solely from traditional religion or from an abundant environment, though there was hardly a Mennonite to whom
both culture and agriculture had not become essential. In both
countries dissatisfied elements became the nuclei of dissenting
movements which almost duplicated the events reported for
North America in the previous chapter.

The reason for recounting the Russian story here does not lie in
the fascinating similarities between the eastern and western Mennonite societies. The parallels, after all, appeared quite in isolation. Whatever desire there might have been for real contact
between the two communities (as for instance by Benjamin Eby),
there could be no easy communication between Mennonite bodies

so distant from each other. Furthermore, few common outside influences have been traced, unless one identifies some commonality in the bi-directional spread of European pietism or unless the wars of 1812 and the mid-century European revolutions created similar stirrings. It might be noted here that there was an exchange of subscriptions between editors J. Mannhardt (*Mennonitische Blaetter*) of Prussia, which had a small Russian readership, and J. Oberholtzer (*Religioeser Botschafter*) of the United States. Another link between East and West was the Dutch Mennonite Mission Association of which Prussian and Russian, as well as American, Mennonites became aware and to which they made contributions around 1851, when the Dutch sent their first missionary to Java.

The main significance of the Russian story arises from the eventual transfer to the West of all the Mennonite institutions, movements and characteristics as they developed in the East. Beginning in the 1870s and continuing for more than 100 years, several major migrations transplanted the Russian experience to North America and thereby substantially affected the Canadian Mennonite story.[2] That story cannot be completely understood without at least a glimpse at the formation and revitalization of those communities which in due course would constitute the bulk of Canadian Mennonitism.

The movement into Russia was itself an experience of revitalization and the shaping of new and different viewpoints. Only a handful of fanatics expected a physical meeting in the East with the returning Christ,[3] but even moderates felt an excitement in their souls at the thought of movement eastward toward new horizons. In that sense, the easterly migrations were as revitalizing for their participants as movements westward were for the westerners. They would not soon come to an end, and the debate between the easternizers and westernizers likewise would continue seemingly endlessly. Indeed, even while some easternizers began to look westward beyond the seas, others became the more determined to find new frontiers still farther eastward beyond the Ural mountain range that divides European and Asiatic Russia.

Apart from the migrations themselves, any major transplant and new beginning required in and of itself a clarification of ideological purpose and intent. To be sure, an abundance of land and satisfactory legal provisions were sufficient attractions, but the formal and official explanation always concerned the maximization of the faith and a unique way of life. For Mennonites, migration was almost always a question of conscience. Rare indeed were the leaders and followers for whom an undertaking as great as movement to a new country did not bring about some soul-searching and rededication.

Aside from the hardships of pioneering in a foreign culture, the conditions for a truly happy Mennonite development existed in Russia from the beginning. The large and exclusive block settlements symbolized by the Chortitza and Molotschna colonies have already been mentioned (Table 1, Chapter 3). Families were allotted over 175 acres of land, a more generous assignment than for other colonists. Other privileges included freedom of location and occupation, loans for farm and industrial purposes, the unrestricted exercise of religion, a permanent exemption from military and civil service, and the right to local self-government.[4]

With productive land and a relative administrative autonomy, and without military obligations, the Mennonites proceeded to establish what later became known as the "Mennonite commonwealth" of Russia.[5] This was a self-contained cultural island in which Mennonites governed themselves, established their own schools and welfare institutions, developed a self-sufficient economy with little outside interference, and practised their religion with few restrictions. (Mennonites were forbidden to proselytize and they never did gain permission to found a theological school.) The characteristic features of the commonwealth were: neatly organized *Strassendoerfer* (street villages); big families in which sons and daughters both had assigned tasks; large and luscious vegetable and flower gardens; sheep and cattle by the thousands collectively supervised by village herdsmen; billowy fields of grain which would eventually necessitate the erection of grist mills; and elected civic and religious leaders. The latter included the *Schulze* and *Oberschulze* (village mayor and colony reeve), and the *Lehrer* (minister) and *Aelteste* (elders, fulfilling the same role as Mennonite bishops in North America).

Although these Russian conditions were favourable and would lead, a century later, to a golden age for Mennonitism, the commonwealth experienced all the growing pains which are common to most immigrant societies. To begin with, the newcomers in Russia were not immediately compatible with one another and with the new environment. The treeless steppes at first permitted only a primitive existence, and the Russian government was slow in keeping its promises of settlement aid. There were great economic disparities among the immigrants and great variations

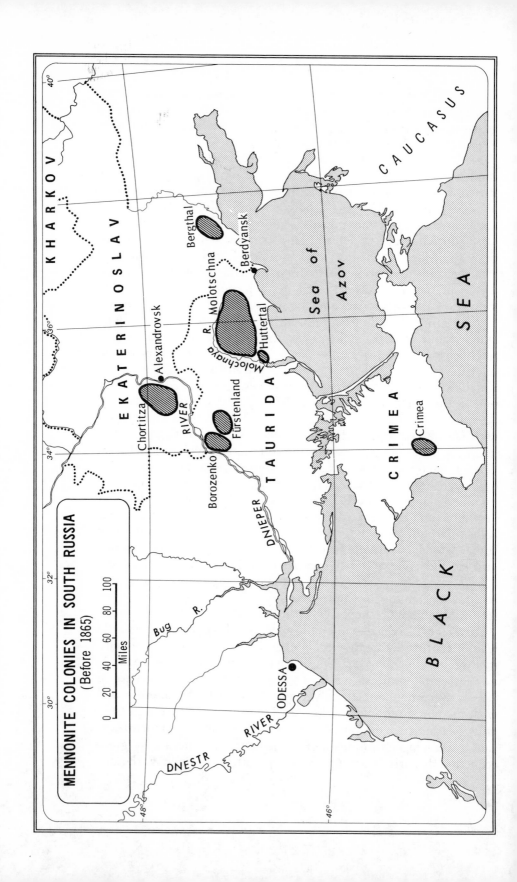

MENNONITE COLONIES IN SOUTH RUSSIA
(Before 1865)

Miles
0 20 40 60 80 100

KHARKOV

EKATERINOSLAV

Bergthal

Berdyansk

R. Molotschna

Alexandrovsk

Huttertal

Chortitza

RIVER

Fürstenland

Borozenko

TAURIDA

DNIEPER

Molochnaya

Sea of Azov

CAUCASUS

SEA

CRIMEA

Crimea

Bug R.

ODESSA

DNESTR RIVER

BLACK

40°

36°

34°

32°

30°

48°

46°

in farming skills. Many of the Prussian landless, for instance, had lost some of the traditional agricultural expertise, though they had become wise in all manner of craftsmanship and trades. Among them were blacksmiths, cartwrights, carpenters, tanners, harness makers, tailors, cobblers, spinners, weavers, millers and brewers. The manifold skills eventually contributed to a diversified economy, but in the beginning all were bound to the land. How best to till the black soils of the steppes remained a contentious issue, until aggressive leadership showed the best way.

There were other differences among these Mennonite immigrants. Varying cultural and religious viewpoints, for instance, were represented by the Flemish and Frisian parties, which had arisen among the Anabaptists in the Netherlands and which had survived 200 years in Prussia. Thus, there were those who eschewed ostentation in the home but allowed luxury in dress, while others reversed the order. One party preferred sermons to be read, the other not to have them read. One baptized by pouring, the other by sprinkling. One *Aelteste* (elder) brought communion bread to the people, while another expected the participating people to come to him. There were also differences of viewpoint in ordination, marriage and excommunication.[6] The traditional parties representing these differences, and some of the differences themselves, disappeared in the Russian environment, but not because Mennonites learned to overcome their squabbles over minutiae. Old ways of differentiation disappeared only when these could be expressed in new ways. In the self-contained commonwealth the continuous struggle for a superior righteousness (i.e. religiosity, real or artificial) expressed itself not so much with reference to outside enemies as with regard to internally felt threats.

One of the earliest religious dissenters was Klaas Reimer (1770–1837), who became dissatisfied with the entire *Grosze Gemeinde* (large church), as he designated the collective church. Reimer brought his protest to a head in 1812, in the same year that John Herr started the Pennsylvania Reform Movement which later came to Ontario. Herr was distant from Reimer, but not entirely unrelated to him. Like Herr, Reimer was a dissenter whose credentials as an ordained leader would come not from the established church but from his family and other immediate followers. Reimer similarly wanted to establish the true church, although not necessarily to modernize it. This meant a reversion to the fundamentals of the faith as expressed in the Scriptures and interpreted by Menno Simons, as well as by Klaas Reimer himself.[7]

Reimer's objections related to the very nature of the commonwealth, though he tended to express his dissent with reference to such particulars as card-playing, smoking and drinking. All such worldly amusements were signs of lax discipline and, consequently, of infidelity and the lack of spirituality. In some ways his dissent was not unlike that of the early Anabaptists who objected to a Grosze Gemeinde and, like the Mennonite commonwealth, baptized all their citizens into the Holy Roman Empire. The Mennonites, of course, baptized not infants but adults. However, so routinized did the baptism of marrying-age young adults sometimes become that the signs of individual faith were not sufficiently evident to the critics. Indeed, it was in Russia that the ethnic quality of being a Mennonite became mixed and sometimes confused with the religious quality.

Reimer's definition of worldliness extended to higher education, to playing musical instruments, to mission work, and to marriage. He also objected strenuously to the use of force and coercion as a disciplinary measure in the Molotschna colony affairs and to contributions, however few in number, made to the Russian government during its war with Napoleon.[8] While objecting to coercive civic measures, Reimer himself practised a strict ecclesiastical discipline. This prevented some sympathizers from joining his movement and others, having joined, from staying with it. The movement remained a small one and his people were derisively called *De Kleen-Gemeenta* in Low German (in High German *Kleine Gemeinde*), meaning little church.

Internal divisiveness, such as usually accompanied narrowness of viewpoint and legalistic discipline, also plagued the Kleine Gemeinde. In due course, the faithful remnant left both Molotschna and Chortitza and began a new settlement called Borozenko south of Chortitza. Another group moved into the Crimea where it adopted an immersion form of baptism and consequently a different identity. None the less, the Kleine Gemeinde as such did not disappear and its peculiar understanding of, and zeal for, the true church was felt by the entire Mennonite brotherhood for years to come.[9] In any event, the Kleine Gemeinde was a prelude to other dissenting movements to follow.

To report that Klaas Reimer and his Kleine Gemeinde stood out against the Grosze Gemeinde requires some qualification. There was no single Russian Mennonite church at the time. As

MENNONITE GROUPS IN RUSSIA
(Nineteenth Century)

KLEINE GEMEINDE

KRIMMER MENNONITE BRETHREN

Independent congregations
collectively known as
GROSSE GEMEINDE

MENNONITE BRETHREN CHURCH

1800   1810   1820   1830   1840   1850   1860   1870

elsewhere in the Mennonite world, the focus of all church life was on the congregation and its leaders, the ministers and the bishop. In Russia, as in America, there was not yet an all-inclusive conference or denomination. The congregational principle was still central to Mennonite thinking and bigness was frowned upon by all. Whenever the population of a congregation, sometimes spread over many villages or over entire settlements, grew too large for one Aelteste, there were divisions and new ordinations to maintain a manageable size for the congregations.

By the mid-1850s there were at least ten such congregations, each with its own Aelteste. Factors contributing to the election of new Aelteste and the formation of new congregations included geography, numbers and differing points of view. The emergence of the Kleine Gemeinde, therefore, was not entirely unique, except in the extent to which it was a nonconformist group and in the severity of its judgement against the rest.

Meanwhile, new life and direction had come to the commonwealth through an entirely different source, again personified in one man. He was Johann Cornies (1789-1848) who "became the most famous man the Mennonites were to produce during the entire period of their life in Russia."[10] Unlike Reimer, Cornies widened the Mennonite horizons, though his efforts were concentrated in economic, agricultural and cultural affairs, rather than ecclesiastical matters. He achieved his earliest renown as a horse and cattle breeder. At age 28 the government named him life-time president of the Commission for the Effective Propagation of Afforestation, Horticulture, Silk Culture and Vine Culture, more commonly known as the Agricultural Union. In this capacity he was given almost unlimited powers as a mediator between Mennonites and the government and as a promoter of all those causes which he held dear. He compelled the Mennonites to do what he considered good "for the economic well-being and cultural advance of the colonies."[11] His co-religionists often referred to him as "that Mennonite tsar" and a later novelist referred to him as Der Steppenhengst (the stallion of the steppes).[12] There was little they could do against the prestige which he had earned as a successful farmer. By the time of his death at the age of 59, he was cultivating about 25,000 acres and caring for 500 horses, 8,000 sheep, and 200 cattle. His nursery became the source of forestation programs which in Molotschna alone meant the planting of over half a million trees, many of them fruit-bearing, by 1845.

Cornies' influence in Odessa and St. Petersburg was so great that his authority was extended to include such diverse groups as Hutterites and Russian sectarians. The latter included the Molokans, Doukhobors, and the nomadic Nogais, 17,000 of whom he helped resettle.[13] The Hutterian Brethren, whose steady eastward movements brought them into the western Ukraine by 1770, were helped to successful resettlement near the Mennonites in 1842.[14] Another minority championed by Cornies was the Kleine Gemeinde. The elders of the Grosze Gemeinde had consistently opposed its recognition and registration by the Russian government. Cornies saw to it that the Kleine Gemeinde was recognized, thus setting a precedent for other separatist movements to follow.

Cornies was as much a child of Mennonite agricultural genius as he was a father of it, and the commonwealth would have prospered without him. Yet, he accelerated that prosperity by disciplining, directing and motivating many young creative farmers. The full flowering of the revitalization which he brought, however, did not appear in his own lifetime. Instead it bore its best fruits in later Russian generations and in North America, where the determined tillers of the Russian steppes would repeat their brilliant achievement on the American and Canadian prairies.

Some results, however, were not wanting in the first half-century of settlement. In the first and second generation of colonization, scores of high Russian officials, including the tsars themselves, and many foreigners came to inspect the commonwealth and to behold the wonderful colonization. As early as 1821 agents of the British and Foreign Bible Society gave extravagant praise for "their industry, the prosperity of their villages," calling them "a light in a dark place" and pointing out how they have "frequently called for the panegyric of the traveller."[15] Another traveller confirmed that "the Mennonites are the most prosperous in their estates . . . having good houses, barns, and with abundance of cattle, fruitful gardens and flourishing plantations. The contrast between these colonies and Russian villages is very great."[16]

In inviting the Mennonites to come to Russia, Tsarina Catherine had intended that they provide a model for an improved agriculture for the native Russians. As the nineteenth century progressed it appeared that her intention could be justified. Through Johann Cornies, at least a modest influence had been extended to some of the peoples of Russia. The possibility that the Mennonite agricultural model would benefit the Russian peasantry as a whole led to a closer examination of the colonies by scores of investigators, both independent and government-sponsored. In the words of D. G. Rempel, the foremost Mennonite scholar of the Russian situation:

> The subjects of Mennonite agriculture in general and of achievements made in grain-farming, stock-raising, and many other farm-related enterprizes in Southern Russia in particular were extensively studied and commented on throughout the nineteenth century by government officials, foreign visitors, agricultural experts of one kind or another, and by publicists.[17]

At one point it was recommended that "all the state peasants of Little and Great Russian stock throughout the northern littoral of the Black Sea area might be placed under the supervision of Cornies."[18] This did not happen. Whatever influence Cornies as an individual and the Mennonites as a people were able to exert, it was insufficient to alleviate the great peasant handicaps which had been produced by generations of agriculturalists. The colonists' failure to help the peasants stemmed partly from the fact that they underestimated the extent to which their own success was due to a rich cultural endowment and to the economics of the Privilegium. In addition, the peasants had been robbed both of a positive development and of most of their privileges.[19]

Historians differ in their views on this aspect of the Russian story. Some writers maintained "that Mennonites were actually living on inherited traits from their one-time homeland, Holland, and now were actually doing everything by rote." Further, they concluded that "were the Russian peasant given even a modicum of the privileges, land grants, educational opportunities, etc., this disadvantaged native son would in a short time surpass the accomplishments of the Mennonites."[20] Others thought that the Mennonite impact upon neighbouring people was salutary and beneficial and that "altogether their value to Russia was unquestionably great."[21]

Seen from another perspective, the Mennonites were becoming part of the Russian problem rather than of its solution by mid-nineteenth century. By 1850 they were rapidly developing their own large class of landless "peasants." The land ownership regulations prevented the division of the colony lands into smaller units. Thus only one son could "inherit" the land, leaving the other sons of the large Mennonite families landless. By 1841, out of the total number of 2,733 families in the Molotschna settlement, only 1,033 were land-owning farmers, and the remaining 1,700 families were either small tenant farmers or were engaged in various trades and businesses.[22]

A similar situation with many landless families was building up in Chortitza, where a solution through the so-called "daughter colonies" was first devised. As early as 1836 a group of 145 families established a new colony, Bergthal, with five villages on 30,000 acres of land. A second such colony was Fuerstenland. But a real solution was not implemented until the mid-1860s when the power of the landowners was broken with the help of the Russian government and the surplus and reserve land funds were used to establish new daughter colonies.[23] The struggle between the landless and the landowners produced much dissatisfaction and bitterness, in both economic and religious terms. As one historian summarized the conflict:

> These land quarrels, therefore, must be regarded as a very sad feature in the history of the Russian Mennonites. The conditions in the colonies were such that they fostered selfishness and rudeness of the human heart, instead of the noble and the good.[24]

Once the problem had been solved, however, with an 1866 statute, a way had been found to spread the Mennonite presence and influence not only into other areas of the Ukraine but also into the Caucasus and even Siberia. After 1869, Chortitza alone founded 37 villages in eight colonies for 1,197 families and Molotschna settled 1,974 families in 62 villages in six separate colonies.[25] Another more independent way in which the colonies were expanded was by the acquiring of large estates from Russian landowners by wealthy families. In this development of a strongly capitalistic *Gutsbesitzer* class (owners of large estates), Johann Cornies had also led the way.

These territorial expansions, however, intensified another problem from the very beginning, namely the relations and obligations of Mennonites to their Russian neighbours. The source of uneasiness, at least for the mission-minded, was the absolute prohibition of evangelism among members of the Orthodox Church, i.e., the majority of Russians. Excluded from this provision, which dated back to 1763, were people of the Islamic faith. Both church and state worked together to prevent evangelical proselytizing among the Orthodox, through administrative measures and, if this did not work, through full application of the punishment provided by the law.[26]

All this dissatisfaction and uneasiness came to a head in the 1860s, when a group of reform-minded Mennonites established a new Mennonite movement, similar to that emerging in America at the same time, though unknown to them. To these revitalizers the new spiritual frontier was as important as, or more so than, the physical frontiers being opened up through the resolution of the land problem.

A fundamental cause of dissent lay in the close ties between the church and colony leadership. In other words, the Mennonites in Russia had become somewhat of a state church. Although adult or believers' baptism was still practised, for all practical purposes one entered the society at birth. The development, to the extent that it was noticed, was not necessarily considered to be a negative phenomenon. On the contrary, was it not the goal of the church to incorporate all of humanity into the community of God? And could not that community be like a Mennonite con-gregational family to which everyone belonged and in which everyone was exposed to Christian teaching? They had also become an elite cultural group. In the words of one scholar, who studied the Russian Mennonites from an anthropological point of view:

> They [the Mennonites] had shifted from viewing themselves as a religious community to an idea of themselves as an elite group of colonists whose task was to present the world with a model image of an enlightened and perfected people. Thus they changed from being an inward looking religious society dedicated to following a narrow path in opposition to the world, to an open culture which was above the world in its advancement, knowledge, and way of life. The sense of "being different" thus shifted from one of a religiously orientated life style to one of a superior cultural tradition in which religious differentiation was no longer the key marker but merely one amongst many.[27]

Whatever virtues the integration of church and society in the commonwealth might represent, there was little allowance for dissent and deviation. Recall that the practically harmless protest of the Kleine Gemeinde was seen by the leaders of the Grosze Gemeinde as a considerable threat. Yet at least a degree of dissent and nonconformity was demanded by the historic Anabaptist theology and also by the existing ecclesiastical situation, which compounded and could easily become the focus of economic unrest. The elders and ministers were of the landed class, and were frequently very well situated. Thus the economics, politics, and religion of the colonies were very much tied together in a single establishment.

It was inevitable that dissatisfaction should surface. The vehicle provided for the protest, however, was not a social gospel or a reform movement that focused on the religio-socio-economic situation, but rather pietism, which emphasized the fine issues of personal morality and personal salvation. Points of mid-century protest were alcoholism, materialism, lack of missionary zeal and frivolity of the kind already frowned upon by Klaas Reimer.

The pietistic religious emphases typical of the followers of the new movement had been introduced to the Russian colonies from time to time since the early decades of settlement, notably by agents of the British and Foreign Bible Society. The church elders had not been entirely closed to this influence. In 1821, for instance, they agreed to the establishment of a branch of the Bible Society in Molotschna.[28] Also, a missioner reported having established "missionary prayer meetings" in Molotschna with the consent of the elders.[29] Similar efforts were being made with success in Chortitza. Incidentally, through these British representatives and their English hymn tunes, the Mennonite colonists in Russia were introduced quite early to a language which they would one day need.[30]

As time passed, the concerns of missions, free prayer and revival meetings were carried by small groups of people who in turn were influenced by the writings of continental pietists. Among these was Tobias Voth, a progressive teacher whom Cornies had persuaded to come from Prussia to help spearhead his educational reforms. Voth organized prayer meetings, *Missionsstunden* (hours devoted to missions), and the production and distribution of Christian literature. Of Voth it was said:

> [he] has given expression for the first time to something
> which we call "brotherhood" (*Brudertum*) or intimate
> Christian fellowship . . .[31]

It was left, however, to a Lutheran pietist, Edward Hugo Wuest, to bring about the stirring that led to the new religious formation. A native of Germany, he had arrived in Russia in 1845 to serve as a Lutheran pastor. A tall man with a winsome personality, Wuest was an outstanding preacher with a deep melodious voice; he had learned well the art of communication.[32] In his oratorical gifts he resembled other leaders of the new Mennonite movements such as John Oberholtzer in Pennsylvania, Daniel Brenneman in Indiana, and Daniel Hoch in Ontario.

Very soon Wuest was accepting invitations from Elder August Lenzmann of the Gnadenfeld Church. He also met with eager Bible students in the Mennonite settlements. Those participating in the gatherings called themselves "Brethren." The centre of their movement was the village of Gnadenfeld in Russia. As in Ontario and in Pennsylvania, there was immediate resistance to the new influences. Some objected because of the disorder which dissent brought to the community, others because they resisted an extremely emotional Christian expression. In the same way that the new Mennonites of Ontario struggled with Pentecostalism, the brethren in Russia wrestled with the *Froehliche Richtung* (the exuberant movement) which they could not easily escape.[33] Neither individuals nor congregations were in a mood to adjust their way of life. Reference to dancing, drinking and disciplining was offensive enough, but downright insulting was the implication that the dissenters were spiritually superior. There was, of course, no way of arriving at a unanimous position, because the viewpoints could be as many as there were elders, ministers, congregations and members.

The Brethren of Gnadenfeld asked Elder August Lenzmann to conduct a separate and private communion for them as true believers. This he declined to do, and thus the Brethren administered it among themselves. They were then called to appear before the elder to give an account of this but instead 18 of their members gathered privately on January 6, 1860, and, in a statement to the Molotschna elders, declared the founding of a new church, as follows:

> We, the undersigned, by the grace of God perceive the
> disintegration of the entire Mennonite brotherhood and
> because of the Lord and our conscience we can no longer be
> part of it; we fear the unavoidable judgement of God ...
> We also fear the loss of the rights and privileges granted to
> us by our benevolent government ... It is sad to see (O
> Jesus, be merciful! Open the eyes of the spiritually blind!)
> the satanic life of our Mennonites at the annual fairs openly

before our neighbours . . . We separate ourselves completely
from these fallen churches, but we pray for our brothers that
they may be saved . . . We have in mind the entire
Mennonite brotherhood, because our imperial government
considers it to be a true brotherhood.[34]

The elders, however, had the whole brotherhood in mind and
perceived the rights and privileges of that brotherhood to be in
danger if they allowed internal dissent to bring about a disintegration. They, therefore, sought to end the protest and secession by
turning the matter over to the *Gebietsamt*, the civic authority in
the colony. The efforts to bring the dissenters back failed, however, even in the face of harassment, persecution, and threatened
exile.[35] After a prolonged effort and in spite of the stiff opposition
from the Grosze Gemeinde, the Mennonite Brethren were granted
legal status and recognition by the imperial government.

One of the ironies of the new formation and the relationship of
August Lenzmann to it was that he had been a proponent of the
movement until its request for a separate communion. Indeed,
Lenzmann's Gnadenfeld congregation had itself been the centre
of a new movement, giving birth among other things to a *Bruder-
schule* (a brotherhood school to nurture the new ideas). It had
also been the cradle for the Mennonite zionists, more properly
called "Jerusalem Friends" or "Templers" who later left for
Palestine.[36]

The new Mennonite Brethren movement confessed the teachings of Menno Simons, emphasizing particularly a baptism upon
confession of the new birth, communion with foot-washing only
for true believers, and discipline and excommunication for car-
nally-minded and intentional sinners. Ministers could be called
directly by God (they could declare themselves) or by the church
(the initiative could come from the congregation). To distinguish
themselves in other ways from the Grosze Gemeinde, the Brethren
adopted an immersion form of baptism, which meant rebaptism
for all the followers of the movement already baptized by the
elder. Before long, especially as they migrated to North America,
they discarded a hierarchical structure in the ministry, though
an early election produced an elder. Ordinary, i.e. unordained,
members of the Mennonite Brethren Church could have leadership roles at public functions. They could serve as *Vorsaenger*
(choristers), speak public prayers, and conduct opening worship
exercises.

Speaking generally, the Brethren thought of themselves as Mennonites, though their borrowings from the Lutheran Pietists and German Baptists were so considerable that a certain theological ambivalence entered the movement from the beginning. In that sense, they shared the identity problem of the new North American movement known as Mennonite Brethren in Christ, whose relation to revivalistic Methodism left doubt about the relation to a pacifistic Mennonitism. The Russian Mennonite Brethren were born of both Anabaptism and Pietism.[37]

The Mennonite Brethren idea and fellowship took hold elsewhere, and congregations were formed at Chortitza. Others were established with new daughter colonies in the Kuban. There was constant growth in Russia and by 1872, the year of the first *Bundeskonferenz*, the membership had passed 600. Eventually, however, when the movement was transplanted to North America, it became the second largest in Canada and the third largest in the United States.

Although the Brethren were the leading renewal movement, there were others closely related. In the Crimea, for instance, a small settlement consisting of Molotschna and Kleine Gemeinde elements adopted a trine-immersion baptism for themselves in 1869. They too emphasized conversion, assurance and salvation experience, and integrated these with the otherwise conservative spirit of the Kleine Gemeinde. The group's Russian membership never exceeded 40 members. They came to be known as Krimmer Mennonite Brethren, appropriate to their Crimean location and to distinguish themselves from the larger group.

In Russia, as in North America, not all the renewal-minded people left the mother church. On the contrary, many whose diagnosis of the church's spiritual condition was similar to that of the Brethren chose not to separate. Among them was a young man, Heinrich Dirks, who became the first Mennonite missionary from Russia to go abroad. Baptized in Gnadenfeld by Elder August Lenzmann in 1860, he went to Germany and the Netherlands for nearly a decade to study before going on to the Dutch colony of Sumatra in 1870 as a missionary under the auspices of the Dutch Mennonite Mission Association. Another was Bernhard Harder, teacher, poet and evangelist, who ardently desired and worked for reform but remained in the Grosze Gemeinde.

Alternatively, not all of the church needed renewing in the Mennonite Brethren sense, unless, of course, the emotional character of crisis conversion experiences and immersion baptism were equated with the desired spirituality. There was among the Russian Mennonites another kind of spirituality expressing itself in more passive and quietistic ways. "Their original simplicity of manners, their purity of faith, and consistency of Christian conduct"[38] was noted early. One who had witnessed the catechetical instruction of over 300 young people praised "their sweetness" and "their tenderness of spirit."[39] And the elders too were not all lacking in pietistic spirituality. One author writing close to the emergence of the Mennonite Brethren movement, in 1855, spoke as follows about a Chortitza elder, just deceased:

> This past autumn I had to lament the loss of a very dear
> and aged friend, the bishop or elder of the Mennonite
> Church at Chortitza ... For a number of years that worthy
> man was a warm friend to Scripture distribution in his own
> community. All the ministers greatly respected him and
> cooperated with him in labours of love, wherefore that
> district is well supplied with Scriptures. There never was any
> difficulty in settling accounts with him ... [After his death
> his books were found to be] in perfect order.[40]

Members of the Bible Society said of the Mennonite people themselves that they "are our chief cooperators in the Bible work."[41] In the words of the Odessa agent who worked primarily in the Chortitza region:

> They are a simple, frugal, well-behaved religious people,
> carefully cultivating elementary education, but not going
> beyond it. Their preachers are uneducated men, chosen from
> among themselves. Their homes present a picture of
> neatness, comfort and plenty, their villages serve as models
> to those around showing what may be done by industry and
> perseverance in turning the barren steppes into a pleasant
> abode, surrounded by trees where formerly for miles around
> not one was to be seen. Their moral condition is high, and
> although not free from prejudices chiefly of a harmless
> nature, their sympathies extend to the well-being of their
> fellowmen outside of their own community ... your agent
> has found them to be those who purchase the largest number
> of Scriptures and among whom is to be found the greatest
> proportion of the friends of Bible circulation.[42]

There were thus not only great differences but also some similarities between the Grosze Gemeinde and the new movements.

The differences of emphasis and style tended to run deep, however, because both groups had so greatly offended each other's religious egos. One denied the other a fair measure of religious spirituality; the other withheld a fair measure of ecclesiastical recognition. These feelings were carried to North America where they were nurtured for years to come and where they were most often defined in doctrinal terms.

The similarities between the old and the new brethren, however, permitted some cooperation in the great migration about to break upon the Russian colonies. Both groups found themselves internally divided on the subject of their future destinies. And some of both groups decided to leave while others decided to stay. Furthermore, the similarity did not end there. Those of the Grosze Gemeinde who migrated to the United States joined the new Mennonite movement there known as the General Conference Mennonite Church. And those of the Grosze Gemeinde who stayed in Russia proceeded to found as another dimension of its own renewal a *Bundeskonferenz*, a General Conference of Mennonite congregations in Russia. That event culminated in 1883, the same year that the new North American movement, the Mennonite Brethren in Christ, completed their own ecumenical assembly.

It is possible, of course, that some of the events in the Grosze Gemeinde occurred only because they first happened in the small new movements — for instance, the Bundeskonferenz was instituted by the Grosze Gemeinde a full decade after the Brethren had initiated *their* Bundeskonferenz. It is in that sense of pioneering that the movement's foremost historian, P. M. Friesen, concluded that the separatist Brethren helped not only themselves but also those they left behind.

Meanwhile, the Mennonite destinies were being affected not only by internal religious ferment and ecclesiastical realignment but also by external imperial rivalries. Russia had been confronted and miserably humiliated by the British Empire and its allies in the Crimean War (1854–56). Recognizing that her weaknesses were due at least in part to her domestic situation, some long overdue reforms had finally been initiated. These were accelerated when a new threat to Russia appeared from the West. At the heart of that threat stood the new German Empire, proclaimed as such by Bismarck in 1871 and feared by both France and Russia. Others, including some Mennonites, admired it. Thus was accelerated a flirtation with German politics that had begun with the Fredericks of Prussia and which survived even the Third Reich.

Some, however, feared the emerging power struggle. The resistance to the 5,000-thaler annual tax for the support of a military school was the cause of a continuous Prussian Mennonite emigration from 1852 to 1870, mostly to Russia but also to America. A further exodus was planned when the Bismarckian laws further reduced Mennonite privileges and ordered them either to accept some national service or to leave the country.

The Prussian Mennonites were torn in two directions. To the majority, acceptance of the situation was the most logical response. Led by Pastor-editor Jacob Mannhardt, the urbanized Danzig Mennonites favoured the formal abandonment of the principle of nonresistance. The young people, who had learned to identify with Bismarck's military successes, likewise favoured integration. There remained in Prussia, however, a minority of determined conscientious objectors for whom emigration now appeared to be the only option. In May of 1870 they delegated Elder Wilhelm Ewert and Minister Peter Dyck to investigate settlement opportunities in Russia. This they did, only to discover that in Russia the climate for military exemption had changed as well. They were encouraged to look to America instead.

Tsar Alexander II viewed German imperial growth with considerable misgivings, and consequently the introduction of universal military service in Russia seemed inevitable. The desirability of such service was reinforced domestically by the great reforms underway since the emancipation of the serfs in 1861. In every area of life there were demands for a greater egalitarianism and the abolition of special privileges. The military system could not remain unaffected. A huge professional army of "volunteers" (many of them peasants forced into service by their lords) had to be replaced by a conscripted force involving several years of military training and service for all Russian males over 21. Alexander proposed not only to distribute equally the national burden but also to increase the strength of the Russian nation in the face of German imperial ambition. He announced his plans on July 16, 1870, implying at the same time that nonconformists would, within a 10-year period, be allowed to emigrate if they could not in good conscience submit to conscription. Thus, the Mennonites were being confronted with fundamental decisions.

The nationalist emphasis on great reforms, however, had other implications for minority groups. The abolition of the Odessa-based German Guardians Committee ended a special administrative link between the foreign colonists and St. Petersburg.

This meant the loss of autonomy for the Mennonites who were not placed under the direct administration of the municipal and provincial authorities. Russification called for the replacement of German by Russian as the official language of instruction in the schools. Land redistribution also was in the offing, though "equalized ownership" through wholesale nationalization had to await a greater revolution.

The Mennonites had no difficulty understanding the negative meaning for them of these measures, positive as they might be for Russia as a whole. The growth of the national spirit and administration had been against them in Prussia, and the same would be true in Russia. Perhaps it would be even more so in Russia, where a language transition meant, in the Mennonite mind, the adoption of an inferior culture. As difficult as had been the transition from Dutch to German in Prussia, that acculturation was eventually recognized as a cultural advancement. In Russia there could only be a cultural debasement. In addition, life without the Privilegium had become quite unthinkable. Thus, the idea that a better future might lie in a new land once again occupied the Mennonite mind.

FOOTNOTES

1. Adapted from P. M. Friesen, *Alt-Evangelische Mennonitische Bruderschaft in Russland, 1789–1910* (Halbstadt, Taurien: Raduga, 1911), p. 165.

2. See C. Henry Smith, *The Coming of the Russian Mennonites* (Berne, Ind.: Mennonite Book Concern, 1927), 296 pp.; and F. H. Epp, *Mennonite Exodus: The Rescue and Resettlement of the Russian Mennonites Since the Communist Revolution* (Altona, Man.: D. W. Friesen & Sons, 1962), 571 pp.

3. See F. Bartsch, *Unser Auszug Nach Mittelasien* (Winnipeg: Echo Verlag, 1948); and Fred Richard Belk, "The Great Trek of the Russian Mennonites to Central Asia, 1880–84" (Ph.D. dissertation, Oklahoma State University, 1973).

4. David G. Rempel, "The Mennonite Colonies in New Russia: A Study of their Settlement and Economic Development from 1789 to 1914" (Ph.D. dissertation, Stanford University, 1933), pp. 44–97.

5. David G. Rempel, "The Mennonite Commonwealth in Russia,

1890–1919" (unpublished manuscript in CGC archives), 72 pp.; see also E. K. Francis, *In Search of Utopia* (Altona, Man.: D. W. Friesen & Sons, 1955), pp. 20–27.

6. Christian Neff, "Flemish Mennonites," *Mennonite Encyclopedia*, II, pp. 337–40; "Frisian Mennonites," *Mennonite Encyclopedia*, II, pp. 413–14.

7. See Friesen, *op. cit.*, pp. 74–6, 106–13; Harold S. Bender, "Kleine Gemeinde," *Mennonite Encyclopedia*, III, pp. 198–200. See also: "Ein Schreiben von Klaas Reimer" (CGC).

8. Bender, *op. cit.* D. G. Rempel has referred the author to a Russian source (Apollon Shal 'kovskii, *Khronologicheskve obozrenie istorii Novorossiiskago Kraia*, Vol. II, 1796–1823, Odessa, 1836) in which appeals to the colonists are quoted and in which contributions from Crimea and Chortitza areas are cited, though without breakdowns. In September of 1812 the colonists, including the Mennonites, had to make a special oath or affirmation of allegiance. Later Mennonite responses in military situations might be noted here. The Molotschna Mennonites contributed 130 horses as a voluntary contribution to the Emperor Tsar Nicholas I for the purpose of restoring law and order in Germany in 1848. During the Crimean War, Mennonites also made extensive contributions — a monument to express recognition was erected in Halbstadt. See Peter G. Epp, "At the Molotshnaya — A Visit, 1890," *Mennonite Life*, XXIV, 4 (October 1969), pp. 151–55.

9. For the complete story of the movement see P. J. B. Reimer, ed., *The Sesquicentennial Jubilee: Evangelical Mennonite Conference (1812–1952)* (Steinbach, Man.: Evangelical Mennonite Conference, 1962), 180 pp.

10. Rempel, "Mennonite Commonwealth in Russia," *op. cit.*, p. 34ff.

11. *Ibid.*

12. Ernst Behrends, *Der Steppenhengst* (Bodensee: Hohenstaufen Verlag, 1969).

13. Walter Quiring, "Johann Cornies," *Mennonite Encyclopedia*, I, pp. 716–18.

14. Victor Peters, *All Things Common: The Hutterian Way of Life* (Minneapolis: University of Minnesota Press, 1966), 233 pp.

15. BFBS. From letters by Doctors Paterson and Henderson (August 4, 1821) in *Reports of the British and Foreign Bible Society*, Vol. 7, 1822–24, London, pp. 1–27. See also John Paterson, *The Book for Every Land* (London: John Snow, 1858).

16. FHL. From narrative of John Yeardley's visit to South Russia, 1853, Case 33, Casual Correspondence, pp. 363–64.

17. David G. Rempel, "Mennonite Agriculture and Model Farming as Issues of Economic Study and Political Controversy, 1870–1917"

(unpublished manuscript, 1973). Rempel's study is based on Russian documents in Leningrad and Moscow Archives. 101 pp. (CGC).

18.   *Ibid.*, pp. 9–10.

19.   For comments on inherited characteristics in this context see Rempel, *ibid.*, p. 25ff.

20.   *Ibid.*, p. 26.

21.   *Ibid.*, p. 25.

22.   Rempel, "The Mennonite Commonwealth in Russia," *op. cit.*, p. 43ff.

23.   *Ibid.*, p. 45ff.

24.   C. H. Wedel, *Abriss der Geschichte der Mennoniten*, Vol. III (Newton, Kans.: 1901), pp. 163–64.

25.   Rempel, "The Mennonite Commonwealth in Russia," *op. cit.*, p. 49.

26.   *Ibid.*, pp. 6–8.

27.   James Urry, Oxford, England, in a letter to the author, February 18, 1974 (CGC).

28.   BFBS. Paterson Letters. See *Reports of the British and Foreign Bible Society*, Vol. 7, 1822–24, London, p. 21. The branch was closed on orders of Nicholas I in 1826.

29.   CCWM. Russian Correspondence 1804–24, Box 1, Folder 5, Jacket c. Letter from Richard Knill to London Missionary Society Bible House, St. Petersburg, April 3, 1822. See also Friesen, *op. cit.*, pp. 113–14.

30.   Dr. J. J. Thiessen of Saskatoon recalls (Letter from James Urry to the author, January 26, 1974) that his grandmother had learned some of these English hymns as a child. See also Reimer and Gaeddert, *Exiled by the Czar*, pp. 19–22.

31.   Friesen, *op. cit.*, p. 79.

32.   J. A. Toews, "The History of the Mennonite Brethren Church" (unpublished manuscript, 1973), pp. 40–41.

33.   See Friesen, *op. cit.*, pp. 221–30.

34.   A. H. Unruh, *Die Geschichte der Mennoniten-Bruedgergemeinde* (Hillsboro, Ka.: General Conference of the Mennonite Brethren Church of North America, 1955), p. 52.

35.   See Friesen, *op. cit.*, pp. 192–220.

36.   Toews, *op. cit.*, p. 39.

37.   See Toews, *op. cit.*, pp. 43–44; Victor Adrian, "Born of Anabaptism and Pietism," *Mennonite Brethren Herald*, March 26, 1965; A. J. Klassen, "The Roots and Development of Mennonite Brethren Theology to 1914" (M.A. dissertation).

38.   Paterson, *loc. cit.*

39.   FHL. Stephen Grellet and William Allens. Account of their visit to Russia in 1819, Case 33, Casual Correspondence, p. 119.

40. BFBS. Foreign Correspondence, 1855, Box K-O. Letter from John Melville to Henry Knolleke, February 19, 1855.
41. BFBS. Russia Agents Book No. 125. James Watt, Odessa to H. Knolleke, March 28, 1871.
42. BFBS. Russia Agents Book No. 149. Report for 1873 on Odessa Agency, pp. 320–22.

Arrival in Manitoba

8. Mass Migration from Russia to Manitoba

*The church chose Canada because [there] it stood under the
protection of the Queen of England, and we believed that our
freedom from military service could be better maintained
and also that the church and school would be under our
control* — GERHARD WIEBE.[1]

A T THE very moment when the Russian Mennonites were
working out new spiritual and ecclesiastical destinies
for themselves, their own and the Prussians' futures were being
significantly affected by circumstances quite beyond their control.
In the early 1870s, the tsar began to withdraw the eternal *Privilegium*; simultaneously, from across the Atlantic, the Mennonites were offered a new version of it. In the resulting negotiations and competitions the Mennonites were lured by at least
three countries, including Russia. The majority chose to stay in
Russia while many others opted for Canada and the United
States.

Among the people to whom the clash between the Russian and
Mennonite societies came as no surprise was Cornelius Jansen of
Berdyansk, a southern Russian seaport. Jansen, himself a Mennonite, had served for nine years as German consul and as an
international contact in general. He counselled the Prussian Mennonite delegation in 1870 to look to America rather than to Russia
for their future, and before that he had received Quakers from

England. Upon their return, the Quakers wrote a letter of admonition, saying that the Russian Mennonites "should be instrumental in spreading the truth of the Gospel of Christ"[2] — in other words, become more mission-minded. Jansen tried to get the letter printed for wide distribution, but Russian authorities prevented this, leading him to the conclusion that the future of Russia looked bleak for nonconformists. He then turned his attention to investigating the prospects for a better homeland, which, according to the best information available, was America.

The Mennonites themselves were not quite ready to plan for such an exodus. Instead they sent a delegation of elders, teachers and administrators to St. Petersburg to remind the authorities of Tsar Paul's *Privilegium*. However, their case was weakened by the fact that neither Elder Leonhard Sudermann of Molotschna nor Elder Gerhard Dyck of Chortitza, the leaders of the delegation, could speak Russian. The president of the imperial council, who received them, declared that failure to learn the Russian language in 70 years of Russian residence was a sin. A promise to correct the neglect met with the rejoinder, "It's too late!"[3] In another sense, however, the delegates had arrived too *early* since the government was still in the process of policy formulation.

The delegates reflected little willingness to compromise, banking rather heavily on the *Privilegium*. When the president held out the possibility of a noncombatant service, the delegates expressed complete disinterest. They knew only what they would *not* do. Consequently, they offered no suggestions as to the kinds of national service they were prepared to perform. Finally, the delegates' defence of their nonresistance, their insistence that they could "embrace" their enemies if attacked, must have left the imperial authorities unmoved. After all, they were well informed on the lack of solidarity and love within the Mennonite colonies themselves — how the various conflicting parties had not been able to embrace each other.[4]

None the less, the members of the delegation were assured of the possibility of an alternative noncombatant service being arranged for their people. The Mennonites, however, doubted everything and wanted strong assurances of total exemption. To this end they attempted to see the tsar personally at his Crimean winter residence in January of 1872 and twice in St. Petersburg in 1873, all to no avail. They gained only a confirmation that Mennonites could be exempted from combatant service in exchange for an alternative form of service. Meanwhile, the Mennonites, having recognized the odds against special privilege, had proceeded to prepare for emigration to other lands, such as Turkestan, Palestine, Australia and the Americas. The tsar, alarmed by the possibility of losing some of his best agricultural-ists, sent his special representative, General von Todtleben, to discourage these plans. But some Mennonites now felt it was their turn to say, "It's too late."

By that time migration plans were well underway and before the decade was out more than one-third of the 50,000 Mennonites had left for North America, along with other Mennonites from Poland and Prussia and Hutterites from Russia. That emigration was encouraged by the intense western competition for good agricultural immigrants, especially Mennonites. Not only were Canadian and American agents zealous in attracting them, but Mennonite leaders in both countries became intensely interested in a possible immigration from Russia. The main communications link for all of them was Cornelius Jansen. Beyond him, the British consul in Berdyansk, James Zohrab, and the American consul in Odessa, Timothy Smith, were eager to help.

The confluence of all these interests was instigated, as mentioned above, by the independent activities of Cornelius Jansen in 1870, before the tsar had made his ominous proclamation. Jansen had begun corresponding with Christian Krehbiel, secretary of the General Conference of Mennonite Churches in North America, and John F. Funk, the Elkhart publisher. Both gave strong reasons for choosing America as a place of settlement, and before long Funk was shipping hundreds of copies of *Herold der Wahrheit* to Russia to help persuade the masses.

Remembering the conditions of military exemption during the American Civil War, Funk assured Jansen that this could be obtained for the payment of 300 dollars per individual.[5] Jansen was pleased with what he heard and proceeded with personal plans to go to America, at the same time encouraging Mennonite leaders also to plan for mass emigration. After the disappointing attempt to see the tsar in the Crimea, Elder Sudermann became willing to examine the prospects. His first interest, however, was Canada, and in January 1872 he and 32 others asked Consul Zohrab about "exemption from all military service," about "grants of land," and about the desirability of dispatching a delegation.[6] In forwarding the inquiry to Earl Granville, the British foreign secretary, Zohrab suggested the resettlement in Canada not only of all the Mennonites, but also of "Germans and other denominations." United States interests were already wooing them and every effort should be made by Canada to gain this "valuable acquisition." Zohrab added:

> The departure of the Germans will, undoubtedly, be a
> serious loss to the country for they are not only much greater
> proficients in agriculture than the native population, and
> consequently produce heavier crops and finer qualities but
> they are very hard working and, therefore, in proportion to
> each man, they bring a much larger quantity of land under
> cultivation and thus increase the produce of the country.
> They employ large numbers of Russian peasants or farm
> laborers and their villages are patterns of cleanliness and
> good order.[7]

A similar inquiry had been made to the United States consul. In April 1872 Timothy Smith told the Mennonites that compulsory military service did not exist in the United States and that lands were available either as free 165-acre homesteads or at about $1.25 per acre if purchased from governments and railway companies. He proposed that a small delegation be sent to inspect the situation.

About two weeks later the official Canadian bid was ready. A Privy Council report quoted from the statutes the Mennonite entitlement to exemption from military service[8] and offered "a free grant of 160 acres of the best land in the possession of the Dominion of the Province of Manitoba, or in other parts of the Northwest Territory . . . to persons over the age of 21 years . . ."[9] The government offered all these possibilities to the Mennonites and expressed readiness to pay the expenses of an official delegation.

Thus, the competing bids for the prospective immigrants had been placed, but before any official delegations were sent a clarification of the military question was requested. The United States consul had avoided speaking to the matter of conscription in time of war. In the Canadian reply, the words "exempt from military service when balloted in time of peace or war, upon such conditions and such regulations as the Governor-in-Council may from time to time prescribe" caused confusion. Bishop Sudermann wanted to know what was meant by "such conditions and such regulations." The termination of "eternal privileges" in South Russia within less than 100 years had made him and all Mennonites wary and extra cautious.

In August the leaders had the opportunity to question directly a personal representative of the Canadian government. He was William Hespeler, a German who had emigrated to Canada in 1850 and who since then had been engaged in business with his brother Jacob, the founder of the Ontario town of Hespeler. An occasional traveller to Europe in search of more immigrants, he arrived in South Russia as an official agent to deliver the government's provisions and invitation in person. He assured them that Mennonites were "absolutely free and exempted from military duty, either in time of peace or war." The Governor-in-Council could prescribe "no conditions or regulations" under which, in any circumstances, these people could be compelled to serve.[10] This interpretation of the military law left no loopholes, and the Mennonites seemed satisfied.

Hespeler remained in South Russia until the police began to interfere with his illegal activities. The British ambassador in St. Petersburg had kept the Russian government informed about the emigration discussion and, though he experienced no obstacle at first, Hespeler soon found himself without the proper permit to carry out his work. Having convinced himself that the Mennonites were immigrants worth having and having arranged for a delegation to visit Canada, he returned home, where he was made a Commissioner of Immigration and Agriculture and placed in Winnipeg to oversee the anticipated immigration. About the Mennonites he wrote to his superiors:

> They are a hard-working, sober, moral, and intelligent people, a great number have accumulated large means, and are owners of from ten to fourteen thousand acres of land . . . they are superior agriculturists, occupy excellent dwellings and have good farm buildings, all erected in brick. In their homes, which excel in order and cleanliness, I found prosperous merchants, manufacturers, and mechanics.[11]

Hespeler's positive assessment of the Mennonite character was further indicated by his reluctance to appoint an agent from among them, as suggested by Ottawa. Such an agent, according to Ottawa, should be paid "a remuneration of $2 per capita for all Mennonites immigrating and settling in Canada." It would not create a favourable effect, Hespeler said. Besides, such an agent would probably not be accepted by any of them "as according to my experience of them, I find them more conscientious than their confessionalists in Canada or the United States. It would in their eyes look too much like dealing in human beings . . . they are a reasoning, thinking, cautious, and to a large extent, an educating people."[12]

The United States government did not send its own representative to Russia, although it seemed to be favoured over Canada. The task of enticing immigrants was left to zealous railroad and land agents. The result was that some Mennonites seemed to choose America before all the evidence was in. In the summer of 1872 a group of four young men from well-to-do families set off on their own exploration of America. Among them was 25-year-old Bernhard Warkentin who travelled extensively in North America in search of the right place to settle.

Meanwhile Canada was becoming more determined. Hespeler had whetted the Canadian government's appetite for immigrants like these Mennonite agriculturalists, needed so badly to settle the new province of Manitoba which had joined the Dominion in 1870. The government hoped to build a railroad along which a chain of settlements was to tie the two ends of Canada together before the Americans could expand into the wide open spaces from the south. Earlier settlement attempts in Manitoba had not been very successful, and the Métis rebellion in that province under Louis Riel had signalled Ottawa not to take the region for granted. What was needed above all was a sizeable group of capable and permanent settlers. The Russian Mennonites appeared to be likely prospects.

To help persuade them to choose Canada the government needed other Mennonites, and so Jacob Y. Shantz, farmer, businessmen and school board trustee of Berlin (later Kitchener), was selected to inspect Manitoba with a view to recommending its suitability for settlement. He made the first of 27 trips in the fall of 1872 in the company of Bernhard Warkentin, who with Shantz had been invited to Ottawa to discuss the plan. Although his three companions had already returned to Europe, Warkentin accepted the Canadian invitation to inspect Manitoba; but then he decided on Kansas, where he settled to prepare the way for other immigrants. Apparently he had not been overly impressed with Manitoba, with its many mosquitoes, untamed Indians, long cold winters, and lack of railroads, though he admitted the land quality to be above his expectations.[13]

Determined to promote Manitoba, Shantz and Hespeler had their work cut out for them. Shantz's 19-page *Narrative of a Journey to Manitoba* served the promotional purpose well; the

Department of Agriculture subsequently had it translated into several European languages and distributed several hundreds of thousands of copies. His five reasons for settlement in Manitoba, expressed in terms of preference over the United States, were as follows: (1) lots of prairie land not requiring clearing and yet plenty of timber near by, (2) land not broken up by land grants to railway companies, making possible compact settlement near transportation arteries, (3) good water communication and navigation and rail lines in prospect, (4) free land grants and options to purchase adjacent areas for one dollar, (5) drier and steadier winters.

Shantz recommended Manitoba as a place for settlement in the strongest possible terms. The "large grants of land *en bloc*" would allow settlements large and compact enough for the Mennonites to "preserve their language and customs."[14] Convinced that Manitoba was the right choice, he now prepared the Canadian government to offer attractive terms. No time was lost in preparing the case. By the spring of 1873 several delegations, as previously recommended, were formed, representing not only Mennonites but also the Hutterites in South Russia, as well as the Swiss and Dutch-German Mennonites in Polish Volhynia and West Prussia (see Table 1).[15]

TABLE 1

MENNONITE DELEGATIONS FROM RUSSIA IN 1873

DELEGA-TION NO.	DEPARTURE DATE	PLACE OF ARRIVAL	MEMBERS	REPRESENTATION
1.	February	Montreal	Heinrich Wiebe	Bergthal
			Jacob Peters	"
			Cornelius Buhr	himself
2.	Early April	New York	Cornelius Toews	Kleine Gemeinde
			David Klassen	"
			Paul Tschetter	Hutterites
			Laurence Tschetter	"
3.	Late April	New York	Jacob Buller	Molotschna
			Leonhard Sudermann	"
			Tobias Unruh	Volhynia/Poland
			Andreas Schrag	"
			Wilhelm Ewert	West Prussia

Hespeler had alerted the Canadian government to the keen American competition for the immigrants and advised them to be ready and waiting in New York since American agents would surely be there to direct them away from their Canadian destination. "Overbalance the inducement," Hespeler counselled, showing exactly what might be done and how the Canadian offer might be stated. He advised, moreover, that they should help representatives to assist and direct the delegates at the European point of embarkation.[16] At Hamburg, therefore, the Canadian government had its servants waiting so that the delegates would not be "surrounded by ever so many agents and runners."[17] Yet those very agents, whose "official duty it was to take care that the Mennonites were not swindled," had allowed the money broker to charge not five per cent commission, which would have been high in any case, but twenty per cent, which was "downright swindle." The result was that delegates paid $495 in exchange on 2,400 American dollars' worth of 3,000 Russian government rubles. The incident was related to, and verified by, a representative of the German society in Montreal who felt that Canada should reimburse the delegates as this would "greatly enhance their confidence in our Government."[18] The special agent in Hamburg denied a swindle, saying that paper, as opposed to silver rubles, fluctuated too much to allow for a more favourable exchange rate.[19]

The first of the three delegations stopped in Berlin and Elkhart to be briefed by Jacob Y. Shantz and John F. Funk, respectively, before going on to Nebraska, Kansas, Colorado, and Texas. The other two followed, stopping en route in Pennsylvania and Indiana, then joining the first group on June 9 at Fargo, North Dakota, for a joint inspection of the northern states and the province of Manitoba. Competing salesmen travelled with them, all doing their part to praise the lands they represented. Hespeler and Shantz promoted Canada; Funk and the representatives of several railroad companies thought that the United States would be best. In his *Herald of Truth* Funk had presented a three-fold reason for the immigrants' choosing the United States over Canada: the milder climate, proximity to commercial centres for the discharge of produce and the republican form of government. On the latter point he said:

> We have examples where, under monarchical governments,
> particularly the Mennonites have lost their dearest, religious
> privileges. . . . Here in the United States, all the oppressed
> followers of Christ have an asylum of the fullest, religious

> liberty ... where they [the Russian Mennonites] may feel
> measurably secure that their privileges will not soon be
> taken from them.[20]

The four-day trip into Manitoba was made by boat on the Red River, winding some 300 miles toward Winnipeg. At the end of the journey the Governor, his entire ministry, five teams, wagons and light camping equipment were waiting to take them to inspect eight townships of uncultivated prairie lands 35 miles southeast of Winnipeg. The sales pitch included liberal references to Queen Victoria, herself a German, and to her daughter, who had married the heir to the German crown. The trek was a discouraging one for most of the delegates. It was the rainy season, the trails were extremely scarce and poorly travelled, the mosquitoes were thick, and much of the land was swampy. Before half the land had been inspected, the delegates asked to be returned to Winnipeg, and immediately the Hutterite, Polish and Prussian delegates returned to the Dakotas. Six days later the Molotschna delegates (Sudermann and Buller) had seen enough of the land along the Assiniboine River west of Winnipeg and also headed for the States.

The Bergthal and Kleine Gemeinde delegates, having previously inspected the States, seemed to be deciding for Canada, even before Shantz and Hespeler had shown them all there was to be seen. The disadvantages of what they saw were obvious but for them the disadvantages did not outweigh the advantages. The lands in Manitoba were free and available in large exclusive blocks. Exemption from military service was guaranteed to be absolute; there would be no objection to the use of the German language. All of these provisions, plus the prospect of living under the British monarchy, John F. Funk notwithstanding, appealed to the representatives of these poorer and more conservative colonies.

An incident, however, that took place at White Horse Plains, 24 miles west of Fort Garry, on July 1, Dominion Day, threatened to ruin the prospective migration to Manitoba. Apparently the incident arose when a Métis struck the faces of horses belonging to a half-breed in Hespeler's party. The drunken Métis, who constituted the majority of the inhabitants in the village, attacked the group so that "the Mennonites, who are noncombatants, were in imminent peril." Their hotel was "surrounded by an infuriated mob,"[21] reported Lieutenant-Governor Alexander Morris to Ottawa. William Hespeler said that if he had not stood guard with pistol and sword while the attackers tried to break into their hotel, the delegates might never have lived to tell their Russian brethren about the land and freedom awaiting them. The government, having been notified of the incident by a fast rider, had immediately dispatched the Fort Garry Chief of Police and a body of troops, who arrested and imprisoned the five ringleaders of the mob. Mr. Hespeler believed that only inclement weather had prevented large numbers of half-breeds from gathering to reinforce the cordon, which had already succeeded in cutting off all roads around the hotel. Attempts to break through that cordon would have been disastrous, perhaps fatal. The Lieutenant-Governor believed the clash to have been unpremeditated, and yet he could not close his eyes to the fact "that expressions of strong hostility were used towards the Canadians, who are crowding into the province in large numbers, by the parties concerned in the affray."[22]

The delegation itself proceeded to Ottawa where, on July 23, 1873, Mr. John Lowe, the Secretary of Agriculture, placed into the hands of Klassen, Peters, Wiebe and Toews the 15-point version of the Canadian Privilegium. It offered the following "advantages to settlers": an entire exemption from military service; eight townships of land available free in quarter-section quantities or less to males 21 years old and over; exclusive use by Mennonites of the reserved land; additional townships if needed and exchange privileges for another eight townships; purchase rights at one dollar per acre of an additional three-quarters to make a section of 640 acres; full exercise of religious principles and education of children without restriction; the right to affirm instead of to swear in taking the oath; transportation credits in the years 1874–1876 of up to 30 dollars for adults (no more than 40 dollars up to 1882) from Hamburg to Fort Garry; and supplies for the sea voyage.[23]

Although most of these provisions were part of the standard immigration policy, some, such as the right to exclusive block settlement and the right to educate their own children, were new.[24] This latter provision was actually outside of federal jurisdiction, education being a mandate of the provinces according to the British North America Act. Its inclusion in the federal offer led to very serious misunderstandings in years to come. Three days after the Privilegium had been handed over, John Pope, Minister of Agriculture, eliminated the education provision from the official document, having recognized its legal discrepancies. The document was placed before the cabinet for approval

without advising the Mennonites of the change.[25] The very important military exemption had existed before in the sense that it
was provided for in the first post-Confederation military service
act in 1868. There it was written:

> Any person bearing a certificate from the Society of Quakers,
> Mennonists or Tunkers, or any inhabitant of Canada, or any
> religious denomination, otherwise subject to military duty,
> but who, from the doctrines of his religion, is averse to
> bearing of arms and refuses personal military service, shall
> be exempt from such service when balloted in time of peace,
> or war, upon such conditions and under such regulations as
> the Governor in Canada may from time to time prescribe.[26]

Although Russian authorities had granted the Mennonites ten
years to comply with its new laws or to emigrate, they had apparently placed their bet on compliance. As the evidence mounted
that they might lose their wager, they discouraged emigration by
every means possible. Hespeler's movements, as already pointed
out, were controlled and limited. His attempted visit to the colonies of 100,000 German Lutherans in Bessarabia, Cherson, and
Crimea, for instance, was cut short by the harassments and
"watchfulness of the police." When it was discovered that the
real culprit might be Cornelius Jansen, he too was sent out of the
country and Zohrab, the British consul, was warned of the severe
penalties provided by the law for "those who seek to induce
Russian subjects to emigrate," penalties from which his official
position would not protect him.[27] Later, St. Petersburg advised
London directly to be cautious. To stifle the emigration the
Russian imperial government could grant "such a relaxation of
the future military law of service as may satisfy the religious
scruples of the German Mennonite colonies." Besides, the British
were told, the Mennonites themselves should be assessed for their
clever strategy. On the one hand, they were exercising

> pressure on the Imperial Government by a threat of
> emigration in order to obtain the fulfillment of their wishes
> whilst, on the other hand, they were simultaneously in
> communication with the Governments of Canada and of
> the United States with the view in case of failure with the
> Imperial Government, to secure the best conditions for their
> future emigration.[28]

On one occasion, when secret and confidential papers from

Ottawa, which were intended for British agents in Berdyansk, reached St. Petersburg through the Russian Post Office, the Canadian government was severely criticized for negotiating with the prospective immigrants without the "sanction of the Russian government." The American government, it was explained, was more prudent.[29] To be sure, the United States officially maintained a non-involvement profile, but immigration activity and promotion was quite considerable. Timothy Smith of the American consulate in Odessa had cultivated excellent relations with the German-speaking peoples in South Russia and, in the fall of 1872, 120 German Lutheran families were on their way, and additional hundreds were preparing to leave in 1873. Consul Zohrab complained that Smith, who knew the Germans and their language well, had a clear field to work in and could therefore "use his influence unchecked to direct current emigration."[30]

Hespeler and Shantz were aware of the strength of American influences, which is why they presented the benefits of Canada in comparison to those of the United States. Their trump cards were "block settlement" and "military exemption." Funk and his Mennonite ministerial colleagues, as well as the exiled Cornelius Jansen, who had already landed in America, were making an extraordinary effort to provide similar possibilities in their country. They appealed to members of Congress to make block settlement possible, not for speculation — "we beg you to prevent it" — but because the Canadian government had made such an offer, and the common pasture was essential to the Mennonite way of farming.[31]

Congress did not respond positively to the petitions, nor were the railroads in a position to give compact settlement guarantees since they owned only alternative sections of land. Neither were guarantees forthcoming on the matter of military exemption, in spite of the fact that the two Tschetters of the Hutterite delegation spoke to President Grant directly. They begged him to guarantee that they would "be free at least 50 years from everything that concerns war." They also requested other privileges, including the right to settle and organize communally and to have the full control of their own German schools. The president, reflecting the weakness of the federal government on these matters, replied that most of their requests relating to settlement and exemptions fell under state jurisdiction and that therefore he could make no promises. He felt, however, "that for the next 50 years we will not be entangled in another war in which military service will be necessary."[32] This assessment of pacifist prospects under a republican form of government proved to be as much in error as that of John F. Funk.

If real assurances on liberty of conscience were lacking, why did the majority of migrating Russian Mennonites in the 1870s none the less choose America? One Canadian historian answers as follows: "Those who placed fertile land above sectarian freedom went to the United States, while those who insisted upon religious liberty at any price, came to Canada."[33] Another said that "some of the most ardent of all defenders of conscientious objection to military service went to the United States."[34]

It is also true that the legal protection of nonresistance and its very strict interpretation was no longer of the highest value to all Mennonites. An ambivalent outlook which had definitely emerged in Prussia also manifested itself in Russia. This ambivalence remained characteristic of those who stayed behind in both Prussia and Russia as well as those who migrated to America.[35]

The historical record of those who chose Canada is clear: their conscientious nonresistance and their German culture were of paramount importance, although they were not unhappy about the fact that both these values related to free land. The legal provisions were so important to them that they felt they could face any environmental handicaps to ensure them. Indeed, when 50 years later those legal provisions broke down, they again had the capacity to forsake the land, even in its developed state, in favour of their cherished values.

Other essential differences between those choosing Canada and the United States concerned economic, social and educational sophistication. The Canadian group consisted primarily of Chortitza people, descendants of those poor and simple pioneers who in the previous century had first left Prussia for Russia. The American group, largely from Molotschna, had not only made a stronger start in Russia but had also benefited more directly from the Cornies reforms in agriculture as well as in education.[36]

After the delegation had left Canada, the government officials felt that perhaps they had lost out to the United States in their bid, even though the delegates had given assurance that it was only a matter of organizing the first immigrants. New York newspapers which were quoted in London, Toronto, and Winnipeg suggested that the selection by the delegates of the "prairie provinces" had been premature and that in actual fact they favoured the United States. The group returning to Russia from New York promised before their departure to "recommend Kansas as the most suitable locality for the 40,000 and that the first instalment of 2,000 will leave Russia next May." Asked the Toronto immigration office: "Which is correct, are there two colonies of Mennonites coming to America, one to Canada and one to the United States? And does each colony number exactly 40,000?"[37]

This was only another case of the newspapers and their readers confusing matters, but they revealed correctly the strong competition for, and high stakes in, the immigration. Canada knew that the final battle might come at points of disembarkation. Cornelius Jansen actually succeeded in persuading 30 families of the Kleine Gemeinde arriving in Toronto to go to Nebraska instead of to their planned destination, Manitoba. The various states and agencies in the United States were also outbidding each other. Several states quickly passed laws to exempt Mennonites from militia duties. The railroad companies eagerly employed Mennonite agents, such as Peter Jansen, son of Cornelius, and others were given free railroad passes and gifts of land to help persuade their brethren.

When the delegations returned to Russia in the fall of 1873 with the report that an abundance of land was available on liberal terms and that there was freedom of religion, emigration fever increased. For those who wanted to migrate immediately there was the difficult question of the sale of land and their properties. Many emigrants sold their properties for half the value or less. Securing the necessary passports permitting emigration was even more difficult. Not only were the fees high, but considerable administrative delays caused problems. Indeed, the imperial government did not really want to grant exit visas until the tsar's personal representative, General von Todtleben, had spoken to the Mennonite leaders to persuade them that their best future lay in Russia. When it became clear that some had their minds made up, he wished them well and sped them on their way.

Sensing the real problem which the Mennonites had with the emerging Russian law, the imperial government acted in 1874 to make concrete the assurances and concessions that Todtleben and other spokesmen were promising. These provisions were that the original Mennonite settlers and their descendants should be exempted from military service but be subject to an alternative service in hospitals or forestry camps where they could work in compact and exclusive groups, in times of both war and peace.

However, new immigrants arriving after enactment of the law, as well as converts, were to be excluded from these privileges.

These assurances were probably related to the fact that in the end only one-third of the Russian Mennonite population emigrated in the 1870s. Among those who decided to stay, there were strong objections to the emigration propaganda. Missionary Heinrich Dirks, for instance, insisted that even in the worst of cultural and political circumstances the Mennonites had a missionary obligation to remain in Russia. The world could not always provide an escape for the Mennonites. He wrote from Sumatra:

> Should there, finally, by the new order of things, much that
> we highly prize, be lost; should the German element more
> and more lose itself in the Russian, . . . and should it finally
> be that most of the Mennonite young men, instead of
> performing hospital service, would voluntarily join the ranks
> of the combatants, it will no doubt, even then yet be possible
> to worship God in spirit and in truth. Hence, whatever the
> result may be, I decidedly advise not to emigrate . . . Those
> who advise too much to emigrate, positively do not know the
> world, neither the character of this present time, otherwise
> they must know that that from which they propose to escape
> will overtake them wherever in this wide world they choose
> to settle.[38]

Johann Epp, a minister at Saratov, similarly voiced his objections in a strong article to John F. Funk. Epp insisted that the acceptance of an alternative service, unrelated to the war ministerium, was truer to the Christian confession than payments for substitute military recruits. His position on these matters was not an isolated one. The extensive assistance given by the nearby Mennonite colonies during the Crimean War in matters of food, medicine and transport suggested itself as a real alternative to direct military service. In Epp's opinion most of the departing emigrants represented elements forever dissatisfied and forever seeking an Eldorado which would eternally satisfy all their desires. His charges support the suggestion that at least some of the migration was motivated by material considerations and perhaps even by Mennonites seeking relief from one another.

> We hear them speaking not so much about freedoms with
> respect to military service awaiting them there but rather
> about the fair, fertile, and cheap lands, and the unusual
> fundamental rights and other worthy institutions of America
> which eliminate all strife and conflict.[39]

Epp conceded some value in the emigration. Not only were the colonies thereby purified of restless elements but the landless also had the opportunity to obtain land in Russia cheaply. But faith or conscience was not a reason for leaving Russia, in his opinion. On the contrary, the Scriptures were clear that Christians had obligations to their country and to the whole of society. This debate over the necessity and desirability of immigration in the 1870s never came to an end. Among those who stayed in Russia, a sizeable number felt the impulse to move into central Asia, as followers of the zealous Claasz Epp, or into Siberia, as pioneers of daughter colonies. Later, the Bolshevik Revolution and its aftermath led some to conclude that the failure to emigrate westward en masse at an earlier time had been a great historical error.

The earliest westward movements consisted largely of small groups leaving from the Crimea, from Volhynia and Prussia (see Tables 2 and 3). However, there were also some larger movements. The entire Alexanderwohl congregations from Molotschna, which had moved as a unit also from Prussia, settled in Kansas. The Canadian immigration consisted for the most part of resettlement of entire colonies, including the Borozenko colony of the Kleine Gemeinde as well as Bergthal and Fuerstenland. The latter two movements attracted others from Chortitza, the mother colony, and from related settlements.

The route for most of the immigrants went overland from Odessa to Hamburg since the imperial government did not permit any shipping companies to take immigrants directly from Russian ports. From Hamburg five shipping lines transported the immigrants either directly to New York, via Liverpool to Quebec, or via Antwerp to Philadelphia. The American groups stopped over either in Pennsylvania or at Elkhart, Indiana, or at both places, before going on to their ultimate destinations.[40]

The Canadian groups were first taken by train from Quebec and Montreal to Toronto. From there they went overland to Collingwood, then by boat to Duluth, overland to Moorehead, and finally by either the International or the Cheyenne Red River boats to their destination in Manitoba. Actually the Dominion government wanted to bring the immigrants over the Dawson Road, a Canadian route, to prevent the possibility of the settlers being sidetracked by American agents between Duluth, Moorehead and the Canadian border.[41] However, Shantz thought the route to the Red River Valley via Lake-of-the-Woods from Lake Superior too hazardous. Passable only from June to September, it

TABLE 2

MENNONITE IMMIGRATION IN THE 1870S TO THE UNITED STATES
AND CANADA

DATE	NUMBER OF FAMILIES*	ORIGIN	DESTINATION

1. THE UNITED STATES

DATE	NUMBER OF FAMILIES*	ORIGIN	DESTINATION
1873, June	Several	Crimea	Illinois
1873, July	27	Crimea	Mid-west States
1874, April	10	Volhynia (Swiss)	Dakota
1874, April	Small number	Prussia Russian Poland	Kansas
1874, June	30	Crimea	Kansas
1874, August	216	Alexanderwohl Molotschna	Kansas Nebraska
1874, August	159	Volhynia (Swiss)	Dakotas, Kansas
1874, late fall	265	Volhynia (Dutch) Poland Russia	Kansas
1874–1879		Crimea Hutterite Bruderhofs	Dakota
1874, June	30	Borozenko (Kleine Gemeinde)	Nebraska

2. CANADA

DATE	NUMBER OF FAMILIES*	ORIGIN	DESTINATION
1874, June	70	Borozenko (Kleine Gemeinde)	Manitoba
1874–1876	1,000	Bergthal Chortitza, etc.	Manitoba
1875	266	Fuerstenland	Manitoba

* Number of families is approximate in a number of instances. There were an average of five members in each family. See Smith, *Russian Mennonites*, pp. 92–131; Gerbrandt, pp. 68–9; Francis, p. 5, and Krahn, *ME*, III, pp. 457–66 (all in the Bibliography).

TABLE 3

MIGRATIONS TO CANADA AND THE UNITED STATES
BY YEARS*

YEAR	CANADA	UNITED STATES
1873	—	150
1874	1,533	5,225
1875	3,261	1,400
1876	1,352	1,241
1877	184	800
1878	324	530
1879	208	726
1880	69	—
Total	6,931	10,000

* United States figures based on Smith and in some cases represent approximations. Canadian figures are compiled from Quebec Ship Lists (PAC, Record Group 76, Lists 9-11, Microfilm C4528-30). Annual Report of Agriculture, *Sessional Papers*, 1875–1881, has slightly different figures for six of the years but the total of 6,930 differs only by one.

took a week at the best of times, and therefore he "vetoed" the plan. Some groups also travelled overland from Toronto via Detroit and Chicago.

The immigrants arrived with a minimum of material goods with which to begin farming anew. While some settlers had come with small tools and implements and even farm wagons, the majority expected to purchase the elemental necessities on the spot, i.e. in Moorehead or in Winnipeg. Again, the agents in both communities, knowing that tens of thousands of dollars were involved, went out of their way to woo the immigrants. Upon the advice of Shantz and Hespeler, however, the first and most of the subsequent groups of immigrants bought their shovels, scythes, hayforks, stoves, coffee mills, frying pans, horses, cattle, flour and other provisions in Winnipeg. The first 65 families spent $20,000 in three days, the most costly items being wagons and horses.

The final point of Canadian disembarkation was the juncture of the Rat and Red rivers, a French parish point called St. Agathe. From there the settlers walked or drove inland about four miles. Immigration sheds and tents had been set up by Shantz. As a reward for this and his many other labours, he received a free section of land on the western edge of the reserve.[42]

While the first group of 65 immigrant families brought with them an average of nearly $1,000 per family, most others did not fare as well. The second group of 85 families averaged less than $100 per family (see Table 4).[43] Not only were there very poor

TABLE 4

RUSSIAN MENNONITES HAVING EMIGRATED TO MANITOBA,
THEIR NUMBER, ARRIVAL DATES, AND CAPITAL

COM-PANY	ARRIVAL IN TORONTO	NO. OF FAMILIES	INDIVIDUALS	CAPITAL
1.	July 19, 1874	65	327	$63,000
2.	July 30, 1874	85	290	8,000
3.	July 31, 1874	100	504	30,000
4.	September 1874	24	120	22,000
5.	September 1874	23	166	20,000
6.	June 27, 1875	28	140	23,000
7.	July 3, 1875	135	664	68,000
8.	July 7, 1875	96	480	40,000
9.	July 15, 1875	111	555	27,000
10.	July 22, 1875	195	998	64,000
11.	July 29, 1875	72	362	20,000
12.	June 21, 1876	42	214	30,000
13.	June 26, 1876	44	224	11,000
14.	June 29, 1876	48	244	20,000
15.	July 12, 1876	14	68	(Branches of families who had been left in Liverpool due to sickness)
16.	July 20, 1876	14	78	
17.	August 1, 1876	82	511	58,000
18.	June 30, 1877	35	183	19,000
19.	July 1, 1878	48	270	—
20.	July 8, 1879	33	207	60,000
21.	August 4, 1880	14	69	7,000
Totals		1,281	6,674*	$591,000

* Based on Philip Wismer.

families in the immigration, but many had to wait for sufficient cash from the final liquidation of their Russian assets. To help meet the needs of the incoming immigrants, the American and Canadian Mennonites organized three aid committees.

In the west and midwest, the General Conference and the old Mennonites combined to form the Mennonite Board of Guardians, with its agent, Bernhard Warkentin, basing his work in New York. In Pennsylvania, both groups of Mennonites combined to form the Mennonite Executive Aid Committee; a similar organization, the Russian Mennonite Aid Committee, was organized in Ontario by Jacob Y. Shantz (see Table 5).[44]

These committees cooperated in the movement of the Russian Mennonites, attending to every detail and placing representatives in Hamburg, New York, and Toronto to make sure that no problem was overlooked and no need unattended to. Although no complete reports are available, it was estimated that the American committees raised up to $100,000 for aid in the early migration years and the Canadian committee, with the help of the Canadian Parliament, produced an equal amount.

In addition, the Ontario Mennonites meeting the immigrants in Toronto ensured that they were resupplied with food and other provisions for the balance of the journey since the Canadian government contribution ended at Collingwood. A group of immigrants arriving late in the fall of 1874 spent the winter in Ontario Mennonite homes before moving on to Manitoba. In 1875 Simeon Reesor of Markham accompanied a group of seven families all the way to Manitoba. The entire journey from Southern Russia to Manitoba took from six to eight weeks, including a sea voyage of about 20 days. The immigrants accepted the privations on the assumption that the new homeland would offer them not only prosperity but permanence with the desired freedoms.

TABLE 5

RUSSIAN MENNONITE AID ORGANIZATIONS AND ARRANGEMENTS

NAME	REGION	DATE FOUNDED	PERSONNEL	TRANSPORT ARRANGEMENTS
Mennonite Executive Committee*	Pennsylvania	April 14, 1874	Amos Herr, chairman John Shenk, secretary Gabriel Bear and Herman K. Godshall, treasurers Casper Hett, agent	Red Star Line Antwerp to Philadelphia
Mennonite Board of Guardians*	West and Mid-west	Nov. 7, 1873	Christian Krehbiel, chairman David Goerz, secretary John F. Funk, treasurer Bernhard Warkentin, agent	Hamburg-American and Inman Lines Hamburg to New York
Russian Mennonite Aid Committee	Ontario	Dec. 22, 1873†	Jacob Y. Shantz, secretary-treasurer Elias Schneider John Gascho Samuel Reesor John Koch Philip Wismer	Allan Line Liverpool to Quebec

* Both American committees were coordinating bodies for numerous local committees.
† Date of first collection.

FOOTNOTES

1. Gerhard Wiebe, *Ursachen und Geschichte der Auswanderung der Mennoniten aus Russland nach Amerika* (Winnipeg, Man.: Druckerei Der Nordwesten, 1900), p. 27.
2. Gustav E. Reimer and G. R. Gaeddert, *Exiled by the Czar: Cornelius Jansen and the Great Mennonite Migration, 1874* (Newton, Kans.: Mennonite Publication Office, 1956), pp. 36–7.
3. P. M. Friesen, *Alt-Evangelische Bruederschaft in Russland, 1789–1940* (Halbstadt, Taurien: Raduga, 1911), p. 493.
4. *Ibid.*, p. 494. See also Wiebe's commentary on spiritual coldness among and between the Mennonites.
5. Reimer, *op. cit.*, p. 46.
6. PAC, *Shortt Papers*, M.G. 30, D45, Vol. 57, Leonhard Sudermann *et al.* to J. Zohrab, January 15, 1872. Original, signed by 33, in Public Records Office, London, Foreign Office files, 65–842. Another similar letter from Fuerstenau, Molotschna, signed by 19 in same file.
7. PAC, *Shortt Papers*, M.G. 30, D45, Vol. 57, J. Zohrab to E. Granville, February 3, 1872. The original, quite extensive Zohrab correspondence is lodged in the Public Record Office in London (PRO), Foreign Office files (FO): 65/842, 65/847, 65/852, 65/856, 65/892, 181/510.
8. 31 Victoria, chap. 40, sect. 17, "Act Respecting the Militia and Defence to the Dominion of Canada."
9. PAC, *Department of Agriculture General Correspondence*, Record Group 17, A1, Vol. 62, #5951½ and 5980. The same as Order-in-Council 827B, April 26, 1872.
10. PAC, *Shortt Papers*, M.G. 30, D45, Vol. 57, William Hespeler, "Report of his Proceedings in Russia," August 28, 1872; and J. Lowe, Secretary, Department of Agriculture, to William Hespeler, September 16, 1872. See also PRO, FO 65/861, "Notizen ueber Amerika, 1872," a printed document from diverse sources on the matter of military service in Canada and the United States.
11. PAC, *Shortt Papers*, M.G. 30, D45, Vol. 57, William Hespeler report to Canadian authorities on visit to South Russia.
12. PAC, *Shortt Papers*, M.G. 30, D45, Vol. 57, William Hespeler to J. H. Pope, October 21, 1872.
13. PAC, *Shortt Papers*, M.G. 30, D45, Vol. 57, Bernhard Warkentin to J. H. Pope, November 28, 1882.
14. Jacob Y. Shantz, *Narrative of a Journey to Manitoba, Together with an Abstract of the Dominion Lands Act, and an Extract from the Government Pamphlet on Manitoba* (Ottawa: Department of Agriculture, 1873).
15. C. Henry Smith, *The Coming of the Russian Mennonites* (Berne, Ind.: Mennonite Book Concern, 1927), p. 51.

16. PAC, *Shortt Papers*, M.G. 30, D45, Vol. 57, William Hespeler to J. H. Pope, April 26, 1873.
17. PAC, *Shortt Papers*, M.G. 30, D45, Vol. 57, Letter from Special Immigrant Agent, Hamburg, to J. H. Pope, March 21, 1873.
18. PAC, *Shortt Papers*, M.G. 30, D45, Vol. 57, Dr. F. Fischer of the German Society of Montreal to Department of Agriculture, April 11, 1873.
19. PAC, *Shortt Papers*, M.G. 30, D45, Vol. 57, J. E. Klotz, Hamburg, to John Lowe, May 10, 1874.
20. John F. Funk, "Minnesota and Dakota, or Manitoba," *Herald of Truth*, 1873, p. 25.
21. PAC, *Shortt Papers*, M.G. 30, D45, Vol. 57, Lieutenant-Governor Alexander Morris, Fort Garry, to the Department of Agriculture, July 7, 1873.
22. *Ibid.*
23. PAC, *Orders-in-Council*, Record Group 2, #959, August 13, 1873. This order-in-council includes the letter of J. M. Lowe, Department of Agriculture, to David Klassen, Jacob Peters, Heinrich Wiebe and Cornelius Toews of July 23, 1873.
24. Norman MacDonald, *Canada Immigration and Colonization 1841–1903* (Aberdeen: Aberdeen University Press, 1966), pp. 197ff.
25. See E. K. Francis, *In Search of Utopia: The Mennonites in Manitoba* (Altona, Man.: D. W. Friesen & Sons, 1955), pp. 48–9.
26. 31 Victoria, chap. 40, sect. 17 (1868).
27. PAC, *Shortt Papers*, M.G. 30, D45, Vol. 57, Lord A. Loftus to J. Zohrab, April 16, 1873.
28. PAC, *Shortt Papers*, M.G. 30, D45, Vol. 57, Lord A. Loftus to Earl Granville, August 18, 1872.
29. PAC, *Shortt Papers*, M.G. 30, D45, Vol. 57, Lord A. Loftus to Earl Granville, November 12, 1872.
30. PAC, *Shortt Papers*, M.G. 30, D45, Vol. 57, J. Zohrab to Earl Granville, February 10, 1873.
31. See January 10, 1874, Petitions to Congress, in Smith, *op. cit.*, pp. 77–8. Cf. Leland Harder, "The Russian Mennonites and American Democracy under Grant," in C. Krahn, ed., *From the Steppes to the Prairies* (Newton, Kans.: Mennonite Publication Office, 1949), pp. 54–67.
32. Reply to Hutterite Petition, Washington, September 5, 1873.
33. Carl Addington Dawson, *Group Settlement: Ethnic Communities in Western Canada* (Toronto: Macmillan Company, 1936), p. 102.
34. Ernst Correll, "Mennonite Immigration into Manitoba: Documents and Sources, 1872, 1873," *Mennonite Quarterly Review*, XI (July 1937), p. 200.
35. J. Mannhardt, "Koennen und duerfen wir Mennoniten der von dem Staate geforderten Wehrpflicht genuegen?", *Mennonitische*

Blaetter, 19:6 (August 1972), pp. 41–3; 19:7 (September 1972), pp. 49–51. See also C. J. Dyck, "For Conscience Sake? Motives Underlying the Mennonite Migration of 1873–1888," manuscript written for *Mennonite Quarterly Review*.

36. H. J. Gerbrandt, *Adventure in Faith* (Altona, Man.: D. W. Friesen & Sons, 1970), pp. 29, 33–4, 37ff.

37. PAC, *Shortt Papers*, M.G. 30, D45, Vol. 57, J. A. Donaldson in Toronto Immigration Office, September 1, 1873.

38. Quoted in "Something to Think About," *Herald of Truth*, 1874, p. 121.

39. AMC, Johann Epp, Koeppenthal, Saratov, to John F. Funk, January 7, 1875, in John F. Funk Collection.

40. For Canadian immigrants see Quebec Passenger Lists, PAC, *Immigration Branch Passenger Lists*, Record Group 76, Lists 9–11 (microfilm C4528-C4530).

41. Francis, *op. cit.*, p. 53.

42. *Ibid.*, p. 52.

43. CGC, Philip Wismer, "A Record of Russian Mennonite Aid Committee for Lincoln County, Ontario, 1873–1880," (unpublished manuscript), 7 pp.

44. C. Henry Smith, *The Coming of the Russian Mennonites* (Berne, Ind.: Mennonite Book Concern, 1927), p. 108. See also H. S. Bender, *Mennonite Encyclopedia*, III, pp. 591–95.

The House-Barn Combination

9. The East and West Reserves

It was these Mennonites who first demonstrated the practicality of farming the open prairie and thus effectively opened much of western Canada to settlement — JOHN W. GRANT.[1]

ONLY ONE-SEVENTH of the 50,000 Russian Mennonites whom Canada had hoped to attract chose the young dominion as their new homeland. But for them it was a very deliberate choice. Having been guaranteed by the government all the essential conditions of a happy settlement, they went about re-creating on their land the Mennonite commonwealth they had left behind. Little did they realize that many of the assumptions with which they began their Manitoba sojourn soon would be questioned from inside and outside of their communities.

The external questioning arose from the fact that for Manitoba and Canada the Mennonites were only a means to an end. The real purpose was to fill the prairies with a united Canadian society, which would prove the possibility of prosperous settlement there and, simultaneously, domesticate the lands in the face of Indian and Métis rebellion and discourage any American incursion, peaceful or otherwise. Whatever early concessions were made to separatist groups they were mainly to build the population base. The government had no intention of forever allowing or even temporarily creating an endless series of unconnected ethnic islands on the vast prairie sea. Those prairies were ultimately intended for a single Canadian humanity premised on undivided British loyalty in politics and culture.[2] Support, and frequently agitation, for a militant prairie Canadianization program would come not only from the politicians but also from the English Protestant churches — Anglican, Methodist and Presbyterian — which sought to homogenize the foreigners into their definition of "His Dominion."[3]

Internally, Mennonite individualism had never been totally forsaken for the benefit of community. Frequent uprootings, latent dissatisfactions or other unexpressed reasons contributed to individualistic tendencies sufficiently to make the re-creation of an unbroken commonwealth impossible. Furthermore, the single-mindedness and solidarity with which the immigrants appeared to decide upon Canada turned out to be more superficial and less enduring than required for Mennonite survival on the community pattern established in Russia. Accordingly, even as the new environment wanted to anglicize and integrate them, the Mennonite communities carried the seeds of their own dissolution.

When one examines the immigrants' new homeland, the internal differences are apparent. The area selected for and by them consisted of eight townships, 36 sections each, with 640 acres in each section. These began 30 miles southeast of Winnipeg and five miles east of the Red River. The land stretched between Niverville and Giroux and coincided with what became known as the Hanover Municipality. The area was then called the East Reserve (a reserve was an unbroken tract of land assigned for exclusive use, at least for a time, by a group of homogeneous settlers).

Two problems presented themselves immediately to the farmers just arrived from the Russian steppes: the heavy covering of brush and trees and the apparently inferior soils. This discovery, tentative at first but later confirmed, led to serious discontent and grumbling from the beginning; it was followed by accusations that the authorities had deliberately misled them. Complaints such as the following were common:

> On this land we drown; this land we cannot cultivate
> because it must first be cleared; this is no place to build,
> etc.[4]

Contrary to popular feeling, the authorities had not intended to deceive the immigrants, because water and wood, which the East

Reserve offered in abundance, were considered as essential for pioneer settlement as the ready-to-plough open, flat and uniformly fertile grasslands farther west. Indeed, the best place for poor people to begin life in a new country was where there were a variety and abundance of natural resources. Most of the settlers arriving from Ontario would desperately avoid the treeless flat-lands stretching, it seemed, endlessly southwest of Winnipeg.

Yet the immigrants were given an area which even "the surveyors regarded as generally unfit for settlement."[5] The woods contained timber of only poor quality and the soils were generally inferior. Indeed, some townships had a great deal of gravel and sand, not to speak of stones and heavy boulders. Large acreages were little more than marshlands. In the words of a Manitoba geographer:

> The advantages gained during the first year or two of
> settlement were far outweighed by the 40 years of struggle
> which the Mennonites spent on land which simply was not
> suitable for farming.[6]

Not surprisingly, therefore, some 32 families, better positioned than the rest, turned their backs on the East Reserve from the outset, and arranged to settle on the west side of the Red River, farther south along the banks of the Scratching River. Others who could afford it looked at possibilities still farther south — to the treeless plain stretching some 40 miles west from the Red along the international border and from there scores of miles northward toward Winnipeg.

Application for a block settlement in the west was made in 1874 and settlement was permitted, but the West Reserve was not officially created, by Order-in-Council, until 1876. However, settlers directly from Russia as well as transfers from the East Reserve began to choose the West Reserve area in 1875. This dismayed other Manitobans, especially those in the Pembina Hills area, who knew it was foolish, if not impossible, to try to survive in open treeless areas, particularly in winter. But, as a chronicler of those years reported:

> In 1875 the few settlers at Pembina Mountain fondly hoped
> that in the course of 15 or 20 years this plain would become
> settled notwithstanding the absence of timber. Before the
> summer was over, a long line of camp fires, extending for
> miles and miles, announced one evening to the lonely settlers

that thousands of Mennonites were locating on seventeen townships.[7]

On both sides of the Red River the Mennonites laid out their settlements in village formations, just as they had done in Russia. There were a total of 59 villages in the east and 70 in the west, though the full number of them did not exist at any one time; some were quite small and incomplete. As the last ones were being founded near the turn of the century, some of the earliest ones had been abandoned (as, indeed, most of them were by 1900). Shantz had tried "to persuade them to abolish the village system," because the particular land area was not sufficiently uniform in quality to lend itself to a uniform distribution of population centres.[8]

However, one of the reasons the Mennonite leaders selected Manitoba instead of the United States was precisely the possibility of block and village settlement. Not only did such settlement represent some distinct economic and sociological advantages, but it also permitted the village communities to set up their own schools and the religious leaders to guide their people more closely. The bishops of three church organizations represented in the immigration (see Table 1)[9] were as insistent on the village system as their delegates had been on block settlement. To them the Manitoba settlement made sense only in those terms.

TABLE 1

MANITOBA IMMIGRANT CHURCHES AND LEADERSHIP

CHURCH	NO.	LOCATION	BISHOP
Kleine Gemeinde	700	East Reserve and Scratching River	Peter Toews
Reinlaender Church*	3,240	Western part of West Reserve	Johann Wiebe
Bergthaler Church	3,403	East Reserve and eastern part of West Reserve	Gerhard Wiebe

* Reinlaender Mennonite Church was the official name. It is often referred to in literature as the Fuerstenlaender or Old Colony group, after the Russian colonies of their origin.

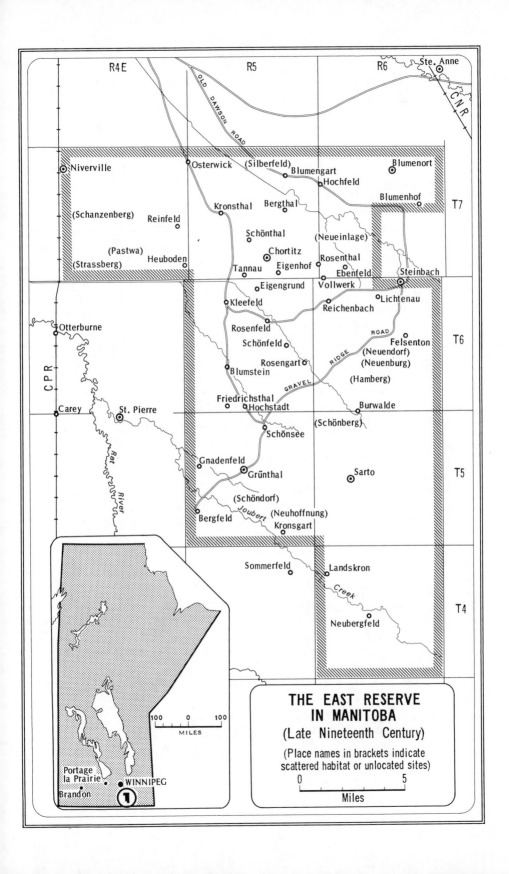

R4E   R5   R6   Ste. Anne

OLD DAWSON ROAD

CNR

Niverville   Osterwick   (Silberfeld)   Blumengart   Blumenort

Hochfeld

Blumenhof   T7

(Schanzenberg)   Reinfeld   Kronsthal   Bergthal

Schönthal   (Neueinlage)

(Pastwa)   Heuboden   Chortitz   Rosenthal

(Strassberg)   Tannau   Eigenhof   Ebenfeld   Steinbach

Eigengrund   Vollwerk

Kleefeld   Reichenbach   Lichtenau

Otterburne   Rosenfeld   ROAD

Schönfeld   Felsenton   T6

(Neuendorf)

Rosengart   (Neuenburg)

CPR   Blumstein   GRAVEL   (Hamberg)

Friedrichsthal   RIDGE

Carey   St. Pierre   Hochstadt   Burwalde

(Schönberg)

Schönsee

Gnadenfeld

Grünthal   Sarto   T5

(Schöndorf)

Bergfeld   Joubert   (Neuhoffnung)

Kronsgart

Rat River

Sommerfeld   Landskron

Creek   T4

Neubergfeld

Portage la Prairie   WINNIPEG

Brandon

100   0   100

MILES

THE EAST RESERVE
IN MANITOBA
(Late Nineteenth Century)

(Place names in brackets indicate
scattered habitat or unlocated sites)

0   5

Miles

The villages were normally laid out in such a way that the buildings of the individual farm units were placed about 200 feet apart and about 100 feet away from the streets to give ample space for trees, gardens, and fences. Unless a village was laid alongside a creek, to which all the farmers wished to have access, the farm buildings would appear on both sides, with lots reserved for schools and/or churches. Hence, they were known as *Strassendoerfer* (street villages).

The farmers of a given village would cultivate the strip of land immediately adjacent to their lots and other similar strips in each of the quarter sections assigned to the village. In that way all farmers had access to the good land and also were obligated to farm some of the poor lands. At the end of a village, a quarter section or more would be reserved for a common pasture, in which all the animals would be cared for by a single cowherd who in winter might also be the village school teacher.

The farm homes constructed later were according to the style to which the Mennonites had become accustomed in Europe. The house, of which the gable end faced the street, was divided into two parts consisting of the *Vorderhaus* (front house) and the *Hinterhaus* (rear house). In the front house was a bedroom or two for the girls and smaller children, as well as the parents' room, which sometimes doubled as a living room. In the rear was the large kitchen/dining room, and a large utility room which might double as the boys' bedroom.

The earliest housing of the immigrants was very primitive. Upon their arrival temporary protection had been provided by shelters erected on the banks of the Red River. Slightly more permanent were the larger sheds, each 20 by 100 feet and divided into 12 rooms, and placed five miles inland near the later site of Niverville. Here mothers and children stayed while the men and boys went out to look over the land, to select village sites, and to dig the first more or less permanent family dwellings. For the most part, these first homes were built of sod — the Russian Mennonites were not accustomed to building log houses. The huts consisted of pits two feet deep surrounded by three-foot sod walls, across which poles were extended to support a sod roof. A normal hut would be about 15 feet wide and 35 feet long, of which a space of 15 square feet might be reserved for livestock. Another early dwelling type consisted of a 25-foot-square area covered by a steeply pitched thatched roof, which touched the ground on one end and was supported by high poles on the other.

TYPICAL FLOOR PLAN OF MANITOBA MENNONITE HOME

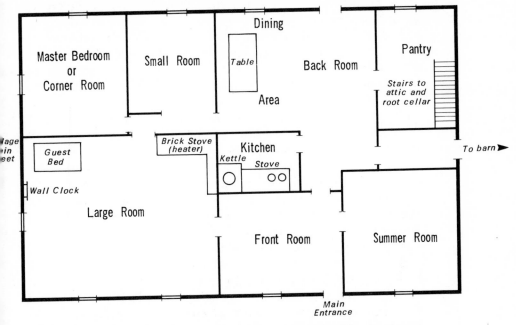

Early agricultural methods were harsh and crude. The land was cleared mostly by hand and with an axe. The first ploughing was done with oxen, as recommended by Canadian authorities. At $60 — one-third of the price of good imported horses — oxen were cheaper. They were better able to survive the winter and resist disease, and more ready to forage for themselves. They were also stronger, though admittedly much slower, often quite stubborn, and predictably thirsty after one or two rounds, but none the less able to break up to one acre of land a day. Horses, of course, were recommended as soon as money, shelter, and feed were available.

In 1874 only very small acreages were ploughed; the next spring seeds were spread by hand and then worked into the soil with small sections of wooden-tooth harrows. The earliest harvesting was done with scythe and flail, but mowers, reapers, twine binders and threshing machines were all introduced within a decade of settlement. In the second year over 5,000 acres were ready for seeding with wheat, oats, barley, rye, flax and potatoes. Some wheat seeds were brought along from Russia, and Canadian grain exchanges became quite excited by the large hard kernel of the Russian wheat. It needed about two weeks longer to mature than the more popular Red Fyfe, however, and therefore soon fell into disfavour when the fall frosts arrived before the grain matured.

The discovery that low-quality lands had been selected was aggravated by the actual physical hardships which the settlers experienced. Crops failed and there was little cash with which to buy supplies. The 7,000 immigrants had brought with them approximately half a million dollars, about $75 per person, but that was barely sufficient for necessities. Besides, it must be remembered that the earliest immigrants had to await a later liquidation of their assets (refer to Table 4, Chapter 8).[10]

During the first winter food was scarce and most meals at best consisted of poor-quality potatoes and bread. Some ministers travelled regularly through the sparse settlements, encouraging the settlers, ensuring that there was no starvation, and otherwise strengthening the conviction that the move from Russia to the East Reserve had been the right one.

The first crop years were almost total failures, with grasshoppers flattening the small plantings in 1875[11] and frosts badly damaging the East Reserve grains in 1876. The result was that the settlers, especially the poorer ones, had to draw heavily on the $100,000 federal government loan negotiated early in 1875 by Jacob Y. Shantz and his Russian Aid Committee, also known as the Committee of Management of Mennonites of Ontario. The loan was guaranteed in varying amounts by a host of Ontario Mennonites. It applied mainly to the purchase of provisions and seed grains. There was an additional $70,000 "for transporting Mennonites and $190,000 toward assisting immigration and meeting immigration expenses" already approved.[12] Although some members of the Canadian Parliament had their reservations about the loan, it was passed as a normal and proper aid to successful competition for immigrants. The assets and reputation of the Ontario Mennonites and the promising role of the immigrants in the economic life of the prairies no doubt contributed to the positive vote. As it was written into the record of Parliament by the loan's promoters:

> The Mennonites in Waterloo and elsewhere, who had become personally responsible for the repayment of this loan, were some of the wealthiest people in the country ... An excellent class of immigrants ... bound together by religious and social ties ... shoulder to shoulder in every difficulty [and] pledged morally to repay it ...[13]

The Mennonites were not without their own internal arrangements for mutual aid and assistance to the needy. One such church institution was the *Waisenamt* (literally "orphans bureau"). In the old country it had originally served in the financial care of orphans and as a manager of estates but the bureau had gradually grown to incorporate such functions as savings, credit, banking and lending. Each of the three churches had a Waisenamt which was supplemented by the charities administered by the deacons, who collected and distributed these funds quite anonymously and privately to protect both donors and receivers.

Another economic institution was a fire insurance program administered by the *Brandaelteste* (literally "fire bishop," but meaning district fire chief) and aided by village representation. Through this insurance a farmer could recover two-thirds of his fire loss, which was collected on a pro rata basis from all other insurers.

The internal commitment to mutual helpfulness made the Mennonites very reluctant to go elsewhere for help. Yet sometimes the poorer members were overlooked, especially in the early months and years when everyone wanted to get a good start. The wealthy settlers were apparently the most eager of all, recognizing the importance of a strong beginning.

The government loans, therefore, were a great encouragement to the pioneers, who proceeded to increase the acreage under cultivation, to purchase more seed grain, and even in 1876 to erect four grist mills in the East Reserve, three of them driven by wind and one by steam. For a while all seemed to proceed according to plan. The increased aid from the government also meant increased attention from government officials, who as early as 1877 looked upon the Mennonite settlements as show places for what could and should be done with the untamed west, thus convincing both themselves and the Mennonites that they had done the right thing.

Heading the list of an unending stream of distinguished visitors as early as 1877 was the Queen's own representative, the Governor General of Canada, who viewed the Mennonite development with "unmitigated satisfaction."[14] Lord Dufferin recognized the tremendous sacrifices made for their religious convictions. Their brave facing of uncertainties rather than surrendering their "religious convictions in regard to the unlawfulness of warfare" qualified them, he said, for another great struggle, "a war, not against flesh and blood, a task so abhorrent to Mennonite religious feeling," but "against the brute forces of nature." In the name of Queen Victoria and the empire, Lord Dufferin extended the hand of brotherhood and fellowship, "for you are as welcome to our affection as you are to our lands, to our liberties and freedom." He expressed hope that the Mennonites would flourish and extend in wealth through countless generations, and that

> Beneath the flag whose folds now wave above us, you will find protection, peace, civil and religious liberty, constitutional freedom and equal laws.[15]

For the settlers these assurances, repeated many times since negotiations with Canada had begun five years before, were welcome words indeed. At that point they did not seem too unrealistic. Manitoba was very distant from the wars of Europe and, as far as relations with the United States were concerned, Lord Dufferin had spoken of "an indissoluable affection" between the two countries, both concerned with common interests and the advance of civilization, not as rivals but as allies.

The settlements which Lord Dufferin had come to inspect on the East Reserve had only been under way three years, but before a farewell banquet for distinguished citizens in Winnipeg he lauded "so marvellous a transformation," explaining that he had seldom beheld any spectacle "more pregnant with prophecy, more fraught with promise of an astonishing future." A great ovation was offered by those assembled, as he praised Mennonite industry and British benevolences:

> . . . in a long ride I took across the prairies which but yesterday was absolutely bare, desolate, and untenanted, and the home of the wolf, the badger, and the eagle, I passed village after village, homestead after homestead furnished with all the conveniences and incidents of European comfort and a scientific agriculture . . . I felt infinitely prouder in being able to throw over them the aegis of the British constitution, and in bidding them freely share with us our unrivalled political institutions, our untrammelled personal liberties.[16]

The Mennonites were not present at that celebration, and it is doubtful that they read the *Free Press* which reported the proceedings in detail. None the less, the way Canada had wooed and welcomed them was etched deeply in their hearts, so that the slightest change in public sentiment or policy was sufficient to stir their basic distrust of governments. For the time being, however, they went about keeping their part of the bargain — proving the agricultural potential of Canadian prairie farmland and the rightness of a liberal immigration policy.

In spite of the progress that was made and the cash that began to flow into the settlements, life on the East Reserve continued to be filled with hardships, except for the few who had settled on good land and started off with ample personal resources. To improve their lot, about 400 families, half of the entire reserve, moved to the west side of the river between 1876 and 1882. Many others, too poor to attempt another uprooting, accepted their misfortune as inevitable and reverted to subsistence agriculture.

The settlements on the West Reserve, on the other hand, though more handicapped in the early years because of lack of timber, made progress more rapidly thereafter. Lacking coal and firewood, they mixed cow dung with straw and dried it in six-inch blocks, burning it as they had been accustomed to do in Russia. This barnyard by-product was a high-heat fuel, clean and without an unwholesome odour. Lumber for building was hauled whatever distance necessary from the groves of the Red River in the east or from the Pembina hills in the west.

In the East Reserve, dairy products, readily marketable in Manitoba's single large trading centre, provided financial resources. The West depended more on poultry products, though both reserves produced both. The dairy and poultry industries helped the women and children to become agricultural producers in a direct way, all of them working with the men and boys from early morning until late at night.

The village communities and building styles likewise contributed to agricultural success. The village protected the poultry from raids by hawks, wolves and foxes, while the heat of the stables encouraged the birds to produce. The joining of the house and barn had the advantage of greater warmth, comfort and protection for humans and animals alike, especially in winter. The disadvantages lay in the greater fire hazard as well as the increased problem of hygiene. Although the rumour was quickly spread abroad that the Mennonites were dirty, they cleaned the barns regularly, allowing no manure to accumulate. Eventually cleanliness was publicly recognized as one of their virtues. As one of the many travellers through the Mennonite colonies wrote:

> We had been told that they were bad settlers, unpleasant
> neighbours, and dirty in their persons and dwellings; but we
> were much pleased to find that the exact reverse was the
> truth . . . All was clean and perfectly neat; indeed it was
> more like a showhouse at an exhibition than an ordinary
> dwelling-room.[17]

Grain and seed shipments, however, became the main source of revenue. By 1878 the settlers were shipping seven carloads of flax to an oil manufacturing firm in Baden, Ontario, all of it hauled to market either at Emerson or at Winnipeg, respectively the southern and the northern shipping points on the Red River. While most of the grain produced in the 1870s was consumed locally by poultry, cattle and horses, or ground into flour for human consumption, some grain was shipped out. By 1883 the West Reserve had produced a surplus.

Healthy progress was also evident in other ways. The villages had become "gems of Sylvan beauty," turning the West Reserve into "one of the loveliest grove-dotted prairies that can be imagined."[18] Immediately after settlement, the immigrants had planted long rows of maple, poplar, and balm of Gilead trees, as decoration and for protection against snowstorms in winter and dust storms in summer. The Mennonite women introduced the dahlia to the prairies, and added to the family income by selling ever-blooming potted roses at Emerson and Morden, the new trading centre on the western fringe. The love for flowers was manifest in the names of villages. Generally brought from Europe, the names were frequently duplicated in the East and West Reserves — Blumenfeld (field of flowers), Blumenort (place of flowers), Rosengart (garden of roses), Rosenort (place of roses), Schoenfeld (field of beauty), etc. Some names, of course, were new — Schanzenfeld, in honour of Jacob Y. Shantz, was the prettiest village, nestled in a natural grove along the Plum Coulee. As time went on, the beauty of Schanzenfeld was surpassed by other villages through Mennonite beautification programs, and Schanzenfeld became a sort of byword among the villagers.

Although in many ways the Manitoba settlements arose as a continuation of the Russian commonwealth, the limitations of the emerging provincial laws and other imperfections appeared quite early. The laws of land ownership, for instance, worked against the Mennonite plan. Those laws provided for individual entitlement to quarter sections of land when the conditions of homesteading were met. These could not be properly fulfilled

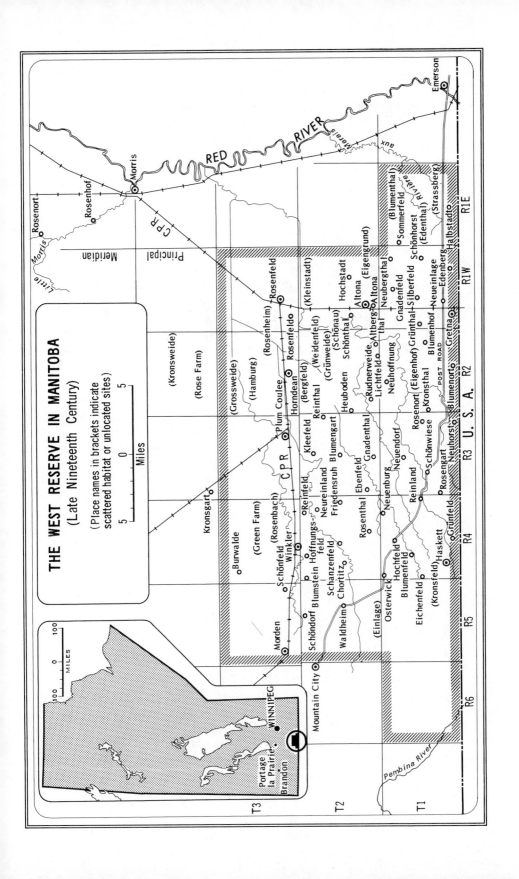

THE WEST RESERVE IN MANITOBA
(Late Nineteenth Century)

(Place names in brackets indicate
scattered habitat or unlocated sites)

Miles
5   0   5

within the village system unless, of course, the Mennonite sense of community was strong enough to negotiate collective owner-ship. Otherwise one could live with neighbours and strip-farm with them on the basis of an understanding until the laws of ownership were changed.[19] For this reason, among others, Shantz had advised against the village system. His counsel was slowly but surely recognized as valid, and one by one the settlers, the most individualistic ones leading the way, abandoned the village system to locate on their own quarter sections, to which they added more land as soon as possible. Among the families moving to the West Reserve a fair number, especially on the eastern end, never settled in village formations at all.

Other obstacles to maintaining the village system were related in the East to marginal lands, as already indicated, and in the West to the advent of the railroads. The Pembina Line, which had built branch lines through Niverville in the East by 1879 and in the West Reserve shortly thereafter, had the option of selling odd-numbered sections of its lands, ten miles on either side of the railway line. In the West alone, 8,640 acres had been sold to Mennonites and others before the sales were temporarily halted in 1880 after the Mennonite leaders had expressed their dissatisfaction over this disruption of the Reserve.

The railway lines, in turn, led to further disruption through the establishment of trading centres. The five in the West Re-serve all became flourishing railway towns (see Table 2).[20] The railway did not pass through the East Reserve, and trading

TABLE 2

TOWNS ARISING ALONG RAILROAD LINE IN WEST RESERVE

1. Rosenfeld	1883
2. Gretna	1883
3. Plum Coulee	1884
4. Winkler	1892
5. Altona	1895

centres such as Steinbach and Grunthal emerged not as "imposi-tions" from the outside but rather as expansions of the most strategically located and trade-minded villages. The grist mills and cheese factories founded in such villages were followed by tanneries, machine shops, lumber yards, and general stores.

In both reserves, however, the trading centres had the effect of breaking down the Mennonite way of isolated self-contained village life. They became the hubs of assimilation with and adjustment to the larger society. However, St. Pierre, Emerson, Winnipeg, and Morden had a clear non-Mennonite identity which Mennonites recognized as foreign and which, consequently, they learned not to adopt. Mennonite towns, on the other hand, could easily incorporate "foreign" elements as part of the total Mennonite culture, as long as this did not happen too rapidly and too completely. Thus, the arrival of German Lutherans, German Catholics, and Jewish businessmen, catering to the Mennonites, represented tolerable influences when compared to the English influence of Morden, the French presence in St. Pierre, or the Ukrainians moving into the southern parts of the East Reserve.

Meanwhile, other external threats to the Canadian Mennonite commonwealth appeared on the horizon in the form of municipal government and public schools. The reserve and village systems, as in Russia, had from the beginning allowed for a good deal of self-government. The village authorities provided for their own schools, common pastures, and streets, and the Reserve attended to the building of essential bridges and roads. The village government was headed by a *Schulze* or mayor and that of the reserve by a reeve or *Oberschulze*. At both levels, ministers and bishops had an important role, especially in the settling of disputes and the setting up of schools and churches. In 1879, however, the provinces passed the municipal act which divided the settled parts of the province into municipalities, with elected councils to run essential services. At first this meant the building of roads and bridges and some weed control, but municipal authority soon extended to where it overlapped with church authority as, for instance, in questions of law and order and the dispensing of charity to the poor.

Some of the Mennonites accepted municipalization while others resisted. The Kleine Gemeinde and Bergthaler bishops in the East were inclined to resist erosion of their autonomy, but since the Hanover Municipality was coterminous with the East Reserve, the problem was lessened by the geography. In the West, the Bergthaler church had among its ranks leaders quite prepared to accept change, while others were more reluctant. Most resistant were the Reinlaender church people in the western part of the West Reserve, especially when they discovered that the whole reserve had been divided into two parts in a way destructive to the commonwealth. The Rhineland Municipality reached beyond the reserve in the west to incorporate English-speaking elements and the Douglas Municipality incorporated non-Mennonite communities up to the Red River at the other end. In due course the two municipalities were joined to become Rhineland and the non-Mennonite areas attached to other municipalities.

Since the Mennonites refused at first to participate in the elections, the first reeves were Anglo-Saxon in Rhineland and German Lutheran in Douglas. Those church members who took part were penalized by the bishops or the church, frequently with excommunication, a rather severe social penalty, inasmuch as the excommunicated were debarred from communication with their own people. Living within the system, however, isolated them from effective association with non-Mennonite people. The penalty of nonconformity, therefore, could be quite a burden, and those who had the courage to invite and withstand it were certainly as heroic as those bishops who, likewise well-intentioned, sought to prevent at all costs the erosion of the commonwealth.

Among the first five Mennonite councillors, four were elected by acclamation. One of them, John Dyck of Osterwick, attempted to take a moderate stand. While accepting the civic position contrary to the church's wish, he sought to act in ways that would not further antagonize it. Responding to his reluctance to act, council not only appointed a replacement for him but also entered a civic prosecution against him. The fine was $40, which the church agreed to pay for him but, according to one source, never did.[21]

At the second election in 1881, Jacob Giesbrecht of Reinland, the largest village in the West Reserve, was elected as reeve. Thereafter the number of voters increased steadily in defiance of the church doctrine and discipline. Those who were excommunicated joined the Lutherans, Baptists, Adventists and other denominations, or waited for more tolerant Mennonite options. Joining other denominations, incidentally, was also a way of rejoining the Mennonites in a social way, because it removed the joiners from the full significance of the church ban and its resulting ostracism. At the same time, it was a way of getting back into the social circle without worrying about getting back into the church.

Another point of tension for the Mennonites was the school system. Although the major clash between the private and public school sectors did not come until some time later, the beginnings of it must not be overlooked. The Mennonites had asked for and obtained from the federal government the permission to set up their own schools, as they had in Russia. Theirs were church-run schools with the emphasis on religious instruction and moral education, in addition to the three R's, all in the German language. The teachers were examined and appointed by the church — 36 in the East Reserve at one time in 1879, one for each village.

Before 1890 the public school system of Manitoba consisted essentially of two sets of officially recognized tax-supported schools, the French Catholic and the Anglo-Saxon Protestant. Mennonite schools could become part of the Protestant system and enjoy a fairer and more adequate tax support base, yet with little interference, simply by registering with the Protestant Board. In the East Reserve such registration took place until 1880, when the more conservative leaders of the West Reserve warned of the dangers and encouraged a united stand against the practice. The public school issue could, however, not be evaded forever, especially after 1890 and the organization of public school districts, which for the Mennonites meant double taxation. However, it also meant the possibility of better schools.

Separation within the Mennonite community and successful defiance of the church by scores of individuals, especially in the West Reserve, was further encouraged by the economic prosperity which came to the community before the end of the century. In 1898 the actual value of property in Rhineland Municipality exceeded six million dollars. Annually, it yielded more than two million bushels of wheat. Up to 100 pounds of butter per family were marketed every year in the Mennonite towns. In material wealth, Rhineland led the 74 municipalities of the province, though it was exceeded in area by at least 14.

The meaning of this prosperity for individual settlers is illustrated by information gathered in 1900. Peter Peters near Winkler had been in the country only 20 years when he owned two sections of land and could buy for cash a steam-threshing outfit costing $3,000. Gerhard Braun near Morden, who began in 1875 with $75, owned 1,600 acres of land, 24 horses and 20 cows, including purebred stallions and bulls. Jacob Siemens of Rosenfeld was worth $50,000. Bernardt Wiebe of Altona accumulated in 25 years what would have taken 100 in Russia. This list was only the beginning. Some, like W. Peters, had even been able to go back to Russia for a visit:

I was in Russia ten years ago on a visit, and I will go again
in a few years more. When I was there before a great many
people were enquiring about this country, and wanted to
know all about it. All my old friends who saw me after 10
years, said I looked healthy, as if this country had been
good to me.[22]

This prosperity enabled the Mennonites to pay off their debts
to the government and to the native Ontario Mennonites, who
had advanced over $50,000 and who agreed to cancel some of
its interest and principal in 1880. The government loan, of which
$90,000 was used, was paid in full in 1892; $24,000 of this was
rebated in consideration of the poorer elements. To the "brethren
in Ontario" Bishop Johann Wiebe addressed the following words
of thanks:

All this which you have done for us humble people, and
what the government has given us in land and money, and
what is still more, that we with our children have the
liberty of exercising our faith according to the teachings of
our Saviour by the providence of God, so moves our hearts,
that we are constrained in praise and thanks to exclaim,
"O Lord, what is man, that thou art mindful of him. Bless
the Lord, O my soul, and forget not all his benefits," which
the great God, the Canadian brethren and the Dominion
Government have bestowed upon thee. The Lord of all grace,
love, and peace be your shield and exceeding great reward.
Amen.[23]

TABLE 3[24]

LOANS ADVANCED TO MANITOBA SETTLERS

RESERVE	FROM ONTARIO MENNONITES*	FROM GOVERNMENT
East†	$23,638.52	$35,329.83
West	26,000.00	54,670.17‡

* Repayable in eight years at six per cent but in 1880 balance of interest
cancelled and principal reduced by 60 per cent.
† Including those transferring to the West.
‡ Francis says "presumably over $60,000," assuming that all of the
$100,000 loan was used. In the repayment, however, a principal of
only $90,000 is mentioned.

The prosperity also produced independence, which further accelerated the breakdown of the villages. By 1891 there were fewer than 25 villages functioning in the East Reserve, breaking up at the rate of one a year. Around 1900 there were not more than 18 complete villages left in the West Reserve.[25] Block settlement also broke down, the Mennonites having sold land to outside speculators. An attempt in 1882 by some leaders to obtain a government ruling, making such sales difficult, had failed. On the fringes of both East and West Reserves, farmers had availed themselves of the opportunity to sell their land if this could be done advantageously. It was also true that the Reserves were opposed by non-Mennonites who saw in them an unfair economic competition.

Recognizing that the Reserves had effectively come to an end, the government passed Orders-in-Council throwing them open for general settlement in 1898.[26] Meanwhile, the Mennonites had themselves been moving out of the Reserves (see Table 4).[27] While the majority of the 15,246 Mennonites then in the province remained in the original settlements, the two Reserves and the Scratching River settlement, hundreds had moved outside, albeit to areas bordering the original settlements. More serious than the population shift, however, was the gradual dissolution of the village system.

TABLE 4

LOCATION OF MENNONITES IN MANITOBA IN 1901

DISTRICTS AND SUBDISTRICTS	MENNONITES*	OTHERS	TOTAL
BRANDON	23	39,282	39,305
LISGAR	10,915	34,037	44,952
Argyle	—	3,869	3,869
Dufferin	—	5,527	5,527
Carman, Village	1	1,438	1,439
Lorne	—	3,286	3,286
Louise	—	4,208	4,208
Pembina	—	3,240	3,240
Manitou, Village	—	617	617
Rhineland†	8,864	1,027	9,891
Plum Coulee, Village†	119	275	394
Gretna, Village†	118	548	666

DISTRICTS AND SUBDISTRICTS	MENNONITES*	OTHERS	TOTAL
Riverside	—	1,601	1,601
Stanley†	1,812	3,357	5,169
Morden, Village	1	1,521	1,522
Turtle Mountain	—	3,523	3,523
MACDONALD	11	37,060	37,071
MARQUETTE	7	34,068	34,075
PROVENCHER	4,267	20,595	24,862
DeSalaberry	—	1,807	1,807
Emerson, Town	9	831	840
Franklin	73	4,617	4,690
Hanover‡	2,373	630	3,003
La Broquerie	468	2,127	2,595
Montcalm	264	2,364	2,628
Morris§	1,007	1,243	2,250
Morris, Town	1	464	465
Ritchot	5	2,035	2,040
St. Boniface	—	585	585
St. Boniface, Town	—	2,019	2,019
Kildonan	—	428	428
Tache	67	1,320	1,387
Unorganized Territory	—	125	125
SELKIRK	10	32,596	32,606
WINNIPEG	13	42,327	42,340
TOTAL	15,246	239,965	255,211

* Hundreds of Manitoba Mennonites moved to the Northwest Territories in 1891–1901.
† West Reserve Area.
‡ East Reserve Area.
§ Scratching River.

After 25 years it was clear that the Manitoba settlement of the Russian Mennonites had not quite turned out the way the leaders had planned it. Solidarity and total community had escaped the Mennonites, though the unique character of their original settlements was not to be erased for a long time. Internally, individualistic tendencies were obviously prepared to sacrifice the Russian Mennonite model of community. The political, economic and social patterns of the surrounding peoples and the Manitoba government proved too forceful to resist.

Canada's further effort to assimilate these immigrants, especially through public schools, proved traumatic for many. Foreign religious influences, including multiple Mennonite intrusions from the United States, brought another round of fragmentation and disintegration into the communities. Some welcomed the influences as the source of a Manitoba awakening which none of the Mennonites should escape. Others viewed them as part of the growing worldly influence against which they were obligated to defend themselves or from which it was their duty to escape.

FOOTNOTES

1. John Webster Grant, *The Church in the Canadian Era* (Toronto: McGraw-Hill Ryerson, 1972). p. 33.

2. See D. G. Creighton, *et al.*, *Minorities, Schools, and Politics* (Toronto: University of Toronto Press, 1969); and Lovell Clark, *The Manitoba School Question: Majority or Minority Rights?* (Toronto: Copp Clark Publishing Company, 1968).

3. N. K. Clifford, "His Dominion: A Vision in Crisis," *Studies in Religion*, II (Spring 1973), pp. 315–26. See also Allan Smith, "Metaphor and Nationality in North America," *Canadian Historical Review*, LI (September 1970), pp. 247–75.

4. Quoted in letter by Peter Dueck, August 12, 1784, in *Gedenkfeier (75) der Mennonitischen Einwanderung in Manitoba, Canada* (Steinbach, Man.: Festkomitee der Mennonitischen Ostreserve, 1949).

5. John Warkentin, "The Mennonite Settlements in Manitoba," Ph.D. dissertation, University of Toronto, 1960, p. 16.

6. *Ibid.*, p. 24.

7. John F. Galbraith, *The Mennonites in Manitoba 1875–1900: A Review of their Coming, their Progress, and their Present Prosperity* (Morden, Man.: The Chronicle Press, 1900), p. 7 (adapted).

8. Canada, *Journal of the House of Commons*, 1886, Appendix 6, p. 34.

9. Jacob Y. Shantz, "From Manitoba," *Herald of Truth*, November, 1875, p. 169.

10. CGC, Philip Wismer, "A Record of Russian Mennonite Aid Committee for Lincoln County, Ontario, 1873–1880," unpublished manuscript, p. 7.

11. *Manitoba Weekly Free Press*, July 10, 1875.

12. Ernst Correll, "The Mennonite Loan . . . ," *Mennonite Quarterly Review*, XX (October 1946), pp. 255–75; and *House of Commons Debates*, February 19, 1875.

13. *House of Commons Debates*, February 26, 1875, pp. 377–91.

14. C. Henry Smith, *The Coming of the Russian Mennonites* (Berne, Ind.: Mennonite Book Concern, 1927), pp. 182–86.

15. *Ibid.*

16. *Ibid.*, pp. 181–86; see also "The Vice-Regal Visit," *Manitoba Free Press*, August 23, 1877, pp. 1–2.

17. Henry W. Barneby, *Life and Labour in the Far, Far West* (London: Cassell & Company, 1884), pp. 358–60.

18. Galbraith, *op. cit.*, p. 35.

19. The Dominion Lands Act was amended in 1876 to enable the Mennonites to settle as they wished, but individual ownership of a contiguous parcel of land was thereby not made easier.

20. E. K. Francis, *In Search of Utopia: The Mennonites in Manitoba* (Altona, Man.: D. W. Friesen & Sons, 1955), pp. 153–60.

21. Galbraith, *op. cit.*, p. 17.

22. *Ibid.*, p. 48.

23. Johann Wiebe, "Address of Thanks from the Mennonite Brethren in Manitoba to their Brethren in Ontario," *Herald of Truth*, XXVII (August 15, 1890).

24. John Warkentin, *op cit.*, p. 213; and Galbraith, *op. cit.*, p. 18.

25. Francis, *op. cit.*, pp. 138–39.

26. East Reserve — August 1, 1898, West Reserve — November 30, 1898, PAC, *Orders-in-Council*, Record Group 2, #1266, June 27, 1898.

27. Canada, *Census of Canada*, 1901, Vol. IV, pp. 26–8, 156–61.

Publishing the Awakening

10. An Awakening at the Centre

*He [John F. Funk] guided the church in gradual changes
down the middle of the road, and is more responsible than
any other one man [teamed with J. S. Coffman] for the
general character of the Mennonite Church . . . between
tradition on the one hand and undirected progress on the
other* — H. S. BENDER.[1]

A s THE nineteenth century drew to a close, Mennonites
in Canada were continuing to move in several directions in search of their future. For some the norm remained
withdrawal and separation, either within established settlements
such as Ontario, or on new frontiers such as the Northwest
Territories. Others, perhaps the majority, were convinced that
Mennonitism in Canada could be saved only through new movements, through spiritual awakenings and aggressive institutional
advances. Such events had previously taken place in other denominations and were beginning among the new Mennonites.
For them the desired destiny seemed to lie along a path which
North American Protestantism as a whole had trod for some
time.

The intention, of course, was not to melt into Protestantism
or other denominations. It is true that adjustments to American
Protestant styles were made in order to enter into evangelistic
and missionary competition on the denominational pattern. However, these adjustments were not made to dissolve the Mennonite

233

way, but to save it. It was believed this could be done if the institution was made palatable for those individuals who had already left, were about to leave, or were tempted to leave. Around the middle of the nineteenth century the Mennonite church as a whole ceased to prosper, and there began a period of conflict and decline which resulted in the loss of many members. This decrease in membership was due to schisms and transfers to other denominations, to the extent that the continuity of the church was threatened:

> The loss was so great that by the end of the nineteenth century the membership of the [Old] Mennonite Church was almost cut in half . . . if the conditions which caused this great decline had been allowed to continue, disaster would have come to the church.[2]

Although estimates vary, there was without a doubt a substantial numerical decline during this period.[3] They numbered in the hundreds or, as some believed, in the thousands. In Ontario this loss was especially felt in the smaller and scattered settlements and where Mennonites had been on the fringe of the church from the beginning. While no exact statistics have been determined, the experiences of two of the larger family groups, who came to inhabit over half of the Mennonite land in Markham Township, are probably typical. They lost about half of their children in the first generation and the percentage rose in the second and third generations (see Table 1).[4]

TABLE 1

NINETEENTH-CENTURY LOSS OF YOUNG PEOPLE FROM THE CHURCH
Illustrated by Two Family Groups in Markham Township

GENERATION	FAMILY GROUP A	FAMILY GROUP B
First	0 per cent	0 per cent
Second	50 " "	45 " "
Third	62 " "	58 " "
Fourth	71 " "	60 " "

The direction necessary to avoid disaster had already been indicated by the "awakenings" or revivalistic movements which had stirred North American religion in the eighteenth and nine-teenth centuries. One by-product of these awakenings had been the growth of voluntary societies to promote evangelical causes of all sorts — Sunday school unions, Bible and tract distribution societies and a wide range of missionary organizations. Another result was the phenomenal growth of the revivalistic denomina-tions, and the subsequent escalation of denominational organiza-tion and programs.[5]

The Mennonites were affected only marginally by the earliest of these awakenings, such as the eighteenth-century emergence of the River Brethren. The larger influence, however, was simply a question of the time required to breach the barriers which habitual separation and withdrawal had erected. Such penetration happened in the mid-1800s and resulted in the emergence of the new Mennonite movements, already identified (see Chapter 6).

At the end of the nineteenth century, the waves set in motion by the various Protestant awakenings and by the activities of the new Mennonites finally and forcefully reached the Mennonite centre. There stood the old Mennonites, the largest Mennonite groups, whose individual congregations and district conferences were not organized into a regular denomination until 1898. As they changed, the fringes were affected and the whole of the North American Mennonite movement was caught up either in accepting change or in resisting it, or both.

The developments among Mennonites in Ontario and Manitoba were strongly influenced by the course of events in the United States, and so that story cannot be overlooked. Indeed, most of the Mennonite organizations or relationships being established or re-established in the latter part of the nineteenth century were continental rather than national in nature. That is, more hap-pened north-south across the border than east-west between Ontario and Manitoba. And thus it would be for years to come. For these reasons the American dimensions of the great awaken-ing must be remembered so that the Canadian story can be better understood.

For those Mennonites ready for an awakening and for change, the preservation and propagation of Mennonitism depended on the adoption of evangelical Protestant models, the vigorous use of the Sunday school, and the promotion of rural, urban, and foreign missions. They also called for a more organized approach to the works of charity both within and without the brotherhood, church publications and colleges, cooperation with voluntary societies of all sorts, and tighter organization of conference offices to go with other programs. Above all, they demanded "protracted meetings" after the style of Charles Finney (1792–1875) and Dwight L. Moody (1837–1899), which made "the pietistic, evangelistic, low-church current of revival" normative in all of North American church life.[6]

In Canada, to be sure, the revivalism of an earlier day had lost some of its momentum, partly because it did not have the rapidly expanding population to work with, partly because the larger denominations had consolidated their programs well. Mennonites, however, remained very much under American influence through their kindred in the States. They were also affected by those sectarian Canadian revivalists who, in the absence of other eager audiences, quickly turned to the ripe fields of malcontent among such groups as the Mennonites.[7]

The new Mennonite movements, such as the Mennonite Brethren in Christ and the General Conference Mennonite Church were, of course, at the forefront of adjusting to Protestantism and of robbing the old Mennonites, though at different levels and in different ways. The Mennonite Brethren in Christ were turned firmly toward an emotional revivalism, climactic conversion, individualistic piety, and strong institutional identity as an expression of the Christian life. The General Conference Mennonites, no less interested in renewal, were, however, more liberally oriented and socially informed. They tended to require a more intellectual examination and presentation of Christian truth. On the other hand, the Conference contained such a great variety within its autonomous ranks that its congregations could not easily be classified.

Both groups of new Mennonites were strong on organization, on uniting widely dispersed congregations in general conferences. The Mennonite Brethren in Christ believed that the missionary cause required a strong superintendency, giving directions from the top. The General Conference Mennonites, on the other hand, undertook nothing which the delegates of the largely independent congregations, meeting in triennial session, had not approved and financially supported. Decisions of General Conference were binding only to those congregations which accepted them and only to the extent that they chose to support them.

The old Mennonite churches were torn in both directions. The Mennonite Brethren in Christ were their most formidable threat in Ontario. By 1897 they had organized seven districts in both

Canada and the United States. They had 79 churches and 176 preaching appointments, a church membership of 3,818 and a Sunday school attendance exceeding 3,000.[8] With the tripling of its membership in the first 25 years, the denomination was threatening to surpass the old Mennonites, both in number of congregations and in members.

Several inherent attractions of the new group greatly aided the successful outreach of its leaders. Not only were the Mennonite Brethren in Christ eliminating the organizational weakness common to all Mennonites through efficient district superintendents, but they were also minimizing the peculiar customs which to open-minded Mennonites had become socially embarrassing. Some of the church's strongest lay leaders, such as Jacob Y. Shantz, were drawn into the movement, partly because of its cultural relationship with the larger community. The Wesleyan-type holiness which was being preached had more to do with correct formulation of doctrine, pious feeling, and spiritual satisfaction, than with nonconformity and nonresistance. The latter were normative for the old Mennonites, though, to be sure, their minimization among the Mennonite Brethren in Christ did not result in their being immediately discarded.

The need among the Mennonite Brethren in Christ for a superior spirituality caused five ministers, including Solomon Eby, and some 80 members to withdraw and form Pentecostal churches at Markham, Vineland, and Kitchener. Those remaining were also convinced that their righteousness exceeded that of other groups. In the words of their historian, "the denomination represented, perhaps not perfection, but surely the best of everything. It had the best givers anywhere. Its foreign missionary effort was second to none. No other church preached a better gospel. Its ministers were among the best to be found, and it represented a work which no other denomination could do."[9] The denominational ego and spiritual arrogance thus expressed was a characteristic by-product of the awakening. But for timid Mennonite people such expressions of self-confidence helped to wash away an apologetic gospel and inferiority feelings, which generations of persecution, isolation and nonconformity had written deep into their souls. To join the Mennonite Brethren in Christ, therefore, or to imitate them, meant the discovery of an identity which was socially more respectable and personally much more satisfying than the old separatist style.

The General Conference, which was similarly expanding its

institutional life and thereby also becoming a convincing denomination, served a similar identity role. Begun in an unpre-
tentious way, the General Conference was becoming a "mighty
movement . . . constantly increasing in power and beneficent
usefulness."[10] It influenced other Mennonites primarily in the
United States, although Canadian delegates from several communities were registered at the triennial assemblies of General
Conference until 1893 (see Table 2).[11]

TABLE 2

CANADIAN REPRESENTATION AT GENERAL CONFERENCE MEETINGS

CONGREGATION	YEARS REPRESENTED
The Twenty	1863, 1866
Waterloo	1861, 1863, 1866, 1872
Stevensville	1884, 1887, 1890, 1893

By the end of the century, the General Conference embraced
61 congregations and 8,789 members. As shown in Table 3,[12] the
General Conference had become a veritable melting pot of North
American Mennonites and represented an attraction for that
reason alone. While the Mennonite Brethren in Christ gave their
best energies to reach beyond the Mennonite borders, the General
Conference was preoccupied with advancing those borders sufficiently to embrace all those in danger of drifting away because of
geographic isolation, cultural differences, and congregational
practices, or doctrinal variance.

Both were being rewarded with success, the Mennonite Brethren in Christ by winning converts and the General Conference by
winning whole congregations. Not only did this Conference
gather up dissenters from the old Mennonites in the old settlements and on the western frontier, but it successfully incorporated in its membership most of the congregations arising from
immigration in the latter half of the nineteenth century from
Switzerland, Prussia, North and South Germany, Holland,
France, and Russia. Indeed, in South Dakota it attracted a congregational unit of dissenting Hutterites.

Theoretically, for missionary purposes the General Conference
included in its plan of expansion all the congregations of North
America. Its union resolutions called for "the hand of fellowship

TABLE 3

ORIGINS OF 61 GENERAL CONFERENCE CONGREGATIONS ATTENDING
THE 1896 SESSION

EUROPEAN ORIGIN	CONGREGATIONS	LOCATIONS OF CONGREGATIONS	MEMBERSHIP
Switzerland	11	Ohio — 2, Indiana — 1, Iowa – 2, Missouri – 1, Kansas — 2, Oklahoma — 1, Oregon — 1, Washington — 1	2,173
South Germany	9	New York — 2, Ohio — 1, Illinois – 1, Iowa — 2, Kansas — 3	1,046
Germany	1	Ontario — 1	25
France	1	Ohio — 1	83
Russia	12	Minnesota — 2, South Dakota — 2, Kansas — 6, Oklahoma — 2	2,024
Prussia	4	Nebraska — 2, Kansas — 2	764
Holland and South Germany	16	Pennsylvania — 15, Ohio — 1	1,819
Russia and South Germany	2	Kansas — 2	362
Russia and Prussia	5	Kansas — 5	493
Total	61		8,789

regardless of minor differences." It overlooked, therefore, all local congregational rules and distinctions as long as they did not conflict with principal doctrines of the faith. It refused to recognize the validity of congregational heresy verdicts and excommunications, unless error could "be established on unequivocal Scripture evidence."[13] It also opposed interference in voluntary transfers from one congregation to another, if these were done only for reasons of dissent against local congregational customs or ordinances.

This assembling of isolated congregations, soon to be extended with the help of "home missionaries" to the Canadian prairies, did not prevent the General Conference from reaching out, but it chose to do so at a somewhat greater distance from home. The readiness of the Mennonite Brethren in Christ to erase Mennonite ethnicity and submerge Mennonite theological identity allowed them a freedom in neighbourhood evangelism which the General Conference did not possess. It is also true, of course, that the General Conference left the neighbourhoods entirely to the congregations.

What the General Conference set out to do was to unite the energies of the congregations for collective action in those regions where congregations could not and should not act alone, and where they would not impinge upon others. Thus, they opened in 1881 a mission station among the Arapahoe Indians in Oklahoma, after thoroughly examining locations in Alaska. At the same time explorations were made about overseas work in cooperation with the Amsterdam Missionary Society. In the end it was decided to work alone, and India was chosen as a mission field.

The influence on the old Mennonites of the General Conference was further enhanced by the coming of the Mennonites from Russia. The majority of immigrant congregations established in the United States in the 1870s had joined the General Conference, and those who did not join formed their own conferences (see Table 4).[14] The Mennonite Brethren in America began with 200 families and the Krimmer Mennonite Brethren with 20 families. A third conference, not institutionally imported from Russia, resulted from early separations of immigrant congregations at Mountain Lake in Minnesota and Henderson in Nebraska. Popularly known as Bruderthaler, after the Mountain Lake congregation, the "Nebraska-Minnesota Conference" went through several name changes and finally became known as the Evangelical Mennonite Brethren. The group very much resembled the Mennonite Brethren in its emphasis except in the form of baptism. The Bruderthaler practised pouring at first and later allowed immersion as an option.[15]

Viewing all of these conference developments and sometimes wooing the Russian groups was John F. Funk, the Mennonite publisher at Elkhart, Indiana. His virtually identical German and English monthly papers had since 1864 been promoting reform among the old Mennonites through Sunday schools, evangelistic meetings, and missionary projects. He had also been promoting a general conference union of all those old Mennonite district conferences, a dozen or more, which in varying degrees of strength tied together the congregations of a given region. His 1864 invitation to this effect read:

TABLE 4

SUMMARY OF MINORITY GROUP CONFERENCES
AMONG THE RUSSIAN MENNONITES

NAME OF CONFERENCE	DATE OF FOUNDING	CONGRE- GATIONS	LOCATION	MEMBERSHIP
Mennonite Brethren	1879	18*	Kansas Nebraska Minnesota South Dakota	1,266*
Krimmer Mennonite Brethren	1880	2	Kansas Nebraska	?
Evangelical Mennonite Brethren†	1889	2	Minnesota Nebraska	?

* 1888 statistics.
† First known as Conference of United Mennonite Brethren in North America and then as Defenseless Mennonite Brethren in Christ. Present name adopted in 1937. Popular name from the beginning was Bruderthaler after the name of the founding Mountain Lake congregation.

> Whereas slight differences exist among the Mennonite brotherhood in different parts of the United States and Canada, both in their views and practices, it would be well to hold a general conference and invite the brethren from all parts of the country, from the east and the west, from the north and the south, that they might meet together and in free interchange of views and opinions become more united and more of one mind.[16]

In most, if not all, instances, the district conferences consisted of periodic meetings of bishops, ministers and deacons. The general conference meeting of the old Mennonite bishops, ministers and deacons, so much desired by Funk, was not easily accomplished. A quarter-century passed before Funk began his earnest campaign to form a general conference. Even then it was not finally accomplished until 1898. Furthermore, at least half of the 16 North American district conferences with a total membership of 25,989 were not fully represented until 1915[17] (see Table 5).[18]

TABLE 5

DISTRICT CONFERENCES OF OLD MENNONITE CHURCHES

NAME	NO. OF CONGRE- GATIONS OR PLACES OF WORSHIP*	MEM- BERS	YEAR FOUNDED
Franconia (Pennsylvania)	21	3,057	c. 1745
Lancaster (Pennsylvania)	76	6,793	c. 1755
Washington County	10	632	c. 1835
Maryland and Franklin County Pennsylvania			
Virginia	26	1,113	c. 1835
Southwestern Pennsylvania	19	1,057	1876
Eastern	19	3,006	1893
Amish Mennonite			
Ohio	22	1,114	1834
Swiss Congregations	2	425	—
Indiana	16	1,187	1854
Indiana Amish Mennonite	9	995	1888
Illinois	6	348	1872
Iowa-Missouri	12	434	1873
Western	30	2,949	1890
Amish Mennonite			
Kansas-Nebraska	16	690	1876
Nebraska and Minnesota (German)	5	156	1889
Ontario	33	1,407	1820
Amish Mennonite (Conservative)	8	626	—
Total		25,989	

* Congregations sometimes embraced more than one place of worship, in which case the latter number is used.

This union might not have happened even at that late date if an inner reorientation had not been achieved in most of the old Mennonite congregations. This adjustment to new ideas happened through the Sunday school and the evangelistic meetings, and their by-products, which Funk promoted so vigorously through his monthly periodicals. His papers were supplemented by a book-publishing program unequalled anywhere in the Mennonite world. In 44 years he published a total of 118 titles, almost equally divided between the English and German languages. Eighty-seven of the titles were original projects and 24 were republished titles from Anabaptist-Mennonite sources and included such mammoth projects as the complete writings of Menno Simons.[19] Funk related his own vision to his experiences in Chicago with Evangelist D. L. Moody, and he offered "a vote of thanks for the influences that he has brought to bear upon the interest of the Mennonite Church."[20] Yet, as indicated in his publications, he was not about to sell out to a militant American revivalism. From his first two volumes on pacifism published during the Civil War[21] to his reprints of Pieter Jansz Twisck countering millennial speculations,[22] Funk sought a conservative path to rejuvenation by means of a strong sensitivity to the Mennonite heritage.

If the criterion of his publication effort be volume alone, Funk's major contribution was in printed material for Sunday schools. By 1892 his six presses were producing about 40,000 copies of the Sunday school materials. Additionally, he published six periodicals with a circulation of 3,000, and 15,000 copies of the annual family almanac.[23]

Among old Mennonites the Sunday school idea gained its earliest and greatest strength in Ontario where, as previously indicated, classes were conducted Sunday afternoons as early as 1841. Progress, however, was slow for half a century due to the solid resistance of the most conservative brethren. Indeed, the Sunday school might have died out altogether after the new Mennonites took most of the progressive-minded people with them, had it not been for the fact that the Sunday school was a way of keeping German-language instruction alive since the public school system had abolished the German *Fibel*. As Historian Harold S. Bender has written:

> Strange as it may seem to us today, one of the chief reasons
> for the organization of the Sunday schools among the
> Mennonites was that the German language might be
> preserved among the rising generation. In the period from
> 1840 to 1890 the Mennonite church was in the midst of a
> serious struggle to maintain the German and avoid
> anglicization. It was a struggle which was hard fought and
> which contributed to the series of old order Mennonite
> schisms which developed in Indiana, Ohio, Ontario,

Pennsylvania, and Virginia from 1872 to 1901. More than one congregation held onto the German language too long in a vain struggle with the English, and either died altogether or lost heavily of its young people.[24]

With the growth of the Sunday school movement in the local congregations came the call for Sunday school conferences to discuss common problems and questions. The first such gathering to be held among the old Mennonites of North America was approved by the semi-annual meeting of Waterloo County clergy in April of 1890 and then held a month later. Soon these conferences were an annual event which, among other things, took statistical note of the progress made. In five years, from 1893 to 1897, Ontario Sunday school enrolment increased from 961 to 2,201.[25]

The addition of Sunday school to the old Mennonite church was an event of revolutionary significance, for it involved the non-ordained people in the work of the church. Noting its great potential, and perhaps fearing it, the bishops and ministers soon insisted that the annual Sunday school conference be held in conjunction with church conference, lest the forces of the church be divided.[26] But the influence of the Sunday school could not be checked. Its contribution to the church was obvious. It helped to hold the young people's interest, increased Bible knowledge, elevated spiritual life, raised moral concerns, especially temperance, created lay-leadership, promoted the missionary movement, and generally enriched church activity and expression.[27]

The Sunday school movement had a powerful ally in the evangelists.[28] Of particular assistance was John S. Coffman, whom John F. Funk had brought to Elkhart from Virginia in 1879 to assist in editorial work.[29] Coffman soon busied himself not only with the *Herald of Truth* but also with the Sunday school materials and with evangelistic work. The result was the formation in 1883 of a Mennonite Evangelism Committee, which within two decades became the mission board of the old Mennonites. The Committee raised funds and sent out evangelists, chief of whom were Coffman and Funk. By 1890 the Committee claimed credit for converting 421 of the 631 members received into the old Mennonite church in that year alone. In 1891 the evangelists were credited with converting 617 of 785 baptismal candidates.[30]

These results did not go unnoticed in Ontario, where evangelistic meetings had been conducted in homes as early as 1885 and where the semi-annual Berlin conference of 1890 noted that "fully

200 young people were standing outside of the church, who should, by some means, be gathered in."[31] Coffman and Funk had already made an appearance in the Waterloo Church earlier that year, and that meeting, as well as reports from the States, commended them highly. The Kitchener *Daily News* reported the event:

> The old Mennonites had a great meeting last evening in the church at the west end of town. The occasion which brought such an immense crowd together was the farewell meeting of visiting brethren Coffman and Funk. Both these gentlemen preached in the English language and gave the most honest advice imaginable to their hearers. Their addresses were earnest and pathetic exhortations to all to come to the Saviour and to follow him the rest of their lives. Anyone who remembers the meeting of this time-honoured church 30 or 40 years ago can hardly believe his eyes or ears at the remarkable change which has taken place in the spirit and style of the services. The meeting would remind one forceably of the old-fashioned Methodist meeting of many years ago when exhortation still had a prominent place in the proceeding of those gatherings.[32]

Coffman came back to Canada in January 1892, and, after his preaching for several weeks in Waterloo, Lincoln and Haldimand counties, 171 persons were baptized and enrolled in the respective churches. With a note of caution from the bishops not to overdo it, Coffman was invited back the following year and this time 146 persons were baptized, most of them in Waterloo County, but some at the Twenty and Markham.[33] The results were soon felt throughout the church. In the words of Burkholder:

> In these two years of evangelistic effort, more than 300 persons were added to the fold and a new era of prosperity for the church in Ontario was begun. From the number converted at this time there have been called four bishops, seven ministers, and five deacons to serve in the Mennonite church, chiefly in Canada.[34]

The Coffman revivals set the pace for the Canadian churches during the next several decades. When he was not available, other evangelists, such as A. D. Wenger from Pennsylvania, were brought in. In a series of meetings at 14 different places in 1904–5

Wenger gained 385 converts.[35] The fruits of the revivals had an immediate invigorating effect on the Sunday school movement, which had prepared the ground for the revivals. It also rejuvenated the young people's Bible movement, which had first emerged in Ontario in 1877. The revivals also led directly to the congregational Bible conferences which were first held in the Weber Church at Strasburg, Ontario, in 1899; to the founding of the Ontario Mennonite Bible School at Berlin in 1907;[36] and in 1907 to the opening of the Danforth city mission in Toronto.[37] Among the leaders participating in all of these developments was Samuel F. Coffman, the evangelist's son who had immigrated into Canada in order to become the minister of Vineland. Though a leader of a different style, the younger Coffman's role in Canadian Mennonite life would soon surpass that of his father.

This "progress" of the Ontario Mennonites did not mean that all the old traditions were suddenly forgotten. On the contrary, to satisfy the conservative and cautious elements, and partly themselves, the clergy passed resolutions in annual conference which ensured the retention of certain customs. Indeed, the steps toward becoming simply another American denomination were sharply curtailed with a new emphasis that moved beyond simplicity in dress to carefully defined uniformity.[38] In parallel decisions, musical instruments were banned.[39] Expensive tombstones and the wearing of badges by pallbearers were disapproved of at funerals.[40] Membership in secret organizations, such as Patrons of Industry, and in labour unions was forbidden,[41] and moustaches were prohibited.[42] Nonpayment of debts meant the forfeiture of church membership.[43] Photography or "having their likeness taken" was forbidden and attendance at the world exhibition in Chicago was discouraged,[44] as was the use of large pictures in Sunday schools.[45] The practice of a head-dress for women was affirmed.[46] Flower-girls at weddings and flowers at funerals were advised against.[47]

On the other hand, the Conference recognized two official languages, German and English,[48] two years after the first Calendar of Appointments had been issued in English. It allowed the various congregations to select their own Sunday school literature,[49] and the districts to decide whether or not fermented or unfermented wine was to be used at communion.[50] Bishops permitted themselves to officiate at weddings of non-church members.[51] A committee was elected to receive volunteer applicants for foreign mission work and one or more annual collections for such work were authorized.[52] The missionary movement, a major by-product of the awakening, was thus officially launched in Ontario.

As the Conference permitted change in some areas, but not in others, certain conflicts and tensions affected the churches, and were intensified in the years to come, when the evangelists themselves became defenders of the status quo in general. John S. Coffman, however, was not one of them. His mind was set on what to him were much bigger questions. He ended up not only promoting liberal education for the church, but also a peace witness in the realm of international politics. In 1896, on the occasion of the opening of the Elkhart Institute, the forerunner of Goshen College, he echoed the larger American social reform and peace movements:

> The occasional World Peace Congresses, in recent years,
> where representatives of all the civilized nations are pleading
> for the "beating of swords into plowshares," for the settling
> of all disputes between nations by arbitration, for the
> reign of universal peace, are but an enlarging of the cloud
> of witnesses which has been hanging as a "man's hand" in
> the religious sky for centuries. May it soon break upon
> the nations with such a deluge of love that will cause even
> bleeding Armenia to look up with joy and say "Behold, at
> last the Prince of Peace reigneth."[53]

Coffman himself was not the founder of the Institute. That credit belongs to H. A. Mumau, another of the men whom Funk had attracted to Elkhart. Still another was G. L. Bender, who pioneered in missionary work in the old Mennonite church. Funk also brought to Elkhart Menno Simons Steiner, another young visionary equal in stature to Coffman. Before his death in 1911 at the age of 45, Steiner had already founded the first old Mennonite city mission in Chicago and served as the first president of the Mennonite Board of Missions and Charities.

Steiner joined Coffman not only in pressing for personal conversions but also in perceiving social implications of the Gospel. In the cities, he said, young women are driven to prostitution because the wages paid by heartless employers "will not keep body and soul together."[54] Steiner urged his readers to "frankly admit the power of sin, and unhesitatingly encourage every good work."[55] Having read the writings of Social Gospel advocates George Herron and Washington Gladden with some enthusiasm, he spoke of the black man as

> a free slave [who] knows no way of ever being emancipated
> . . . many colored people know not virtue . . . they are
> strangers to it. If they were better housed, clothed, fed, and
> educated, they would in one or two generations rise to the
> moral standards of the whites.[56]

With the passage of Coffman and Steiner from centre stage
and with controversy surrounding the aging Bishop Funk, which
resulted in his retirement at the age of 67,[57] leadership passed
to Daniel Kauffman, one of Coffman's 1890 converts. Ordained
a minister in 1892 and bishop in 1896, his gifts as speaker,
teacher, writer and leader soon made him "the outstanding
leader of the old Mennonite Church and for over 40 years he
made an impact on the church not even approached by any
other person."[58] At the age of 33 he became the first moderator
of the old Mennonite General Conference in 1898. In 1908 he
became editor of the *Gospel Herald*, a periodical which continued
Funk's *Herald of Truth*, and which became the official organ of
the new conference. The new generation of leadership, symbolized by Kauffman, reintroduced a conservatism which muted
the progressiveness introduced by Funk, Coffman and Steiner.
It was a conservatism that became allied with theological fundamentalism in its battle against the theological modernism which
raged in early twentieth-century America.[59]

Yet social responsibility had been permanently reawakened.
When famine struck in India in 1899, the old Mennonites, the
General Conference Mennonites, and the Mennonite Brethren
sent relief workers who in turn became missionaries to that
country (see Table 6).[60] Other areas of activity were similarly
stimulated. They founded their colleges almost all at the same
time (see Table 7),[61] and they established their own denominational periodicals, often with a similar content and format (see
Table 8).[62]

The various Mennonite denominations believed themselves to
represent differences significant enough to validate their independent organizations and institutions. But the similarities in
style and emphasis were many. All promoted the Sunday school,
evangelistic meetings, the youth movement and Bible conferences. They even duplicated one another, quite unknowingly
perhaps, in the choice of church names. Zion and Eben-Ezer, for
instance, were used by five and six groups respectively (see
Table 9).[63]

TABLE 6

SOME BEGINNINGS OF FOREIGN MISSIONS
AMONG NORTH AMERICAN MENNONITES

DATE	PLACE	SPONSORING GROUP
1898	Armenia	Mennonite Brethren in Christ
1899	India	(Old) Mennonite Church
1899	India	Mennonite Brethren Church
1900	India	General Conference Mennonite Church
1901	China	Krimmer Mennonite Brethren Church
1901	Nigeria	Mennonite Brethren in Christ
1911	Congo	Congo Inland Mission*
1917	Argentina	(Old) Mennonite Church

* Started by Defenseless Mennonites (Evangelical Mennonite Brethren) and Central Conference Mennonites (GC).

TABLE 7

COLLEGES FOUNDED BY NORTH AMERICAN MENNONITES AROUND 1900

DATE	NAME	PLACE	AFFILIATION*	ANTECEDENTS OR ORIGINAL IDENTITY
1893	Bethel College	Newton, Kansas	GC	Forerunners were Wadsworth (1868), Halstead (1883) Seminaries.
1900	Bluffton College	Bluffton, Ohio	GC	Known as Central Mennonite College from 1900 to 1913.
1903	Goshen College	Goshen, Indiana	OM	Forerunner was Elkhart Institute in 1894.
1903	Freeman Junior College	Freeman, South Dakota	GC	Known at first as South Dakota Mennonite College.
1908	Tabor College	Hillsboro, Kansas	MB	The Mennonite Brethren supported McPherson College of the Church of the Brethren, 1898–1905.
1909	Messiah College	Grantham, Pennsylvania	BC	First known as Messiah Bible School and Missionary Training Home.
1909	Hesston College	Hesston, Kansas	OM	Known first as Western Mennonite School, then as Hesston Academy and Bible School.
1917	Eastern Mennonite College	Harrisonburg, Virginia	OM	Known as Eastern Mennonite School until 1947.

* GC — General Conference Mennonite Church; OM — (Old) Mennonite Church; MB — Mennonite Brethren Church; BC — Brethren in Christ Church.

TABLE 8

PERIODICALS ESTABLISHED BY MENNONITES AROUND 1900

DATE	NAME	LANG-UAGE*	PLACE	AFFILIA-TION†	HISTORY
1878	Gospel Banner	E	Goshen, Indiana (1878–1885), Kitchener, Ont. (after 1885–1909), Elkhart, Indiana (1809–)	MBC	Preceded by Gospel Messenger, a private venture, in 1877.
1882	Christlicher Bundesbote	G	Newton, Kansas	GC	Founded as Religoeser Botschafter, later Christliches Volksblatt, by J. H. Oberholtzer in 1852 and merged with others in 1882.
1884	Zionsbote	G	Hillsboro, Kansas	MB	Founded by Conference.
1893	The Mennonite	E	Quakertown, Pennsylvania	GC	Founded in 1883 in Eastern District from where it moved to Newton, Kansas, in 1902.

1897	Heilsbote	G	Flanagan, Illinois	EMC	Founded by Conference.
1891	Botschafter der Wahrheit	G	Steinbach, Manitoba	CGCM	Founded by John Holdeman.
1903	Messenger of Truth	E	Kansas	CGCM	Founded by Conference.
1908	Gospel Herald	E	Scottdale, Pennsylvania	OM	A merger of Gospel Witness (1905) and Herald of Truth (1864).
1910	Evangelizations-bote	G	Mountain Lake, Minnesota	EMB	Founded by Conference.
1913	Zion's Call	E	Flanagan, Illinois	EMC	Founded by Conference.
1915	Der Wahrheits-freund	G	Chicago, Illinois	KMB	Founded by city missionaries.

* E — English; G — German.
† MBC — Mennonite Brethren in Christ; GC — General Conference Mennonite Church; MB — Mennonite Brethren; EMC — Evangelical Mennonite Church (see next chapter); CGCM — Church of God in Christ Mennonite (Holdeman); OM — (Old) Mennonite Church; EMB — Evangelical Mennonite Brethren; KMB — Krimmer Mennonite Brethren.

TABLE 9

USE OF CONGREGATIONAL NAMES SUCH AS "ZION" AND "EBEN-EZER"

PLACE	CONFERENCE	DATE OF FOUNDING
A. Zion		
Hubbard, Oregon	Amish Mennonite	1883
Goodland, Indiana	General Conference	1895
Dinuba, California	Krimmer Mennonite Brethren	1911
Vestaburg, Michigan	(Old) Mennonite	1914
McPherson, Kansas	Holdeman	c. 1920
B. Eben-Ezer		
Henderson, Nebraska	Evangelical Mennonite Brethren	1882
Stayner, Ontario	Mennonite Brethren in Christ	c. 1900
Dalmeny, Saskatchewan	Mennonite Brethren	1902
Gotebo, Oklahoma	General Conference	1903
Halifax County, Virginia	(Old) Mennonite	1904
Doland, South Dakota	Krimmer Mennonite Brethren	1919

The parallel developments can, of course, be explained by the common heritage, by the common appeal to the Bible as authority, and the common influence from the American religious environment. The mission, the periodicals, and, indeed, most of the emerging institutions in the Mennonite world were now part of the common denominational pattern. Perhaps more than anything else in the Mennonite world the colleges were "a product of the North American environment" and an indicator of the extent to which Protestant models in education as well as in evangelism were becoming normative for the Mennonites.

The years of emergence for the Mennonite colleges followed closely a boom in college building generally. About one-fourth of the nearly 500 colleges in the United States by 1900 were founded, most of them by churches, in the last two decades of the century.[64] The Mennonites in Canada were not without educational visions of their own. For the foreseeable future, educational, literary, and missionary leadership in Ontario and Manitoba would come from the United States, as would also the resistance to all of these endeavours.

FOOTNOTES

1. H. S. Bender, "Funk, John Fretz," *Mennonite Encyclopedia*, II, p. 422.
2. William W. Dean, "John F. Funk and the Mennonite Awakening" (Ph.D. dissertation, University of Iowa, 1965), pp. 42–3. See also: L. J. Heatwole, "The Mennonite Church — Her Past and Present Conditions Compared," *Mennonite Year-Book and Directory*, 1907, p. 14; J. S. Hartzler and Daniel Kauffman, *Mennonite Church History* (Scottdale, Pa.: Mennonite Book and Tract Society, 1905), p. 371.
3. Dean, *op. cit.*, p. 42.
4. Grove compared the date in the Christian Reesor (1747–1806) and Henry Wideman (1757–1810) genealogies (see Family History Bibliographies) with church records. A much more extensive study, but covering a later period, is reported by John A. Hostetler, *The Sociology of Mennonite Evangelism* (Scottdale, Pa.: Herald Press, 1954), p. 287.
5. Sidney S. Mead, "Denominationalism," in *The Lively Experiment: The Shaping of Christianity in America* (New York: Harper & Row, 1963).
6. See Bernard A. Weisberger, *They Gathered at the River* (Boston, 1958).
7. The story of revivalism in Canada before the twentieth century is best reported by S. D. Clark in his study *Church and Sect in Canada* (Toronto: University of Toronto Press, 1948).
8. Everek Richard Storms, *History of the United Missionary Church* (Elkhart, Ind.: Bethel Publishing Company, 1958), p. 281.
9. *Ibid.*, p. 260: "Today members of the United Missionary Church are among the best givers to be found anywhere . . . missionary effort . . . is second to none. Here at home the work of the Church is under the leadership of some 250 ministers, who are among the best to be found anywhere."
10. H. P. Krehbiel, *The History of the General Conference of the Mennonites of North America* (Berne, Ind.: Mennonite Book Concern, 1898), Vol. I, p. 30.
11. *Ibid.*, p. 397ff.
12. The one Ontario congregation was not represented at the 1896 session but it was counted. Krehbiel gives the European origin as North Germany, but the reason for this is not clear, inasmuch as Ontario Mennonites were mainly Swiss Mennonite and South German in origin. The parents of Jacob Krehbiel, the usual delegate, came from the Weierhof.
13. *Ibid.*, p. 57.
14. J. H. Lohrenz, "Mennonite Brethren Church," *Mennonite Encyclopedia*, III, pp. 595–602; H. S. Bender, "Krimmer Mennonite

Brethren," *Mennonite Encyclopedia*, III, pp. 242–45; H. F. Epp, "Evangelical Mennonite Brethren," *Mennonite Encyclopedia*, II, pp. 262–64; E. E. Rupp, "Evangelical Mennonite Church," *Mennonite Encyclopedia*, II, pp. 264–66.

15. H. F. Epp, "Evangelical Mennonite Brethren," *Mennonite Encyclopedia*, II, pp. 262–64.

16. J. S. Hartzler, "John F. Funk," *Gospel Herald* (October 24, 1929), pp. 32–49.

17. Dean, *op. cit.*, p. 238ff.

18. *Mennonite Year-Book and Directory*, 1905, Goshen College, Goshen, Ind., pp. 32–49.

19. John A. Hostetler, *God Uses Ink* (Scottdale, Pa.: Herald Press, 1958), pp. 53–4.

20. Dean, *op. cit.*, p. 62.

21. J. M. Brenneman, *Christianity and War*, and John F. Funk, *Warfare, Its Evils, Our Duty, Addressed to the Mennonite Churches Throughout the United States, and all Others who Sincerely Seek and Love the Truth* (Markham, Ont.: printed at Economist Office, 1863).

22. Robert Friedmann, *Mennonite Piety Through the Centuries* (Goshen, Ind.: Mennonite Historical Society, 1949), pp. 262, 263.

23. Dean, *op. cit.*, p. 238ff.

24. H. S. Bender, "New Life Through the Sunday School," in J. C. Wenger, *The Mennonite Church in America* (Scottdale, Pa.: Herald Press, 1966), p. 167.

25. L. J. Burkholder, *A Brief History of the Mennonites in Ontario* (Markham, Ont.: Mennonite Conference of Ontario, 1935), pp. 157–61.

26. *Ibid.*

27. H. S. Bender, "New Life Through the Sunday School," *op. cit.*, pp. 174–81.

28. Daniel Kauffman, "48 Years in the Mennonite Church: The Rise of Evangelism," *Gospel Herald*, XXXI, 16 (July 21, 1938), p. 1ff. (This was a series of articles ending on September 29, 1938.)

29. Barbara F. Coffman, "John S. Coffman," *Mennonite Encyclopedia*, I, pp. 633–34; and her *His Name was John* (Scottdale, Pa.; Herald Press, 1964); and M. S. Steiner, *John S. Coffman: Mennonite Evangelist* (Spring Grove, Pa.: Mennonite Book & Tract Society, 1904).

30. Dean, *op. cit.*, p. 166.

31. Burkholder, *op. cit.*, p. 162ff.

32. "Great Meeting," *Kitchener Daily News*, Berlin, Ont. (June 10, 1890).

33. Burkholder, *op. cit.*, p. 163.

34. *Ibid.*

35. *Ibid.*, p. 164.

36. *Ibid.*, pp. 164–67.

37. John H. Hess, "Toronto," *Mennonite Encyclopedia*, IV, p. 739.

38. Melvin Gingerich, *Mennonite Attire Throughout Four Centuries* (Breinigsville, Pa.: The Pennsylvania German Society, 1970), pp. 34–5.

39. Semi-Annual Conference Resolutions, Berlin, Ont., April 16, 1886 (CGC).

40. Annual Conference Resolutions, May 19–20, 1892, also 1901.

41. Annual Conference Resolutions, 1895–1898.

42. *Ibid.*

43. Annual Conference Resolutions, May 25–26, 1893.

44. Semi-Annual Conference Resolutions, April 13–14, 1893.

45. *Ibid.*, April 11, 1895.

46. Annual Conference Resolutions, May 23–24, 1901.

47. Semi-Annual Conference Resolutions, April 7, 1904.

48. *Ibid.*, September 8, 1892.

49. Annual Conference Minutes, May 25–26, 1893.

50. *Ibid.*, May 30–31. 1895.

51. *A Manual of Conference Resolutions* (Berlin, 1904), Resolution of 1897, p. 10.

52. *Ibid.*, 1900 and 1904, p. 7.

53. John H. Yoder, "Evangelism and Latin American Politics: A Document," *Gospel Herald*, LXI (January 2, 1973), pp. 4–5.

54. M. S. Steiner, *Pitfalls and Safeguards* (Elkhart, Ind.: 1899), p. 23.

55. *Ibid.*, p. 211. On giving Steiner his rightful place as a leader in the "Mennonite Awakening," see G. F. Hershberger, "The Founding of the Mennonite Central Committee" (unpublished manuscript, n.d., AMC).

56. *Ibid.*, pp. 21–2.

57. H. S. Bender, "John F. Funk," *Mennonite Encyclopedia*, II, p. 423.

58. Paul Erb, "Daniel Kauffman," *Mennonite Encyclopedia*, III, pp. 156–57.

59. Rodney Sawatzky, "The Influence of Fundamentalism on Mennonite Nonresistance, 1908–1944" (M.A. dissertation, University of Minnesota, 1973).

60. S. F. Pannabeck, "Foreign Mennonite Missions," *Mennonite Encyclopedia*, III, pp. 712–17.

61. Most of the data gleaned from Melvin Gingerich, "Colleges," *Mennonite Encyclopedia*, I, pp. 636–39, and *Mennonite Encyclopedia* articles on individual institutions: P. J. Wedel, "Bethel College," I, pp. 304–8; C. H. Smith, "Bluffton College," I, pp. 368–70; J. S. Umble, "Goshen College," II, pp. 546–48; J. D. Unruh, "Freeman Junior College," II, pp. 389–90; W. J. Prieb, "Tabor College," IV, pp. 679–80; H. S. Bender, "Messiah College," III, p. 658; M. Miller, "Hesston College," II, pp. 729–30; H. A. Brunk, "Eastern Mennonite College," II, p. 134.

62. See following articles in *Mennonite Encyclopedia*: J. T. Wiebe,

"Botschaft der Wahrheit," I, p. 396; Cornelius Krahn, "Christlicher Bundesbote," pp. 584–85; Nelson P. Springer, "Der Wahrheitsfreund," IV, p. 870; H. F. Epp, "Evangelizationsbote," II, p. 268; J. A. Huffman, "Gospel Banner," II, p. 550; Paul Erb, "Gospel Herald," II, p. 550; H. S. Bender, "Gospel Tidings," II, p. 550; H. S. Bender, "Gospel Witness," II, p. 551; E. E. Zimmerman, "Heilsbote," II, p. 693; P. G. Hiebert, "Messenger of Truth," III, pp. 657–58; J. N. Smucker and Maynard Shelly, "The Mennonite," III, pp. 587–88; P. H. Berg, "Zionsbote," IV, p. 1033–34.

63. See Zion and Eben-Ezer articles in *Mennonite Encyclopedia*, IV, pp. 1031–33; and II, pp. 135–36, respectively.

64. Melvin Gingerich, "Colleges," *Mennonite Encyclopedia*, I, pp. 636–39.

Martin's—Home of the Old Order

11. The Stand of the Old Order

*The old order groups originated through a reluctance to
accept cultural change and the determination not to adopt
the newer agencies for Christian education and evangelism*
— J. C. WENGER.[1]

THE GREAT awakening of the nineteenth century was not
recognized or accepted as such by great numbers of
Mennonites, who saw in the manifold adjustments little more
than accommodations to strange values and customs. Fearing
the destruction of their cherished traditions, they vigorously
resisted the gospel of progress, which pressed hard on them from
religious and secular sources. The resistance movement became
general throughout North America wherever Mennonites were
found — including Ontario and Manitoba. But most important
for our discussion here is that just as the old Mennonites had
resisted the *new* Mennonite movements earlier in the century,
the defenders of the *old order* among the old Mennonites started
to stand up against their progressive brethren who had been
affected in the great awakening. This old order movement became as universal as the awakenings and renewal movements
had become.

The reluctance to accept change was, and remains, a universal
phenomenon. Times of social transition and rapid secularization,

shifting values and changing styles, have always met with conservative recalcitrance in religious as well as in secular societies.
Those who insisted on preserving the old ways were sometimes in
the majority, sometimes in the minority. Sometimes they remained within the larger movement as an ever-present conservative force; sometimes there occurred a separation when the
conservatives coerced others or were themselves squeezed out.[2]
There are many illustrations of this practice in other movements,
some distant from and others close to the Mennonites. The
Russian Orthodox Church, for instance, had its minority group
known as Old Believers. Similarly, the Jewish tradition has always had its Orthodox rabbis, some of them ultra-orthodox. The
coming of the first great American awakening and the new
Presbyterian movement revealed the residual strength of the old
Presbyterian movement.

During the latter part of the nineteenth century the conservative Quakers, who held ecclesiastical power in Canada,
crossed from their lists hundreds of members who were accepting change much too quickly.[3] Similarly, the fragmented
Brethren in Christ, still known at mid-century as River Brethren
in the United States and as Tunkers in Canada, gave birth to an
old order movement as a reaction to the renewal movement in
that group. From the Brethren in Christ, some groups gravitated
toward the Mennonite Brethren in Christ or to the Pentecostal
Church; others became known as the Yorkers or Old Order
Brethren, the conservative group. The Old Order River Brethren
refused to build churches, to decorate their homes with art or
music, to change even minutely their style of clothing, and to
adopt Sunday school.[4]

The particular points of old order dissent among Mennonites
have, by non-old-order historians, normally been referred to as
"slight differences" or "minor points" — issues of contention only
because of clashing personalities, and which might easily have
been negotiated, given a less egotistic leadership and a more
patient brotherhood.[5] There is some evidence to support this
view, particularly from Goshen-Elkhart, Indiana, where the new,
the old and the old order movements all crystallized successively
in an extended period of congregational conflict. In that controversy the four principal leaders involved were, over a period
of time, either discredited, demoted, defrocked or rejected in
some other way. One of them was Jacob Wisler, the first old
order bishop, after whom those of the order were also called

Wislerites. Bishop Wisler's first opponent, the exuberant and evangelical preacher, Joseph Mohrer, whose Methodist spirit was so offensive to Wisler, left and, like Bishop Jacob Gross at the Twenty in Ontario, joined the Evangelical Church. Then Wisler himself was voted out, at which point the Wislerite old order movement came into being in Indiana. Shortly thereafter Daniel Brenneman, Wisler's chief foe after Mohrer, was also voted out of Conference, which then led, as noted in Chapter 6, to the formulation of the Mennonite Brethren in Christ. John F. Funk, who had pronounced the expulsion order on Wisler, was himself suspended as bishop.[6]

It therefore seems that a good case can be made for blaming the emergence of the various new and old movements on strong stubborn personalities with schismatic tendencies. It also seems true, however, that all or most of these leaders or would-be leaders were struggling quite seriously and, in their own minds, sincerely for the best future for the Mennonite church at such a dynamic time. Wisler was not alone in his doubts about the pervasive changes. There were also doubters among the so-called progressives. While Mohrer, Brenneman, and Funk all saw the need for changes, they were not in agreement on them, nor the speed with, or extent to, which they could be adopted. Funk, for instance, also had a passion for some of the old traditions and was anxious to preserve them. Indeed, he was constantly fluctuating between "conservatism and progress" for "he had a deep historical sense" and was anxious to anchor the church more firmly "in its great historical heritage."[7] And, when by 1900 more progressive men were becoming leaders of the church, he was identified as a definite conservative with an authoritarian bent. The latter trait cost him, in 1902, the office of bishop which he had held for 10 years; it was never restored to him.[8]

Wisler's position must, therefore, not be seen as existing entirely outside of the Mennonite world. Although his conservative rigour moved beyond the general tradition, in many ways he stood squarely within the Mennonite theological and cultural traditions. And he had his immediate sympathizers. After his ouster from the church in 1872, he experienced no difficulty in organizing followings in Indiana, Ohio and Michigan, and through more local leaders in Ontario, Pennsylvania, and Virginia (see Table 1).[9] In all of these regions the old order followers were also known as Wislerites.

Whether the defenders of the old foresaw some of the ultimate-

TABLE 1

SUMMARY OF NINETEENTH-CENTURY OLD ORDER OR WISLERITE DIVISIONS
IN THE (OLD) MENNONITE CHURCH

LOCATION	DATE	LEADER
Indiana-Ohio	1872	Jacob Wisler
Ontario	1889	Abraham Martin
Pennsylvania	1893	Jonas H. Martin
Virginia	1900	Gabriel D. Heatwole

ly undesirable implications of following the new order, or whether they viewed such results as inevitable, is not entirely clear. It was not one of their strengths, or, from their point of view, weaknesses, to clearly articulate their position and to document it, at least not for the outside world. Yet one must suspect that they sensed at least some of the eventual directions of those who chose progressive ways. In any event, some of those directions led the Mennonite Brethren in Christ and other evangelical groups to minimize Jesus' Sermon on the Mount, which for the old order people was the heart of the Scriptures, and to completely neglect the nonresistant position. The new movements also led all the new Mennonites to adopt styles of church architecture and liturgy which militated against the simple and intimate community that since frontier days had characterized the worship of the congregation.

Moreover, the Christianity of the new Mennonites began to express itself increasingly in terms of organization, constitutions, programs, committee meetings, statistics, and reports. By contrast, the old order emphasized attitudes and relationships, a Christianity that was more felt and acted than verbalized. It was one that was local and immediate, one that consisted of people simply living their faith rather than promoting endless layers of church program, which would always be points of contention and whose constant revision might forever sap the spiritual energies of the church. To the old order, the Sunday school had the effect of removing responsibility for Christian instruction from the home. The revival meetings, once begun, required fresh restoration of the spiritual glow, which apparently could not maintain itself apart from revivalism.

It was not foreseen, but perhaps the old order people deeply felt that technological change and innovation would some day produce endless cycles of obsolescence and pollution, that the telephone would some day be man's master as much as his servant, and that the cities would some day prove to be as anti-human as the rural old order thought them to be.

Also unforecast was how the preoccupation of the new movements with "personal salvation, personal ethics, and personal evangelism" would tend to a breakdown of the total community in which the Christian culture was thought to pervade all of life. Increasingly, the new Mennonites would be torn between two worlds with two different cultures, one sacred and one secular, the one requiring personal faithfulness to Christ, the other allowing, sometimes demanding, easy adaptation to the economic, social, educational and political values of surrounding society.[10]

One scholar analysed the changes that came to the Brethren in Christ denomination and their effects on the Christian expression. Martin Schrag observed that, in the period from 1870 to 1910, the Brethren had accepted six major innovations: the Sunday school, revivalism, a church periodical, a formal missionary program, Wesleyan holiness and a church-sponsored educational institution. These six innovations had a profound effect upon the denomination's concept of the church. The early idea of the separated community, an obedient and faithful social organism, was to a large degree replaced by an individualistic understanding of the faith concerned primarily with a salvation that was personalized, an ethic that was internalized, and a community that was millennialized or postponed.[11]

As already indicated, the proponents of the old order had no such sophisticated rationale or explanation of their stance. If they possessed it, it was a deep internal feeling rather than an intellectual analysis or theological statement. In the absence of a clear articulation of what they instinctively felt to be the unwanted direction, the resistance to change and their stubbornness often appeared quite ridiculous, if not stupid. Those unsympathetic with the old order view saw only obstinate bishops, whose clashing personalities and petty power struggles met in silly confrontation over minor issues.

There were many minor issues. If change was to be introduced or resisted, this could be done only at the many specific junctures of human experience. Moreover, the conservatives as well as the progressives created these issues. In fact, the progressives probably created more minor issues than the conservatives. Progressive insistence on accepting change usually preceded the conservative insistence on resisting it. The plain coat, the German language, singing in unison, and the preaching table became issues for the conservatives only after the suit, the English language, four-part singing, and the pulpit had been made into issues by the progressives. Cultural changes of all sorts made their inroads through small innovations. If change was to be resisted, how else could it be done than on the very same terms that it was promoted, namely on fine points or issues, and the little events of everyday life.

On the other hand, both progressives and conservatives were concerned with major issues. Each side was advocating a fundamentally different way of life and approach to religion. Thus, many minor issues really signified major ones. The language issue, for instance, was more than a language issue. In the social context of the times, the changing language really meant the exchanging of total cultural packages. As Harold S. Bender has written:

> The English language was synonymous with "pride," for "pride" had come to mean to many "being like other people," and society was divided into two classes, the "Dutch" and the "English" or worldly people. In sober fact, the German language really was a barrier of considerable efficacy against the encroachment of "world" society and aid to "separation" from it. It should not be forgotten also that the struggle to maintain the German was the common experience of practically all German-language religious groups.[12]

Not all the "awakened" Mennonites viewed the defenders of the old order with disparagement. Daniel Kauffman, for instance, was careful, at least in his later analysis as editor of the *Gospel Herald*, to give credit where credit was due. Differences in approach did not necessarily mean lower or higher degrees of spirituality if different methods were employed or if different degrees of aggressiveness in "bringing the gospel message to the people were manifested." The old leaders, he said, were not lacking in "zeal and loyalty." On the contrary, there were church leaders whose self-sacrificing zeal for the cause led them to make "sacrifices that most of our present-day active workers would refuse to make." In the course of their duty some bishops travelled for hundreds of miles, either on horse-back or by buggy, sometimes on foot; they paid their own expenses. Their only weakness, in the words of Kauffman, was

> ... their tendency to cling to old methods — such as meeting monthly instead of weekly, German preaching, not many night meetings, no revival meetings, etc., etc. — when the changed conditions demanded also a change in at least some of these methods.[13]

In Ontario the old order movement had been in preparation for some time; as early as the 1840s, a small old order group of about 10 Waterloo families, all from Woolwich township, was organized into a separate congregation.[14] These old order families worshipped alternately in each other's homes and elected their ministers and a bishop, Jesse S. Bauman. Their main emphasis, in contrast to the Mennonite churches, was on plainness of clothing, simplicity of life, and greater strictness in discipline. It was difficult, however, to exercise this discipline, since the larger church always provided a way of escape for nonconformists. This entire Woolwich old order group, therefore, migrated to Iowa in the years 1887 and 1888, precisely at the time when the larger old order movement under discussion here was taking shape.

In Waterloo County, as in certain parts of the United States, there had for some time been considerable uneasiness about the changes that were being adopted. These included religious changes such as prayer meetings, protracted evening services, Sunday schools, and the use of English in preaching, as well as social-secular changes: new falling-top buggies, new dress styles, and other such innovations. Not infrequently the religious and the social-secular changes appeared simultaneously.

Although the focus of the Ontario movement was in Waterloo County, there were actually three centres of dissent, of which the bishops were the leaders or for which they became the rallying points. They were Christian Gayman of Cayuga, bishop of the Niagara district since 1875; Christian Reesor, bishop of the Markham district since 1867; and Abraham Martin, bishop since 1867 of the Woolwich sub-district, one of the three sub-districts in Waterloo.[15]

Bishop Gayman had been a problem to his colleagues for some time. Meeting in conference, they supported that part of his congregation which had found him "disobedient."[16] Since Gayman and his followers were later found in the old order camp, one may speculate that it had to do with differences over such issues as language, Sunday school, and protracted meetings. Thereafter, however, the differences in the church came up at almost every annual and semi-annual conference. Repeatedly it was resolved not to divide the church but to attempt to follow through on "a peace resolution" formulated in 1882 and reaffirmed in 1885.[17] Reconciliation at the time concerned not only differences between the old Mennonites and the old order Mennonites but also those between the old Mennonites and the new Mennonites. The church was being pulled very much in two directions. The old Mennonites, flanked by new Mennonites and old order Mennonites, attempted to hold things together.

The departure of members in both directions usually relieved tensions only partially and only temporarily, because not all those who empathized with the old order or with the new order saw fit to leave the church. They hoped to move the church in their direction from within. Thus, the conflict between the old and the new remained. Though the conflict receded whenever people at the extremes of old and new thought left the church, it tended to resurface again and again.

One immediate cause of the division that came to Waterloo County in 1889 seems to have been the protracted meetings conducted in 1885 in a home just north of Waterloo, which resulted in 30 applications for baptism. Most of these converts lived in the district over which Bishop Abraham Martin had the oversight. Martin declined to instruct and baptize the applicants because they were coming to him under the influence of these evening meetings. They then went to Bishop Elias Weber who baptized them at Breslau.[18]

This incorporation of a group of young people into the church by one bishop, after they had been rejected by another bishop, proved to be a major source of irritation. It had happened once before in 1871 when Bishop Hagey refused and Bishop John Lapp consented to baptize those converts prepared for baptism by a revivalist. Such acute differences of opinion could not be held together forever, and in the heated discussions of the semi-annual conference in Berlin in September of 1887, Bishop Abraham W. Martin, supported by a number of ministers and sympathizers, withdrew. In the spring of 1888, Bishop Martin held a separate conference at the Martin meeting-house between Waterloo and St. Jacobs. Four ministers and six deacons stood with him.

Apparently, however, the efforts at reconciliation continued until the full and final break in the spring of 1889, which was precipitated by confusion and disagreement over the dates of the annual conference. The traditional date for meeting was the last Friday in May. That year, however, May had five Fridays, the last of them preceded on Thursday by Ascension Day, traditionally a day on which church services were held. The result was that two conferences were held, one on the fourth Friday and the second on the fifth Friday, both at the Wideman meeting-house in Markham. The first was attended by Bishops Amos Cressman (Wilmot), Elias E. Weber (Waterloo), and Daniel Wismer (ordained in Kansas, no particular field of assignment), all progressives, and the second by Bishops Christian Reesor, Abraham Martin, and Christian Gayman, conservatives. Both sets of bishops were supported by ministers and deacons, with the majority siding with the former group. Counselling the conservatives, and assisting them in their organization, was Christian Schumm, an associate of Daniel Wismer.[19]

The religious division which resulted did not cut across geographic boundaries. In the Markham and Niagara areas, the majority of the people still left after the Evangelicals, the Mennonite Brethren in Christ, and the Pentecostals had reaped their share, sided with the bishops. In Waterloo County, most of the people supporting Bishop Martin were in the township of Woolwich, north of Waterloo.

Since the defenders of the old order were largely in the northern part of Waterloo County (only about 30 families in Woolwich stayed with the old Mennonites) they were referred to in Pennsylvania Dutch as "die Overa" (the Uppers) and those to the south, east and west, were called "die Unera" (the Lowers). The northerners were also called old order or Woolwichers, while the others preferred to call themselves "of the Mennonite Conference of Ontario," though their popular designation remained old Mennonites for a long time.[20]

Neither group ever officially accepted the name which popular usage attached to them. Both groups, the old Mennonites and the old order Mennonites, continued to use the same name, *Mennoniten Gemeinde*, in their respective calendars of appointments. Both continued the same sequential dating of those calendars, which had begun around 1834. Yet, both groups could not avoid living with, and to a certain extent even accepting, the popular names. In the plethora of Mennonite groups, some commonly accepted identifications were necessary. Slowly but surely the names Old Mennonite and Old Order Mennonite became part of the denominational literature that originated in the United States. As time went on the "Old" of the Old Mennonite was placed in brackets, as (Old) Mennonite. In due course it was dropped in favour of the simple Mennonite Church.[21] In this history, however, the Old and Old Order names will continue to be used for reasons of clarity in identification.

At the time of the Old Order break it was still customary to look upon the membership under a single bishop as a single congregation. Even though a number of meeting-houses might be used, they would not all be used on a single Sunday. Most had meetings every two weeks and some only once a month. The larger number of meeting-houses prevented geographic discrimination against the families farther away from the centre but the fewer number of services prevented the break-up of the congregation into units much too small to be meaningful. It also permitted a limited number of ministers and deacons to work together as teams. The meeting-houses used by the Old Order after the break in the three regions are indicated in Table 2.[22]

The vacancy of some meeting-houses on some Sundays raised the issue of their use by others, notably those (Old) Mennonites in the area who had not gone along with the Old Order or who, having gone along at first, soon had a change of heart and left. In Woolwich there were at least 30 such families. At first they conducted their worship services and Sunday school in an old farm house north of Conestoga. Finding the space too crowded and inconvenient, they soon asked for permission to use the Conestoga Old Order meeting-house, but in vain. Since the (Old) Mennonite group persisted, the Old Order people finally decided in 1892 to give up their building and to build their own half a mile away.

One of the problems which the Old Order groups had was to maintain unanimity of viewpoint on, and uniformity of practice in, the new disciplines and rules of simplicity and orthodoxy that had been adopted. The more specific and detailed these rules were, the greater the potential for division and dissension. The Old Order groups were therefore given even more to internal dissension than some of the new more progressive groups who had accepted change and adjustment.

Those who became dissatisfied went in one of two directions.

TABLE 2

OLD ORDER MEETING-HOUSES IN ONTARIO AFTER 1889

NAME	DATE CONSTRUCTED	LOCATION	1906 MEMBERSHIP
A. WATERLOO COUNTY			
Martin's	1830	Waterloo Township	160
Conestoga	1848–1892 1894†	Woolwich Township	60
West Woolwich	1853	Woolwich Township	60
North Woolwich	1872	Woolwich Township	60
South Peel	1901	Peel Township	30
B. YORK COUNTY			
Risser	1848	Markham Township ⎫	
Cedar Grove	1867	Markham Township ⎬	100
Wideman	1848	Markham Township ⎭	
Almira	1860	Markham Township	?*
C. ONTARIO COUNTY			
Altona	1852	Pickering Township	?*
D. WELLAND COUNTY			
Bertie	1873	Bertie Township	3
E. HALDIMAND COUNTY			
Cayuga	1873	South Cayuga	20
Rainham	1850	Rainham Township	?*
F. HURON COUNTY			
Stanley	1887	Stanley Township	?*
G. LINCOLN COUNTY			
Moyers	1840	Clinton Township	15

* Indicates unknown memberships. It is very likely that they were very small since they eventually disappeared.
† "Surrendered" to (Old) Mennonites in 1892. Old Order built in 1894 on nearby land donated by George Hoffman.

The more progressive-minded Old Order people tended to migrate in their church affiliation toward the (Old) Mennonites. Already in the 1890s the congregation at Conestoga (later at St. Jacobs) was swelling, while a new one was emerging at Floradale, where a meeting-house was constructed in 1895. By 1907 the Woolwich (Old) Mennonites were ready for their first bishop, who was Abraham Gingerich.[23]

The more conservative-minded Old Order, however, tended to split off into ever smaller factions, sometimes migrating to maintain the separation, sometimes only using stricter discipline to maintain their cause. Thus the group that moved from Ontario to Iowa ended up going from there to Michigan, Pennsylvania, and Alberta.[24]

In Waterloo County the church survived a serious 1908 controversy over a government drainage ditch through central Woolwich, the factions aggressively promoting it and those opposing it being about equally divided. The resulting tensions, however, led to a series of breaks for other reasons. Preacher Daniel M. Brubacher supported his married son who had been charged with and excommunicated for "disorderly" affection toward an unmarried girl. Consequently, the new Old Order bishop, Paul Martin, who succeeded Abraham Martin in 1902, excommunicated Daniel Brubacher, who promptly proceeded to conduct his own services with the support of a number of families.

About 15 years later the Brubacher group affiliated with the David Martin group at Wallenstein, which had begun separate services. David B. Martin was a preacher and his son David W. Martin a deacon. The group elected Daniel Brubacher as bishop, his son Menno became a minister, and a meeting-house was built for what became known as the David Martin Old Order group. A few years later Daniel Brubacher "went separate again" because the rules of the David Martins were too strict. The Martins elected Enoch Horst as bishop, but he too left over the question of the ban and excommunication. At that point David W. Martin became bishop and was able thereafter to hold the group together, though it increased only by the baptism of direct descendants.[25]

The net effect of all the separations that occurred in the Ontario Mennonite churches in the nineteenth century was the production of many small congregational units. In the three conference groups — Mennonite Brethren in Christ, (Old) Mennonite Conference of Ontario, and Old Order Mennonites — only four congregations (single places of meeting) had 100 members

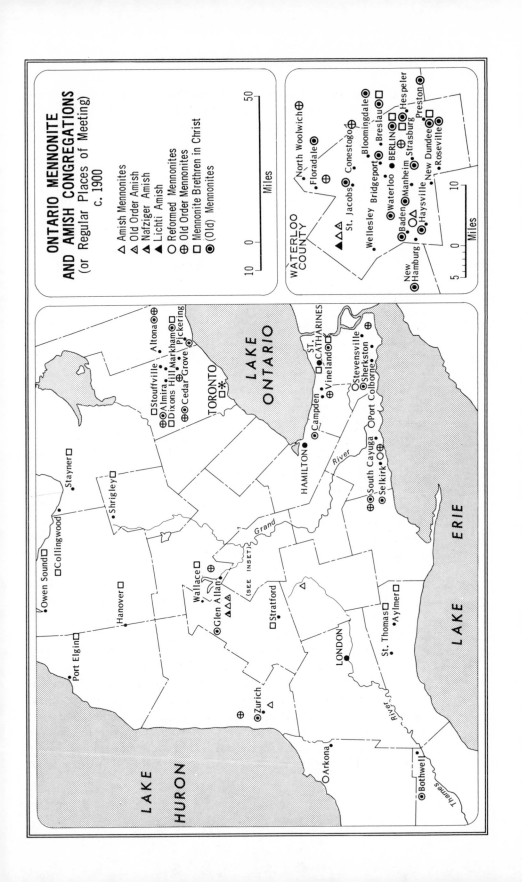

ONTARIO MENNONITE AND AMISH CONGREGATIONS
(or Regular Places of Meeting)
c. 1900

△ Amish Mennonites
△ Old Order Amish
▲ Nafziger Amish
▲ Lichti Amish
○ Reformed Mennonites
⊕ Old Order Mennonites
☐ Mennonite Brethren in Christ
◉ (Old) Mennonites

Miles

WATERLOO COUNTY

North Woolwich
Floradale
St. Jacobs
Conestogo
Bloomingdale
Hespeler
Wellesley
Bridgeport
Breslau
Preston
Waterloo
BERLIN
Haysville
Manheim
Strasburg
New Dundee
Baden
Roseville
New Hamburg

Miles

LAKE HURON

Owen Sound
Collingwood
Stayner
Shrigley
Hanover
Port Elgin
Wallace
Glen Allan
Stratford
Zurich
Arkona
Bothwell
LONDON
St. Thomas
Aylmer

LAKE ONTARIO

Stouffville
Altona
Almira
Dixons Hill
Markham
Pickering
Cedar Grove
TORONTO

Campden
Vineland
ST. CATHARINES
Stevensville
Sherkston
Port Colborne
South Cayuga
Selkirk
HAMILTON

Grand River
Thames River

LAKE ERIE

or more and the majority of the preaching places had less than 50 (for comparisons see Table 3).[26] The 500 Markham area Mennonites, for instance, were distributed over at least 17 congregational units or preaching places.

TABLE 3

COMPARATIVE STATISTICS FOR THREE MAIN MENNONITE GROUPS
IN ONTARIO 1905–06*

GROUP	NO. OF CONGREGATIONS OR PREACHING PLACES	NO. OF MEMBERS
Mennonite Brethren in Christ	48	1,518
(Old) Mennonites	29	1,353
Old Order Mennonites	16	508

* Old Order statistics for 1906 (first year available); others for 1905.

While the Mennonite Brethren in Christ and (Old) Mennonites rearranged their churches to include a pulpit and horizontally arranged Protestant pews, the old order maintained the plain meeting-houses, with benches arranged in a U-pattern, with the preaching table placed in its neck. The Mennonite Brethren in Christ deliberately introduced musical instruments; the Old Order deliberately kept them out.

Thus it was in every area of life. In the new order the weddings were transferred to the church and considerably shortened, though in some ways made more elaborate. For the old order, weddings and flowerless funerals were all-day events, with three-hour ceremonies followed by meals and visiting. For the old order the social circle and the institution of visiting was definitely limited to the community — to friends, relatives, and neighbours, on Sunday afternoons and at barn-raisings and quiltings. The mobility of the new order, on the other hand, introduced Mennonites to conventions, fairs and marketplaces in small and large cities, to the professions and even to public life.

The old order championed the rural way of life, without the new machinery and technology. Farming was done with horses and road transportation limited to buggies. Homes remained simple without curtains, pictures or wallpaper. Clothes stayed plain, homemade, and usually dark, and were not adorned with jewellery. The pantries and cellars, on the other hand, would be fanciful with hundreds of fruit jars reflecting both the industry and creativity of the home.

The old order resisted education beyond the elementary school level, since it contributed nothing useful or necessary to the rural way of life. All frills and luxuries were avoided, while a premium was placed on productive work during weekends and abundant socializing on Sundays and other church holidays. An existence in many ways austere and limited, the old order way of life none the less produced a people unusually industrious and temperate, peace-loving and tranquil, benevolent and kind, well-mannered and pious. All involvement with the outside world was avoided, and this became possible in an economy nearly self-sufficient and a community both closed and content.

Meanwhile, the struggle of "the new against the old" and "the old against the new" had surfaced also among the Amish of North America, whose settlements by the end of the nineteenth century had spread from Pennsylvania as far west as Oregon, with strong concentrations in Indiana, Illinois, Nebraska, and Kansas.[27] A very brave attempt, unprecedented in North American Mennonite circles, to reconcile the emerging differences was made in a series of Amish general conferences, called *Diener-Versammlungen*, over a period of 16 years, but with only partial success.[28] Again, the development of the Amish community in the United States had immediate and long-term implications for the Amish in Canada, and therefore the American background is reported once again.

The discussions of the Diener-Versammlungen, covering a wide range of issues, began with baptismal form and the membership status of those Amish who were accepting government pensions for service in the civil war for which service repentance had already been made. The Versammlungen found church membership and military pensions to be incompatible. They also decided that members should not participate in the erection of memorial monuments to soldiers; that political activity and public office, either judicial or military, requiring the use of force, was to be prohibited; and that attendance at political meetings, flag-pole raisings and even voting was to be discouraged as being unseemly for a nonresistant people. Unequal business alliances were discouraged and business contacts tabooed, including the holding of bank stock and the managing of a store, post office or express office. Other objectionable innovations were lightning rods, lotteries, photographs, insurance and large meeting-houses.[29]

The Diener-Versammlung did not bring complete accord on a number of questions, and so after 1878 the Amish tended to go in three directions. The conservative elements retained all the old traditions and practices and became known as the Old Order Amish, or Conservative Amish if they were less orthodox than the Old Order. There was no complete unanimity among the "progressives" either and they, therefore, also tended in different directions, those same directions which have been observed among the Swiss Mennonites (see comparisons in Table 4).[30]

Nor were the conservative Amish unanimous in their conservatism. One group of congregations, which in 1910 formed the Conservative Amish Mennonite Conference, saw themselves as standing "more closely together in the work of the Lord" somewhere between the more progressive and the Old Order Amish churches.[31] The Old Order Amish, who eventually spread to over 50 settlements in North America with over 225 church districts, each with about 75 baptized members, never organized themselves into conferences. They did, however, maintain an informal relationship because of their similar nonconformist attitudes and resistance to social changes, their strictly rural way of life, their horse-and-buggy culture, their plain dress and their use of a peculiar German dialect. Their nonconformity has been described as follows:

> Among the culture traits which the Old Order Amish have resisted are the following: buttons on coats and vests, wearing of a mustache, men's suspenders in various forms, hats for women, "store" clothes, talon fasteners, "bosom" shirts, detachable collars, modern styles of underwear, patterned dress goods, fine shoes, low shoes, ladies' high-heeled shoes, parted hair, parted hair except in the center, meeting-houses, four-part singing, hymnbooks with printed musical notes, laymen's use of Bibles at preaching services, Sunday schools, revival meetings, high-school education, central heating, carpets, window curtains, storm windows and screens, writing desks, upholstered furniture, brightly painted farm machinery, painted wagons, top-buggies, "falling" buggy tops, buggy springs, rubber-tired buggies, buggy steps, fancy buggies, whipsockets, dashboards, sausage grinders, lawn mowers, bicycles, windmills, sewing machines, steam threshers, tractors with tires, tractors for field work, tractors at all, elaborately decorated harness, musical instruments, telephones, electricity, automobiles, and many others.[32]

TABLE 4

AMISH MENNONITE GROUPS
ARISING IN THE GREAT AWAKENING

NAME AND LOCATION	HISTORY	EVENTUAL AFFILIATION
Defenseless Mennonite Church — Indiana, Ohio, Illinois	Emerged as Egli (after founder) Amish in 1864 but met in regular conference only after 1895 and later known as Evangelical Mennonite Church.	A 1898 breakaway group, the Missionary Association, eventually affiliated with Mennonite Brethren in Christ.
Central Illinois Mennonite Conference	Emerged in stages after 1872, but organized with 12 congregations in 1909.	General Conference Mennonite Church.
Indiana-Michigan Amish Mennonite Conference	Emerged 1889–1919.	(Old) Mennonite Church.
Western Amish (Mennonite Conference (Kansas-Nebraska)	Emerged 1890–1920.	(Old) Mennonite Church.
Eastern Amish Mennonite Conference (Pennsylvania)	Emerged 1893–1925.	(Old) Mennonite Church.

Note: The progressive Amish of Ontario followed the route of the latter three groups, though at a much later date.

The clash between Amish progressives, also called Church-Amish, and the conservatives, also called House-Amish, did not leave the Canadian communities in Ontario untouched. Barely had the Amish migration to Ontario come to an end around 1870 and the original five communities been shaped when the quarrel erupted. As Orland Gingerich, the group's historian, has written:

> The changes which came to the Amish world on the outside
> and on the inside were not accepted by all, at least not
> without some complaint and a great deal of internal
> dissatisfaction. New styles of clothing and grooming, the
> increasing use of the English language, and differing
> approaches to worship eventually led to a serious gap
> between the more progressive and more conservative of the
> Church.[33]

The more serious differences arose in regard to so-called worship issues, which included church music, Sunday school, and, most importantly of all, meeting-houses. There were several reasons why some wanted meeting-houses. The houses, or even barns, tended to be too small and impractical as meeting places for a variety of reasons. Besides, church buildings were becoming the fashion not only in society generally but also among the Mennonites, whom some Amish were inclined to imitate. The conservatives resisted, precisely for reasons of fashion and the tendency of the Church-Amish to place more importance on buildings than on the gathering of people. Modestly, the progressives referred to their buildings as *Versammlungs-haeuser* (meeting-houses or places of gathering), but conservative names for progressive symbols could not accommodate all the defenders of the old order.

During the period from 1883 to 1886, all the original five settlement-congregations began to worship in meeting-houses (see Table 5).[34] They were plain to be sure and, with one exception, of frame construction. Sheds for the parking of horses and buggies were also erected. The meeting-houses did not immediately lead to such innovations as characterized the Mennonite awakenings — evening services, protracted meetings, Sunday school, etc. In that sense, the progressive Amish of Ontario could be compared not with the progressive Mennonites of Ontario but with the conservatives. In cultural accommodation, the progressive and conservative Amish remained a decade or two "behind"

TABLE 5

SUMMARY OF ORIGINAL AMISH SETTLEMENT-CONGREGATIONS AND EARLY CHURCH BUILDINGS

NAME	DATE OF FOUNDING	COUNTY LOCATION	ORIGIN	FIRST BISHOPS	DATE OF CHURCH BUILDING
Wilmot*	1824	Waterloo	Pennsylvania Europe	Peter Nafziger (1825–1831) John Oesch (1831–1848)	1884 1885 (St. Agatha)
East Zorra	1837	Oxford Perth	Europe Wilmot	Joseph Ruby (1853–1897)	1883
Hay	1848	Huron	Wilmot East Zorra	John Oesch (1818–1850)	1885
Wellesley	1859	Waterloo	Europe Wilmot	John Jantzi (1859–1881)	1886
Mornington	1874	Perth	Europe Wilmot East Zorra	Joseph Gerber (1875–1893)	1886

* Names also indicate township location, since Amish settlements and congregations were known by the townships in which they resided.

their progressive and conservative Mennonite cousins, respectively.

There was one exception to the above, namely the Hay Amish congregation, where Peter Ropp, a Mennonite minister from the Ontario Mennonite Conference congregation in Michigan, used his influence with his father-in-law, John Gascho, the Hay minister, to arrange evening meetings. Ropp's evangelistic meetings resulted in 19 conversions. When the young men in the group refused to wear traditional dress for baptism, a real congregational crisis developed. In the end a Mennonite bishop from Waterloo County baptized the group of new converts and with 50 additional progressive Amish members organized a new Mennonite congregation at Zurich, thus dividing the Hay group.

Although there was opposition to Versammlungs-Haeuser in the East Zorra, Wilmot and Hay congregations, no permanent rift resulted, partly because of wise leadership. Such, however, was not the case in Mornington and Wellesley, where the ordained ministerial leaders were of different opinions. Thus it happened that in those two situations the "House Amish" who insisted on the old ways came to be known as the Old Order Amish. They were also known as "Holmsers" after Holmes County, Ohio, from which the bishop came to serve them until 1891 when they finally "made their own bishops" in each of the two Old Order congregations, Christian L. Kuepfer for Mornington and Peter Jantzi for Wellesley.

The departure of the Old Order, however, did not leave the Mornington and Wellesley congregations without bothersome conservatives. On the contrary, as progress opened the door to other innovations, such as young people's singing and music schools, four-part harmony, English songs, and Sunday School around 1900, the congregations divided once more (see Table 6).[35] Nicholas Nafziger led some conservatives out of the Mornington congregation in 1903, but although they built their own meeting-house they did not otherwise innovate. The same was true in 1911 in Wellesley where Bishop Jacob Lichti vowed "to leave the church precisely as he had received it."[36] For him this meant separating from the main group and building a new, though more conservative, meeting-house. Others escaped the modernizations and tensions by migrating to various Amish communities in such far-flung places as Michigan, Minnesota, Nebraska, Colorado, Virginia, Oregon, New York or western Canada.[37]

TABLE 6

DIVISIONS IN MORNINGTON AND WELLESLEY CONGREGATIONS

DATE	MORNINGTON	WELLESLEY
1886	Old Order "house churches"	Old Order "house churches"
1903	Nafziger congregation	
1911		Lichti congregation

In one way the various Amish church families, however, refused to be separated from one another, namely in their program of mutual aid. The Fire and Storm Aid Union, which had been formed in 1872, grew and continued its service to the entire Amish community under the leadership of a broadly representative board of directors. Whenever human need called the neighbours together the many organizational fragmentations tended to be reversed. Indeed, some day it would be not only mutual aid within the community but also relief action in the international arena which would bring the fragmented Amish and Mennonites into closer fellowship again. Meanwhile, the conflicts between the old ways and new movements surfaced also in Manitoba, and there too they left lasting structural scars on the Mennonite body.

FOOTNOTES

1. J. C. Wenger, "Old Order Mennonites," *Mennonite Encyclopedia*, IV, pp. 47–9.
2. E. K. Francis, "Tradition and Progress Among the Mennonites in Manitoba," *Mennonite Quarterly Review*, XXIV (October 1950), pp. 312–38.
3. As told to the author by Quakers in Conference at Grindstone Island, Portland, Ontario, August 12, 1972.
4. Arthur W. Climenhaga, *History of the Brethren in Christ Church* (Napanee, Ind.: Evangelical Publishing House, 1942), pp. 127–31.
5. See C. N. Hostetter, Jr., "Brethren in Christ," *Mennonite Encyclopedia*, I, pp. 424–25; Climenhaga, *op. cit.*, p. 127ff.
6. The successive controversies are detailed by Helen K. Gates *et al.*, *Bless the Lord, O My Soul: A Biography of Bishop John Fretz Funk, 1835–1930* (Scottdale, Pa.: Herald Press, 1964), pp. 146–

87; John C. Wenger, "Old Order Mennonites," *op. cit.* See also William War Dean, "John F. Funk and the Mennonite Great Awakening" (Ph.D. dissertation, University of Iowa, 1965), especially "The Expulsion of Daniel Brenneman," p. 281ff.

7. H. S. Bender, "John Fretz Funk," *Mennonite Encyclopedia*, II, p. 122.

8. Gates, *op. cit.*, pp. 175–87. See also A. C. Kolb, "John Fretz Funk, 1835–1930: An Appreciation II," *Mennonite Quarterly Review*, VI (October 1932), pp. 250–63.

9. Wenger, "Old Order Mennonites," *op. cit.*, p. 47.

10. See Martin Schrag, "The Brethren in Christ Attitude Toward the World" (Ph.D. dissertation, Temple University, 1967), 388 pp. This "historical study of the movement from separation to an increasing acceptance of American society" in the Brethren in Christ Church has relevance also to the new Mennonite movements, not least of all because the change of orientation in the various Anabaptist renewal groups happened approximately at the same time.

11. *Ibid.*, pp. 295–97.

12. H. S. Bender, "New Life Through the Sunday School," in J. C. Wenger, *The Mennonite Church in America* (Scottdale, Pa.: Herald Press, 1966), p. 167.

13. Daniel Kauffman, "48 Years in the Mennonite Church: The Rise of Evangelism," *Gospel Herald*, XXXI (July 21, 1938), p. 1ff. See also Mary Martin, "The Church of Christ and the Old Order Mennonites in Waterloo County" (unpublished manuscript, University of Waterloo, 1970), 47 pp. (CGC).

14. Isaac G. Martin, *The Story of Waterloo-Markham Mennonite Conference*, p. 9.

15. See Table 2, Chapter 6.

16. *Semi-Annual Conference Minutes,* Berlin, September 12, 1884. Nature of disobedience not specified. Minutes of April 18, 1884, and September 14, 1883, not available (CGC).

17. See L. J. Burkholder. *A Brief History of the Mennonites in Ontario* (Markham: Mennonite Conference of Ontario, 1935), p. 198.

18. Isaac G. Martin, *op. cit.*, p. 4.

19. Burkholder, *op. cit.*, pp. 199–200.

20. Isaac G. Martin, *op. cit.*, p. 5.

21. H. S. Bender, "Mennonite Church," *Mennonite Encyclopedia*, III, pp. 611–16. The designation "Mennonite Church" died slowly, however, because there were too many Mennonite Church families to make the identification of any one of them acceptable or practical without at least one adjective in the name.

22. Isaac G. Martin, *op. cit.*, pp. 5–6. For membership figures see *Mennonite Yearbook and Directory*, 1906, p. 57.

23. Isaac G. Martin, *op. cit.*, p. 6.
24. *Ibid.*, pp. 9–10.
25. *Ibid.*, pp. 9–10. These events regarding David Martin transpired between 1917 and 1923, somewhat ahead of our story, but they are best told here. A major later division occurred in 1939 (see Volume II).
26. See *Mennonite Yearbook and Directory*, 1905–06, and *General Journal of the Mennonite Brethren in Christ*, 1905.
27. H. S. Bender, "Amish Mennonite," *Mennonite Encyclopedia*, I, pp. 93–7.
28. C. H. Smith and H. S. Bender, "Diener-Versammlungen," *Mennonite Encyclopedia*, II, pp. 56–7.
29. *Ibid.*
30. E. E. Rupp, "Evangelical Mennonite Church" (Defenseless Mennonite Church), *Mennonite Encyclopedia*, II, pp. 264–66; J. H. Fretz, "Eastern Amish Mennonite Conference," *Mennonite Encyclopedia*, II, pp. 130–31; W. B. Weaver, "Central Conference Mennonite Church," *Mennonite Encyclopedia*, I, pp. 540–41; J. S. Umble, "Indiana-Michigan Amish Mennonite Conference," *Mennonite Encyclopedia*, III, p. 29; M. Gingerich, "Western District," *Mennonite Encyclopedia*, IV, pp. 932–33.
31. Ivan J. Miller, "Conservative Amish Mennonite Conference," *Mennonite Encyclopedia*, I, pp. 700–2.
32. J. A. Hostetler, "Old Order Amish," *Mennonite Encyclopedia*, IV, p. 44.
33. Orland Gingerich, *The Amish of Canada* (Waterloo, Ont.: Conrad Press, 1972), p. 75.
34. *Ibid.*, p. 39.
35. *Ibid.*, pp. 80–83.
36. *Ibid.*, p. 82.
37. *Ibid.*, pp. 83–85.

The Threat of Progress

12. The Church Struggle in Manitoba

The struggle between the old and the new is perhaps the one principal theme or leitmotif which can be discovered in the history of the Mennonites as a whole. The driving power behind their migrations . . . was always a heroic desire to preserve their sacred traditions . . . against the allurements of a larger society — E. K. FRANCIS.[1]

ANOTHER parallel exists in Canadian Mennonite history — while the conflict between the old and the new was being staged in Ontario, a similar drama was being enacted in Manitoba. As the Mennonites and Amish in the East opted for progressive or conservative ways, so the Western Mennonites made decisions which stemmed from their varying response to the issues confronting them. There was one important difference, however. In Manitoba, the majority rather than the minority insisted on the old ways. The minority, however, was quite vocal and convinced of the rightness of its position. The developing differences, together with geographic distance, resulted in the separation of the three Manitoba ecclesiastical organizations into no less than eight before the end of the century (see Table 1).[2]

The emergence of new organizations, however, was not the only manifestation of the differing points of view. For Mennonites, religion continued to embrace the whole of life, and thus the appearance of variant church symbols reflected variant values and approaches to the issues of life. The Anabaptist idea that

TABLE 1

MEMBERSHIP OF EIGHT MANITOBA MENNONITE CHURCHES IN 1912*

NAME	LOCATION	MEMBER-SHIP	SOULS†
Kleine Gemeinde	East Reserve	270	825
	and Morris	123	299
Holdemaner	East Reserve	154	389
(outgrowth of Kleine	and Morris	27	89
Gemeinde)			
Bruderthaler (EMB)			
(outgrowth of Kleine			
Gemeinde)	East Reserve	67	150
Chortitzer	East Reserve	835	2,037
Sommerfelder	West Reserve	2,085‡	5,214
Bergthaler	West Reserve	488	1,112
Reinlaender			
(Old Colony)	West Reserve	1,545	3,808
Mennonite Brethren	West Reserve	277	?§
Total		5,871	13,023

* First census available.
† "Souls" was term commonly used by Mennonites to designate entire population, including all family members.
‡ Estimate.
§ Unknown because converts to Mennonite Brethren Church did not necessarily transfer as families.

all of life was to be governed by religious principles had in some ways been strengthened by the commonwealth integration of the economic, cultural and religious facets of the Mennonite experience. Thus, differing views on community, land holding, public schools and culture played as great a role, if not greater, in the fragmentation as did creedal and liturgical questions.

The Kleine Gemeinde, smallest of the groups in Manitoba, was located partly in the East Reserve and partly west of the Red River, along the Scratching River, an area also known as the Morris area. The Bergthaler likewise were located on both sides of the Red River (the Red River separated the two reserves). They had begun settling on the East Reserve, but had transferred to the eastern end of the West Reserve as soon as the better land was discovered. Filling the western end of the West Reserve was the Reinlaender church, whose settlers came from Chortitza, the Old Colony in Russia, and from Fuerstenland, one of the daughter colonies. For this reason they were also known as Fuerstenlaender.[3] The name for this group that most entered into common usage, though it did not become official until the 1930s, was Old Colony. Thus, a designation which formerly carried only a geographic meaning took on an ecclesiatical connotation.

Of the three, the Old Colony was the most conservative church among the Russian Mennonites of the first migration. They strongly resisted the coming of municipal government, public schools, the breaking up of the villages, and the adoption of the English language.[4] On matters such as language, these Dutch-German Mennonites most resembled the Old Order of the Swiss-German tradition. Both manifested a simple and steadfast faith in the provident God who had called on them to be his faithful people. Since they would often have to suffer for their faith, a sombre seriousness typified the spirit of the Old Colony. Joy and satisfaction lay in conforming to the will of God as interpreted by the bishop, in raising large families, keeping a good household, and otherwise exemplifying a well-ordered life in social conformity and agricultural productivity. Social conformity for the most part came easily because socializing itself was a happy occasion, especially on Sunday afternoons when it was customary for relatives and friends to gather for story-telling and otherwise catching up on the events of the past week. In this the Low German language, being the language of social intercourse, served them well.

The weekly Sunday morning services, usually two to three hours in length, were filled with admonition from one major preacher and several minor ones, and hymns with many verses reinforced the mood of obedience and devotion. Exceptions to the weekly service were Christmas, Easter and Pentecost, when people attended church three days in a row. In addition to Epiphany and Ascension Day, these were the only holidays the Old Colony ever knew. Sunday morning highlights were the annual baptism of the eligible young people, who had undergone intense catechetical instruction and memorization; this was followed by communion, which included a foot-washing ceremony. Ordinations, weddings and funerals were the other church events which involved the entire community.

Community and *Gemeinde* (church) were the all-important
words. The Old Colony knew themselves to be a people of God
who had made a covenant with Him. Salvation was more
corporate than individual, hence the great emphasis on conformity and on group separation from the world, on keeping
the villages intact, and on keeping faith with the brotherhood.
The Old Colony did not practise common ownership of goods
but in other ways they were a total social organization similar
to that of the Hutterites.

Generally speaking and seen from the outside, the Mennonites
of the Kleine Gemeinde and the Bergthaler in Manitoba followed
many ways similar to those of the Old Colony. All had their
bishops and ministers, and, in their villages, elected officials. All
were farmers and had large families. For all, religious instruction
and baptism of the young people were an essential way of maintaining and perpetuating the way of life. The Kleine Gemeinde
was perhaps given more to legalistic moralisms affecting the life-
styles of individual members, while the Old Colony took its
stand on the economic, educational and national-cultural issues
of the day, as it sought to maintain the village, the private
school and the German culture.

The Bergthaler were difficult to classify since there were both
progressive and conservative factions among them. The progressives accepted urbanization, public schools and the changing
styles. They also were the earliest to pick up the English language. In their church life they tended to sing more rapidly and
have fewer verses, and occasionally they invited outside speak-
ers.[5] New ideas, however, had to be treated cautiously because
the majority of the Bergthaler leaned toward either the firmness
of the Old Colony on cultural-educational issues or the rigidity
of the Kleine Gemeinde on personal ethical issues. Indeed, the
religious differences within the Bergthaler were sufficient to
threaten ecclesiastical division, as the so-called progressives and
conservatives confronted each other inside that group.[6]

In Manitoba, as in Ontario, Mennonites began to be known as
progressives or as conservatives, though the sharpest distinction
between those two groups was not made until the second major
migration from Russia. Progressive and conservative, however,
are relative terms, as indicated in the previous chapter. The
conservatives in Manitoba themselves resented the use of the
term, inasmuch as they believed themselves to be the defence of
Mennonite values against an encroaching world and unfaithful

brethren. In the context of the times, however, conservative and progressive appeared to be terms properly descriptive and, though inadequate here, quite unavoidable. The varieties of conservatism in Manitoba, to be described here, had their roots in the Prussian emigration and in the Russian experience. For the most part, the Manitoba Mennonites had been poor and landless in Prussia and, for the longest time, the least educated in Russia. Cornies' reforms had affected the Chortitza elements only indirectly. Besides, many of the Manitoba people had spent all of their energies pioneering in Russia first in Chortitza, then in the daughter colonies of Bergthal and Fuerstenland. The main contingent of the Kleine Gemeinde in Manitoba had a Molotschna heritage, to be sure, but in their case too it was a heritage made ultra-conservative by the teachings of Klaas Reimer.

Even the choice of Canada was a conservative act since the progressives tended to choose the United States. The conservative orientation of the Manitoba migration was also exemplified in the expressed conservative intention. Two of the immigrant bishops explicitly insisted that migration meant a clean and pure start, a sure return to the old ways. Indeed, the two cousins, Bishops Gerhard Wiebe of the Bergthaler and Johann Wiebe of the Reinlaender, had vowed to reverse the accommodation to outside influences that had gone too far in Russia. Specific reference was made to *hohe Gelehrsamkeit* (high learning) in the schools, *Notengesang* (singing of notes), and *die grosse Gleichstellung dieser Welt* (the great conformity to the world).[7] Not surprisingly, not all of the immigrants were ready to return to or confirm such an ultra-conservatism, so that the seeds of dissent and a relative progressivism were present from the beginning. By their rigid recalcitrance, conservatism in the extreme, the bishops ensured the emergence of progressive elements.

Their position on hymnbooks with notes is a case in point. Bishop Johann Wiebe and his ministerial colleagues were determined to go back to the *Kirchengesang nach alter Sitte* (church singing according to the old tradition).[8] This meant not only avoiding hymnbooks with notes but also abolishing the books with *Ziffern* (numbers to indicate pitch) which had become commonplace in Russia.[9] There was consequently much unhappiness and dissension. Although most of the immigrants were ready to preserve a cultural status quo, only a very few were actually ready to turn the clock backward.

The intention of the bishops to hold the line was only intensified by the influences which became manifest early in the new environment. The reader has already been introduced to the breakdown of the village system in the Manitoba reserves, the coming of railroads and trading centres, the imposition of municipal government and the constant suggestions from official government quarters that the private German-language schools would have to go. Pressures to Anglicize and Canadianize were appearing much sooner in Canada than had those of Russification in Russia.

This development was painful particularly because the church bishops had in the beginning had much more authority in the Manitoba environment than had been the case in Russia. To be sure, a close relationship existed in Russia between the *Aelteste* (church leader) and the *Oberschulze* (civic leader), but the latter was appointed by Russian authorities following his public election. In Manitoba the *Kirchendienst* (bishops, ministers and deacons) nominated the civic leaders, who were then acclaimed by the *Bruderschaft* (church assembly).[10]

In this context, it can be seen why any outside interference affecting the status quo was viewed with great misgivings. Public schools, municipal government, and law enforcement agencies all represented unwanted intrusions, as did any influence or spokesman that opened the door wider to these disruptions of the commonwealth. To head off early disintegration and total disaster for the Manitoba experiment later on, the bishop applied a very strict discipline from the beginning and rather "lavish and indiscriminate use of excommunication not only for serious offences . . . but also for minor infractions of old customs."[11]

> Among the many "sins" and "crimes" which were punished
> in this drastic manner, the following have been mentioned:
> sending children to a public school, seeking employment
> with Anglo-Saxons, selling land to outsiders (even to
> Mennonites of other churches), mortgaging one's property,
> insuring it with the mutual fire insurance associations
> established by the Bergthal people, adopting such novelties
> as bicycles, buggies, musical boxes or sleigh bells.[12]

Among the outside influences so troublesome to the Manitoba conservatives were the constant intrusions from south of the border. As the conservatives saw it, progressives had compromised precious principles by going to the United States, but especially aggravating was their insistence that they had light and truth to bring to the north. The fragmentation of the Mennonite communities was assisted by the progressive American Mennonites.

Since the major dissenting Manitoba groups were soon tied in varying degrees to similar Mennonites in the United States, the whole Manitoba struggle must be told in the context of North American Mennonites in general. The (Old) Mennonites were among the first American brethren to influence the new immigrants in Manitoba. Although John F. Funk of Elkhart had not encouraged settlement in Canada, he respected the choices that had been made and considered also the needs of these people in his literary program. This meant, above all, an even wider distribution of the *Herold der Wahrheit*, though he soon recognized that a more specialized publication could better serve the Russian Mennonites.

His opportunity came in 1880 when the *Nebraska Ansiedler* (Settler), a railroad-subsidized publication printed in his shop, was about to expire. He made the paper his own, renamed it the *Mennonitische Rundschau* (Mennonite Observer), and two years later converted it into a weekly paper with special appeal for the people from and in Russia. One of his regular features was the Russian correspondence column, which carried communications to and from the Russian Mennonites in both the old and new worlds for nearly a century.

The *Rundschau* also dealt, more than the *Herold,* with everyday life, with crops, animal husbandry, markets and settlement news. It was thus more in keeping with the way the Russian Mennonites viewed their total existence — namely as a single religious cultural expression — especially on the reserves. The *Rundschau*'s entry into Manitoba was slow, but sure, and eventually its strength there increased to the point where the transfer of its publishing base to Winnipeg was advised.[13]

Funk and his (Old) Mennonite friends followed their papers with other literature (books, pamphlets, hymnals, catechisms), advertised therein, to Manitoba, but apparently no effort was made to organize (Old) Mennonite congregations. Funk deeply resented the schismatics, the "church accusers" as he called them in his own counter-attack.[14] In Manitoba as elsewhere he was interested in moving the church, but not breaking it, though indirect contribution to tension and disruption must not be overlooked.

An American contemporary of Funk's did not shy away from

open breaks. For Johannes Holdeman of Ohio, the pursuit of the "true church" meant what it had meant for John Herr and Klaas Reimer — a very precise return to some cherished doctrines and ethical norms, if necessary, by separating. His approach appealed to some Kleine Gemeinde people in the United States. It also appealed to Bishop Peter Toews in Manitoba who had corresponded with him and also travelled all the way to Kansas to hear him. Apparently, Holdeman's practice of very exactly defining the requirements of the "true church" gave him his opening in Manitoba with Toews and some of his people.

Not only had the insecurities and the uncertainties of pioneer settlement brought doubts about the rightness of their cause, but it also meant the rather wearisome observance of many rules and regulations. Holdeman was able to provide religious assurance while bringing about meaningful, though slight, change. With his dogmatism, Holdeman linked up with the basic conservatism of the Kleine Gemeinde. With his revivalism he helped them to get away from sterile forms. Above all, he could once again convince people that if they took a certain course of action they could be right and true again.

Toews welcomed Holdeman to Manitoba and allowed him to define the true church for him. The visiting evangelist advised the bishop that he needed to be rebaptized and reordained, so as to be in the apostolic succession of truth. Otherwise Toews needed to accept Holdeman's synthesis of American revivalism and Anabaptist conservatism.

The Holdeman approach appealed not only to Toews but to at least one-third of the Kleine Gemeinde people in the East Reserve and the Morris area. They followed Toews, who decided to follow Holdeman after he conducted evangelistic meetings in the winter of 1881–82. The result was a more emotional and verbally expressive Christianity with unwritten sermons and more public prayers. In some ways it also represented a more specific conservatism, such as mandatory wearing of beards and tie-less shirts by the married men and a new consistency in church discipline.[15] The meaning of the break-up of the smallest of the three immigrant congregations in Manitoba was summarized by the group's historian, as follows:

> There was much heartache and bitterness in the division. Families were separated and close relatives and friends estranged from each other. For a good many years it was unthinkable, even at funerals to come to each other's

meetings . . . It was the most progressive-minded and
spiritual-minded group that left . . . a very conservative
branch of the Mennonite church, at first spiritually
bewildered and then firmly resolved to isolate themselves
more than ever.[16]

The small Kleine Gemeinde group, which had separated from
the main group in Toronto and had gone to Nebraska with
Jansen, was likewise beset by differences of opinion, thus opening
it up to outside influences. John Holdeman won over a few
families, and the Reformed Church of John Herr (with the Kleine
Gemeinde dating back to 1812) also gained a few adherents,
though both failed to organize congregations. Other Kleine
Gemeinde families joined the Mennonite Brethren and the
Krimmer Mennonite Brethren. Much more successful were the
Bruderthaler, who established a congregation in their midst after
1879.[17]

What remained of the Kleine Gemeinde in Nebraska and
Manitoba now became reconciled in the mutual reinforcement
of their conservatism — the Nebraska elder came to Manitoba
to reorganize the group — but the end of their troubles was not
in sight. The Nebraska group, fearing further attrition to outside
influences, moved as a body to Kansas. There it maintained
itself for several decades, but then gave up its Kleine Gemeinde
identity, one part of the congregation becoming independent
and the other part joining the Bruderthaler.

The Bruderthaler also gained a foothold in the East Reserve,
more precisely at Steinbach, before the end of the century. The
intentional conservatism of the Kleine Gemeinde was not acceptable to all the people. Among those not going with Holdeman
were other restless people, who in some ways, but not all, could
be sympathetic to the Holdeman approach. They included the
business types, those people most ready to see one or more of the
villages develop into expanding centres, most specifically those
who were founding what later became the dynamic commercial
community of Steinbach. The conservatism of the Kleine Gemeinde, which later excommunicated J. R. Friesen for being
the first of their church men to buy a factory-built car (and
likely the first Ford dealer in western Canada), did not allow for
that kind of commerce and modernity.[18] Among the Kleine
Gemeinde:

Houses, furniture, and dress was plain and there was a
great emphasis on humility. It was wrong to take pride in

material possessions and consequently the shining brass
buckles that came with the horse-harnesses and later even
the chrome-plated lamps and radiator caps on the auto-
mobiles were painted black, and new inventions like the
telephone, top buggies, bicycles, and window curtains were
also forbidden at first until they were more commonly in use
and no longer status symbols.[19]

The governing principles of the Kleine Gemeinde were shaped
in a discussion process which began in 1898 and which resulted
several years later in the acceptance of a document signed by
three bishops (East Reserve, Morris, and Nebraska), nine ministers, and deacons. It was a six-point statement of negatives
in the Klaas Reimer tradition, which now became a desperate
attempt to hold the line. Expressly forbidden were acceptance of
government employment and participation in elections, attendance at non-Kleine Gemeinde services (unless the minister had
been approved and was accompanied by one of their own), and
attendance at non-Christian weddings. Also disallowed were
funeral sermons, except ordinary ones, and other innovations,
including graveside services.[20]

This general mood of negativism and some of the specific rules
not surprisingly caused some of the modern villagers of Steinbach
to raise questions about the rigid status quo. A group of laymen
led by Henry Rempel took the initiative in getting a revival
started. For this purpose they invited two ministers from the
Minnesota and Nebraska Bruderthaler congregations to come to
Manitoba. In Steinbach, a Bruderthaler congregation began in
1897 with only four couples. There were serious growing pains
and reorganization was required a decade later, but then a fresh
inflow of young people from the Kleine Gemeinde ensured a
permanent place in the East Reserve for the Bruderthaler.

The fragmentation of the Kleine Gemeinde was a matter of
considerable concern to Bishop Gerhard Wiebe of the Bergthaler
in the East Reserve. Actually, his own group had already become
known as the Chortitzer Church after the village in which he
resided. Gerhard Wiebe had been recognized, both by himself and
by others, as the leader of the East Reserve in the same way that
Bishop Johann Wiebe was from the beginning the leader of the
West Reserve. Both looked upon the Mennonite development in
Manitoba in commonwealth terms. At least their views in this
regard were stronger than those of the Kleine Gemeinde or
Bergthaler independents in the West Reserve, who tended to

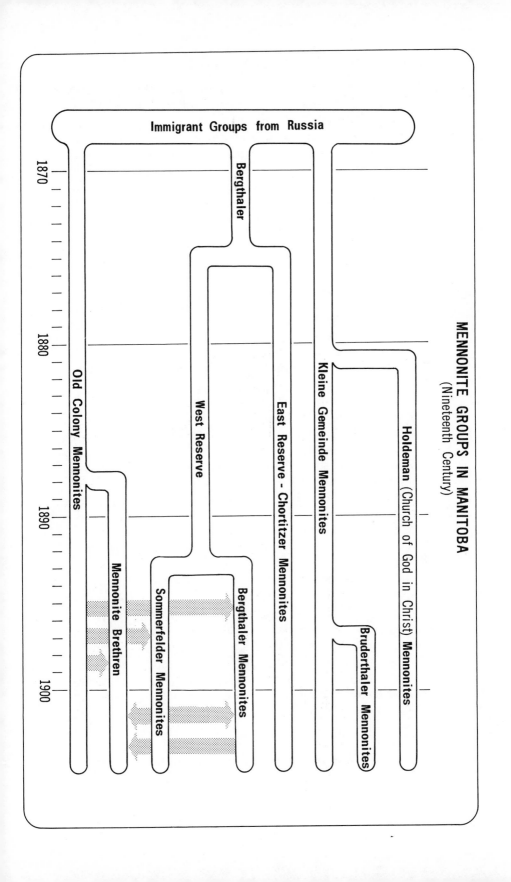

MENNONITE GROUPS IN MANITOBA
(Nineteenth Century)

Immigrant Groups from Russia

1870
1880
1890
1900

Old Colony Mennonites

Mennonite Brethren

Sommerfelder Mennonites

West Reserve

Bergthaler Mennonites

Bergthaler

East Reserve - Chortitzer Mennonites

Kleine Gemeinde Mennonites

Bruderthaler Mennonites

Holdeman (Church of God in Christ) Mennonites

separate religion and church affairs from the social-cultural and
the economic ones. The atomization of the Kleine Gemeinde
now made more difficult than ever a unified approach on the
school question and on other communal and district-wide matters.
Bishop Wiebe remembered Russia and the greater peace that had
been maintained there between Mennonites and their Russian
neighbours:

> Our neighbours; to the west Russians, to the north
> Catholics, to the east Greeks, and to the south Cossacks;
> were surrounded by three or four confessions, and it
> happened occasionally that things were stolen, but we did
> live with each other in peace and quiet. Oh, if only we could
> now live likewise with the Kleine Gemeinde and the
> Holdeman people and have spiritual fellowship with them,
> then the evil enemy could not injure us in so many ways
> through the district schools as is now the case.[21]

Bishop Wiebe's troubles extended to the West Reserve, where
some members of his Bergthal group had ideas of their own. The
centre of dissent among the Bergthaler on the West Reserve was
Johann Funk, a man whom Gerhard Wiebe had in 1887, for
reasons of distance, ordained to be his assistant bishop. This
ordination, however, soon resulted in an independent church organization, partly because of distance, partly because of Funk's
independent thought. He was not opposed to public district
schools and other so-called progressive movements. Indeed, he
became a rallying point for all those independent Bergthaler who
had from the beginning welcomed the break-up of the villages,
the coming of railroads, trading centres, municipal organizations,
and, last but not least, the visits of the General Conference "home
missionaries" from the United States, who had made their first
appearance early in the 1880s.[22]

The home mission work of the General Conference was from
the beginning defined as contact with outlying Mennonite congregations. This activity was accelerated by the immigration and
the needs of immigrant settlements. In 1881 a plan was adopted
which would see eastern ministers travelling west and westerners
travelling east for periods of time. Before too long this also meant
going north, especially after the first full-time home missionary
was appointed in the person of J. B. Baer, a graduate of Union
Theological Seminary.

In 1887 Baer spent two months in Manitoba and it was subsequently reported that "having found an open door, [he] was enabled by the Lord's aid to make the beginning for the revival of spiritual life in that extensive Mennonite settlement."[23] His work gave rise to the *Reiseprediger* (itinerant ministry) concept which would be so widely employed in the scattered Canadian communities in years to come. Itinerant ministers would conduct services, Bible studies, and home visitations, and some of them would also dispense medicines. In 1890 Manitoba as a special field was assigned to N. F. Toews, and many others followed Baer and Toews.[24]

The Reiseprediger of the General Conference was not able to tie any of the Russian immigrant groups to itself organization-ally as had so successfully been done in the United States, but their influence was felt none the less. Among the people who found much support from and for them was Johann Funk of the West Reserve. By 1888 Funk was insisting on the founding of a teacher-training school in Manitoba to provide teachers for the elementary schools. But not all of the Bergthal people of the West Reserve, not to mention the Old Colony, were ready to go that far. He proceeded to organize a school society which would support him, and in 1889-90 such a school was actually in session at Gretna under the leadership of William Rempel, a trained teacher recently arrived from Russia. The opposition grew, however, and after one year the school closed again. Then the Manitoba government took an interest in the founding of a normal school which would train teachers especially for the Men-nonite districts. The result was that a fresh start was made in 1891, with H. H. Ewert, a General Conference educator newly arrived from Kansas, at the helm.

Ewert stayed for over 40 years, in spite of the bitter con-troversy that ensued immediately after his arrival. Both Funk and Ewert encountered massive opposition. Suffice it to say here that in the spring of 1892 four West Reserve communities once again asked the bishop from the East to come and baptize their young people, a total of 98. A year later these same communities called upon Gerhard Wiebe to ordain a new bishop more to their liking. He was Abraham Doerksen from the village of Sommerfeld, and the majority of the Bergthaler people of the West Reserve left Funk and followed him. Immediately they became known as the Sommerfelder Church after the village in which the bishop resided, to distinguish themselves from the Bergthaler Church led by Funk.[25] Thus the Bergthaler people who had migrated from Russia in the 1870s came to be divided into three ecclesiastical groups: Bergthaler and Sommerfelder in the West Reserve, and Chortitzer in the East Reserve.

Of the three groups, the Sommerfelder was the largest, more than four times the size of the Bergthaler and more than twice the size of the Chortitzer. In terms of cultural and spiritual affinity the Chortitzer and Sommerfelder were close and, except for their geographic separation by the river and the Reserves, they might have been a single unit. Because of its size and because of the educational strife which focused on the West Reserve, the Sommerfelder, who tended toward the Old Colony in educational matters, became much more prominent than the Chortitzer. The Chortitzer, like the Kleine Gemeinde, hardly participated in the cultural conflicts which descended on the West Reserve.

In spite of the large defection, Funk did retain a core of supporters, including some of the people defecting from the Old Colony group who rallied to his support. In the village of Hoffnungsfeld was a progressive-minded schoolteacher by the name of Jacob Hoeppner, who two decades later would succeed Funk as bishop of what had become a minority Bergthaler church. His interest in four-part harmony singing and in Bible study led to the termination of his teaching contract, but he soon found a new opportunity in Schanzenfeld. In the end, the entire village of Hoffnungsfeld was lost to the Old Colony, in part to the Bergthaler and in part to the Mennonite Brethren Church, which found its first opening in Canada there. Begun as a minority movement, the Bergthaler were destined to grow both from their own population and from the influx of progressive-minded Sommerfelder. The progressive-minded Old Colony, on the other hand, might end up either with the Sommerfelder or with the Bergthaler.

There appeared, however, another ecclesiastical option on the West Reserve, similar to that provided by the Bruderthaler on the East Reserve. This option was the Mennonite Brethren Church. There were at that time Mennonite Brethren communities in Dakota, Kansas, Minnesota and Nebraska with 18 places of worship, 1,266 members, seven elders and 52 ministers and deacons.[26] These were all organized together into a Conference. As in Russia the Mennonite Brethren in the United States adopted a policy of seeking converts in other Mennonite groups, as well as in society generally. The Russian development of the movement had proved the conversion potential among conservative groups. The success of John Holdeman in Manitoba had not gone unnoticed, nor had the movement in Manitoba of Mormon and Swedenborgian evangelists. The southern Manitoba communities had become somewhat of a free-for-all to the extent that access could be gained not only by government officials, settlement agents, inspectors of all kinds, and "tourists," but also by evangelists. The southern Manitoba reserves shared this experience with the colonies in southern Russia earlier in the nineteenth century.

The 1883 Conference of Mennonite Brethren authorized two ministers to visit the communities in Manitoba. They were Heinrich Voth of Minnesota because of his proximity, and David Dyck of Kansas because he had relatives in Manitoba. Their contacts in 1884 led to further Conference authorization, and for the next five years Elder Voth visited Manitoba at least once annually. Voth's first preaching services were in Hoffnungsfeld, where he gained an immediate opposition. On one occasion three "visitors" to his service planned to seize the American, take him to the border, and send him back to Minnesota. Their plans fell through when at least one of the three was converted.[27]

Voth's visits led to conversions and the rebaptism by immersion of eight persons in 1886. Two years later the organization of the first Mennonite Brethren Church in Canada took place at Burwalde, north of the present site of Winkler and well outside the West Reserve. Voth continued his work, though not without opposition, which came in the form of personal harassment and official Old Colony warnings to the faithful that they should stay away from him. The itinerant minister, however, found many people "who were afraid of being lost and who feared eternal punishment" and these opened their doors to him, not least of all because he was a kindly gentleman, sincere and well versed in the Bible.[28]

The first Mennonite Brethren congregation was organized with 16 members in 1888. By 1895 David Dyck had consented to move to Manitoba. A meeting-house was erected at Burwalde, near Dead Horse Creek, the place of the first baptism. By 1897 the group was ready to move the church to Winkler, though not everybody wanted it right inside the little town for fear that "urban" influence would be corrupting. A compromise was reached and the church brought to the edge of town, but only after its move had been halted a mile away for several days.[29]

Thereafter the Mennonite Brethren became the urbanizers in the Winkler area, the role played by the Bruderthaler in the Steinbach area and the Bergthaler in the Altona area. Indeed, the Brethren would soon establish a Mennonite outpost in Winnipeg, thus anticipating the time a half-century later when Mennonites by the thousands would make the big city their home. For immediate growth, however, the Brethren had to move into the rural areas, where two satellite congregations for Winkler were established on the northern fringes of the West Reserve at Grossweide near Horndean and also at Kronsgart.[30]

The Canadian beginnings for the Mennonite Brethren were small, but the prospects and optimism were such that the Mennonite Brethren Conference of North America decided to hold their 1898 session at Winkler. The real advance in Canada, however, would depend on immigration, first from the United States to Saskatchewan and later to all the prairie provinces from Russia. For the time being, only small numbers could be persuaded to leave the Old Colony and Sommerfelder for a church community, which was allegedly more spiritual. In the West as in the East Reserve, the overwhelming majority of Mennonites believed that a greater spirituality lay in resisting revivalism, acculturation and the breakdown of community which inevitably came with it.

Thus, the Brethren as well as the Bruderthaler and the Bergthaler had to be satisfied with minority positions for quite some time. The majority groups, however, were far from secure. The conservative spirituality was being challenged not only by progressive Mennonites but also by the government. The possibility of preserving it elsewhere became evident — both the Old Colony and the Sommerfelder were joining the movement of settlers into the Northwest Territories.

FOOTNOTES

1. E. K. Francis, "Tradition and Progress Among the Mennonites in Manitoba," *Manitoba Quarterly Review*, XXIV (October 1950), pp. 312–28.
2. First reliable statistics available. See *Der Mitarbeiter*, VII (February 1913), p. 37.
3. Francis, for instance, uses the Fuerstenland name frequently. See

E. K. Francis, *In Search of Utopia: The Mennonites in Manitoba* (Altona, Man.: D. W. Friesen & Sons, 1955), pp. 87–96.

4. For the best description of the Old Colony way of life see Calvin Redekop, *The Old Colony Mennonites: Dilemmas of Ethnic Minority Life* (Baltimore: Johns Hopkins University Press, 1969), 302 pp.

5. For the most comprehensive treatment of the Bergthaler, see H. J. Gerbrandt, *Adventure in Faith* (Altona, Man.: D. W. Friesen & Sons, 1970), 379 pp.

6. For the story of the Kleine Gemeinde see P. J. B. Reimer, ed., *The Sesquicentennial Jubilee: Evangelical Mennonite Conference, 1812-1962* (Steinbach, Man.: Evangelical Mennonite Conference, 1962), 180 pp.

7. Isaac M. Dyck, *Auswanderung der Reinland Mennoniten von Canada nach Mexico* (Cuahtemoc, Chihuahua, Mexico: Imprenta Colonial, 1970), p. 21. See also Gerhard Wiebe, *Ursachen und Geschichte der Auswanderung der Mennoniten aus Russland Nach Amerika* (Winnipeg: Druckerei der Nordwesten, 1900), 58 pp.

8. An account of the event as experienced by an opponent is "Schriftmaessige Erwaegung ueber den Zustand unserer Gemeinde," an 1878 document of which an Abraham Buhler was the author and Wilhelm Rempel the scribe. Copy at CGC; original with Bishop Abram J. Buhler, Warman, Sask.

9. *Ibid.*

10. See Francis, *op. cit.*, pp. 84–5.

11. *Ibid.*, p. 90.

12. *Ibid.*

13. See H. B. Bender, "Mennonitische Rundschau," *Mennonite Encyclopedia*, III, pp. 647–48; see also Frank H. Epp, "The Making and Unmaking of Inter-Mennonite Periodicals" (unpublished research paper, Bethel College, 1956) (CGC).

14. John F. Funk, *The Mennonite Church and Her Accusers* (Elkhart, Ind.: Mennonite Publishing Company, 1878), 210 pp.

15. Clarence Hiebert, "The Holdeman People: A Study of the Church of God in Christ Mennonite, 1858–1969" (Ph.D. dissertation, Case Western Reserve University, 1971), pp. 260–61.

16. P. J. B. Reimer, *op. cit.*, p. 23.

17. H. S. Bender, "Kleine Gemeinde," *Mennonite Encyclopedia*, III, pp. 196–99.

18. A. Warkentin, *Reflections on Our Heritage: A History of Steinbach and the R.M. of Hanover from 1874* (Steinbach, Man.: Derksen Printers, 1971), pp. 106–7.

19. *Ibid.*, p. 207.

20. P. J. B. Reimer, *op. cit.*, pp. 26–7.

21. Gerhard Wiebe, *op. cit.*, p. 21.

22. H. J. Gerbrandt, *op. cit.*, pp. 80–91.
23. H. P. Krehbiel, *The History of the General Conference Mennonite Church of the Mennonites of North America* (Canton, Ohio: published by the author, 1898), Vol. I, p. 21.
24. H. J. Gerbrandt, *op. cit.*, pp. 85–6.
25. *Ibid.*, p. 90.
26. J. H. Lohrenz, "Mennonite Brethren Church," *Mennonite Encyclopedia*, III, pp. 595–602.
27. See Frank Brown, *Mennonite Brethren Church, Winkler, Manitoba, 1888–1963; 75th Anniversary Publication*, p. 4; and J. A. Toews, "History of the Mennonite Brethren Church" (unpublished manuscript, 1973), pp. 232–33.
28. Frank Brown, *op. cit.*, pp. 3–4.
29. *Ibid.*, p. 42, and J. A. Toews, *op. cit.*, pp. 25–55.
30. A. H. Unruh, *Die Geschichte der Mennoniten–Bruedergemeinde* (Hillsboro, Kans.: General Conference of the Mennonite Brethren Church of North America, 1955), 491 ff.

To New Homesteads by Rail

13. Settlement in Alberta and Saskatchewan

*A few conservative leaders thought if they could place a
greater distance between their settlements and Canadian
influences they could still return to the insular life that they
had led in Russia. . . . However, not all were fleeing
"progress." Many land-hungry Mennonites were also
heading West to homestead again* — JOHN H. WARKENTIN.[1]

THE PRESSURES which Mennonites felt in Manitoba and
other parts of the world around the turn of the century
once again coincided with new settlement opportunities. Once
again a new frontier allowed the beginning of a new life, which
for some meant a better preservation of the old life. As new railroad lines were built and the northwest territories were organized
into two new Canadian provinces (1905), thousands of Mennonites from Manitoba, Ontario, and various American states, as
well as Prussia and Russia, once more undertook the hardships
of homesteading in order to enjoy the freedoms of the frontier.

These new migrations were characterized, however, not so
much by mass movement and block settlement as by individual
effort and the action of small family or congregational units who
selected widely scattered lands and regions as they deemed best.
The result was that over a period of two decades numerous new
Mennonite settlements dotted the western Canadian map, with
one as far away as the interior of British Columbia (see Table
1).[2] While the Mennonite population in Ontario and Manitoba

remained relatively stable from 1901 to 1911, the regions farther west enjoyed manifold increases.

TABLE 1

MENNONITES IN CANADA IN 1901, 1911, 1921*

PROVINCE	1901	1911	1921
British Columbia	11	191	173
Alberta	546	1,555	3,131
Saskatchewan	3,787	14,586	20,568
Manitoba	15,289	15,709	21,321
Ontario	15,257	12,861	13,655
Quebec	50	51	6
Nova Scotia	9	18	2
New Brunswick	–	1	4
Prince Edward Island	–	–	3
Yukon and Northwest Territories	–	–	1
Total	31,949	44,972	58,874

* Total population according to Dominion Census.

This distant scattering was of some concern to those leaders who still felt that Mennonites could and should survive as a group. The extraordinary spreading out of their people prompted some leaders to make a great effort to tie them all together. The result was the formation of new conferences, notably the Conference of Mennonites in Central Canada, which would some day be the largest of the Canadian conference families. Since no single conference, however well-intentioned, could embrace all the diverse congregations and their members, any comprehensive Mennonite unity was at best a dream of a very distant reality.

Some activity, predicting the westward move, had already been evident in the West Reserve of Manitoba, during its second decade as a settlement. By the end of 1888, a deputation from Gretna had inspected lands in California, Oregon, and Washington, as well as in British Columbia, but none of the ten families who subsequently ventured to the west coast stayed there.[3] However, if the far west held no attraction at this point, the mid-west did, especially after the Dominion government and the land agents decided that the northwest territories, newly opened by the Trans-Canada Railroad, were a good place to live.

In the Northwest Territories, as in Manitoba, settlement began slowly but surely after the lands of the Hudson's Bay Company were incorporated into the Dominion in 1870. The Indians, and the Métis who completely identified with them, were placed on reserves. Other Métis followed a settlement pattern similar to that of the new immigrants although dissatisfaction with their new lot reached rebellion proportions on several occasions. The most famous of these rebellions happened in 1885 in the Saskatchewan Valley, which the Mennonites were about to select as another homeland. The defeat of Louis Riel at Batoche and his trial and hanging in Regina finally pacified the 2,500 Indians, Métis and French people in the Valley at the time.[4]

Important agents of the national policy of pacification and occupation were the Northwest Mounted Police. A peaceful, non-violent West was essential to the building of railroads and to the permanent attraction of settlers, which were, in turn, necessary for the establishment and maintenance of a separate Canadian nation on the North American continent.[5] This was not an easy task because the nation to the south, partly caught up in the international imperialist mood of the times, had expansionist designs of its own.[6]

The permanent peace and protection sought by the Canadian authorities against native uprisings and American intrusions depended on permanent settlement. In some ways Canada faced a problem similar, albeit not quite as acute, to that of Catherine of Russia a century earlier. Unless permanent agricultural settlers were brought in, the nomadic natives indigenous to the area and troublesome Turks from the south would make nation-building difficult if not impossible. The part which Mennonites played in the Canadian domestication program, first in Manitoba and later in Saskatchewan, led one sociologist to conclude that "the Mennonite farming invasion" was essential to the national policy:

> Each time when the hunters and trappers had been cleared
> away, the Mennonites moved in . . . It was a struggle
> between the food gatherers and the food growers — the
> hunters and the farmers. The Mennonites were part of the
> farming invasion.[7]

A key factor in opening the new Mennonite areas was the

advent of the east-west and north-south railroads, the latter being connected to the trans-Canada line at such new sites as Regina and Calgary. The line from Regina through Saskatoon to Prince Albert opened up the Saskatchewan Valley in 1890, and in the same year a similar line reached from Calgary to Red Deer and later all the way to Edmonton. Within a few years 13 German settlements were established along this line, a few of them Mennonite.[8]

As part of this settlement promotion the Canadian Pacific Railway had in 1889 sponsored a "homeseekers' excursion" for prospective settlers. Among the prospectors were Elias W. Bricker of Woolwich Township in Ontario[9] and, in all likelihood, some Mennonites from Manitoba. Within a year, West Reserve Mennonites were applying to the Dominion government for exclusive reserve lands north of Calgary and some Ontario Amish and Mennonites were inquiring about homesteading in the Peace River district.[10] A Mennonite petition for homesteading rights in the Peace River district of Alberta was denied.[11] Since similar bids with respect to Saskatchewan proved successful, one can only speculate that there may have been some regional opposition in Alberta. The *Edmonton Bulletin*, for instance, seriously questioned the establishment of reserves:

> This is a favor that is not extended to ordinary Canadian or British settlers, and the question naturally arises, is a Mennonite so much more desirable a settler than any other man that he should be accorded privileges not accorded to others? If Canadian-born Mennonites are so prejudiced against their fellow citizens that to induce them to remain in the country it is necessary to give them a reservation by themselves, it is evidence that there are disadvantages as well as advantages connected with a Mennonite population.[12]

The Mennonites, however, were not barred from the region altogether. On the contrary, they were given some informal concessions which allowed them to settle more or less by themselves, particularly in the Gleichen area, where a number of families arrived from southern Manitoba in 1891 and temporarily made their home.[13] Others, mostly Bergthaler, moved to Didsbury which became the most permanent settlement of Mennonites in Alberta. At the same time Elias Bricker moved his family to High River, south of Calgary, to be followed by a dozen others within the decade, enough to form an (Old) Mennonite congregation.[14] Another (Old) Mennonite settlement including settlers from Ontario emerged at Carstairs near Didsbury in 1893.[15]

The Didsbury-Carstairs area represented a merger not only of Bergthaler Mennonites from Manitoba and the (Old) Mennonites from Ontario, but also of the Mennonite Brethren in Christ from Ontario. Although Jacob Y. Shantz, the already-famous colonizer, had preceded the (Old) Mennonites by one year when, in 1893, he made his twenty-sixth trip to the west, he did not actually bring settlers in until 1894 when 34 persons, including some of his relatives, left Waterloo by train. Seven carloads were necessary to transport the group and their equipment for what must have been one of the best settlement starts in the west.[16] Nevertheless, the group did not escape the rigours of pioneering as reported then:

> We started to look for the iron stakes that indicated our
> homesteads. These stakes were surrounded by four square
> holes about a foot deep. In many instances these holes
> were grown over with grass and brush. We had no compass.
> We were supposed to take 900 steps to the quarter section
> in length but we did not always hold to the right direction
> . . . The tent was burned a day later in the prairie fire . . .
> Everybody went out to assist in back firing from the
> plowed furrow, but very often the wind picked up a bunch
> of burning grass and threw it over our heads behind us . . .
> We used to walk nearly two miles to the railway track to
> pound out our steel plowshares cold . . .[17]

The first group of Mennonite Brethren in Christ settlers was followed by others. But the denomination's most rapid expansion was due to vigorous missionary activity from the outset; six congregations were founded in the first two decades, including a mission in Edmonton (see Table 2).[18]

The (Old) Mennonites, who lost some converts to the Mennonite Brethren in Christ, gained some of their own, mainly through immigration from the States. Not only did the Iowa and Nebraska Amish who settled at Tofield become an (Old) Mennonite congregation, but so did the people at Mayton whose Old Order background was with the Stauffer people who migrated from Waterloo to Iowa in the 1880s. The conservative Mennonites who came to Duchess from Pennsylvania likewise became part of the (Old) Mennonite fold – largely due to the work of Ontario

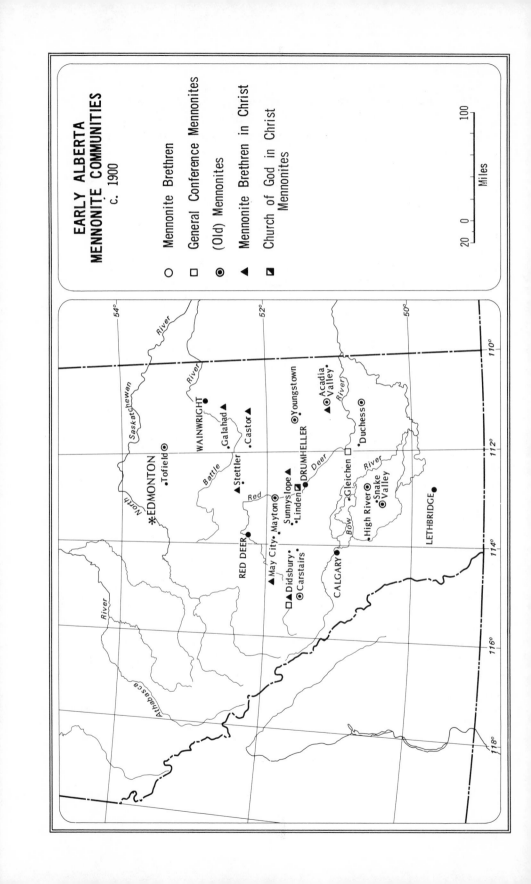

EARLY ALBERTA
MENNONITE COMMUNITIES
c. 1900

○ Mennonite Brethren

□ General Conference Mennonites

◉ (Old) Mennonites

▲ Mennonite Brethren in Christ

◪ Church of God in Christ
    Mennonites

20   0   100

Miles

*EDMONTON

•Tofield◉

WAINWRIGHT•

Galahad ▲

•Castor ▲

▲Stettler

RED DEER•

•Youngstown

▲◉Acadia Valley•

Sunnyslope ▲

•Linden   DRUMHELLER◪

Mayton◉

•May City

▲Didsbury•

◉Carstairs•

□▲

□□

CALGARY◉

•Gleichen□

Duchess◉

High River•

•Snake Valley

LETHBRIDGE•

North Saskatchewan River

Battle River

Red Deer River

Bow River

Athabasca River

54°

52°

50°

110°

112°

114°

116°

118°

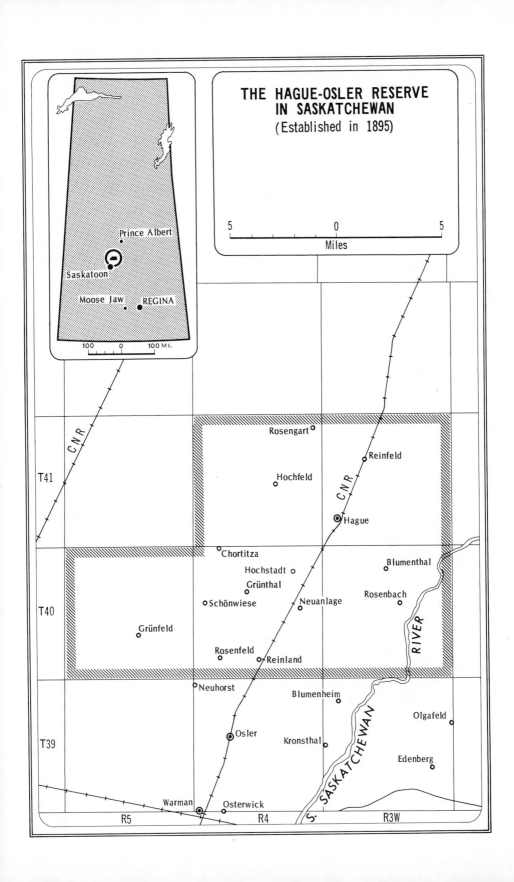

THE HAGUE-OSLER RESERVE
IN SASKATCHEWAN
(Established in 1895)

5   0   5
Miles

Prince Albert

Saskatoon

Moose Jaw   REGINA

100   0   100 MI.

T41

CNR

Rosengart

Reinfeld

Hochfeld

CNR

Hague

Chortitza

Hochstadt

Grünthal

Blumenthal

Schönwiese

Neuanlage

Rosenbach

T40

Grünfeld

Rosenfeld

Reinland

RIVER

Neuhorst

Blumenheim

Olgafeld

T39

Osler

Kronsthal

Edenberg

SASKATCHEWAN

Warman

Osterwick

S.

R5   R4   R3W

TABLE 2

NEW SETTLEMENTS IN ALBERTA AROUND THE TURN OF THE CENTURY*

PLACE	DENOMINATIONAL FAMILY†	DATE	ORIGIN
Acadia Valley	OM	1908	Ontario
	MBC	1913	Ontario
Carstairs	OM	1893	Ontario
Castor	MBC	1906	Ontario
Didsbury	MBC	1894	Ontario
	GC	1901	Manitoba
Duchess	OM	1915	USA
Galahad	MBC	1915	Alberta
Gleichen	GC	1891	Manitoba
High River	OM	1891	Ontario
Linden	CGCM	1902	USA
May City	MBC	1906	Didsbury
Mayton§	OM	1901	USA
Snake Valley	OM	1910	Ontario
Stettler	MBC	1909	Ontario
Sunnyslope	MBC	1909	Didsbury
Tofield‡	OM	1910	USA
Youngstown	OM	1910	USA

* The Alberta region was founded as a province in 1905.
† OM — (Old) Mennonites; MBC — Mennonite Brethren in Christ; GC — General Conference; CGCM — Church of God in Christ Mennonite.
‡ Of Old Order origin, including some who moved to Iowa from Ontario; most moved to Tofield by 1918.
§ Original settlers of Amish origin, including some who had moved to Iowa-Nebraska from Ontario.

bishops such as S. F. Coffman and Elias Weber who were sent to minister to the distant and scattered frontier flock.

The settlement of both American and Canadian families also took place at Linden where some Holdeman people from Oregon and other American states arrived by 1902, soon to be joined by their counterparts from Manitoba. The result was a more intimate gathering of Swiss and Russian Mennonites of Holdeman persuasion than had happened anywhere before.[19]

Settlements emerging simultaneously in Saskatchewan and

Alberta were similar in that they represented a wide scattering of small and diverse communities. However, the Saskatchewan Mennonite population turned out to be predominantly Dutch-German while the Alberta people were mostly of Swiss-German background. Alberta had one Dutch congregation at Didsbury, while Saskatchewan had one Swiss congregation at Guernsey and another small one at Alsack.

In Saskatchewan the earliest centre of activity was the Saskatchewan Valley north of Saskatoon. There, Abram Buhr of Gretna, who had already staked a claim at Gleichen in Alberta, claimed the first Mennonite homestead just north of a railroad landing called Rosthern.[20] He was not allowed to retain it since he did not settle on it, so it passed into the hands of Gerhard Ens, a young and energetic immigrant from Russia who became a most vigorous immigration agent himself.[21]

Born in Russia in 1863, Ens had migrated to Canada in 1891 and had been among the first in a new wave of about 900 to arrive in the 1890s.[22] After spending the winter in southern Manitoba, he joined five Bergthaler families who were ready to homestead in the new area. Ens not only took up a homestead, but he also opened a store and the town's first post office — both in a boxcar loaned to him by the Canadian Pacific Railway. Soon he was vigorously promoting settlement on the frontier, becoming an agent for Clifford Sifton who, as a member of Wilfrid Laurier's cabinet after 1896, was the most vigorous promoter of immigration that Canada had yet seen. Ens travelled in the United States as well as back to Russia, where he predicted absorption into Russia for those Mennonites who would not emigrate.[23] He anticipated that the assimilation would be so complete that even "the finest microscope will not be able to spot them."[24]

Ens found a partner in settlement promotion in Peter Jansen of Nebraska, who joined him in the formation of the Saskatchewan-Manitoba Land Company. Like Jansen, who became a Nebraska senator, Gerhard Ens entered politics and became an elected member of the first Saskatchewan legislature in 1905.[25] His wide-ranging interests, however, centred around Rosthern, which he felt could become the wheat capital of the world. By 1905, when the population of the incorporated town was still less than 1,000, there were no fewer than eight grain elevators, making the town one of the largest grain shipping centres in the new provinces. Most of that grain was grown by Mennonites.

A variety of Mennonites had settled in the Rosthern region by then and the majority of them found a common community in what became known as the Rosenorter Mennonite Church. At the head of the community stood Peter Regier, a bishop of the Rosenort congregation in Prussia, which he had left in 1893 because of his uncompromising desire to avoid the pressures of militarism. (Apparently many others in Prussia had felt otherwise and re-accepted into the congregation those young men who had returned from active military service.)[26]

Like Ens, Regier spent the winter in southern Manitoba before taking up a homestead at Tiefengrund, near Rosthern. On July 2, 1894, a few months after his arrival, he conducted the first brotherhood meeting, which led to the organization of the Rosenort church. This, in turn, helped to bring together the diverse elements among the immigrants, that is, those coming directly from Russia and Prussia, and those arriving from Manitoba and later from the United States. Three weeks later, the first election of preachers took place at Eigenheim, six miles west of Rosthern. The first church was built in 1896 on a 20-acre plot donated for that purpose by the railway company. However, Eigenheim was only one of the worship centres that arose as immigrants rapidly filled up the regions around Rosthern.

Meanwhile, a mass movement of Old Colony people from Manitoba's West Reserve had been partially accomplished. Petitioned by the Mennonites, the Dominion government had, on January 23, 1895, reserved for their exclusive settlement the even-numbered sections of four townships in the Hague-Osler area which lay along the railway line between Saskatoon and Rosthern (odd-numbered sections had to be obtained from the railway).[27] The government justified the reservation on the basis of precedents set in Manitoba and on the grounds that this was the way of reaching the goal of filling Canada with expert agriculturalists:

> These people had prospered to a remarkable degree since their arrival in Manitoba, and have fulfilled with singular good faith all the obligations undertaken by them in that relation, repaying the advance of money made to them, with interest, to the last cent, and fully colonizing their reservations with the choicest settlers . . . it is important, in the public interest, that the efforts of the Mennonites to induce the immigration of their friends in Europe and elsewhere to the Northwest should be encouraged, and to do this it is necessary to give the intending settlers an assurance that they will be enabled to carry out the

principles of their social system, and to settle together in hamlets (for which provision is made by Section 37 of the Dominion Lands Act) by obtaining entries for contiguous lands.[28]

In May of 1895 the first trainload of Old Colony Mennonites from the West Reserve arrived at the Hague siding, where they lived in railroad cars for two weeks until the first homes could be erected.[29] Others followed and within three years the Mennonites were requesting reservation of another adjoining township which was granted to them for similar reasons and on similar terms.[30]

Population pressures within the Manitoba reserves continued, however, in spite of the fact that numerous farmers were buying land just outside the Manitoba Reserves and moving to Saskatchewan. In the East Reserve the pressure was relieved by movement into the empty French-Canadian municipalities to the north and east of the Reserve. In the West Reserve in 1897 farmers were buying land as far north as Lowe Farm.[31] Others, however, looked farther afield for reasons stated by John Warkentin:

> Many of the conservative Mennonites wanted to leave the reserve because they felt that they and their children were exposed too directly to outside influences. Others were not satisfied with the climate, and wanted to move to the West Coast. But the strictly economic reasons were the most important. Some Mennonites were so poor that they couldn't start farming in the reserve where farm prices were high, so they were anxious to homestead in the West. Many found it to their advantage to sell their farms at a good price (often to outsiders), move west and homestead again, thus making a handsome profit by the move.[32]

The Old Colony leaders hoped for as much collective movement and settlement as possible and thus, in 1904, they were once more appealing to the Dominion government for a reservation — this time for vacant lands south of Swift Current. These lands were vacant because they were believed to be of poor quality. The Mennonites, however, claimed that they would be able to work the lands successfully.[33] The Crown believed them from the beginning and granted them, for exclusive use, both the even-numbered and the available odd-numbered sections in

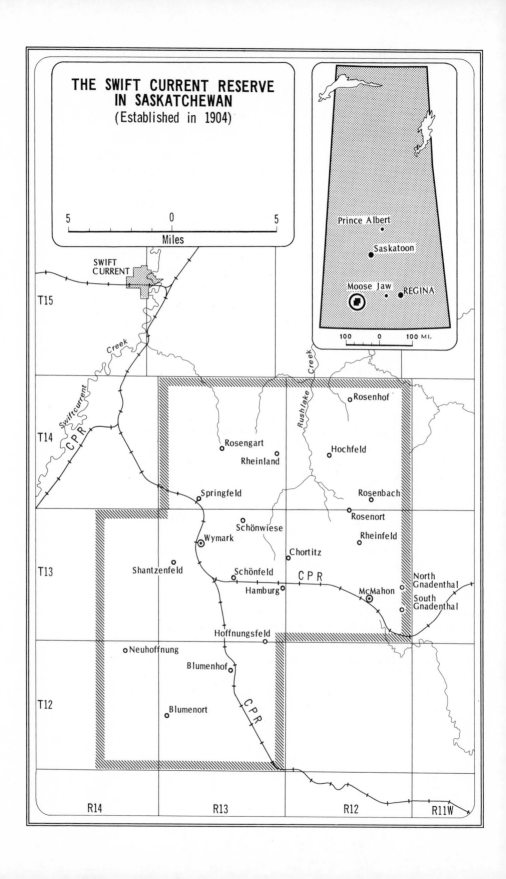

THE SWIFT CURRENT RESERVE
IN SASKATCHEWAN
(Established in 1904)

six townships. The odd ones were to be purchased at $3 per acre in ten annual instalments with interest at five per cent.[34]

In both areas, Hague-Osler and Swift Current, the Old Colony people sought to reconstruct the intimate and closed Mennonite communities as they remembered them from Russia and as they hoped to keep them in Manitoba. In the two reservations, 29 villages were founded,[35] and the old style of community and religious life was restored.[36] The Old Colony Mennonites who settled on reserves were followed by the Sommerfelder, whose individual homestead settlements were near the reserves in the Aberdeen area east of the Hague-Osler reserve, as well as near Rosthern and in the Herbert area north of the Swift Current reserve. By 1906 there was movement also toward a large area of land east of Prince Albert, known as the Carrot River Valley Mennonite Reserve.

The government concessions made to the Mennonites at this time had several parallels which had arisen from the government's satisfactory agricultural experience with the Mennonites. In 1898 and 1899, respectively, special concessions were made to 7,000 Russian Doukhobors who were about to arrive in Saskatchewan, and to the Hutterites who had already begun to arrive in Manitoba from South Dakota.[37] Since these were religious pacifist groups, they both required assurances that they would be granted military exemption. Both groups were exempted by separate Orders-in-Council on the basis of the statutes which had given similar privileges to Quakers, Mennonites and Tunkers.[38] Since the three groups — Doukhobors, Hutterites and Mennonites — shared a pacifistic doctrine as well as a Russian origin, a strange language, and communal organization of some degree, it was not surprising that, in the public mind, they should attain a common identity. In Canadian law, the nineteenth-century "pacifist trinity" (Quakers, Tunkers and Mennonites) was, in the twentieth century, replaced by a strange new grouping (Mennonites, Doukhobors and Hutterites), which will be seen more clearly in the context of the Great War. This latter trio, however, associated less with each other in western Canada than did the former three groups in eastern Canada.

The migration of the Doukhobors began in 1899, assisted by Leo Tolstoy and the British Quakers. Nearly six thousand detrained at Yorkton and formed three colonies with 47 villages. Two other settlements were founded in the Saskatchewan Valley with 10 villages. Of these new settlers it was said that they were excellent gardeners and craftsmen. Their settlements were more largely self-contained than those of any other people. They made good farmers, though their lives too were disrupted by pressures against the communities.[39]

The Hutterites, who numbered about 100 families or 700 individuals at the time of their immigration in the 1870s from Russia to the Dakotas, had doubled their population by this time, in spite of some defections to the Mennonites. About a dozen colonies had been established in South Dakota and plans were underway for moves to Montana. They were, therefore, experiencing population pressures of their own, but in 1898 they turned their sights on Manitoba due to the threat of the Spanish-American War. They sought and obtained from Canada the right to establish colonies and the right to military exemption. In 1899 they established themselves on the Roseau River east of Dominion City in Manitoba. However, after five years they returned to South Dakota. The war between Spain and the United States had been of short duration, while the land in Manitoba was poor and floods were frequent.[40]

Canada, which one day soon would think negatively about the Hutterites, was sorry to see them go since the departure to the United States of good agriculturalists was entirely contrary to the Sifton plan. At that time of drought in Kansas, Sifton was wooing the Mennonites not only from the United States but also from Russia. In 1898 Peter Krahn and Peter Braun, a delegation from Russia, had arrived to tour the Northwest and there was optimism that another great flow from Russia would result. Said Sifton's German immigration agent in Winnipeg:

> This will, no doubt, have a very great effect upon
> immigration from that quarter, as until now, the people of
> Russia have only had the letters of friends in this country
> to depend on.[41]

The immigration from Russia had, however, nearly run its course for the time being, probably because the times were good for the Mennonites in Russia and most did not see the dark clouds on the horizon, in spite of the war with the Japanese and revolutionary ferment everywhere.[42] Immigration from the United States, however, was a different story, and though the groups that came were not large there were numerous Russian Mennonite contingents from various states that made their homes in Saskatchewan during these years (see Table 3).[43]

TABLE 3

MENNONITE SETTLEMENTS ESTABLISHED IN SASKATCHEWAN AROUND 1900

PLACE	CONGREGATION	DENOMINA-TION†	DATE*	ORIGIN
Aberdeen	Aberdeen	MB	1906	USA
	Bergthaler	SM	1902	Manitoba
	Rosenorter	GC	1910	Prussia
Alsack	Alsack	MBC	1910	Alberta
Borden	Hoffnungsfeld	MB	1904	USA, Russia
Carrot River	Bergthaler	SM	1908	Saskatchewan, Manitoba
Dalmeny	Ebenezer	MB	1901	USA
Drake	Nordstern	GC	1906	USA
	Drake	GC	1913	USA
Eigenheim	Rosenorter	GC	1894	Russia, USA
Flowing Well	Gnadenau	MB	1907	USA
Fox Valley	Fox Valley	MB	1914	USA
Great Deer	Bethel	GC		
Greenfarm	Greenfarm	MB	1912	Russia
Guernsey	Sharon	OM	1905	Ontario, USA
Hague-Osler	Rosenort	GC	1911	Manitoba
	Old Colony (14 villages)	OC	1895	Manitoba
Hepburn	Hepburn	MB	1910	USA
	Brotherfield	MB	1898	Russia, USA
Herbert	Herbert	GC	1904	Manitoba
	Herbert	MB	1905	Russia, USA
Herbert Area‡	Sommerfelder	SM	1900	Manitoba
Kelstern	Elim	MB	1907	Russia, USA
Laird	Laird	MB	1898	Manitoba
	Rosenort	GC	1894	Russia
Langham	Bruderthaler	EMB	1912	USA
	Emmanuel	KMB	1901	USA
	Zoar	GC	1912	USA
Main Centre	Main Centre	MB	1904	Russia
Rosthern	Rosenorter	GC	1891	Russia, Manitoba
Swift Current	Old Colony (15 villages)	OC	1905	Manitoba
	Emmaus	GC	1914	Manitoba
Tiefengrund	Rosenorter	GC	1910	Prussia
Turnhill	Bethania	MB	1913	
	Bruderfeld	MB	1901	USA
Waldheim	Salem	KMB	1899	USA
	Waldheim	MB	1918	USA
	Zoar	GC		USA
Woodrow	Woodrow	MB	1909	USA

* Date of founding may refer to beginnings of settlement, congregational organization, ordination, or first church building.

† MB — Mennonite Brethren; MBC — Mennonite Brethren in Christ; SM — Sommerfelder Mennonites; GC — General Conference Mennonites; OM — (Old) Mennonites; OC — Old Colony Mennonites; EMB — Evangelical Mennonite Brethren; KMB — Krimmer Mennonite Brethren.

‡ Including Main Centre and Gouldtown.

General Conference Mennonites from Kansas, Oklahoma, and Minnesota established congregations (settlements) at Drake, Waldheim, and Langham, while others joined Manitoba Mennonites moving to Herbert and Swift Current and the Rosenort groups around Rosthern. Mennonite Brethren from Minnesota, Nebraska, Kansas, and Oklahoma settled at Aberdeen, Borden, Dalmeny, Hepburn, Herbert, Laird, and Waldheim. The Krimmer Mennonite Brethren from Nebraska and Kansas found a home at Langham and Waldheim, while the Evangelical Mennonite Brethren or Bruderthaler (as they were still known in Minnesota) founded one congregation at Langham.

Some (Old) Mennonites from Lancaster, Pennsylvania, joined their friends from Ontario in establishing a congregation of about 50 members at Guernsey in the first decade of the century.[44] The letters which American immigrants sent to their friends had the effect of confirming what the land and immigration agents were saying — that it was possible to survive in Canada. The following is a sample of such correspondence:

> The Giver of all good is showering blessings, both naturally and spiritually upon us . . . When some of our eastern friends hear of the grain grown in this land of snow, as some term it, they think it hardly possible to mature grain in so short a season . . . We had little work done on the land before May 1 and wheat that was sown at that time started to head from 60 to 70 days from time of sowing; and wheat sown as late as May 20 started heading in from 50 to 55 days from time of sowing. We expect wheat harvest to be here about August 20.[45]

With the start of the First World War in 1914, migration to Canada from Europe was terminated, but the Mennonites continued to trickle in from the United States. The movement nearly reached flood proportions when American harassment of conscientious objectors turned Canada into a place of political refuge.

The implications of the Mennonite scattering into scores of new little communities across the prairies were not lost in the minds of certain Mennonite leaders. They realized increasingly that unless special efforts were made to hold the Mennonite family together, its separate parts would be assimilated and disappear into the rest of the Canadian society. The general answer which Mennonitism had given to such drifting was a

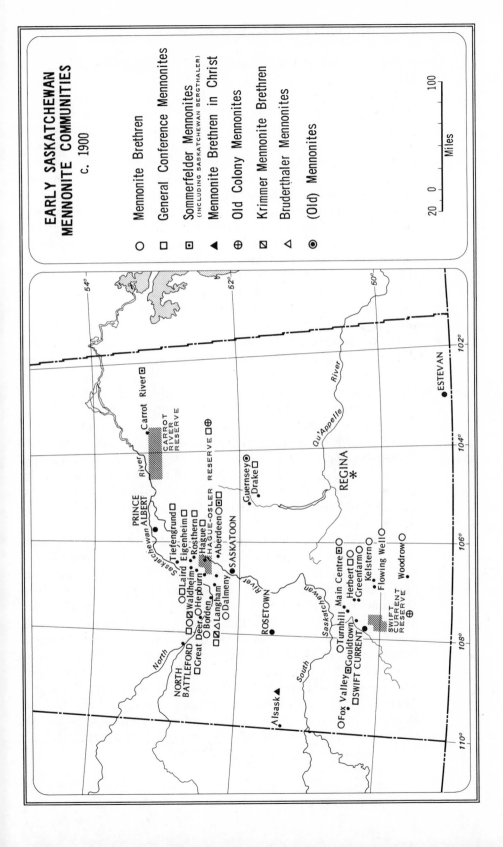

EARLY SASKATCHEWAN
MENNONITE COMMUNITIES
c. 1900

○   Mennonite Brethren

□   General Conference Mennonites

▣   Sommerfelder Mennonites
(INCLUDING SASKATCHEWAN BERGTHALER)

▲   Mennonite Brethren in Christ

⊕   Old Colony Mennonites

▨   Krimmer Mennonite Brethren

△   Bruderthaler Mennonites

◉   (Old) Mennonites

20   0   100
         Miles

closer community of the people and their congregations by forming conferences.

As yet, there was little hope of forming a single conference,
though the idea was current in some areas and among some
people. In North America the first of a series of unofficial All-
Mennonite Conventions had been planned; it was held in 1913
at Berne, Indiana.[46] Generally speaking, however, the Mennonite
world was not ready for any serious ecumenicity in the early
twentieth century, even though in the wider Christian universe
there were ecumenical stirrings. The historic 1911 international
and ecumenical Missionary Conference in Edinburgh was then
in preparation and Canadian newspapers publicized the participation of Canadian churchmen in such events.[47] For Mennonites,
the divisions resulting from the awakenings and denominational
competitions were still too fresh and, besides, the whole idea of
"conference" was still being questioned almost everywhere it was
promoted.

The organizational character of Canadian Mennonitism around
1912 may be described in two different ways. On the one hand,
there were the independent congregations led by bishops, and on
the other hand, the conferences which tied like-minded congregations together, regionally and/or continentally. The conservative
groups retained the strong emphasis on the congregation that was
led by one bishop and several ministers and deacons, all of them
elected for life. In Ontario these included all the Amish groups,
the Reformed Mennonites, and the Old Order Mennonites. In
Manitoba and Saskatchewan, they were the Old Colony and the
Sommerfelder as well as the Kleine Gemeinde and the Chortitzer,
shown in Table 4.[48]

It should be indicated here that the Bergthaler of northern
Saskatchewan were most closely aligned with the Sommerfelder
family, which had been constituted in the West Reserve of
Manitoba in 1892-93 by Bishop Abraham Doerksen of the village
of Sommerfeld. However, in 1893, when the first Sommerfelder
began moving into the Northwest Territories, the name was still
new in Manitoba and thus the immigrants carried the old name
Bergthaler with them. The Saskatchewan Bergthaler (or Sommerfelder), therefore, must not be confused with the Bergthaler
who stayed in Manitoba or with those who moved to Didsbury,
Alberta. The Saskatchewan Bergthaler appear to have had an
element of liberality about them, and thus were able to absorb
at least some of the immigrants coming to the Saskatchewan

TABLE 4

MENNONITE CONGREGATIONAL GROUPS
ORGANIZED AROUND BISHOPS (1912)

NAME	PLACE	BISHOP	MEMBERSHIP*
	Ontario		
Old Order	Waterloo North Markham Cayuga	Paul Martin Christian Reesor Freeman Rittenhouse	408
Amish	Wilmot East Zorra Blake (Hay) Wellesley Mornington	Daniel H. Steinman Jacob M. Bender Jacob M. Bender Jacob Wagler Elias Frey (Ohio)	1,362
Old Order Amish	Wellesley Mornington	Peter Jantzi Christian L. Kuepfer	
			200
Beachy Amish	Mornington Wellesley	Nicholas Nafziger Jacob F. Lichti	
Reformed Mennonites	Stevensville, Port Colborne, Rainham, Wilmot, Arkona.	Wilmer Steele (1917)	300
	Manitoba		
Kleine Gemeinde	East Reserve Morris Area	Peter R. Dueck Jacob M. Kroeker	393
Chortitzer	East Reserve	Peter Toews	835
Sommerfelder	West Reserve	David Stoesz	2,085
Old Colony	West Reserve	Peter Wiebe	1,545
	Saskatchewan		
Old Colony	Hague-Osler Reserve Swift Current Reserve	Jacob Wiens Abram Wiebe	1,668
Bergthaler	Aberdeen-Rosthern Area Carrot River Area	Aron Zacharias Cornelius Epp	80† 30†
Sommerfelder	Herbert Area	David F. Doerksen	70†

* Includes baptized membership only. To obtain approximate total number of "souls" multiply by 2.4.
† Estimate.

Valley from other regions. One Johann J. Friesen, who had been born in Nebraska, became one of the leading Bergthaler ministers in 1914, serving them well for 30 years.

Among all these bishop-centred congregations, it was common in new settlements to elect new bishops and thereby to form independent congregations which were not linked to others by conferences. Only very rarely did all the bishops (and sometimes the ministers and deacons) come together to discuss common problems. Minutes were rarely kept. Thus, to give one example, the different Old Colony congregations in Manitoba and Saskatchewan could, even in their conservatism, develop different styles and outlooks, the particular congregational character being for the most part determined by the bishop. Only major questions, such as public school, militarism, and immigration, or the death of a bishop, might bring them together. The times when they met with leaders of other Mennonite groups were even rarer; not even the First World War brought them all together for consultation on its implications for them.

All the other Mennonite groups adopted, to a greater or lesser extent, the conference or denominational system. This system was characterized by the linking together of congregations through elected representatives who would meet annually, eventually under the guidance of a constitution, to discuss matters of common concern. The progressive development of the conference system saw ministers and deacons added to the bishops as representatives. Later, unordained lay delegates were added, and women and young people were involved in some instances.

All the conference systems had a North American context (see Chapter 10). Several of the congregational families in Canada remained small enough not to consider any regionalism. They were: the Church of God in Christ Mennonite (Holdeman), the Evangelical Mennonite Brethren (Bruderthaler), and the Krimmer Mennonite Brethren. Their American counterparts, however, quickly agreed to conduct their North American conferences at Canadian locations as soon as possible and as often as a proper rotation made it feasible (see Table 5).[49]

The larger Canadian groups, however, saw the need to establish regional conferences, such as those that had existed in Ontario for some time (see Table 6).[50] Four such conferences came into being in the West as a direct result of the new settlements in Saskatchewan and Alberta (see Table 7).[51] For the (Old) Mennonites and Mennonite Brethren in Christ this simply meant repeating in Alberta and Saskatchewan what they already had in

TABLE 5

EARLY CANADIAN GATHERINGS OF SMALLER NORTH AMERICAN GROUPS

NAME	FIRST CONFERENCE IN CANADA	CANADIAN MEMBERSHIP (1912)
Church of God in Christ Mennonite (Holdeman)	1921	247
Bruderthaler (EMB)	1911	242
Krimmer Mennonite Brethren (KMB)	1912	72

TABLE 6

ONTARIO MENNONITE CONFERENCES*

NAME	DATE OF FOUNDING	MEMBERSHIP (1913)
Mennonite Conference of Ontario	1820	1,543
Canada District, Ontario Mennonite Brethren in Christ	1874	1,589

* Note that the Amish Mennonites, named in Table 4, did not organize a Conference until 1923.

TABLE 7

CONFERENCES ORGANIZED AS A RESULT OF MIGRATION INTO NORTHWEST TERRITORIES

NAME	NORTH AMERICAN AFFILIATION*	DATE	MEMBERSHIP (c. 1912)
Conference of Mennonites in Central Canada	GC	1903	1,936
Alberta-Saskatchewan Conference	OM	1907	217
Canadian Northwest District	MBC	1908	349
Northern District Conference	MB	1910	1,200†

* GC — General Conference Mennonite Church; OM — (Old) Mennonites; MBC — Mennonite Brethren in Christ; MB — Mennonite Brethren.
† Estimate.

Ontario. For the members of the General Conference and the Mennonite Brethren this meant forming completely new regional entities. The Mennonite Brethren formed a Canadian (it was at first called Northern) district of their North American denomination.

The congregations with a General Conference identity founded a completely autonomous Canadian entity, of which not all congregations would relate to the General Conference Mennonite Church of North America. It must be remembered that the General Conference, from its beginnings in 1860, was a most flexible and diverse organization, allowing maximum autonomy and heterogeneity at the lowest level. This was quite unlike the Mennonite Brethren and Mennonite Brethren in Christ who insisted on tight organization and discipline throughout.

In the larger General Conference context, the Conference formation in Canada must, therefore, be seen as working at three levels, at least in the early 1900s. There was, first of all, the activity of the General Conference "home missionaries" who had visited Manitoba in the 1890s and Saskatchewan as soon as American settlers arrived at Waldheim, Langham, Herbert and Drake. Seen at first as mission outposts, the congregations became independent and self-sustaining in a decade or two. They also became members of the General Conference Mennonite Church.

Some other congregations who easily fell into the General Conference orbit and who were readily placed on the circuit of General Conference home missionaries were, however, much slower in affiliating because, at their core, they were not constituted by settlers from the United States. This was especially true of the Bergthaler congregations in Manitoba and Alberta and of the Rosenorter congregation in Saskatchewan.

The Bergthaler of Manitoba were the most progressive of the Russian Mennonites of the 1870s. Although a minority, they were constantly attracting new individuals and families from the Sommerfelder and Old Colony, especially on the frontiers of Manitoba settlement. Eventually there would be more than 20 local congregations under one bishop — in other words, a Bergthaler conference by itself.

Bergthaler leaders in Manitoba encouraged their settlers in Saskatchewan to join the Rosenorter congregation led by Bishop Peter Regier of Prussia; many of them did. In the Saskatchewan Valley the Rosenorter congregation served the same function as the Bergthaler in the Red River Valley, a community to which the progressives could migrate. As a great synthesizer, therefore, the Rosenorter congregation soon included people recently migrated from Prussia and Russia and others from both the United States and Manitoba.

Like the Bergthaler in Manitoba, the Rosenorter in Saskatchewan were developing many local congregations under one bishop; both shared their pattern of congregational organization with the conservatives (see Table 4). Soon there were too many units for one bishop and so the Rosenort church was divided into districts as follows: (1) Rosthern with Bergthal and district; (2) Hague with Osler and district; (3) Aberdeen and district; (4) the school districts Eigenheim, Danzig, Silberfeld, Friedensfeld, and Ebenfeld; (5) Laird and district, Carman, Springfield and Snowbird; (6) Tiefengrund with Johannesthal and Hamburg. The rules of the reorganization were: ministers worked within their own districts; each district was in charge of its own baptismal candidates; the elder served at baptism and communion; and each district had its own church, its own administration, and its own church book.[52]

Both Rosenorter and Bergthaler leaders felt, however, that an even greater fellowship was needed and so they entered into conversations leading to the organization, in 1903 at Hochstadt near Altona, Manitoba, of the Conference of Mennonites in Central Canada. In the years immediately following, it met alternately in Manitoba and Saskatchewan. Congregations, including the one at Didsbury, Alberta, began to relate to it one at a time, even as they likewise related, if they so chose, to the General Conference. The earliest sessions of the Central Canada Conference were not very concerned with program, except for the founding of the monthly periodical known as *Mitarbeiter* (Co-Worker). Rather, the goal seemed to be to reach a common understanding on such matters as the purpose of the Canadian and General Conferences, the ministry to the widely dispersed settlers, involvement in civic, legal, and political affairs, participation in worldly amusements, and keeping the young people.[53]

The (Old) Mennonite congregations in Alberta-Saskatchewan were organized into a conference in stages, with the earliest initiative coming from Ontario. In 1903 Bishop S. F. Coffman of Vineland, who had already been to Alberta on his own in 1901, was commissioned to visit the remote and scattered settlements, to ordain ministers, and to organize congregations. A year later the Alberta conference was organized and when, in 1907, Eli S. Hallman of Guernsey joined it, the name Alberta-Saskatchewan Mennonite Conference was adopted.[54]

It must have been wise statesmanship, the greater tolerance of the frontier, or the diminished need to strictly maintain old positions that brought the various (Old) Mennonite groups together. Though they were few, they were quite diverse. On the one hand, there were the conservative groups derived from the Old Order and the Amish at Mayton and Tofield, respectively. On the other hand, there were the more liberal groups at Carstairs and Guernsey. The Pennsylvania group at Duchess was relatively moderate.

At Didsbury-Carstairs all three groups — Mennonite Brethren in Christ, (Old) Mennonites, and Bergthaler — appear to have been unusually community-minded, perhaps since, as Mennonites, they were the dominant groups in the area and they themselves became involved in friendly competition. Not only did they assume leadership in business, education, and civic affairs, but some members of each of the three groups joined secret orders, a sin almost unforgivable elsewhere among the Mennonites. Since Dordrecht, such membership was expressly forbidden on the ground that secret societies were oath-bound fraternities and thus compromised exclusive loyalty to the church.[55] Several Bergthaler people were members of the King Hiram Lodge and J. E. Stauffer of the Mennonite Brethren in Christ was its secretary. Some (Old) Mennonites were members of the Masonic Lodge. This deviation has been explained as follows:

> No doubt the pioneer environment which accentuated the spirit of liberty and individualism, as well as the desire to retain a position of leadership and acceptance in an evolving community, led to such a deviation from one of the principles of the Mennonite faith.[56]

The Didsbury-Carstairs people, comprising the Rosebud constituency, elected two Mennonites as their first two representatives in the provincial legislature, both having distinguished themselves in farm organizations. Cornelius Hiebert was elected as a Conservative in 1905, the year Alberta became a province. During his term of office he fought, among other things, for prohibition and for the flag to be flown over every school. His choice of the Independent label to fight for his second election was to free himself to criticize government measures if, in his opinion, they were unfavourable. Hiebert, however, was not returned. In the 1909 election, J. E. Stauffer, of the Mennonite Brethren in Christ, running as a Liberal, won the Rosebud seat. In time Stauffer became deputy speaker of the Legislative Assembly but, while still legislator, was killed overseas as an enlistee in the First World War forces.[57]

The Mennonite Brethren in Christ likewise organized their Northwest District with the help of Ontario. In 1906, Henry Goudie, a veteran organizer and district superintendent in Ontario for five years, designated Alberta as a mission district for Ontario; a year later it became a district conference in its own right.[58] Immediate attention was given to mission activities in Alberta, as in Ontario. Also in 1906, a mission was opened in Edmonton; in 1909 it became the Beulah Home for unmarried mothers, and other "appointments" or mission stations were begun. Very soon the Mennonite name was believed to be a handicap to overcome, but efforts of the Northwest Conference to get the denomination to drop the name would not succeed until 1947. Yet the "progressive spirit" of the Canadian Northwest District experienced some early triumphs. Soon the District founded its own training school for ministers, later known as Mountain View Bible College. It would also host the first young people's convention of the denomination and be the first to organize women's missionary societies on a district-wide basis.[59]

The Mennonite Brethren Churches in Canada were organized into the Northern District Conference at Herbert, Saskatchewan, in 1910; at the same time four other district conferences within the North American General Conference of Mennonite Brethren Churches also came into being.[60] At that time, the 50th anniversary of the Mennonite Brethren Church's founding, the church had a total of 6,000 members in Russia, India, the United States and Canada. About one sixth of them were in Canada.[61] When the Northern District was organized there were 13 churches in Saskatchewan with nearly 1,000 members. The two Manitoba congregations, Winkler and Winnipeg (the latter recently founded as a city mission), joined in 1913, at which time the membership exceeded 1,200.[62]

The first conference at Herbert was held in a 50-by-90-foot tent to accommodate the many visitors, 85 of whom had come by train on reduced fares. The language was German except on the evening of the *Festsonntag* when one English sermon was given. Most of the concerns of the conference could be summarized by the word "mission" — foreign, home and city. Collections were assigned equally to these causes. The home mission work was carried on mainly through colporteur-evangelists, one in the Rosthern and one in the Herbert area. At that first meeting the monthly salary for missionaries was raised from $30 to $40 because "the wages for farm labour had gone up and because in the north (Canada) everything cost more."[63]

Thus, the new settlements and conferences that profoundly helped to shape the Canadian Mennonite destiny were formed. It was a destiny which saw the Mennonites not fully united precisely at a time when the larger Canadian society was beginning consciously to absorb and mould them. As attempts were made to assimilate the aliens, especially for reasons of patriotism, the Mennonites became sorely pressed on every side. Some accepted the assimilation as good; most resisted it as being very bad. Whatever the stance, the impending war forced Mennonites to reconsider their relationship to the world outside, as well as to the state.

FOOTNOTES

1. John H. Warkentin, "The Mennonite Settlement of Southern Manitoba" (Ph.D. dissertation, University of Toronto, 1960), pp. 209–10.
2. Canada, *Dominion Census Reports*, 1901, 1911, 1921.
3. Warkentin, *op. cit.*, p. 200; and J. F. Galbraith, *The Mennonites in Manitoba, 1875–1900: A Review of their Coming, their Progress, and their Present Prosperity* (Morden, Man.: The Chronicle Press, 1900), p. 36.
4. Leo Driedger, "A Sect in a Modern Society: A Case Study: The Old Colony Mennonites of Saskatchewan" (M.A. dissertation, University of Chicago, 1955), p. 13.
5. R. C. Brown, *Canada's National Policy, 1883–1900: A Study in Canadian-American Relations* (Princeton: University Press, 1964), p. 12.
6. See David Healy, *US Expansionism: The Imperialist Urge in the 1890s* (Madison: University of Wisconsin Press, 1970).
7. Leo Driedger, "Louis Riel and the Mennonite Invasion," *The Canadian Mennonite*, XVIII (August 28, 1970), p. 6.
8. A. S. Morton, *History of Prairie Settlement* (Toronto: Macmillan Company, 1938), p. 96.
9. Aron Sawatzky, "The Mennonites of Alberta and their Assimilation" (M.A. dissertation, University of Alberta, 1964), p. 28.

10. PAC, *Dominion Lands Branch*, Record Group 15, Vol. 232, p. 3129, L. Lynwode Pereira to David Gascho, April 30, 1891.
11. Warkentin, *op. cit.*, p. 200.
12. *Edmonton Bulletin*, October 24, 1898, p. 2. The *Bulletin*, edited by Frank Oliver, Member of Parliament, editorialized on the establishment of reserves in Saskatchewan.
13. Warkentin, *op. cit.*, p. 200.
14. Sawatzky, *op. cit.*, p. 28.
15. *Ibid.*, p. 29.
16. M. Weber, "The Part Played by Immigrants from Waterloo County to the Didsbury, Alberta Settlement, 1894," *Waterloo Historical Society*, XXXVIII (1950), pp. 13–21.
17. *Ibid.*, p. 16.
18. Everek Richard Storms, "Acadia Valley," *Mennonite Encyclopedia*, I, p. 9; J. W. Toews, "Linden," *Mennonite Encyclopedia*, III, pp. 349–50; Melvin Gingerich, "Alberta," *Mennonite Encyclopedia*, I, pp. 31–3; Ezra Stauffer, "Clearwater," *Mennonite Encyclopedia*, I, p. 620; Everek Richard Storms, "Didsbury," *Mennonite Encyclopedia*, II, p. 52; Ezra Stauffer, "Duchess," *Mennonite Encyclopedia*, II, p. 105; Ezra Stauffer, "Mayton," *Mennonite Encyclopedia*, III, p. 546; Milo D. Stutzman, "Tofield," *Mennonite Encyclopedia*, IV, p. 736. See also: Peter F. Bargen, "The Mennonites in Alberta" (M.A. dissertation, University of British Columbia, 1953); and Aron Sawatzky, *op. cit.*
19. Clarence Hiebert, "The Holdeman People: A Study of the Church of God in Christ Mennonite, 1858–1969" (Ph.D. dissertation, Case Western Reserve University, 1971).
20. Frank H. Epp, "The Story of Rosthern Junior College" (unpublished manuscript in possession of the author, 1969), pp. 9–10.
21. *Saskatoon Star Phoenix*, XLV (January 2, 1947), p. 3.
22. Warkentin, *op. cit.*, p. 201.
23. Frank H. Epp, *Mennonite Exodus: The Rescue and Resettlement of the Russian Mennonites Since the Communist Revolution* (Altona, Man.: D. W. Friesen & Sons, 1962), p. 61.
24. George Dyck, "I Remember Gerhard Ens," *The Canadian Mennonite*, XV (June 13, 1967), p. 44; J. G. Rempel, "Gerhard Ens," *Mennonite Encyclopedia*, II, p. 225.
25. *Saskatoon Star Phoenix*, XLV (January 3, 1947), p. 3.
26. J. G. Rempel, *Die Rosenorter Gemeinde in Saskatchewan: In Wort und Bild* (Rosthern, Sask.: D. H. Epp, 1950), p. 13.
27. *Order-in-Council*, Record Group 2, 1, 188 (January 23, 1895).
28. *Ibid.*
29. Margaret Heinrichs, "Hague in Saskatchewan," *Mennonite Life*, XIII (January 1958), pp. 18–19.
30. *Order-in-Council*, Record Group 2, 1, 1627 (June 24, 1898).
31. Warkentin, *op. cit.*, p. 193 ff.
32. *Ibid.*, p. 198.

33. *Order-in-Council*, Record Group 2, 1, 1605 (August 13, 1904).
34. *Ibid.*
35. J. G. Rempel, "Hague and Osler," *Mennonite Encyclopedia*, II, p. 628; Cornelius Krahn, "Swift Current," *Mennonite Encyclopedia*, IV, p. 669.
36. See Leo Driedger, "A Sect in Modern Society . . ." *op. cit.* Also see Leo Driedger, "Hague-Osler Settlement," *Mennonite Life*, XIII (January 1958), pp. 13–17; Leo Driedger, "Saskatchewan Old Colony Mennonites," *Mennonite Life*, XIII (April 1958), pp. 63–6.
37. *Order-in-Council*, Record Group 2, 1, 2747 (December 6, 1898) and 1676 (August 12, 1899).
38. *Revised Statutes of Canada*, Militia Act, c. 41, Sect. 21, Sub-Sect. 3.
39. Morton, *op. cit.*, pp. 112–13.
40. Victor Peters, *All Things Common: The Hutterian Way of Life* (Minneapolis: University of Minnesota Press, 1966), pp. 47–8.
41. PAC, *Immigration Branch*, Record Group 76, 1, Vol. 173, 58764, 1. Charles A. Jones to Commissioner of Immigration, January 6, 1899.
42. See Epp, *op. cit.*, p. 3.
43. J. G. Rempel, "Saskatchewan," *Mennonite Encyclopedia*, IV, pp. 424–26; J. H. Epp, "Aberdeen MB Church," *Mennonite Encyclopedia*, I, p. 7; J. H. Epp, "Borden," *Mennonite Encyclopedia*, I, p. 389; J. H. Epp, "Dalmeny," *Mennonite Encyclopedia*, I, p. 4; G. G. Epp, "Eigenheim," *Mennonite Encyclopedia*, II, p. 170; J. Gerbrandt, "North Star," *Mennonite Encyclopedia*, III, p. 922; Ezra Stauffer, "Sharon," *Mennonite Encyclopedia*, IV, p. 512; J. G. Rempel, "Hague and Osler," *Mennonite Encyclopedia*, II, p. 628; J. G. Rempel, "Herbert," *Mennonite Encyclopedia*, II, p. 708; J. H. Epp, "Herbert MB Church," *Mennonite Encyclopedia*, II, p. 708; P. R. Toews, "Hepburn MB Church," *Mennonite Encyclopedia*, II, p. 706; J. H. Epp, "Laird MB Church," *Mennonite Encyclopedia*, III, pp. 268–69; J. G. Rempel, "Laird," *Mennonite Encyclopedia*, III, p. 268; Melvin Gingerich, "Langham," *Mennonite Encyclopedia*, III, p. 290; Valentine E. Nickel, "Emmaus," *Mennonite Encyclopedia*, II, pp. 204–5; J. G. Rempel, "Waldheim," *Mennonite Encyclopedia*, IV, p. 876; J. H. Epp, "Waldheim MB Church," *Mennonite Encyclopedia,* IV, p. 876.
44. E. S. Hallman, *The Hallman-Clemens Genealogy with a Family's Reminiscence* (Tuleta, Kans.: E. S. Hallman Family, n.d.).
45. Martin D. Musser, "Correspondence: Guernsey, Saskatchewan," *Gospel Herald*, VI (August 14, 1913), p. 313.
46. C. H. Smith, "All-Mennonite Convention," *Mennonite Encyclopedia*, I, p. 62; *Echoes of the First-All-Mennonite Convention in America* (Hillsboro, Kans., 1913); P. E. Whitmer, "The All-Men-

nonite Convention," *Yearbook of the General Conference of the Mennonite Church of North America,* 1931, pp. 42–3; N. E. Beyers, "The All-Mennonite Convention," *Mennonite Life,* III (July 1948), pp. 7–8, 10.

47. "World Conference on Church Union: Big Project to Unite Religious Forces of Christendom," newspaper article found in J. F. Funk Collection.

48. Source of membership figures: "Statistik der Mennoniten-Gemeinde," *Der Mitarbeiter,* VII (February 1913), p. 37; J. H. Lohrenz, "Canadian Conference," *Mennonite Encyclopedia,* I, p. 505; *Mennonite Yearbook,* 1913.

49. "Statistik der Mennoniten-Gemeinde," *Der Mitarbeiter,* VII (February 1913), p. 37.

50. *Mennonite Yearbook,* 1913.

51. "Statistik der Mennoniten-Gemeinde," *Der Mitarbeiter,* VII (February 1913), p. 37; also *Mennonite Yearbook,* 1913.

52. J. G. Rempel, *Die Rosenorter Gemeinde in Saskatchewan, op. cit.,* p. 25.

53. Minutes of Conference of Mennonites in Central Canada, July 20–21, 1903. See also J. G. Rempel, *Fuenfzig Jahre Konferenz-bestrebungen, 1902–1952,* Part I.

54. Melvin Gingerich, "Alberta-Saskatchewan Mennonite Conference," *Mennonite Encyclopedia,* I, p. 34; Ezra Stauffer, "The Alberta-Saskatchewan Mennonite Conference," Ryley, Alberta, 107 pp.

55. *The Complete Works of Menno Simons* (Scottdale, Pa.: Mennonite Publishing House, 1956), Vol. II, pp. 410, 412. Based on such scripture passages as John 18: 19–20 and II Corinthians 6: 14–17.

56. Sawatzky, *op. cit.,* p. 44.

57. *Ibid.,* pp. 51a–56.

58. Everek Richard Storms, *History of the United Missionary Church* (Elkhart, Ind.: Bethel Publishing Company, 1958), p. 158.

59. *Ibid.,* pp. 157–64; S. F. Pannabecker, "Canadian Northwest Conference," *Mennonite Encyclopedia,* I, p. 509. The school was founded in 1921 and the youth convention was held in 1925.

60. A. H. Unruh, *Die Geschichte der Mennoniten-Bruedergemeinde* (Hillsboro, Kans.: General Conference of the Mennonite Brethren Church of North America, 1955), pp. 547–54.

61. J. H. Lohrenz, "Mennonite Brethren Church," *Mennonite Encyclopedia,* III, pp. 595–602.

62. J. H. Lohrenz, "Canadian Conference of the MB Church of North America," *Mennonite Encyclopedia,* I, pp. 505–6.

63. *Yearbook of the Northern District Conference of the Mennonite Brethren Church for the Year 1911,* p. 9.

Flag-raising for an Empty School

14. Education: Church v. State

The rationale for the public schools was expressed with the following slogan: one king, one God, one navy, one all-British empire . . . For us it was unthinkable that we should educate our children with [such implications] — ISAAK M. DYCK.[1]

A s we have seen, the Mennonites were intimately involved with opening up the western parts of Canada. This fact and the geographical scattering of their settlements had cultural implications which both Canada and the Mennonites tried to avoid. They were both interested, for their own reasons, in maximizing the agricultural opportunity, but the long-term cultural interaction, or the lack of it, could not be ignored. Because of felt national needs, the tension of an uneasy relationship mounted and reached a critical peak during the First World War. It eventually led to yet another emigration.

This clash of values reached its greatest intensity in the school struggle between the conservative-minded groups on the reserves and the governments of Manitoba and Saskatchewan. It was not limited, however, to those two provinces or to the conservatives. Progressive-minded Mennonites, who made many accommodations and accepted a degree of assimilation, were also concerned about the preservation of precious values. The confrontation of cultures could, therefore, be identified as a universal Mennonite phenomenon, with its internal as well as external manifestations.

333

On the surface the confrontation seemed to be merely the jealous opposition of the English and the German languages. But at its deepest levels it was much more than that. The value systems which opposed each other were nothing less than the British military imperium and a pacifist sect which believed itself to be espousing the kingdom of God and its righteousness. For Canada as a whole, it represented a first round in the long battle between Anglo assimilation and integrationists, and non-Anglo ethnic separation and religious dissent. The official Canadian policy of multi-culturalism had not yet suggested itself either to the federal or to the provincial governments, except for the short-term purpose of settling the prairies.

The Mennonite cultural problem was not limited to Canada. In Russia, for instance, the non-emigrating group had after the 1870s developed a vast and sophisticated school system as its own defence against Russification. Its people did not, however, oppose the learning of the Russian language. On the contrary, after they had been thoroughly scolded by the Imperial Council of St. Petersburg for their neglect, they turned with considerable zeal to learning Russian for its own sake and so as not to lose the respect of the tsar. Some Mennonite educators developed so great a love for certain Russian writers that they were not only read and quoted with regularity, but also translated with enthusiasm. The poet, Lermontev, for example, became a challenge to several Mennonite poets.[2]

The Russian Mennonite school system, which by 1914 included 400 elementary schools, 13 high schools, several colleges, and a variety of specialized schools, was therefore not intended to avoid the Russian language. Rather, the intention was to learn new culture while strengthening the old one. That old culture was then described as *Deutsch und Religion* (German and religion), representing the twin concepts of the Mennonite value system and consequently of education.[3] By offering in their schools a strong German curriculum of literature, language and religion, the Mennonites saw themselves surviving in the midst of the Russian influence. And if Russia, the national mother of the Mennonites, had not been opposed to Germany, their cultural parent, this formula for cultural and religious survival might very well have been adequate.

The outbreak of the First World War brought a clampdown on the public use of the German language as well as property liquidation proceedings against Russian Germans nearest the front.

Mennonites managed to escape the harsh treatment accorded to other Germans by stressing their Dutch ancestry. This *Hollaenderei*, as the Dutch lobby became known, aroused controversy among the Mennonites and suspicion in Russia generally. After all, there had been no Dutch nationality in the modern sense since the Anabaptists had first fled to Prussia in the sixteenth century. Furthermore, the Low German dialects in use, especially for everyday parlance, were only a remote reflection of the Dutch language and were popular in some form in most of the north German areas. Besides, the identity with German culture, a priority for some, and Russian citizenship obligations, a priority for others, militated against any genuine *Hollaenderei*. Although *Hollaenderei* was resorted to as an expedient in times of cultural and national crisis,[4] it did have some basis in fact. It symbolized an ongoing process of acculturation despite the attempt to use language as a vehicle in the process of group maintenance and separation from the world.[5]

The Mennonites during the Prussian sojourn were initially Dutch in language and culture, and acculturated in the direction of the literary High German only under the protests of the traditionalists. For the less educated and more conservative Mennonites, the more common and less literary Low German remained the dominant language with a more cultural High German gloss appearing slowly and then only for formal occasions. The Mennonites who came to Manitoba fell into this latter category. And for their cause of maintaining separation from the world, both High and Low German were as functional in Canada as in Russia.

The educational system emerging at the college level among American Mennonites served a role similar to that of the vast network of schools in Russia. The colleges were intended to fortify Mennonite religious values so that any cultural accommodation to American society would not threaten the essential core. There was a critical difference, however, between the American and Russian Mennonites. The former, already influenced by the melting-pot, were assuming the inevitability, perhaps even the desirability, of a language transition, while the latter insisted that the cultural pressures would never make them Russian.[6] The Americans assumed that the linguistic cultural forms of Mennonitism could be changed without great peril to the content of their religion. To the Russian Mennonites, however, it was quite clear that their cultural environment could not be radically changed without drastically affecting its religious content.

The first five Mennonite schools founded in Canada (see Table 1)[7] generally shared the American assumptions. The three Bible schools at Kitchener, Herbert and Didsbury, founded primarily for the training of church workers, represented in themselves three different positions. The Didsbury school of the Mennonite Brethren in Christ, the farthest west and, of the five, the most recent, aligned itself — linguistically, culturally and, to a degree, theologically — with the denomination on the frontier of assimilation. The Institute at Kitchener likewise accepted the language transition, but in every other cultural and theological way it intended to prevent Mennonite assimilation with surrounding society. A simple life-style, nonconformity in clothing and nonresistance remained paramount. The Herbert school was influenced by recent immigrants from Russia and from the United States and was, therefore, bilingual from the beginning, though, when in doubt, it gave way to English. The strong missionary impulse of the Mennonite Brethren and the Mennonite Brethren in Christ justified an earlier anglicization at Herbert and at Didsbury respectively than might otherwise have been acceptable.

The two Mennonite high schools at Gretna and Rosthern were in a class by themselves. They were not sponsored by individual Mennonite denominations, as was the case with the Bible schools, though Bergthaler and Rosenorter people, respectively, stood at the heart of the school societies which founded them. Both schools were inspired by the American educational assumptions and drew their strong leaders from Kansas. Neither attained the college level to which they aspired.

As opposed to the Bible schools, the high schools — at first really teacher training institutions — stood at the crossroads of the Mennonite and Canadian cultures. They were intended to be substitutes for the public system; teaching a government curriculum, they partially overlapped it. As teacher training institutes, they accepted and promoted the public elementary schools but hoped to keep them as Mennonite as possible. As the name of the Rosthern German-English Academy implies, these schools assumed a cultural dualism for the Mennonites. Along with their American cousins, they accepted the English culture more strongly than the Russian Mennonites had accepted the Russian. However, they insisted much more vigorously than the

TABLE 1

EARLY POST-ELEMENTARY MENNONITE SCHOOLS IN CANADA

NAME	PLACE	DATE OF FOUNDING	CHARACTER
Mennonite Collegiate Institute*	Gretna, Man.	1889	High school and teacher training.
German-English Academy	Rosthern, Sask.	1905	High school and teacher training.
Ontario Mennonite Bible Institute	Kitchener, Ont.	1907	Bible school and training of church workers (OM).†
Herbert Bible School	Herbert, Sask.	1913	Bible school and training of church workers (MB).
Mountain View Training School for Ministers	Didsbury, Alta.	1921	Bible school and training of church workers (MBC).

* First known as Gretna Normal School, and from 1898 to 1908 as Mennonite Educational Institute. In 1908 the MEI became two schools temporarily (until 1926); the Altona school was called MEI and the Gretna school Mennonite Collegiate Institute.
† OM — (Old) Mennonite; MB — Mennonite Brethren; MBC — Mennonite Brethren in Christ.

Americans on the retention of the German culture. In that sense they were like the Russian schools, which built their hope on a strong *Deutsch und Religion* curriculum.

In their biculturalism these schools had the potential of averting, or at least diminishing, the cultural clash that was mounting between the majority of the Mennonites and the Canadian government. However, they represented only a minority Mennonite movement. In Manitoba and Saskatchewan a well-defined Mennonite majority refused to accept the Gretna and Rosthern schools. In Manitoba, particularly in the West Reserve where the school was located, the Old Colony and most of the Sommerfelder stood aloof. The Kleine Gemeinde and the Chortitzer of the East Reserve were of a similar mind, but their geographic distance made an explicit expression on the question unnecessary.

In the Saskatchewan Valley the Rosenorter supporters of the German-English Academy were joined by isolated individuals from the Mennonite Brethren, the Bruderthaler, and the Krimmer Mennonite Brethren. There too the Old Colony and the Saskatchewan Bergthaler remained bitterly opposed.

The popular interpretation of these opposing stances was, and still is, that the Old Colony and the Sommerfelder were against education. In fact they were opposed only to a certain kind of education. To be sure, they were inclined to limit elementary school to six or seven, at most eight, years. In their minds more than eight years was related to a change in quality; further formal education pointed away from the agricultural way of life. It is in this context that their own saying must be understood: *"Je gelehrter, desto verkehrter"* (more education, more confusion).[8]

Additionally, the conservatives believed that education was the responsibility of the family and the church. The moment they surrendered this responsibility to the state, they felt that they surrendered to a qualitative difference in education, to urban rather than rural values, to a vocational rather than a moral orientation, to the goals of government rather than those of the church. The Old Order Mennonites and Old Order Amish in Ontario held a similar view on education, though their quarrel with the public school system reached the breaking point many years later when it became clear to them that the creation of larger districts had wrested from them all educational control.

In the negotiations of 1873, the Mennonites arriving from Russia thought they had been permanently guaranteed a church-oriented rather than a state-oriented education. Clause #10 of the letter that John M. Lowe wrote to delegates David Klassen, Jacob Peters, Heinrich Wiebe and Cornelius Toews in 1873 had remained very precious to them. It read:

> The fullest privilege of exercising their religious principles
> is by law afforded the Mennonites, without any kind of
> molestation or restriction whatever, and the same privilege
> extends to the education of their children in schools.[9]

The Mennonites did not know, nor were they told, that authority over schools had been given to the provinces by the British North America Act.[10] Neither were they told that three days after the Secretary of Agriculture had confirmed an agreement with the delegates it was changed by the Minister of Agriculture and that this change, rather than the original agreement, was given the strength of law by Order-in-Council, which read as follows:

> That the Mennonites will have the fullest privileges of
> exercising their religious principles, and educating their
> children in schools, as provided by law, without any kind of
> molestation or restriction whatever.[11]

The difference between the two statements was a fundamental one. The first, which the Mennonites thought had the force of law, entitled them to their own private schools without "any kind of molestation or restriction whatever." The second limited their freedom to such schools as would be provided for by law. As the legal provisions shifted from private to public schools, the Mennonites felt certain that their rights were being violated. The federal government may well have been acting in good faith and assumed that the provincial governments would not contradict their agreements. None the less, there is no evidence that the Mennonites were ever informed that their *Privilegium* stood on contested ground and that it was amended, perhaps quite innocently by legal clerks, to match the language of existing laws in the secret chambers of Ottawa.[12]

The repeated efforts of Manitoba government representatives since the late 1870s to introduce publicly financed district schools had, therefore, been viewed with suspicion and opposition. The financial advantages in the arrangement militated against the jurisdictional disadvantages, and it had therefore been most difficult for the Mennonites to come to a unanimous and consistent position. Most of the Manitoba Mennonites rejected the district schools some of the time. A few always rejected them, and a few were favourably disposed toward them from the beginning. This vacillation brought on governmental interference. The result was a gradual undermining of the Mennonite position and the erosion of the private school situation. As Gerhard Wiebe of the East Reserve later wrote:

> We were in Canada for only a few years when money was
> offered to us for the support of our schools. This however
> seemed hazardous to us for we feared to lose our school
> freedom which had been promised to us by the government;
> but Hespeler said, "There is no danger." Hence we agreed
> to accept it. We went to him with the entire lists of the

names of our school teachers and Hespeler told us to divide
our school teachers into three classes. "Why," we asked.
"Well," he said, "you don't think that the government will
give its money to men who are cowherds in summer and
school teachers in winter." Then, the author gathered his
papers together and said, "Mr. Hespeler, now we understand,
we will keep to the arrangement which our deputies have
made for us."[13]

A definite turning point came in 1890 with passage of the
Manitoba Public Schools Act. The Act ended the denominational
public schools, Protestant and Catholic, and made English the
official language of instruction in the secular, state-controlled
and tax-supported school system.[14] To pacify the French Catholics, certain concessions to religious and bilingual instruction
were made. These benefited also the Mennonites; they could
join the district school system and still cultivate *Deutsch und
Religion*. If more than ten pupils in a given school — a requirement easily met in the solid Mennonite districts — had a mother
tongue other than English, instruction could with official sanction
be given in a limited way in that language. Religion could be
taught by lengthening the teaching day.

For the progressive Mennonites these compromises were acceptable; for the conservatives they were not. They took advantage, therefore, of the loopholes in the law which left open
the matter of compulsory attendance at public schools.[15] The
government for its part embarked on the promotion and, as much
as possible, on the institution of district public schools in all the
ethnic areas of Manitoba, including the East and West Reserves.
Whereas in 1879 all 36 schools had been registered with the
Protestant Denomination Board, there were in 1891 only eight
listed as district schools in a total of at least 100.

At that point the progressive-minded Mennonites, who had
founded the Gretna school in 1889, joined their interests with
those of the government, as we have seen. With the Rev. Dr.
George Bryce of the Department of Education leading the way
and with the encouragement of the Hon. William Hespeler, Heinrich H. Ewert of Kansas was persuaded not only to head up the
Gretna Normal School which was refounded in 1891, but also to
be promoter and inspector of district schools among the Mennonites.[16]

For the conservative Mennonites, Ewert's identity with the
United States was in itself almost enough reason to reject him.

After all, the Manitoba immigrants believed that those going to America had made a fundamental compromise in their faith and thus they did not look kindly upon American efforts to teach them a better way. Besides, they thought Ewert had been educated for too long in the schools of America. Not only had he attended the State Normal School at Emporia, Kansas, and the Des Moines Institute of Iowa, but also the theological seminary of the Evangelical Synod of Missouri. On the other hand, Ewert was not a Russian Mennonite and could be seen, therefore, as not having shared totally the identity of the Russians in the United States. He had been born in Prussia and his father, Wilhelm Ewert, had been the Prussian member of the 12-man delegation that had toured North America in 1873.[17] It could also be said that Ewert himself had made a fundamental decision not unlike that of the conservatives, by accepting the offer in Manitoba. It was clear from the beginning that he meant to identify himself with the people of Manitoba and that he had turned his back on Kansas. He and his brother, Benjamin, whom he recruited as a teacher for a district school, allowed themselves to be quickly enrolled with the Bergthaler. Soon they were both on the preaching circuit lists of Bishop Johann Funk and Benjamin was ordained a minister. They were, therefore, adaptable, but as E. K. Francis has said of the senior Ewert:

> He was also in a way a marginal man and shared the fate
> of the marginal man. While he was working for a
> compromise, he was blamed by his own people for betraying
> their best interest and by the Anglo-Saxons for not
> achieving enough.[18]

H. H. Ewert took charge of his office on September 1, 1891, and immediately made a tour of all the Mennonite settlements of Manitoba. Since he had had no immediate predecessors, there were no statistics, reports or other information available to him. Eight district schools had been in operation, four in the east and four in the west. "These schools had given good satisfaction to the people, and considered by most of them an improvement on the private schools still maintained by the vast majority of Mennonites," he said in his first report.[19] While most villages or settlements had private schools, there were several localities where no schools of any kind were maintained. The reason for this state of affairs was lack of agreement on whether the schools would be private or public, and, if private, which church organization would be in charge.

Ewert began his task of establishing district schools precisely in those areas where outside initiative could shift public opinion, which he did in the direction of the government. An important instrument in the advancement of the district schools was the Gretna Normal School, of which he was the principal. Ewert, salaried by the government, proceeded to conduct five-week "normal sessions" for prospective teachers, who eventually were certified to teach in Mennonite schools. Ewert prepared them for the teaching profession by giving them a command of both the German and the English languages and introducing them to methods of religious instruction. The curriculum included Bible, church history, apologetics and ethics, as well as subjects outlined in the program of studies by the Department. At the beginning of the first year Ewert had eight students and this rose to 28.[20]

Very carefully and diligently Ewert worked at the task of preparing teachers for teaching, and the Mennonite people for the acceptance of district schools in which his teachers would be installed. By 1895 there were 24 district schools in operation, an increase of 16. Two of the 25 Mennonite teachers placed therein had permanent departmental certification, the others holding interim certificates. Seven of these brought teaching credentials with them from the United States, Russia and Prussia.[21] It was Ewert's conviction that the best way to preserve Mennonite values was to accept public schools for Mennonite areas but to place well-qualified teachers in them. They could supplement the government requirements with the curriculum and language of the church.

For the conservatives, however, the Ewert approach represented too much compromise and an unacceptable erosion of values. After all, the final direction and quality of education was determined by those who controlled the schools. To them the ultimate direction, if not the immediate application, of the Ewert formula was totally unacceptable. A meeting of one set of village farmers, as later recorded anonymously (perhaps by Ewert himself), reveals the flow of the conservatives' thinking:

> *An Older Neighbour*:   We do not wish to have an inspector.
>   Our schools are good enough.
> *A Younger Neighbour*:   I believe it would be well if we
>   could have some English in our schools.
> *Several Voices*:   What! English?

Other Younger Neighbours: Why not? We should know
    how to read and write English. That is necessary. Who
    now can really decipher the government letter that has
    been sent to us?
An Older Person: That is entirely unnecessary. Our
    schools are private schools and the government has
    nothing to say to them.
A Voice from the Rear: No, he must not be allowed to do
    that. We must treat the government with respect.
A Neighbour: Have they not promised religious freedom
    to us?
A Voice from the Rear: And in Canada one must know
    how to speak Canadian, that is English.
An Older Person: That shows the new spirit. Beware of
    such suggestions. That is the beginning of the end. For
    twenty years we have not learned English and were
    happy without it. But today many are getting along
    too well. They are becoming proud. The younger men
    know better than their elders the things that ought
    to be done.
Another Older Person: The Bible has been written in
    German, why then should we have to learn English.
    My children at least shall not do so.
A Third Elderly Person: Neither shall mine.[22]

In spite of great opposition, Ewert continued his work. He
instituted teachers' conventions and introduced a travelling
library, both designed to further increase the resources of the
teachers and to improve their teaching. At the same time he
persuaded more and more areas to accept the district school. The
promise of public tax support helped. In 1902 the number of
district schools had risen to 42, approximately one-third of the
total number of Mennonite schools, both private and public,
then in existence in Manitoba.

Not all the district schools were of equal quality. The attitudes
of the trustees and the qualifications of the teachers differed a
great deal. Salaries varied from $400 to $500 per annum. Some
trustees continued their resistance to every innovation, while
others were liberal enough to pay for the students' textbooks.[23]

Ewert's steady progress was, however, rudely interrupted by a
strange combination of forces and events, both internal and external, which appeared on the scene in rapid succession in the
first decade of the twentieth century. In 1903 Ewert was dismissed as inspector of schools by the newly elected Conservatives,

who had compaigned in conservative Mennonite areas with the promise to do just that. As it turned out, most of these Mennonites had not voted anyway. As the *Free Press* editorialized, the unconventionality and unpredictability of Mennonite political behaviour was a problem for every politician.

> What was to be done with the people who for years refused even to vote? What was to be done with the people superbly indifferent to the political plums that made the mouths of English-speaking constituencies water even to think of. When the travelling salesman displayed his wares to the Mennonites they turned away in disgust. Even "job" lines failed to impress them. The ordinary avenues of political approach to the foreign immigrant, were, in the case of the Mennonites, obviously out of the question.[24]

Ewert's dismissal as inspector did not mean that his work had come to an end. Members of the school association immediately pledged $25,000 to underwrite the school which in 1898 had been renamed the Mennonite Educational Institute. That fund, however, became internally divisive because it raised the issue of enlarging the school facilities, which in turn raised the question of the school's permanent location. All of these were most fundamental issues since the responsibility for the school and its principal rested clearly with interested Mennonites.

On May 22, 1905, a meeting was held at Altona to decide the issue. But unconstitutional, or at least confusing, procedures were adopted and had the effect of making every decision disputable. The constitution of the school society, adopted in 1888, had specified two-thirds majority approval for matters as important as relocation. This meeting, however, determined by a show of hands that a simple majority, rather than absolute (not to speak of two-thirds) majority, should be decisive. The result was 117 votes for locating the school in Winkler, 179 votes for Altona, and 151 for Gretna. Soon after the count had been entered in the minutes and the meeting adjourned, the decision was questioned with regard to both its constitutionality and a possible improper vote count. The meeting had awarded one vote for every $5 donation, but apparently failed to produce donor lists or to clarify the status of monetary pledges, oral or written. The result was that some questioned the voting, others the counting. Most were confused. The problems created by procedural ineptitude were compounded many times by existing Altona-

Gretna rivalries — the two towns were separated by only seven miles. There were clashes between Ewert and leading Altona families and differences of opinion between Bishop Funk and his assistant, Bishop Hoeppner (both of whom alternately, though never together, sided with Ewert and opposed him). Provincial politics may have also been involved again.[25]

The end result was that the relocation of the school in Altona was delayed until 1908. Ewert apparently supported the 1905 decision, but the endless wrangling that followed led him and his supporters to resign in the spring of 1908 when the relocation was to take place. Thus, while the Mennonite Educational Institute was transferred to Altona, the pro-Gretna group that same year founded a new society and built a new facility which became known as the Mennonite Collegiate Institute.

Both schools faced difficult times. The Altona school had the advantage of a larger constituency — even the Sommerfelder bishop supported it — and government support. The new inspector of Mennonite schools was located there. But Gretna had the strong-willed, single-minded, completely dedicated lifetime principal in its favour. Thus, while principals came and went in Altona, Ewert continued his steady forward plodding, seizing every opportunity to advance the educational cause. In his own words: "Men may come and men may go, but I go on forever."[26] When the Altona school burned down 18 years after its founding, never to be rebuilt, Ewert once again had the field to himself.

Meanwhile, the number of Mennonite elementary schools in the public sector had again diminished. Some school trustees had previously been persuaded to go public because Ewert was the inspector. It had taken a long time, but gradually some conservatives had come to the conclusion that Ewert could be as sincere about Mennonite values as they were, though following a different approach. When he was removed, their interest in the public school also vanished.

Another reversal for the public school came with the 1907 election campaign. The election manifesto of Premier Rodmund P. Roblin announced his intention to "inculcate feelings of patriotism" and to blend "together the various nationalities in the province into a common citizenship, irrespective of race and creed."[27] Subsequently, he decreed that the Union Jack, the symbol of the British Empire, be flown over public buildings and raised in public schools daily. This, Roblin suggested, would help the young people to become "filled with the traditions of the British flag" and in their manhood willing and able to defend those traditions. Roblin's patriotism coincided with British imperial overtures to its various colonies to participate in strengthening the British armed forces. The use of the classroom for the nurturing of such sentiments, however, was precisely what the Old Colony and other conservative Mennonites feared. Militarism, including the German militarism against which the British were arming themselves, had its roots in the classroom. As Bishop Isaak Dyck explained years later:

> We could hear the peoples and nations of this world
> preparing anew for war, more vigorously than ever before,
> to counteract the unprecedented military might of Germany
> . . . That might itself have originated in the classrooms where
> militarism and the arts of war were implanted in the
> students with unquenching zeal . . . And this example
> Canada wanted to follow . . . The rationale for the public
> schools was expressed with the following slogan: one king,
> one God, one navy, one all-British empire.[28]

Other parts of the Canadian Mennonite world were aware of the imperial power-play of the times, the increased militarism and jingoism. In Ontario, church leaders were disturbed by Great Britain's attempt to persuade Canada to develop an indigenous defence force. This force would have close military ties to Great Britain and would allocate troops to a special imperial reserve. This reserve "would be under the control of the imperial government, and available for employment in any part of the world."[29]

In 1909, a peak year for the imperial defence conferences, the Mennonite Church of Ontario, in session at Vineland from May 26 to May 28, took note of "much agitation and excitement among the citizens of our land and neighbouring countries, owing to the many rumours of war." The conference resolution commended "the peaceable attitude and friendly relationship which our Dominion sustains toward all nations" but criticized the "strong demand made upon our government and upon the people of this country, to take steps to defend our country and the empire by extensive naval and military establishments." Steps had already been taken to introduce military training in the public schools and military expenditures had increased enormously, all of which was noted with sorrow:

> [We] regret the steps taken to inculcate the spirit of
> militarism in the minds of the rising generation, and . . . we

hereby express ourselves in favour of inculcating the
principles of peace and good will to all men in the minds of
our children, using every means to spread the cause of
peace. . . .[30]

A copy of the resolution was sent to the government through
W. L. Mackenzie King, the young Member of Parliament since
1907 for Waterloo North. A native of Berlin, he promised to do
everything in his power "to further the wishes of the Mennonite
Church in safeguarding this country from the evils of militarism,
and in restricting expenditures in the matter of defence, to such
point only as may be necessary for our security and as a nation
having a like protection and responsibilities within the empire."[31]

Apparently King was well aware of the possible political effects
for him of the Liberal defence policies. When he was defeated
in 1911, a confidential letter to Governor General Lord Grey
stated that his riding had very large numbers of Mennonites
who were opposed to war and the government's naval policy.
Many believed that it was King's support of these policies that
contributed to his defeat. Twice he said he had denied the false
reports that he was furthering militarism, but his denials, he
complained, had not been noted by the press.[32]

There were other indications of the strength of Mennonite
opinion. Between 1906 and 1909, a Mennonite "peace and arbitration association" was formed with headquarters in York
County. The association was founded on the principle "that war
is contrary to true religion and morality, and the best interests
of humanity." Its object was "the promotion of universal and
permanent peace, by means of arbitration and by cultivating the
spirit of peace and good will among men."[33] Perhaps it was precisely this association which promoted individuals such as Isaak
Wideman and L. J. Burkholder, in private correspondence with the
Prime Minister, to "regret the continued education for increased
military practice in the schools in Canada," and "to discourage
this false military spirit and all jingoism."[34] They and the conservative leaders of Manitoba shared this sensitivity about militarism in the schools, though the former had accepted the public
schools while the latter had not.

The flag legislation in Manitoba produced an immediate Mennonite reaction. Eleven schools which had gone public immediately reverted to private status. Others, which had considered going
public, had their minds made up. Where the public schools were
closed down by local Mennonite trustees, they were forcibly

kept open by the government under its own official trustee. But the results were the same in that the parents refused to send their children. The experience of the teacher at Altbergthal near Altona, where a school was kept open by the government, was typical. The appointed district teacher, who all year long had not a single student, wrote:

> When I hoisted the flag on the first of September, there wasn't a child in school. The old people got together, fixed up a log cabin and hired a private teacher for the 45 children of the district. They paid him the salary I was getting, $80 a month, but I stuck to it and hoisted the flag every one of the 202 days but I did not have one pupil.[35]

The *Free Press*, quite consistently opposed to the Conservative government, blamed the "pig-headedness, blusteringly manifested in that connection" for the loss of the schools "to the national system."[36] Everyone knew that Mennonites would not be coerced and that any attempt in that direction was very unwise. The Winnipeg daily newspaper warned that undue pressure could lead to the emigration of these people:

> It is asserted quite positively that the conservative people, who constitute the large majority of the people, are to this day so tenacious of their principles that if any attempt should be made on the part of the government to force public schools upon them or even to force them to teach English in their private schools — not that they have any conscientious scruples against learning English, but because they resent all outside, that is government, interference — they would leave the country in spite of the large material interests which they have there.[37]

Meanwhile, the government, recognizing its own folly, or pursuing still another expediency, had reappointed Ewert as inspector of Mennonite schools in May of 1908 only to drop him, again for political reasons, three months later. It was a time of severe trial and testing for Ewert. Less than a month before his dismissal Ewert had received a letter from the Minister of Education "expressing full confidence in his ability and promising to support him in every legitimate way."[38]

During this time Ewert's strong commitment to education was bearing fruit in the second generation of his own family. Every one of his four sons and his daughter Elma moved on to advanced schools after graduation from the Mennonite Collegiate Institute, the latter to Royal Victoria Hospital in Montreal. The two oldest sons, Paul and Karl, were becoming medical doctors and Wilhelm, the youngest son, a dentist. Receiving the greatest recognition and distinction was Alfred, third son in the family. At the age of 20, Alfred Ewert was selected Manitoba's Rhodes Scholar. Moving on to Oxford he distinguished himself not only as a brilliant student but also as a professor of Romance languages from 1921 until the day of his retirement nearly 40 years later. On the occasion of his being awarded the Rhodes Scholarship, the *Winnipeg Free Press* lauded not only the many gifts of the young man and the service record of his father, but also the people from which he had sprung:

> In his second year his record was even better. On the total standing in the spring examination he had led his year in the university, being the only student to secure a 1A standing . . . His devotion to sports had gained him a robust constitution, which had stood admirably the strain of continuous and severe study. In other departments of college life he has been equally prominent. He is a clear and forceful speaker, and is this year president of the University Debating Union. He has also served as treasurer of the college literary society, and is the organizer and leader of the college orchestra. He has a great love for music, and is a skilled pianist. He has unusual powers of imagination and expression, and recently won a prize for verse in a college competition. Mr. Ewert is remarkably fortunate in having an absolute command of the two languages which afford access to the greatest intellectual wealth of the modern world — England and Germany. A former student of the Mennonite Collegiate Institute at Gretna, his appointment gives representation to a people of high intellectual powers, from whom no Rhodes scholar has previously been chosen.[39]

Such achievements and accolades established a reputation for educational excellence not only for the Ewert family but also for the Mennonite Collegiate Institute, thus helping to vindicate H. H. Ewert's steadfastness of purpose, which his progressive critics had mistaken for a stubborn streak. None the less, for the most conservative critics the Ewert family record proved their point. Education led the young people far away from the Mennonite community, its way of life and its value system. The inevitable destiny of young university students was the non-Mennonite world. Paul Hiebert, the award-winning 1916 University of Manitoba chemistry graduate, later the famous author of the best-selling *Sarah Binks*, was a case in point. The rural, agrarian, German-speaking and often legalistic Mennonite community was not about to follow the students; nor did the students want it to follow. Connections between farm and city, village school and university, pious sermon and learned lecture, and agrarian simplicity and urban sophistication were for the most part non-existent. Decades would pass before these gaps would begin to be closed.

Meanwhile, the Mennonites in Alberta and Saskatchewan were also responding in varied ways to the surrounding pressures of Canadian culture. In Alberta, the community involvement of the Didsbury pioneers, and the election to the provincial legislature of their best representatives, generally set the pace. From the beginning the district school was accepted as inescapable and not undesirable even at Mayton and Tofield, where Old Order and Amish Mennonites had settled. The same was true in Saskatchewan except on the two reserves, Hague-Osler and Swift Current, where the Old Colony bishops, like their colleagues on the West Reserve of Manitoba, insisted on the private elementary school under the control of the church leaders. Here and there were small exceptions. At Herbert, for instance, a group of 12 Mennonite families in 1905 appealed to the federal government for permission to establish their own school "because we are called *deutsche Mennoniten* [German Mennonites] and this is what we want to be before God and the highest governmental authorities . . ." Should their wish have been granted, the petition read, "we [will be] the quiet in the land."[40] The federal government referred such matters to the provinces, whose jurisdictional authorities covered education. These Mennonites had difficulty understanding such referrals because they had in 1873 made what to them was a fundamental agreement with the federal government.

The year of that request was the birth year of the Province of Saskatchewan and of the German-English Academy at Rosthern, Saskatchewan. Like the Mennonite Collegiate Institute at Gretna, the Academy represented the attempt of the progressive-minded Mennonites to preserve as many of the best values of the past as possible, while accepting the future. Thus, with the acceptance of the public school, came a concerted effort to equip those schools in the Mennonite districts with bilingual teachers who could also teach a religious curriculum.

In Rosthern, one man came to symbolize the school and the progressive spirit. He was David Toews, who, like H. H. Ewert of Gretna, was the second man in the school. (The first was Herman Fast, "the man with the beard," as he became known, one of the Mennonite Brethren missionaries to Russian-language immigrants in the Saskatchewan Valley.) Also like Ewert, Toews had Manitoba, Kansas and Europe in his background. He had been born at the Trakt settlement in the Middle Volga province of Samara in Russia in 1870, one year after his parents, Jacob and Maria Toews, had migrated from Prussia to escape military service for their sons. Ten years later the Toews family joined the notorious Claasz Epp, Jr., who was leading a band of followers to a *Bergungsort* (place of refuge) for Christians in the Turkestan of Central Asiatic Russia, where Christ was to meet them all. The two-year trek turned out to be a very tragic one; hardships were many, the millennium did not arrive, and Claasz Epp became more unbalanced in his claims, finally insisting on his own identity with the divine trinity. After a twenty-month stay at Khiva below the Aral Sea, the Toews family, along with 20 others, decided that their salvation lay in the west rather than the east. Via their Samara homeland, Moscow, and Berlin, the Toews family migrated to Kansas where they arrived in October of 1884.

Toews studied at Halstead under H. H. Ewert, and in 1893 he followed him to Manitoba as one of a number of American teachers whom Ewert was attracting to his newly established district schools. After three years in the Gretna district school, Toews studied for a year in Winnipeg, and, after another teaching year in rural Manitoba, moved on to Saskatchewan where he was afforded a field of opportunity nearly as wide as that which Ewert had in Manitoba.[41] In a sense his opportunity was even wider. Toews had married into the Rosenort community, his wife being from the Friesen family recently arrived from his own parental home in Prussia. Toews became both a teacher and a homestead farmer and in 1900 a Rosenort minister. Within thirteen years he would succeed Peter Regier as bishop of the church. So outstanding and widely recognized was his leadership ability that he became not only the moderator of the Conference of Mennonites in Central Canada in the first year of the First World War, but also the unofficial "bishop of Canada" for the Mennonites in the west.

As principal of the German-English Academy he was the rallying point for progressives in the Saskatchewan Valley in much the same way that Ewert was in Manitoba. Toews had determined that the Saskatchewan Board of Education had the power to authorize a half-hour period at the end of a school day for German-language instruction and to prescribe the texts to be used in such instruction. Since, however, the two-hour noon recess was unnecessarily long for farm children, who brought their lunch and stayed all day, Toews recommended that the hour from one to two o'clock be utilized for classes in the German language. This would leave the half-hour at the end of the day for religion, also in German. In other words, there were unusual opportunities for teachers properly trained by the German-English Academy:

> Anyone can see that an able and diligent teacher can achieve much in the present circumstances. Friends of education can draw their own conclusions. We need teachers from among our *Volk* [people] whose heart-felt desire it is to serve our *Volk*. For these reasons do not become weary in support of the Academy.[42]

Dissenters among the conservatives not only sent their children to public schools and to his Academy, but they were also starting to join his church. If they came from the Old Colony reserve at Hague-Osler, however, this presented special problems. Bishop Jacob Wiens excommunicated those families who left the private school and otherwise adapted to modern ways. The loss of Old Colony membership in itself was not serious, because a new church home could always be found in the Rosenorter melting-pot. But excommunication among the Old Colony meant economic boycotts and social ostracism as well, and this affected the merchants who, as townspeople, were the first to make accommodation to the education system and the general culture.

Leading a group of about 30 dissident families were two merchants, one by the name of Isaac P. Friesen, who later became a minister and evangelist in the Rosenort church, and Jacob J. Friesen. Both were placed under the ban. The latter Friesen was the son of another Jacob Friesen, whom Hespeler had once appointed as the first organizer of district schools in Manitoba.[43]

In a letter of excommunication, Bishop Wiens regretted that repeated efforts to bring about repentance from worldliness and reconciliation had been ignored and that the only way open to him was "to separate you from our community as you have separated yourself from us through your disobedience."[44] Jacob Friesen undertook to take his own grievances and those of his group to Hon. J. A. Calder, Saskatchewan Minister of Education. Reminding Calder that a dominion election was nearing and that he had always been a supporter of liberalism, Friesen asked the government to do something about his plight:

> Having the future welfare of my children in view I took the necessary steps to join a more progressive branch of the Mennonite church. As soon as the leaders of the Old Colony Church got notice of my steps they excommunicated me and forbade all the members to have any more dealing with me. The consequence was that I had to give up my home, my business, and everything for the sake of giving my children a better education and this in a land of the free. Now my dear Mr. Calder, don't you think that existing conditions are an insult to our liberal constitution.[45]

The government expressed interest in saving the Mennonites from each other but only after the autumn by-elections. Meanwhile, Premier Walter Scott suggested to Calder that he inform "the Mennonite heads . . . unless they leave free those of their people who wish to use the public school we will deprive them of the legal right to solemnize marriages."[46]

The warning fell on deaf ears and the provincial government launched a full investigation into the Old Colony educational system and attitudes. Meeting at the Warman schoolhouse, the Commission of Enquiry on December 28–29, 1908, heard over 100 pages of testimony from Old Colony leaders and teachers, as well as from the excommunicated and their teachers.[47] There were few immediate results, but the long-term consequence was a stiffening of the various positions. On the government side, a case was slowly being built up for the introduction of public schools in all the areas and the enactment of legislation requiring compulsory attendance, which came during the war. Newspapers helped with headlines such as "Progressive Mennonites 'Barred from heaven and cursed forever' by Bishop of the Sect in Saskatchewan."[48] The *Regina Leader* editorialized on "Mennonites and Excommunication" by linking the Saskatchewan events to an excommunication incident in Ontario. Apparently a Mennonite at Altona, Ontario, by the name of Lehman, had taken another to court for seducing his under-age daughter and successfully sued for the support of her child. The church elders threatened Lehman with excommunication for taking a case against a brother to court. Said the *Regina Leader*:

> . . . there must appear to all right-thinking men something
> radically wrong in the tenets of a church which, while
> looking upon an action at law as a heinous crime, for the
> commission of which a member of the church runs a risk of
> losing his own soul, appears to look with comparative
> lenience upon the seduction of a child . . . In no country
> in the world is greater tolerance shown towards people's
> religious beliefs than in Canada, and we would be slow to
> recommend interference with the church policy of any sect.
> Such a case, however, as is under review would seem to call
> for the modification of that tolerance as being subversive
> both of morality and common justice . . .[49]

The story was not altogether correct, for among Mennonites few sins were as unforgivable as adultery and seduction. Disciplinary actions, however, were undertaken in private. Taking brothers to courts of law was also a sin because the church had its own way of dealing with disputes between brethren. Bishop Jacob Wiens and his colleagues paid dearly for their intransigence and for their reluctance to defend themselves in court. Jacob Heinrichs of Osler, who had been excommunicated by Wiens, successfully sued him for $1,000 for "conspiracy resulting in the loss of business." Five Old Colony leaders subsequently went to Ottawa to complain about this and other infringements on their religious principles. The Solicitor General offered only to appoint counsel on their behalf and at their expense "to guard against unjust action at law of any kind against our people."[50] All of this activity became public knowledge and severely damaged the image of all Mennonites.

The negative publicity was bound to increase with the coming of the First World War. Public concerns about enemy aliens, pacifism, German culture and private schools comprised a single cause against which British patriotism and Anglo-Saxon culture had to take a firm stand. The schools were one place where a firm stand could be taken, and the first to experience this were in Manitoba where less than 58 per cent of the population were of British origin. A premonition of things to come was provided by the election campaign, which led the Liberals under T. C. Norris to defeat Roblin and his Conservatives. At the pre-election convention, Norris had demanded "national schools, obligatory teaching of English in all public schools and compulsory school attendance."

Fearing the worst for their schools, the Mennonites had begun to coordinate their efforts. Under Ewert's leadership a *Schulkom-*

mission (school commission) had been organized in 1913. Consisting of official Bergthaler, Sommerfelder and Brethren representatives, the Commission set as its task the encouragement of instruction in German and Bible in all Mennonite schools, district or private, and the negotiation with the authorities to this end.[51] Very soon the Commission confronted both Conservatives and Liberals. The first meeting was with the Premier. To him the Commission expressed gratitude for the continued right to have their own private schools and to teach German and religion in the public district schools. Promising to encourage better attendance at the latter, the Commission explained its main goal as follows:

> Our main task, however, is to see to it that religious
> instruction in all our schools be thorough and adequate and
> that our right to teach German in all our schools be
> exercised everywhere.[52]

The Hon. Valentin Winkler, southern Manitoba representative in the legislature, was advised by the Schulkommission that the majority of Mennonites had hitherto placed their trust in the Liberal party, that they had consistently returned a Liberal member to the provincial legislature, but that this would change should they find school legislation unsatisfactory. The Mennonites were not asking for special privileges but rather the simple continuation of the existing laws, which the Liberal government had no mandate to abrogate.[53]

As adverse legislation threatened, however, representatives of all the congregations, with the exception of the Old Colony, banded together on the educational question under the auspices of the School Commission in an unprecedented display of unity (see Table 2).[54] Meeting in Winnipeg with the Premier, they laid before him and his ministers the high value Mennonites placed on the education of their children. They contended that the norms of this education could not be established by outsiders because Mennonites considered themselves responsible to God alone in this matter, that instruction in religion and the German language were indispensable ingredients in the right instruction of the children and that education provided continuity of spiritual fellowship between the generations. To reinforce the strength of their conviction on this matter they expressed readiness to emigrate rather than surrender these values, in spite of the fact that they were otherwise fond of Canada as a homeland.[55] In all these ways they were really expressing Old Colony

TABLE 2

EMERGENCY DELEGATION ON EDUCATION TO MANITOBA GOVERNMENT

CHURCH GROUP	REPRESENTATIVES
Chortitzer	Bishop Joh. K. Dyck
	Rev. Heinrich Derksen
	Rev. Joh. Schroeder
	Mr. Jacob Kehler
Kleine Gemeinde	Bishop Peter R. Dyck
	Mr. Jacob Reimer
Holdemaner	Rev. Jakob T. Wiebe
	Mr. Johann Barkman
Bruderthaler	Rev. Peter Schmidt
Sommerfelder	Messrs. H. J. Friesen
	Joh. D. Klassen
	H. Friesen
Bergthaler	Rev. H. H. Ewert
	Rev. Benj. Ewert
	Mr. B. Loewen
Mennonite Brethren	Rev. P. H. Neufeld
	Mr. J. M. Elias

sentiments, differing only in degree and in the basic acceptance of district schools.

Their efforts availed little against the tide of patriotic public opinion and the government's determination. A School Attendance Act was passed on March 10, 1916. The Laurier-Greenway Compromise of 1897 was thereby repealed, English was made the sole language of instruction in all public schools, and children aged 7–14 were compelled to attend public schools unless satisfactory private education was provided. Saskatchewan followed Manitoba with similar legislation in 1917. The legislation once again reversed the trend to public schools, a trend which remained unchecked to the end of the war. A new inspector of Mennonite schools in Manitoba, a German from Ontario by the name of A. Weidenhammer, had made considerable progress since 1909 in establishing district schools. His years of greatest progress were 1909–1913, when the number of district schools advanced from 37 to 64 and attendance from 1,124 to 1,858.

Following passage of the Attendance Act, 20 ministers and

deacons of the Bergthaler and Sommerfelder churches met immediately under the chairmanship of Sommerfelder Bishop Abraham Doerksen and together agreed *in groeszter Einmuetigkeit* (in the spirit of complete unity) to work for a return of all district schools to the private school system.[56] Subsequently, the representatives of the 2,500-member Sommerfelder church unanimously endorsed the program. The 500-member Bergthaler church was more divided, though the majority wanted a return to private schools. The Mennonite Brethren delayed a decision on the matter pending the formulation of curriculum and a plan for the financing of private schools.[57]

Private schools, it must be remembered, were still permitted, though they faced the prospect of being judged unsatisfactory and being closed for that reason. Also, the Mennonites were not the only ones thus to react to unilingualism in education. The French Catholics likewise "believed that the language, religion, and nationality were closely tied together and that religious instruction was largely defeated unless it was imparted through the medium of the pupil's mother tongue."[58]

The new policy was argued in the courts but without success. One Judge Curran, of Irish descent, expressed the hope "that the government will never yield one jot or tittle of its determination to make the teaching of English alone prevalent in our public schools." Judge Pendergast, of French ancestry, countered: "If such a solemn binding agreement as the Laurier-Greenway settlement can be so lightly violated, why should our soldiers go away to fight because another agreement was violated by Germany."[59]

In Ontario, and more particularly in Waterloo County, the question of German in the schools had been a difficult one throughout the latter half of the nineteenth century, but by 1900 a successful compromise had been adopted. German became an additional subject of study "within the school system, but on a voluntary basis, and supervised by the parents themselves."[60] Anti-German sentiments connected with the war weakened the voluntarism necessary to keep German studies going and gradually they faded altogether. Such anti-Germanism was strong enough to effect a change of name, in 1916, for the former Ebytown from Berlin to Kitchener. It was strong enough to eclipse all remaining enthusiasm for the German language.

The loss of the German language, however, did not mean diminution of the religious values of the Ontario Mennonites. On the contrary, military conscription, which started in 1917, demonstrated that the anglicization of the Ontario Mennonites did not mean their militarization and that not all the traditional ingredients of the Mennonite cultural package were essential to it. It was different on the reserves in the west. The more the government tied anglicization, patriotism, militarism and education together in a single cultural package, the more the Mennonites were convinced that German, religion, and the private school also belonged together, inseparably linked.

FOOTNOTES

1. Isaak M. Dyck, *Die Auswanderung der Reinland Mennoniten von Canada nach Mexico* (Cuahtemoc, Chihuahua, Mexico: Imprenta Colonial, 1970), pp. 43–4.
2. H. Goerz, "Wenn in des Lebens Angst und Not," in *Gedichte* (Winnipeg: published by the author, n.d.), 62 pp.; Gerhard Loewen, "Gebet," in *Feldblumen* (Steinbach, Man.: Arnold Dyck, 1946); G. H. Peters, "Das Gebet," in *Blumen am Wegrand* (Gretna, Man.: published by the author, n.d.), 270 pp. The Peters book contains five translations from Russian poetry.
3. Frank H. Epp, *Mennonite Exodus: The Rescue and Resettlement of the Russian Mennonites Since the Communist Revolution* (Altona, Man.: D. W. Friesen & Sons, 1962), p. 25.
4. The Hollaenderei argument will appear again in Canada in the late 1930s and early 1940s and in post-Second World War Europe.
5. Joshua A. Fishman, *et al.*, *Language Loyalty in the United States: The Maintenance and Perpetuation of Non-English Mother Tongues by American Ethnic and Religious Groups* (The Hague: Mouton & Company, 1966).
6. It is true, of course, that the American Mennonites also had a whole series of German Preparatory Schools, the links between the public elementary schools and the Mennonite colleges, sometimes the forerunners of the latter. Americanization came fast, however, and the parochial preparatory high school declined rapidly in favour of the American school system and the English-language Mennonite colleges. See J. E. Hartzler, *Education Among the Mennonites of America* (Danvers, Ill.: Central Mennonite Publication Board, 1925), 195 pp.
7. P. J. Schaefer, *Heinrich H. Ewert: Lehrer, Erzieher, und Prediger der Mennoniten* (Gretna, Man.: Mennonite Youth Organization, 1945); P. J. Schaefer, "Mennonite Collegiate Institute," *Men-*

nonite Encyclopedia, III, p. 617; J. G. Rempel, "Rosthern Junior College," *Mennonite Encyclopedia*, IV, pp. 362–63; O. Burkholder, "Ontario Mennonite Bible School," *Mennonite Encyclopedia*, IV, p. 66; J. G. Rempel, "Herbert Bible School," *Mennonite Encyclopedia*, II, p. 708; E. R. Storms, *History of the United Missionary Church* (Elkhart, Ind.: Bethel Publishing Company, 1958), pp. 162–67; Frank H. Epp, "The Story of Rosthern Junior College" (unpublished manuscript, 1970); A. J. Klassen, *The Bible School Story: Fifty Years of Mennonite Brethren Bible Schools* (Mennonite Brethren Bible College, 1963), 20 pp.

8.   E. K. Francis, *In Search of Utopia: The Mennonites in Manitoba* (Altona, Man.: D. W. Friesen & Sons, 1955), p. 168. See also "Memorandum Concerning Mennonite Schools" in Calvin Redekop, *The Old Colony Mennonites: Dilemmas of Ethnic Minority Life* (Baltimore: Johns Hopkins University Press, 1969), pp. 245–50.

9.   PAC, *Immigration Branch*, Record Group 76, 1, Vol. 173, 58764. Copy of letter of John M. Lowe, Secretary, Department of Agriculture, to David Klassen, Jacob Peters, Heinrich Wiebe and Cornelius Toews, July 23, 1873.

10.   See BNA Act, Sect. 95; the Manitoba Act, 33 Vict. chap. 3, Sect. 22; Imperial Act, 35 Vict. chap. 28, 34–5.

11.   PAC, *Order-in-Council*, Record Group 2, 1, 957, July 28, 1873.

12.   See letter by William Kaye Lamb, Dominion Archivist, May 11, 1950, to John J. Bergen, reproduced in "An Historical Study of Education in the Municipality of Rhineland" (M.Ed. thesis, University of Manitoba, 1959), Appendix M, "Communication with Dominion Archivist," pp. 135–36.

13.   Gerhard Wiebe, *Ursachen und Geschichte der Auswanderung der Mennoniten aus Russland nach Amerika* (Winnipeg: Druckerei der Nordwesten, 1900), p. 17.

14.   W. L. Morton, "Manitoba Schools and Canadian Nationality, 1890–1923," in D. G. Creighton, *Minorities, Schools, and Politics* (Toronto: University of Toronto Press, 1969), pp. 10–18.

15.   Francis, *op. cit.*, p. 170.

16.   "The Bi-lingual Schools of Manitoba," *Manitoba Free Press*, February 5, 1913; see also Bergen, *op. cit.*, p. 47.

17.   P. J. Schaefer, "Heinrich H. Ewert — Educator, of Kansas and Manitoba," *Mennonite Life*, III (October 1948), pp. 18–23; see also P. J. Schaefer, *Heinrich H. Ewert; Lehrer, Erzieher, und Prediger der Mennoniten, op. cit.*

18.   Francis, *op. cit.*, p. 169.

19.   Manitoba, *Report of the Department of Education, 1891*, p. 37.

20.   Bergen, *op. cit.*, p. 48.

21.   *Ibid.*, p. 55.

22.   "A Description of the First Reaction of the Conservative Men-

nonites to the Appointment of a Mennonite School Inspector as given by Novokampus," in *Kanadische Mennoniten — Zum Jubilaeums-jahr*, quoted in I. I. Friesen, "The Mennonites of Western Canada with Special Reference to Education" (M. Ed. thesis, University of Saskatchewan, 1934).

23. Bergen, *op. cit.*, pp. 56–7.
24. "The Bi-lingual Schools of Manitoba," *Manitoba Free Press*, February 5, 1913, p. 3.
25. See P. J. Schaefer, *H. H. Ewert . . . , op. cit.*, pp. 65–7, and H. J. Gerbrandt, *Adventure in Faith* (Altona, Man.: D. W. Friesen & Sons, 1970), pp. 253–72.
26. As recalled by G. H. Peters, Ewert's successor, and remembered by the author from the days when he was Peters' student.
27. Francis, *op. cit.*, p. 174.
28. Dyck, *op. cit.*, p. 43. Compare W. L. Morton, *op. cit.*
29. George F. G. Stanley *Canada's Soldiers: The Military History of an Unmilitary People* (Toronto: Macmillan Company of Canada Ltd., 1960), p. 449.
30. PAC, *Mackenzie King Papers*, M.G. 26, J. 1., Vol. 12, 11886–11884.
31. *Ibid.*; W. L. Mackenzie King to Noah Stauffer, Moderator, Conference of Mennonite Churches in Ontario, August 4, 1909.
32. PAC, *Mackenzie King Papers*, M.G. 26, J.1., Vol. 17, No. 15652–15653, Letter of W. L. Mackenzie King to Lord Grey, Governor General.
33. CGC. "Constitution of the Mennonite Peace Arbitration Association," from L. J. Burkholder papers.
34. PAC, *Laurier Papers*, M.G. 26, G. 1a., c-900, Vol. 668, p. 18168, Letter of L. J. Burkholder and Isaak Wideman to Hon. Sir Wilfrid Laurier, February 20, 1911.
35. Bergen, *op. cit.*, p. 74.
36. *Free Press News Bulletin*, November 26, 1910.
37. *Ibid.*
38. "The Bi-lingual Schools of Manitoba," *Manitoba Free Press*, February 7, 1913. See also Bergen, *op. cit.*, p. 66.
39. Elizabeth Bergen, "Rhodes Scholar from Gretna," *Red River Valley Echo*, January 10, 1973, p. 4, as quoted from *Winnipeg Free Press*, August 30, 1912.
40. PAC, *Privy Council Dormants*, Record Groups 2, 3, Vol. 155, P.C. 2302. Letter from P. W. Harder and Peter H. Penner, Herbert, Saskatchewan, to "Geehrter Herr," December 11, 1905.
41. Epp, *op. cit.*, pp. 81–92.
42. David Toews, "Etwas ueber die Schulverhaeltnisse in Saskatchewan," *Der Mitarbeiter*, VIII (February 1914), pp. 36–7; David Toews, "Wie koennen wir versuchen durch unsere hoeheren

Schulen den Beduerfnissen unseres Volkes mehr zu entsprechen,"
Der Mitarbeiter, VIII (August 1914), p. 83, and VIII (September 1914), pp. 93–4.

43. Andrew Willows, "A History of the Mennonites, Particularly in Manitoba" (M.A. thesis, University of Manitoba, 1924), p. 102.

44. SAB. Letter of Bishop Jacob Wiens to Friend Jacob Friesen, January 20, 1908.

45. SAB. Letter from Jacob J. Friesen, Rosthern, to Hon. J. A. Calder, Regina, October 1, 1908.

46. SAB. Memorandum from Premier Walter Scott to Hon. J. A. Calder, Regina, September 2, 1908.

47. SAB. "Proceedings of Commission of Inquiry at Warman," December 28–29, 1908.

48. *The Regina Leader*, January 5, 1909, p. 3.

49. "Mennonites and Excommunication," *The Regina Leader*, January 20, 1909, p. 4.

50. PAC, *Borden Papers*, M.G. 26, H. RLB 1167 (C-342), 121065-121078a.

51. C. Krahn, "Manitoba School Commission," *Mennonite Encyclopedia*, III, p. 467.

52. "Uebersetzung der Schrift, welche die Beamten der mennonitischen Schulkommission der Regierung vorgelegt haben, February 18, 1914," *Der Mitarbeiter*, VIII (March 1914), pp. 43–5; H. H. Ewert, "Schulzwang in Manitoba," *Der Mitarbeiter*, VIII (May 1914), pp. 62–3.

53. B. Ewert, "Bericht von der Spezialsitzung der mennonitischen Schulkommission, abgehalten Freitag den 7. Januar, 1916," *Der Mitarbeiter*, X (January 1916), pp. 2–4.

54. Joh. D. Klassen, "Bericht ueber die Taetigkeit der mennonitischen Schulkommission . . . ," *Der Mitarbeiter*, X (March 1916), pp. 1–4.

55. *Ibid.*; H. H. Ewert, "Ansprache als einer der Wortfuehrer der mennonitischen Delegation an die Regierung," *Der Mitarbeiter*, X (March 1916), pp. 4–6; H. H. Ewert, "Schulzwang in Manitoba," *Der Mitarbeiter*, X (February 1916), p. 4; H. H. Ewert, "Die Aussichten fuer das fortbestehen der zwei-sprachigen Schulen in Manitoba," *Der Mitarbeiter*, X (February 1916), pp. 4–5.

56. "Bewegung unter den Mennoniten Manitobas zur Abschaffung der Distriktschulen in ihrer Mitte," *Der Mitarbeiter*, X (May 1916), pp. 2–3; "Bericht von der Zusammenkunft und Beratung der beiden Lehrdienste der Sommerfelder und Bergthaler Gemeinden in Angelegenheit unsere Schulen," *Der Mitarbeiter*, X (May 1916), pp. 2–3.

57. B. Ewert, "Bericht ueber die abgehalten Bruderschaften einiger Gemeinden in Manitoba in Angelegenheit der Privatschulen," *Der Mitarbeiter*, X (June 1916), p. 3; H. H. Ewert, "Warum die

Mennoniten-Gemeinden in Manitoba wieder zu den Privatschulen zurueckheben," *Der Mitarbeiter*, X (July 1916), p. 4.

58. G. M. Weir, *The Separate School Question in Canada* (Toronto: Ryerson Press, 1934), p. 7; Bergen, *op. cit.*, p. 46.

59. "Judges of King's Bench Clash on Bilingualism," *Winnipeg Tribune*, February 6, 1916.

60. Patricia McKegney, "The German Schools of Waterloo County, 1851–1913," *Waterloo Historical Society*, LVIII (1970), pp. 54–61.

A People Opposed to War

15. The War and Military Exemption

Compulsory military service channeled a mounting resentment toward Mennonite sectarians who, before the turn of the century, had been exempted from military service by a government anxious to settle Canada's prairie west with hard-working agriculturists whether of pacifist persuasion or not — J. F. C. WRIGHT.[1]

THE FIRST World War, begun in August of 1914, affected the Mennonites adversely not only because of their German identity, but also because of their religious insistence on being exempt from military service. Their claim, of course, was supported as a right granted to them in Canadian law. But the war affected the interpretation of that law and the people's feelings about it. Before long, it became clear to the Mennonites that the laws which favoured them might not be much stronger than the public opinion, which in the end failed to support them.

Actually, the early months of the war showed an amazing tolerance, which some Canadians and Canadian leaders maintained to the end. Prime Minister Borden had described the half-million Canadian citizens of German origin as "the very best" in the land.[2] But then came the national call to all Canadians to "stand shoulder to shoulder with Britain and other British dominions . . . to uphold principles of liberty, and to withstand forces that would convert the world into an armed camp."[3] This could not help focusing the attention of Canadians on those immigrants in their midst who spoke the language and appreciated the culture of their enemy. The so-called "alien enemy question" therefore became a very live one throughout the war with repeated calls for disfranchisement, compulsory work at low wages, internment and censorship of foreign language publications. Some of these measures were actually carried out.[4]

In organization and structure, the Mennonites were ill-prepared for the onslaught of federal legislation, administrative regulations and adverse public opinion which was about to burst upon them. They had no united approach to government authorities of any kind. Consequently, they had no common secretariat to mediate the many messages that of necessity flowed between the federal authorities and the people. Indeed, only Ontario authorized a secretariat in the person of S. F. Coffman and then only in the last year of the war. He even had to type his own letters, using only low-budget worn-out carbon papers to duplicate the many messages intended for all the church leaders and all the young men. In the prairies, similarly inadequate "secretariats" were symbolized by David Toews and Benjamin Ewert, who became the chief correspondents, not because they were appointed but because they were the most knowledgeable and, consequently, most able and willing.

As the crisis deepened, at least four different groups of Mennonites, one from Ontario and three from western Canada, made their representations in Ottawa. Mennonite leaders learned to regret very much this divided state of affairs, but somehow east and west did not establish contact with each other until the war was over. For the public at large, Mennonite disunity was a constant source of confusion; for public officials it meant unending irritation and nuisance. As the *Ottawa Citizen* reported, quoting a Regina dispatch:

> Fred Ivay struck a popular chord when he cried: "Who are the Mennonites exempted under the original arrangement? . . . We have nothing but the word of the several Mennonites, and there are exactly 16 branches. So who will undertake to solve the puzzle the problem presents?"[5]

In theological and spiritual ways, the Mennonites were fully prepared, for the doctrine of nonresistance was still strongly held by all the groups, as the developments of the war revealed. Such publications as the *Gospel Herald*, circulating in both Canada and the United States, had, since its founding in 1908, regularly published articles on the biblical teaching of nonresistance.[6] War was no more in harmony with Christian civilization than was slavery, which had already been abolished, and duelling, which had also been prohibited.[7] One of the chief obstacles to the removal of war, it was pointed out, was the theological sentiment "that the rules of the gospel of Jesus Christ, which apply to individuals, are not applicable to nations."[8] The principle of nonresistance was "a practical rule of life" and it applied "to nations as well as to individuals." Its true meaning could be seen in the life and death of Jesus Christ who "exemplified nonresistance."[9] The *Christian Monitor*, a monthly publication founded in 1909, gave special attention to the analysis of world events, attacking the question of war with regularity many months before it actually broke out.

When the war came it was not immediately clear how the Mennonites would be affected. Throughout the nineteenth century they had become quite accustomed to a clear and complete protection from military service in the statutes of Upper Canada and of the Dominion, which specifically named Mennonites, Quakers and Tunkers.[10] The 1868 post-Confederation statute had become the basis for the 1873 Order-in-Council, issued on behalf of the migrating Russian Mennonites. It stated that "an entire exemption from any military service, as is provided by law and Order-in-Council, will be granted to the denomination of Christians called Mennonites."[11]

In the twentieth century, however, the Militia Act had been changed to exclude any mention of specific religious groups. The Act of 1906 said only that such persons were exempted, who "from doctrines of their religion, are averse to bearing arms or rendering personal military service, under such conditions as are prescribed."[12] The Mennonites viewed this provision in the light of their tradition and consequently were not particularly concerned. Besides, Sir Sam Hughes, Minister of Militia and Defence (1911–1916) stated publicly that under the law Mennonites could not be forced to take up arms.[13]

The War Measures Act of 1914, however, did give broad powers to the Governor-General-in-Council to censor publications and communications, to arrest, detain, exclude and report enemy aliens. An intensive recruitment campaign was immediately begun and enemy aliens were registered and interned if they were considered dangerous. A complete Canadian change of attitude to the non-British immigrant population seemed to be under way. As recently as May of 1914 the Governor General, in addressing a Berlin audience, had exalted "the thoroughness, the tenacity, and the loyalty of the great Teutonic race" to which he was "so closely related." The "inherited qualities" would go far "in the making of good Canadian and loyal citizens of the British Empire."[14] But with the coming of the war the substance and tone changed.

Before August 1914, people of German ancestry had been "thrifty, intelligent, industrious, sober, thorough, loyal, good citizens." After August 1914, they were derided for the reasons for which they had earlier been praised.[15] The resulting suspicions of Germans led the people of Berlin to name their city Kitchener and to demonstrate their loyalty in other ways also. The enlistment campaign, which in less than a month produced 100,000 volunteer male recruits, included many Germans and also some Mennonites. Kitchener was proud that the great-great-grandson of its founding father gave his life in battle on March 20, 1915. He was Alexander Ralph Eby, of the Fifth Battalion, First Canadian Contingent, a direct descendant in the line of oldest sons from Bishop Benjamin Eby.[16]

There were other Mennonite military heroes, much to the dismay of the fathers. Herman Fast, the Saskatchewan missionary and teacher, who had come to Canada in 1901 precisely to avoid for his sons the militarisms of Eastern Europe, found himself confronted by their voluntary enlistment. Nicholas fell in the battle at Vimy Ridge and during the War Ernest contracted tuberculosis, of which he died years later.[17]

The Mennonites as a whole, however, were not easily moved. From the most conservative Amish to the most accommodating Mennonite Brethren in Christ, the teaching on nonresistance remained relatively strong. This became clear in the publicity of the deportation in November 1916 to the United States from Windsor of a party of ten Amish Mennonites, who were coming to Huron County for the express purpose of conducting a revival. Bishop E. L. Frey, of Ohio, had been to Ontario several times before to minister to the Amish. Consequently, he freely admitted that once again he would be conducting services in the German language and that his meetings would strengthen historic Mennonite teachings. In a signed statement to the immigration officials at Windsor, he said:

> We take no part in war. We believe that war is wrong in any country. Any member of our church that would volunteer

for military service would be forthwith dismissed from membership in our body. We do not encourage recruiting, we rather discourage it among our people. I have referred to the present war as a calamity in my sermons. I am expressing the views of the Mennonite people in the war.[18]

Asked about the incident by the *Toronto Daily Star,* the Rev. J. N. Kitching, of the Toronto Mennonite Brethren in Christ Church, confirmed that his congregation's views were "the same with regard to going to war — strongly opposed."[19] Opposition did not, however, for his church mean intolerance or excommunication. At least two young men and a minister had enlisted and they freely attended Sunday services. Even their khaki uniforms were accepted in church. In Kitching's words, "We are opposed to our members enlisting, but we have not endeavoured to stop them. In the event of conscription, Mennonites might consent to dig trenches or drive teams but they would not kill. We would sooner die — sooner give our life blood — than take the life of a fellow man." This position, he explained, was based on religion and not actuated by any sympathy for the Germans.[20]

The Russian Mennonites in the west were banking on the 1873 Order-in-Council, but not without some concern, since education legislation, as they saw it, had already destroyed part of the *Privilegium.* Their first premonition of trouble on the military question came in December of 1916 when R. B. Bennett, the Director General of National Service under the War Measures Act, called for a January inventory of every male in Canada between the ages of 16 and 65. National Service Cards available at the post offices were to be filled out and returned within 10 days.

The first to respond negatively to this order was the Old Colony Manitoba bishop, Johann J. S. Friesen. He and his colleagues from Saskatchewan, Bishop Jacob Wiens from Hague-Osler and Bishop Abram Wiebe from Swift Current, had been in Ottawa in November and, in their opinion, received assurances from Prime Minister Borden that Mennonites were totally exempt on the basis of the 1873 Order-in-Council. In a letter to Borden, Bishop Friesen expressed every gratitude for the continued exemption and confirmed that Mennonites desired only to be "the quiet in the land" and to pray to God for the welfare of the country. The National Service Cards were therefore being returned uncompleted, but in no way, said the bishop, should this be interpreted as disloyalty to the British Crown.[21]

Bishop Jacob Wiens from Hague wrote similarly, expressing appreciation for the peace which the community enjoyed in Canada, and enclosed a $1,383 cheque with the instruction that it be applied where it was most needed to relieve victims of the war. Prime Minister Borden assured him of "the determination of the government to adhere fully to the obligations of honour incurred by this country at the time of admission of your people." He also indicated that the money so generously donated would be applied to the Canadian Patriotic Fund "as a free and loyal donation from the community of Mennonites."[22] Subsequently, the Old Colony community of Saskatchewan and Manitoba held a meeting of bishops, preachers and laymen at Reinland, Manitoba, at which time it was decided not to fill in their National Service Cards, which were viewed as the first step toward military enlistment. The church was, however, not averse to providing a list of male members apart from the cards.[23]

Meanwhile, a more representative delegation of western Mennonites had gone to Ottawa to "get definite information relating to questions that agitate the minds of our people." The members of the delegation, meeting with Mr. R. B. Bennett and other officials of the National Service, were Bishop Abraham Doerksen of the Chortitzer Church and Rev. Benjamin Ewert of the Bergthaler Church, both from Manitoba, and Bishop David Toews of the Rosenorter Church and Mr. Klaas Peters, both from Saskatchewan. Peters, of Mennonite heritage, had actually joined the Swedenborgian Church, but for purposes of exemption he readily identified again with the Mennonites. The delegation reviewed the history of the Mennonites and their theology of nonresistance based on the Christian gospel. They reminded the Ottawa authorities of the 1873 Orders-in-Council and also of the contents of the Lord Dufferin speech, given to the Mennonite pioneers on August 21, 1877, especially the memorable words "the battle to which we invite you is the battle against the wilderness . . . you will not be required to shed human blood." The delegates assured Ottawa of their "unflinching loyalty to the land." Since they anticipated a further large migration from Russia, they asked for "a clear statement assuring us of the continued exemption from military service."[24]

Replying on the same day, Director General Bennett gave a four-point answer, which, in the first instance, promised Canada's "respect to the utmost" of that Order-in-Council. Secondly, members of the Mennonite community were requested to fill in the National Service Cards, though they could also write across the face of each card the word "Mennonite" to ensure special treatment. The cards would thereby indicate how many men between the ages of 16 and 65 might be available for agricultural production. And finally, Mennonites who had joined overseas battalions under false assumptions or pressures and desiring to be released could obtain this release if application were made in writing by the applicant himself.[25]

Overjoyed to receive this new official assurance, the delegates immediately sought from their constituency a financial contribution, a special expression of gratitude toward the support of war victims, invalids, widows and orphans. Within three months $5,577.17 was sent; it was likewise applied to the Canadian Patriotic Fund.[26] Intended mainly for the dependants of war victims, the Fund had a history dating back to the Crimean War.[27]

The expression was very timely, because police detachments had already informed Ottawa of strong pro-German factions in southern Manitoba and that one member of the Gretna community had been sent to an alien internment camp. Although he had been allowed to return home in three weeks, there was a strong feeling that hundreds "if not thousands" of young Mennonites on the reserves should be dispatched throughout the Dominion to alleviate the manpower shortage in agriculture. Should these Mennonites not help in this crisis, then the only privilege they should be accorded was the privilege "to get out."[28]

There is no evidence that young men were officially recruited and dispatched for agricultural service elsewhere in the country, but the financial expression of appreciation and loyalty became normative for the Mennonites. On one occasion $4,000 was raised and two freight cars full of feed grain were dispatched to Deloraine, an English settlement community in western Manitoba, which had experienced total crop failure on account of grasshoppers.[29] Large sums amounting to about half a million dollars would later be raised for the Red Cross and the Victory Loan campaigns.

The year 1917 also began with somewhat of a crisis in Kitchener. Mayor-elect David Gross announced a return to the name of Berlin, and promptly the Canadian press used this incident to accuse Kitchener of being pro-German and failing to do its duty in the war effort. Mayor Gross then boasted that Waterloo North constituency had already provided 1,100 men for the services, that 50 per cent of the enlistees were of German extraction, that the city had already given $124,000 to a war fund and paid $31,000 in soldiers' insurance. In a city of 20,000 where 12,000 were of German origin, this was not a bad record.[30] Needless to say, Kitchener remained Kitchener.

A greater crisis, however, was in the making for Ontario and, indeed, all of Canada. Although many more volunteers had been enlisted in Canada's armed forces than had at first been sought and expected, voluntary enlistments were lagging by the summer of 1917 when the manpower needs of the British Empire were sharply increasing. Enlistments were behind especially in French Canada, and Prime Minister Borden felt that he needed a conscription bill, which after much debate was assented to on August 29, 1917. The Act, however, was most controversial and threatened to divide the country. Borden therefore proceeded to form a union government in October with 13 Conservatives and 10 Liberals in his Cabinet. There was some dissent, however. Sir Wilfrid Laurier, the Liberal leader, decided with Quebec backing that he could not possibly go along with the conscription bill and consequently with a union government. Otherwise he supported the war effort in every way.

Anticipating an election, Borden was also warned from the west in June that anti-conservative and anti-conscription votes could swing large areas against him.[31] How critical the opposition vote could be was also suggested by the editor of *Der Nordwesten* in Winnipeg. He counselled Prime Minister Borden before the Act was passed to promise the Mennonites the government's good will in exchange for their not voting in the forthcoming election, the chief issue of which would be conscription.[32] However, the Prime Minister in September armed himself with the Wartime Elections Act. Thereby aliens in general and conscientious objectors in particular were disfranchised. The Act also made clear that anyone who voted lost his exemption privileges.

In Ontario, particularly in Waterloo and York counties, the Elections Act produced considerable confusion. The Act excluded Mennonites from voting, but G. W. Weichel, the Conservative Member of Parliament for Waterloo North, sought to persuade his electorate that it was only aimed at Russian Mennonites. W. L. Mackenzie King, who was trying to regain a seat in Parliament, this time in York County, also was overly anxious for the Mennonite vote. He had a "committeeman's book and instructions for agents" prepared, which emphasized that Ontario

Mennonites had the right to vote. Letters to constituents advised that "even if they should be struck off the lists they ought to render their ballots and have them recorded for purposes of re-count later."[33] Both Weichel and King were wrong in their inter-pretation of the Wartime Elections Act, which in the relevant clause read as follows:

> All persons who on the sixth day of July, 1917 were
> members of the religious denomination or sect called
> "Mennonites" (the members of which denomination or sect
> were exempted from military service by Order-in-Council
> of August 13, 1873 . . .)[34]

The Act meant all Mennonites. The bracketed reference to the 1873 Order-in-Council was everywhere else understood to serve the functions not of limitation but of identity and to justify from history the naming of Mennonites as a general class. Only Weichel and King gave to the reference a restrictive interpretation, but in so doing they unleashed a confusion which twice did disservice to the Mennonites whom they were so anxious to help. In the election campaign they confused those Mennonites who were anxious to vote but who by the general public interpretation of the Act were excluded. In the later conscription program, the King-Weichel interpretation was conveniently resurrected by those of the general populace and public officialdom who wanted to exclude from the exemptions of the conscription act as many as they possibly could.

The unusual re-election efforts of King and Weichel were not successful. Both had gone to great effort and in the end Weichel had even dissociated himself from the Borden Club in Kitchener and announced himself as a Labour candidate for Waterloo North. Winning the election, however, was a Laurier Independent Liberal candidate, W. D. Euler, who was against the conscription bill and who insisted that his pro-Germanism had to do with the Germany of Beethoven and Schubert and not with the Germany of Kaiser Wilhelm. A former mayor of Kitchener and president of the Kitchener Board of Trade, Euler was a popular man and was able to render great assistance to the Mennonites not only in the war years but after, for he held his seat until 1940.

Perhaps anticipating the conscription crisis, the Mennonite Conference had been formulating anew their historic position on war. The Ontario Executive Committee urged each minister to discourage members from engaging in the manufacture of munitions of war or any similar work.[35] Forty-eight Mennonite bishops, 104 ministers, and 22 deacons of the Mennonite General Conference assembled at Goshen, Indiana, and framed "a statement of our position on military service."[36] They expressed gratitude "for the exemption clause for nonresistant people in the new [U.S.] selective draft law" and expressed the hope that the clause referring to noncombatant service would be modified.

"We cannot participate in war in any form; that is, to aid or abet war, whether in a combatant or noncombatant capacity," the statement said, emphasizing that this was not an act of disloyalty or disobedience or of cowardice. They appealed, therefore, to the American president to "grant unto us full liberty of conscience and the free exercise of our faith" and asked "the brethren liable for military service" not to accept any form of military service and to submit "to any penalty the government may see fit to inflict, trusting the Lord for guidance and protection."[37]

Officially at least, the opposition to any form of noncombatant service was a universal position among Mennonites of North America during World War I, the Mennonite Brethren in Christ being a possible exception. In Russia, by contrast, the alternative service provisions worked out since the 1870s involved at least 12,000 young men during the World War, of which about 6,000 served in hospital or ambulance corps, including many in the front lines. The Russian Mennonites underwrote the complete cost of the program and it was said to be under civilian direction. Later, however, all the participants qualified for veterans' pensions just like other members of the armed forces.[38]

The Military Service Act of 1917 received royal assent in Canada on the same day, August 29, that the Mennonites declared their position. Thus, as the Goshen delegates returned to Canada with a clarified theological stand, they faced the need to clarify their legal position. In a sense the Act was unambiguous. It contained a schedule of seven clauses which spelled out seven exceptions to the Act, that is, seven categories of persons, including those "exempted from military service by Order-in-Council of August 13, 1873 and by Order-in-Council of December 6, 1898."[39] The 1873 Order-in-Council, it may be remembered, provided "an entire exemption from military service . . . to the denomination of Christians called Mennonites."[40] The 1898 Order-in-Council, passed on the occasion of the admission of the Doukhobors from Russia, gave the same right also to the Doukhobors upon the production of a certificate of membership in the

Doukhobor society.[41] These Orders-in-Council in turn were based on statutes which specifically exempted Quakers, Mennonites and Tunkers.[42]

It seemed clear, therefore, that neither the Militia Act of 1906 nor the Military Service Act of 1917 had any intention of undoing for religious pacifists what the eighteenth and nineteenth centuries had in Canadian law repeatedly given to them. It could, consequently, be concluded that the Mennonites of Ontario were *excepted from* the Military Service Act. Failing that, however, there was another escape clause in the Act, namely an "exemption clause" in distinction from the foregoing "schedule of exceptions." According to the exemption clause, application could be made to any of the local or district military tribunals being set up across the country for a certificate of exemption. Such exemptions were made available to any person who

> conscientiously objects to the undertaking of combatant
> service and is prohibited from so doing by the tenets and
> articles of faith, in effect on the sixth day of July, 1917, of
> any organized religious denomination existing and well
> recognized in Canada at such date and to which he in good
> faith belongs.[43]

There were several problem clauses in the exemption provision, however. One, immediately obvious, was the limitation of exemption to "combatant service." The Mennonite Conference of Ontario and the Amish Mennonites therefore sent a joint delegation of eight people to Ottawa to request Prime Minister Borden and Secretary of State Meighen to achieve clarification of the Military Service Act for them. The delegation's appeal to the government was attached to the Goshen statement which reinforced their position on both combatant and noncombatant service. However, in expressing themselves on the Military Service Act the Mennonites did not base their claims on the "*exceptions*," but rather on the "*exemption*" clauses. The significance of this delicate distinction had not yet become obvious. The delegation going to Ottawa and the correspondents subsequently handling Mennonite affairs might have benefited from the help of a lawyer. It soon became obvious that the case for either exception or exemption from all forms of service would have to be made by the Mennonites and not by the government. The government authorities were not about to disburse privileges and rights allowable under the law when the people themselves were not ready to claim or "fight" for them. Some legal assistance would have aided immeasurably in the clarification of relatively simple points of law. On the other hand, why should a people trusting a government spend much time and energy clarifying minute legalities?

Nevertheless, the trip to Ottawa resulted in a most favourable ruling. On November 3, the Deputy Minister of Justice, E. L. Newcombe, informed Bishop S. F. Coffman, the spokesman for the delegation, that Mennonites came under "the schedule of exceptions to the above act, and have no duty to perform thereunder." Newcombe hastened to add that the provision would not relieve them of any annoyance caused by prosecution for non-compliance. There could be and probably would be prosecution, but the defence against that prosecution would be to claim identity as a Mennonite, "and on proof of the fact, undoubtedly the prosecution would be dismissed."[44]

The Ontario Mennonites' response to this good news from Ottawa was similar to that of Western Canada Mennonites earlier in 1917. They wanted immediately to raise an offering of gratitude or a memorial gift for war relief as an expression of appreciation. The idea of receiving special offerings for war relief had previously been aired by various leaders, among them Thomas Reesor of Markham and Noah A. Bearinger from Elmira, but now the time to act had come.[45] Bearinger, one of the very few Mennonites with a college education, had been troubled for some time by the inactivity of the Mennonites as well as by their ignorance pertaining to the protection that they had under the law, an ignorance which he said was matched only by the ignorance of the authorities in Ottawa. He felt that the services of a lawyer and of duplicating equipment would unquestionably have benefited the Mennonite cause. As it was, persons like himself typed away into all hours of the night with a "hunt and peck" method producing copies of the Military Service Act and other important documents.[46]

The idea of the memorial gift now brought together the various nonresistant factions, first on November 17 and again on December 11, to form the common enterprise known at first as "the Non-Resistant Relief Movement of Ontario." The formal organization took place in Kitchener on January 16, 1918, at which time the name "Non-Resistant Relief Organization" (NRRO) was adopted for the common task of the Mennonites and the Tunkers. It was resolved that a generous fund be raised among the churches interested in donating to the government for relief and charitable purposes "as a memorial of appreciation for the privilege of religious liberty, and our freedom from military service."[47] Another delegation was authorized to go to Ottawa with a double purpose in mind:

> to clarify purpose and procedures for the memorial gift and at the same time to receive assurance "that the total exemption from those of our faith from all military service is still the purpose of our government."[48]

The NRRO hoped to raise at least $100,000 from the 7,000 members in the nonresistant churches, this being only $15 per member. S. F. Coffman calculated the $100,000 in another way. If each young man called and given exemption paid $50 a year for each year that the war had been in progress, then the $100,000 goal would also be met. He reminded the Mennonites and Tunkers that in the past males between the ages of 21 and 60 had annually paid from $15 to $25 to be free from militia service.[49]

The formation of the Non-Resistant Relief Organization was a big step for the Ontario Mennonites, inasmuch as it brought together the various factions who had been separated from each other in the nineteenth century. They set about immediately to raise the projected memorial gift (eventually about $80,000 was disbursed), but for nearly a year the effort was side-tracked by the uncertainties of the Mennonite position under the law. While the Justice Department had given a rather clear ruling on their status, the ambiguities in the situation were sufficient to allow for almost total confusion once public opinion began to affect the interpretation of the law and the rules and regulations emanating from it.

Public opinion, as it related to public policy, was an omnipresent factor. Even while the Justice Department was giving a favourable reply to S. F. Coffman, he was under surveillance by the police, who became informed on the content of some of his Sunday morning sermons. The specific statements which Sir Percy Sherwood of Ottawa, the Chief Commissioner of the Dominion Police, wanted explained were the following:

> What good are the soldiers, they produce nothing, they earn nothing, they don't earn the clothes they wear, they do nothing but destroy. If any of you are producing food to

> help win the war, don't do it. If you are producing food to
> feed the needy, alright go on.[50]

The bishop insisted that the statements were made to encourage people to continue steadfastly in the nonresistant principles of faith. There was no intention to speak against the government, their soldiers or their methods. Besides, this could not possibly have any recruiting effect since in his church of 70 members there was only one young man eligible to be called and he had made exemption claims on the grounds of being a church member.

Coffman was personally excused, but very soon he was wrestling with the problem of the young men facing conscription. Within a month after the last deadline for the first recruitment (November 10, 1917), there were problems of interpretation and application of the rules. The instruction from the London district tribunal, the main one for the Mennonites, to local tribunals was sufficiently precise. The director, W. E. Wismer, a man of distant Mennonite extraction whose family had joined the Evangelical Association, advised local tribunals as follows:

> All those Mennonite people, of course, are excepted from the
> Act, and as long as you are fully satisfied that they are in
> fact Mennonites you have no option but to grant them
> exemption.[51]

Wismer did not speak with such clarity again, nor did his superiors of the provincial tribunal in Toronto. The Central Appeal Judge in Ottawa did not bring about a final and consistent ruling until the end of the war. Before that, though, a whole series of problems emerged in the local tribunals. In the first place, the tribunals were under great pressure to produce recruits for the services. This is why under the Act every male British subject in Canada between the ages of 20 and 45 was automatically a "soldier." These soldiers were absent without leave — and without pay — until called up by royal proclamation. The first such proclamation, issued on October 13, 1917, called into active service all unmarried men between the ages of 20 and 34. All had to report by November 10, and in the filling out of the induction forms either waive or claim exemption. As it turned out, all across the land an average of 95 per cent claimed exemption. Apparently, all young men with any interest at all in the war effort had already volunteered. The local tribunals were under great pressure, therefore, to give the government the benefit of any of their doubts when it came to processing exemptions.

The first area of doubt, when it came to processing Mennonites, had to do with the differences between "exceptions from the Act" and "exemptions under the Act." Under the former provision, the Mennonites could remain essentially outside the tribunal process. The Justice Department had ruled that the former applied, but at the same time allowed for an administrative process which easily erased the difference. Unless the young Mennonite was unusually well-informed, alert and courageous, which most of them were not, or unless the local tribunals were unusually considerate or sympathetic, which was unlikely given the pressures of conscription, there were no exceptions to the Act.

Thus, Mennonite claims tended to come under the "*exemption*" clause rather than under the "*exception*" schedule. Under the exemption clause there were at least eight possibilities, including the dictates of religion and the demands of the farm and food production. Both of these came into play. Although the real issue for Mennonites was religion and conscience, both they and the tribunals would sometimes choose the farm option to avoid complexities. But even a farm exemption was only a postponement of service for young men whom the Act had already identified as soldiers.

The religious option presented several problems. The first concerned the definition of who was a Mennonite. Under the exemption clause Mennonites were not specifically named, but since a religious claim had to be related to a denomination whose tenets of faith on July 6, 1917, included opposition to war, the processing of Mennonite claimants as Mennonites was unavoidable.

Seeking the strictest possible application of the Military Service Act, some tribunals immediately made the July 6 date crucial. They applied the date not to the faith or existence of the denomination, as the law specified, but to the faith and membership status of the claimant. This latter interpretation was not entirely without precedent, inasmuch as the July 6 date had been used in that sense in the War-Time Elections Act. In the resulting confusion, the press and the public even used October 13, the day of the first recruitment proclamation, as the membership cut-off date.

Whatever use was made of dates, however, a more fundamental issue of religious identity was raised by the Military Service Act. Who was a Mennonite? It was a question not only for the authorities who needed some reliable certification, but also for the Mennonites themselves. In one sense, only those who had been baptized upon confession of faith and entered into the church register as bona-fide members were Mennonites. No attempt would have been made to enlarge on that definition — except for the fact that the baptismal age in most of the Mennonite groups was the marrying age, around 21. This meant that some men were of military age before reaching the normal time for baptism.

The problem arose not only in Ontario, where it came to defining who was *exempted by* the Act, but also among the Russian Mennonites in the West, where it came to defining who was *excepted from* the Act. None of the leaders in Ontario seem to have recalled the precedent set in Upper Canada legislation in 1809 providing relief from militia taxes for minors, but S. F. Coffman did make a strong appeal to common sense. When he saw how the tribunals were "splitting hairs" regarding the definition of Mennonite, he told government officials:

> No one ever intimated to me, nor tried to make me believe, that a young man whose father was a Mennonite all his life and belonged to the Mennonite church was not also considered a Mennonite.[52]

There were two relatively quiet ways of dealing with the problem. One concerned lowering the baptismal age, which by mid-1918 was happening in both the east and the west, but apparently nowhere more dramatically than among the Old Order Mennonites. Before long the London district office sent out someone to investigate. The investigation on June 11, 1918, produced much fear in the Elmira congregation, but Noah Bearinger had nothing but praise for the visit and he asked the London authorities to place the investigating officer in charge of military affairs in that district:

> Instead of our fears being justified, we find that the officer whom we had supposed would subject our boys to every inconvenience that his authority would permit, has entered a strong plea in our favour with the authorities at London; and, no doubt, as he has personally seen and experienced the true state of affairs, his pleas will not be ignored . . . We were impressed with the quiet manner in which he performed his duties, which hardly disturbed our divine services and avoided all publicity.[53]

The other quiet way was to certify young men as Mennonites whether they were baptized or not. But this procedure too could not be kept quiet, and soon David Toews, who did most of the certifying in Saskatchewan as an unofficial "bishop of Canada," was being accused of turning many good-for-nothings into Mennonites.[54] The misunderstandings that resulted brought Mennonites of Saskatchewan together for a conference in mid-1918, out of which came a strongly worded petition to the Governor General to have the public harassment, official and unofficial, lifted:

> We are accused of fraud. We are referred to by leaders of
> our fellow citizens from public platforms as outlawed
> parasites. We cannot even cast a vote in our protection.
> Any one can afford to slight or insult us or to assault or
> neglect us. We are not outlaws in the sense of disobedience
> to constituted authority. In fact, as we shall show in a
> moment, it was largely our desire to take instruction from
> the authorities that has caused our troubles. Parasites we
> are not. We are earning our bread by honest labour, and if
> we mistake not, our labour has assisted materially in
> advancing the material welfare of our country. We do not
> depend for our living on the sustenance or efforts of others
> excepting as we give and take. We do not require any one
> to shed his blood for us. We would rather die ourselves or
> languish in prison or leave our home and again settle
> in some wilderness, the same as our forefathers have done,
> than to require a sacrifice of any kind by any one on our
> behalf. Every one knew at the time of the last Dominion
> elections who were Mennonites and who were not. Neither
> the registrar nor the tribunal nor the public seem to
> know it now.[55]

The Manitoba bishops were called to Winnipeg to explain the matter of unbaptized young people and their status as Mennonites. The authorities apparently were of the opinion that unbaptized youths did not qualify for exemption and to prove their point they had one Abraham Dyck of Lowe Farm tossed into the barracks in order to turn him into a soldier. The bishops were now expected to declare in the presence of a lawyer the rules and regulations defining the relationship of the churches to their young people and vice versa.

The requested statement, drawn up by bishops Abraham Doerksen of the Sommerfelder church and Jacob Hoeppner of the Bergthaler church, reviewed the strong theological tradition of nonresistance, recalled the agreements made in 1873, and explained the ecclesiastical organization of the Mennonites. They pointed out (a) that a child's name was entered into the church register the day of his birth, (b) that instruction in nonresistance was given in the homes as well as in the schools and churches, (c) that baptism was given approximately at age 21 to those voluntarily requesting it on confession of faith and after a period of intense instruction, (d) that unbaptized young people took part in all church activities except communion and voting, and (e) that in the teaching of the church unbaptized persons could be saved. In short:

> Our *Gemeinschaft* has always considered its children and
> young people its own as much as the baptized members
> and petitions for exemption from military service have
> always intended to include young people of military age
> whether they were baptized or not. Any assurances which
> provided for less than that would never have persuaded
> us to accept the invitation of the Canadian government to
> settle in this country.[56]

The statement turned out to be acceptable to the authorities and Abraham Dyck was immediately released. Henceforth, all Mennonites in Western Canada were *excepted from* the Act upon simple proof of identity. This provision included all those who had come not only from Russia, directly or indirectly, but also those who had migrated westward from Ontario.

While the matter of Mennonite identity was being clarified across the land, in June of 1918 another issue aroused the suspicion of the Russian Mennonites. A second registration of manpower had been scheduled for June 22, this one more thorough than the first. This time all males and females between 16 and 60 were required to answer an 18-point questionnaire. Those failing to do so were to be fined $100, imprisoned for as long as a month, and fined an additional $10 daily until registration was submitted to.

Twenty-four Manitoba ministers, representing six church groups, met on June 11 at Altona to discuss the matter. Some were convinced that the demand could be compared to the registration by "the beast" in the New Testament Book of Revelations, chapter 13, but in the end they agreed to cooperate.[57] The Old Colony church, however, was not so inclined. The superintendent of registration in Manitoba, P. C. Locke, made a strong effort to persuade them otherwise. He called their representatives to Winnipeg and also dealt with their legal representative, Mr. McLeod in Morden, all to no avail. Finally, he arranged to meet with Saskatchewan and Manitoba representatives of the Old Colony in Reinland on June 13. As he approached the village he was met by many buggies going in the opposite direction. One driver told him: "The meeting is over. We met at six o'clock this morning and prayed to the Lord and he told us not to register."[58] Locke was advised that he could meet the bishops and some ministers at a home in the village. According to Locke the following conversation took place:

> I used every argument I could think of. The answer was
> "No, we cannot register, the Lord will not let us." Mr.
> McLeod said to me, "I am afraid we cannot do anything."
> I said to the bishop, "Bishop, I have known the Mennonite
> people since my childhood. If you refuse to register it is my
> duty to enforce the Act and I purpose to do so. The Act
> provides for ten days imprisonment for failure to register,
> and for a fine of so much a day for each day after the 22nd
> of June you fail to register. I propose to enforce that. I
> cannot have the authority of the Dominion Government
> flouted." The old Manitoba bishop then broke the silence.
> He said to me in English, "You cannot put all the
> Mennonite people in jail." I said, "No, but I can guarantee
> you one thing, and that is that you and every man present
> in this room who fails to register on the 22nd of June will
> be imprisoned on the 23rd." Again the old bishop spoke. He
> said, "I want you to clearly understand we do not blame
> you for doing your duty. If we don't register, any man
> of us whom you want will report to Mr. McLeod's office at
> Morden on the morning of the 23rd ready to go to jail."
> I said, "Bishop, there is also a fine." He said, "Yes, and we
> will bring you in our bank books, the titles to our farms
> and lists of our stock."[59]

In the end Locke picked up the German Bible translated by Luther, and, reading from Luke 2 the account of Caesar Augustus ordering a registration, he proceeded to persuade the Old Colony leaders that the Lord really wanted them to register. Having persuaded them, they not only agreed to cooperate but they actually volunteered the assistance of their young people.

Will you let us register our own people under your
direction? We will give you all our young people who read
and write and speak English well and they will do whatever
work is necessary without expense.[60]

The various confrontations with government officials in Ontario, Manitoba and Saskatchewan led to mutually acceptable
ways of certifying Mennonite identity by the middle of 1918.
After they had clarified the meaning of membership and of
ministerial ordination, the various groups drew up lists of people
qualified to sign certification cards. Those lists were then submitted to government officials who recognized no other signatures
and no other forms than those that had been agreed to.

By June 25, the situation of the Tunkers had also been
clarified. Although recognized as a pacifists' church along with
the Quakers and Mennonites in the nineteenth-century militia
law, the Tunkers and Quakers had been almost forgotten. For
the Tunkers, and for S. F. Coffman who laboured on their behalf
(as he did for all the NRRO groups), the breaking point was
reached early in May when one of their most promising young
men was detained in the Hamilton barracks.

Ernest J. Swalm of Collingwood, who later became the
Canadian bishop for the Tunkers, had asked for exemption as a
farmer and as a member for eight years of a pacifist religious
sect. The Ontario registrar had wrongly ruled that Tunkers were
not exempted under the Act. They were not specifically named,
but they were in existence on June 6, 1917, as a denomination
whose tenets opposed participation in war and had been in
existence as such for over 100 years.

When called, Swalm had reported to the military officer but
even under threat refused to report for military duty. He was
then forcibly stripped and clothed in military uniform. Still un-
cooperative, he was on June 5 sentenced to hard labour for two
years. The persistent effort of Coffman and D. W. Heise of the
Tunker church led to Tunker recognition on June 25 and to
Swalm's release on July 3. At least two other Tunker men shared
Swalm's experience.[61]

In Ontario the proper identification of Mennonites and Tunkers, however, was not the end of their troubles. If and when
exemptions were granted they were from combatant services
only, according to the law. Therein lay the difference between
Ontario and Western Canada. When the western Mennonites

were properly identified as Mennonites, they were *excepted from* the law; in Ontario they were *exempted within* the law from combatant service. They were, therefore, still "soldiers" in the definition of the Act and expected to perform noncombatant duty, unless they were granted farm exemptions, i.e. postponements.

Those who were not granted farm exemptions were sent to the camps as "soldiers" to do noncombatant service. Young men who, like Swalm, resisted were sent to the guardhouses and after court-martial to military prison. As time went on, Coffman and his friends in the House of Commons were able to arrange for "leave of absence" which became automatic with proper Mennonite identification. "Leave of absence" was an administrative procedure, allowable under the law, by which the tribunals could avoid forcing Mennonites into service, without either excepting or exempting them.[62] The application of this provision depended on the good will of officials at some authoritative level.

The legal position of the Ontario Mennonites with respect to the conscription laws remained inconsistent and unclarified until the end of the war. On the one hand, the Central Appeal Judge as late as September 1918 dismissed some exemption appeals because the applicants were excepted from the Act, consistent with the November 1917 ruling of the Justice Department. One Ezra Boshart from Milverton, for instance, was advised September 13 by the Clerk of the Central Appeal Judge that he did not come "within the application of the Military Service Act 1917 . . ."[63]

Yet the Ontario and London district registrars continued to insist as late as September 25 that the "Eastern Mennonites, according to the ruling of the Central Appeal Judge, do not constitute an exception to the Act and will be exempt only from combatant service."[64] And on October 5, five weeks before the war came to a conclusion, the Central Appeal Judge office itself advised that Ontario Mennonites were not excepted.[65] Ten days later the Governor-General-in-Council ruled that immigrant Mennonites and their descendants not specifically covered by the 1873 Order-in-Council "shall not be deemed to be exempted from military service or within the 7th exception to the Military Service Act 1917."[66]

Perhaps the inconsistency and confusion was due in part to a new debate that was raging in Western Canada and in Ottawa concerning the influx of Mennonite and Hutterite conscientious objectors from the United States. The presence of these "draft-dodgers" added fuel to the fires of public opinion, thoroughly aroused by a people insisting not only on military exemption, but also on German culture in their churches and schools. Although the war came to an end, those fires were not quickly quenched.

FOOTNOTES

1. J. F. C. Wright, *Saskatchewan: The History of a Province* (Toronto: McClelland & Stewart, 1955), p. 170.
2. Various authorities, *Canada in the Great World War*, Vol. II, *Days of Preparation* (Toronto: United Publisher of Canada, c. 1918), p. 30.
3. *Ibid.*
4. "The Alien Enemy Question of 1918," *Canadian Annual Review* (1919), pp. 579–81; "German Propaganda and Plots in the United States," *Canadian Annual Review* (1919), pp. 254–69.
5. "Western Furore Over Exemption of Mennonites," *Ottawa Citizen*, September 25, 1918, p. 6.
6. W. I. Powell, "Nonresistance," *Gospel Herald*, VI (May 29, 1913), pp. 130–31, 133; John Horsch, "A Popular Objection to Nonresistance," *Gospel Herald*, V (March 27, 1913), pp. 819–20; J. A. Ressler, "What the Bible Teaches," *Gospel Herald*, V (May 9, 1912), p. 82.
7. George S. Grimm, "What is War?" *Gospel Herald*, III (March 16, 1911), p. 790.
8. "Carnegie on War," *Christian Monitor*, III (March 11, 1911), p. 93.
9. J. A. Ressler, "What the Bible Teaches," *Gospel Herald*, V (May 9, 1912), p. 82.
10. 48 George III, Chap. 1, Sect. 27 (1808); I Victoria 8, Sect. 50 (1837); II Victoria, Chap. 9, Sect. 52 (1839); IV and V Victoria, Chap. 2 (1841); IX Victoria, Chap. 28, Sect. 31 (1846); XII Victoria, Chap. 88 (1849); XVIII Victoria, Chap. 77, Sect. 7 (1855); Consolidated Statutes of Upper Canada, Chap. 35, Sect. 73 (1859); XXXI Victoria, Chap. 10, Sect. 17 (1868); XLVI Victoria and *Revised Statutes of Canada*, 1886, Chap. 1, Sect. 26.
11. PAC, *Order-in-Council*, Record Group 2, 1, 957, July 28, 1873.
12. The Militia Act, *Revised Statutes of Canada*, 1906, Chap. 41, Sect. 11.
13. "Rather Die Than Slay, So Mennonites Will Not Fight," *Toronto Daily Star*, November 25, 1916.

14. "A Visit of Governor General," *Berlin Daily Telegram*, May 9, 1914, p. 1.

15. W. H. Heick, "The Lutherans of Waterloo County During World War I," *Waterloo Historical Society*, L (1962), pp. 23–32.

16. *Waterloo Historical Society*, III (1915), p. 8.

17. Frank H. Epp, "The Story of Rosthern Junior College" (unpublished manuscript, 1970), Chap. 2, p. 28.

18. PAC, *Immigration Branch*, Record Group 76, 1, Vol. 173, 58764, 1. Statement of E. L. Frey, Bishop of Amish Mennonite Church, November 14, 1916.

19. "Rather Die Than Slay, So Mennonites Will Not Fight," *Toronto Daily Star,* November 25, 1916.

20. *Ibid.*

21. PAC, *Borden Papers,* M. G. 26, H, RLB 1167, 121078. Bishop Johann J. S. Friesen, Neuenburg, Winkler, to Sir Robert L. Borden and Arthur Meighen, January 4, 1917.

22. N. W. Bahnmann, "Der Ausgang des Prozesses gegen den Lehrdienst der Altkolonier Gemeinde bei Hague, Sask.," *Der Mitarbeiter*, XI (November 1916), p. 3.

23. PAC, *Borden Papers,* M. G. 26, H, RLB 1167, 121098. Report of the RNWMP, Rosthern Detachment, April 5, 1917.

24. CMBC. BE. "A Petition of the Mennonite Delegation to the Government at Ottawa, January 8, 1917, signed Rev. Abraham Doerksen, Rev. Heinrich Doerksen, Rev. Benjamin Ewert, Rev. David Toews, Mr. Klaas Peters, representatives of Mennonite settlers of Western Canada."

25. CMBC. BE. Letter of R. B. Bennett to representatives of Mennonite settlers in Western Canada, January 8, 1917, Ottawa.

26. CMBC. BE. Letter from Abraham Doerksen, Heinrich Doerksen, David Toews, Klaas Peters, Benjamin Ewert, to R. B. Bennett, Director General, National Service, April 27, 1917.

27. Philip H. Morris, editor, *The Canadian Patriotic Fund: A Record of its Activities*, n.p., n.d. 367 pp.

28. PAC, *Borden Papers*, M. G. 26, H, RLB 1167, 121086. Letter of Director General of the National Service to Robert L. Borden, January 22, 1917.

29. Isaak M. Dyck, *Auswanderung der Reinlander Mennoniten Gemeinde von Canada nach Mexico* (Cuahtemoc, Chihuahua, Mexico: Imprenta Colonial, 1970).

30. Gerhard Enns, "Waterloo North on Conscription 1917," *Waterloo Historical Society*, LI (1963), pp. 60–69.

31. PAC, *Borden Papers*, M. G. 26, H, RLB 1414, 123093. Letter of John R. Lavell to Robert L. Borden, June 19, 1917.

32. PAC, *Borden Papers,* M. G. 26, H, RLB 1414, 123252. Letter of G. G. Maron, editor of *Der Nordwesten*, to Robert L. Borden, August 24, 1917.

33. PAC, *Mackenzie King Papers*, M. G. 26, J. 1, Vol. 37, 32696. Letter of W. L. Mackenzie King to Isaak Pike (Bethesda, Ont.), Newmarket, December 14, 1917. Also Vol. 36, 31148–31551. Letter of W. L. Mackenzie King to C. W. Davidson, Newmarket, November 26, 1917. Also Vol. 35, 31149–50. Letter of W. L. Mackenzie King to J. D. Aitchison, Stouffville, November 27, 1917.

34. 7–8 George V, Chap. 39, Sect. 154(f), "War-Time Elections Act."

35. Minutes of the Executive Committee of the Mennonite Conference of Ontario, August 4, 1917, David Bergey, Secretary.

36. *Mennonites on Military Service: A Statement of our Position on Military Service*, as adopted by the Mennonite General Conference, August 29, 1917.

37. *Ibid.*

38. Frank H. Epp, *Mennonite Exodus: The Rescue and Resettlement of the Russian Mennonites Since the Communist Revolution* (Altona, Man.: D. W. Friesen & Sons, 1962), pp. 28–9.

39. Military Service Act 1917, 7-8 George V, Chap. 19.

40. PAC, *Order-in-Council*, Record Group 2, 1, 957, August 13, 1873.

41. PAC, *Order-in-Council*, Record Group 2, 1, 247, December 6, 1898.

42. *Revised Statutes of Canada*, Chap. 41, Sect. 21.

43. 7-8 George V, Chap. 19, Sect. 11(f).

44. CGC. SFC. Letter of E. L. Newcombe, Deputy Minister of Justice, to S. F. Coffman, November 3, 1917.

45. CGC. SFC. Letter of Noah M. Bearinger to W. C. Weichel, M.P., May 23, 1917.

46. Interview with Noah M. Bearinger on August 6, 1969.

47. CGC. Minutes of the Non-Resistant Relief Movement of Ontario, January 16, 1918.

48. Blodwen Davies, "From Militia Tax to Relief," *Mennonite Life*, V (October 1950), pp. 27–8; "A Request of a Committee of the Non-Resistant Relief Organization to a Committee of the Cabinet Regarding a Donation from Non-Resistant Churches made to the Government for Charitable Purposes," signed S. F. Coffman, D. W. Heise, and Thomas Reesor. There is no date on it, but the date should probably be March 27, 1918.

49. CGC. SFC. Letter of S. F. Coffman to Noah M. Bearinger, September 26, 1918.

50. CGC. SFC. Letters of S. F. Coffman to L. J. Burkholder, November 7, 1917; and to Sir Percy Sherwood, Chief Commissioner of Police, November 7, 1917.

51. CGC. SFC. W. E. Wismer, Deputy Registrar under Military Service Act at London, as told local tribunal #263 at Milverton, Ontario, November 10, 1917.

52. CGC. SFC. Letter of S. F. Coffman to the Hon. Arthur Meighen, November 23, 1917.

53. CGC. Letter of Noah M. Bearinger to Seargeant H. Wray, June 11, London, to Lieutenant Col. Smith, London, June 12, and to M. F. S. Scott, Member of Parliament, June 12.

54. Epp, *Mennonite Exodus, op. cit.*, p. 98.

55. CGC. SFC. Petition "To His Excellency, The Governor-General of Canada in Council, Ottawa," 24 pp., 14 exhibits.

56. Benjamin Ewert, "Bemuehungen zur Sicherung der Wehrfreiheit fuer unsere ungetauften Juenglinge," *Der Mitarbeiter*, XII (June 1918), pp. 3–7.

57. Benjamin Ewert, "Predigerzusammenkunft in Altona, Manitoba," *Der Mitarbeiter*, XII (June 1918), p. 7.

58. PAC, *Lacelle* Files, Record Group 27, Vol. 132, 601 (Justice Adamson File). Article by P. C. Locke. The event is also referred to by Isaak Dyck, *Die Auswanderung der Reinland Mennoniten . . . , op. cit.*

59. *Ibid.*

60. *Ibid.*

61. CGC. SFC. Letter of D. W. Heise, Gormley, Ontario, to Hon. J. A. Calder, May 10, 1918.

62. CGC. From S. F. Coffman Papers.

63. CGC. Central Appeal Judge ruling re: Ezra Boshart, Milverton, September 13, 1918.

64. CGC. Letter of H. F. Beresford, Deputy Registrar, London, to Ezra A. Baer, R. R. #2, St. Petersburg, Ontario, September 25, 1918.

65. CGC. Letter of J. Lorne McDougall, Clerk to the Central Appeal Judge, to C. Lesslie Wilson, Registrar, Toronto, October 5, 1918.

66. PAC, *Order-in-Council*, Record Group 2, 1, 2622, October 25, 1918.

Parliament—For and Against

16. War's Aftermath and Mennonite Exclusion

If there are in the United States or Europe people of any class, whether they be called Mennonites, Hutterites, or any other kind of "ites," we do not want them to come to Canada . . . — JOHN WESLEY EDWARDS.[1]

CANADIAN SENTIMENT against Mennonites was aggravated not only by aliens speaking foreign languages in their schools and churches and by their exemption from military service, but also by the amplification of both of these irritations from the United States. From the beginning, Canada guarded herself against possible subversion from the United States, but when that country entered the war Canada was forced to cope with an influx of pacifists and their families. Once again, Mennonites and Hutterites were caught in the middle of the ensuing conflict, which reached its peak with the return of the veterans from Europe. The result was that Mennonites, Hutterites and Doukhobors were barred in 1919 from entering Canada, months after the war had come to an end, and just when over 100,000 Mennonites in Russia, being uprooted by the Revolution, were hoping for a better homeland.

The United States had not entered the war until April 6, 1917, but, as a member of the British Empire, Canada had become concerned about her southern neighbour. Of the 100 million or more Germans in the world, at least 20 million were living abroad, many of them in the United States. Among this large group of *Auslanddeutsche* (Germans abroad) were five million who had been born in Europe and who had migrated to the West during the decades immediately preceding the war. Many of these American Germans or German Americans had intimate ties with the motherland: i.e. family, culture, business and politics.

Indeed, so influential and strategically placed was the German populace in the United States that Britain viewed its presence with great concern. Suddenly "a skilled and world-wide espionage system" was seen at work everywhere. The mail from relatives, the travels of businessmen, the activities of consular offices, were all viewed with suspicion. Even barbers, governesses and domestic servants were linked to the network of spies. Not least of all, education and publishing were seen as instruments serving the purposes of propaganda:

> . . . school books . . . were used along subtle lines of
> education regarding the greatness of the German mind, the
> historic nobility of the German rules, the sympathetic
> geniality of the German character, the wonderful leaps of
> German science; the German professor was omnipresent in
> universities everywhere . . . ; books were written and
> published . . . to build up and perpetuate the belief in
> German military, scientific, educational and philosophical
> supremacy . . . ; newspapers in every centre of the United
> States were found in war-years to have been started, or
> helped or bribed or otherwise influenced to further German
> propaganda . . .[2]

Parallel to a vast German espionage system, as the British and Canadians saw it, were a multitude of pacifist organizations. While these were variously motivated and had a variety of complexions, including an Irish one, in the minds of the patriots these were linked to the internal and external German threat. Pacifists were automatically assumed to be pro-German, making them guilty by association until somehow their innocence was proven. With few exceptions Mennonite and Hutterite political loyalties did not involve Germany, but this is not how much of the American or Canadian public tended to see the situation.[3]

With the War Measures Act, Canada had taken immediate steps to protect herself against a southern threat. The powers of censorship were first applied to German publications originating in the United States and circulating in Canada. In one six-month period no fewer than 67 German-oriented papers, most of them from the U.S., were barred from entering Canada.[4] Included in the group was *Christlicher Bundesbote* (Messenger of Christian Union) which, as the weekly German organ of the General Conference Mennonites, was entering western Canadian communities. The Secretary of State declared that the *Bundesbote* contained "objectionable matter" and barred its Canadian circulation, which was not restored until at least a year after the war had come to an end.

The decision was, of course, not readily accepted by the Mennonites. Bishop David Toews, speaking for prairie readers and for the publishers in Berne, Indiana, questioned the cessation of the German paper, saying that "we want this paper for church and mission work, not for political ends."[5] Bishop Toews' case, however, was not helped by the allegation that his father, Bishop Jakob Toews of Newton, Kansas, remembered his Prussian heritage and expressed rather strong pro-German views. The words of the Newton bishop were reported to the Canadian chief press censor second-hand. An agent of the censor quoted the senior bishop as saying the following:

> I know it is wrong and sinful to read war news, and form opinions, but I cannot help it; my sympathies are with the Germans, and I hope to see Germany win.[6]

The chief press censor took the view that church papers were "the most dangerous media" for communicating enemy propaganda and causing disaffection "among the foreign population residing in Canada." While the "incorrect and disturbing statements" of *Bundesbote* were contained in paragraphs "more or less obscure," the inclinations and intentions of the publication were to the censor very evident. It contained "gross misrepresentations of the actions and attitudes of Great Britain" and "flagrant manifestations of unreasoning hatred" toward the Empire.[7]

As the war progressed and anti-German feeling swept Canada, other American Mennonite publications were affected. The *Mennonitische Rundschau* entering Canada from Scottdale, Pennsylvania, was excluded.[8] And a pamphlet of the Holdeman people (Church of God in Christ Mennonite), containing resolutions passed at Lonetree, Kansas, in 1917, was barred from Canada after its circulation in the mails had also been prohibited in the United States. The doctrinal pamphlet set forth and rationalized the more conservative Mennonite view, which espoused total non-participation and refusal to take part even in food pledges and the Red Cross. Biblical texts were cited by chapter and verse to support the point being made.

Several Canadian publications were also affected. In *Der Mitarbeiter*, the monthly periodical of the Conference of Mennonites in Canada, published at Gretna in the West Reserve, editor H. H. Ewert continued to promote bilingual schools, both private and public. The *Steinbach Post*, a German Mennonite community newspaper for the East Reserve, founded as a private venture in 1913 at Steinbach, was suspended in its fifth year. Both papers were disqualified under a general censorship rule prohibiting "publication in enemy languages" unless they were "standard works of religious, artistic, literary and scientific reference, etc." Matters of "a religious character" were being very narrowly defined, much too narrowly for the Mennonite view of religion which at that time was still quite comprehensive. Religious publications, the censor said, could partake "in no sense of the character of a newspaper." All features of a newspaper had to be eliminated "such as trade advertising, news of all kinds, even views of church or denominational meetings."[9]

Der Mitarbeiter had more of a devotional character than did the *Steinbach Post*, but to exclude from its pages all the problems of education and culture would for Ewert have meant its total emasculation. And the *Post*, by its very nature, needed to include all the facets of community life, which in one way or another all touched on religion and the Mennonite view of the world.

The greatest American disturbance in Canada, however, was not caused by German publications but rather by German-speaking people whose identity was compounded by their pacifism. Such German-speaking immigrants were the Mennonites and Hutterites, chiefly those Mennonites and Hutterites or their descendants who had come to America from Russia in the 1870s, and who had discovered that the United States was not the haven for pacifists that they had expected it to be. The Hutterites who had entered Canada from the United States in 1898 had returned a few years later, but American Mennonites by the hundreds had since the 1890s made Canada their permanent home by forming new communities in Saskatchewan and Alberta. In a sense, therefore, the war-motivated migrations were simply an acceleration of interest and movement that had begun before the war.

How many were actually involved in the war-time migrations northward has never been established with accuracy, partly because some of them later accepted the presidential amnesty and returned south. The exaggerated figures quoted in the press and in the House of Commons ranged from 30,000 to 60,000, but the Hon. J. A. Calder, the Minister of Immigration, claimed that no more than 500–600 Mennonites and about 1,000 Hutterites had entered Canada in 1918, the year of the greatest influx.[10] No more than 200 arrived before 1918 and by mid-November of that year the war was over.[11] Furthermore, these numbers represented not individual draft-age men, but their families as well, and those families, especially the Hutterite ones, were large. Whatever the number, they came to Canada expecting privileges which apparently were not forthcoming in the States.

The United States entered the war much later than Canada, but for some reason was much more intolerant of pacifists within her borders. Much of this intolerance was probably due to the unclear nature of American law on this matter, and the American public's not having had the educational advantage of that clarification. Recall that President Grant referred the delegates from Russia to the militia laws of the individual states and to the likelihood of America's never being at war, certainly not for 50 years. Besides, there were precedents in the American Revolution and the Civil War, in which conscientious objectors fulfilled their military obligations through the employment of substitutes or the payment of commutation fees.

Times had changed, however, and the imperial rivalries of the day affected America much like the emergence of new empires a half-century earlier had affected Russia. During the First World War, military conscription in America had to be "absolute and universal."[12] The laws that were written into the statute books were supported by public sentiment, which was very much conditioned by the imperialisms of the day and a growing American nationalism.

Before the passage of the Selective Service Act on May 18, 1917, the American Mennonites sent delegates and petitions to Washington asking for exemption for pacifist people, and not without some success. The Act did provide for a certain exemption in the form of an alternate noncombatant service for conscientious objectors. The definition of noncombatant service, however, was left to the President, and when this definition was finally given on March 20, 1918, it had a military context. Pacifists were expected to enrol in the military, though in a non-combatant role. In that sense the American Selective Service Act was very much like the Canadian Military Service Act, and it is possible that the latter was modelled after the former.

Meanwhile, drafting of young men had been proceeding in the United States since September of 1917. Draftees were placed in military camps, and those unable to accept the conditions of the draft were held in detention until their case could finally be decided. For the 503 who claimed to be conscientious objectors, 360 for religious reasons, the decision came by way of court martial, usually resulting in prison sentences ranging from one year to life. The maximum term was given to 142 men and 17 were sentenced to death, though none were executed; all received a presidential pardon a few months after the close of the war.[13] More might have been court-martialed, except for new rulings after June 1918. In March, Congress had legislated that military men could be furloughed to alleviate farm labour shortages, and in June the Secretary of War applied the law to conscientious objectors. A civilian board of inquiry was established to review all the cases. After that about 60 per cent of the conscientious objectors were assigned to farm work in America or to relief projects in France. The process was a slow one, however, and the cases of at least 30 per cent of those detained in camps were not reviewed when the war ended.

Thus, during the course of the war, the law was adjusted in favour of conscientious objectors. But for the American public at large and for camp and prison officials in particular, adjustment did not come easily; intolerance remained entrenched. The result was brutal treatment in camps, guard-houses and jails, molestations of the families, and harassments of entire Mennonite and Hutterite communities.

> Anything that smacked of "Germanism" or "slackerism"
> was attacked with unmitigated fury; mob action dotted the
> experience of Mennonites in Montana, Illinois, Kansas,
> Iowa, Ohio, and particularly Oklahoma. For a man of
> German ancestry who happened also to be a conscientious
> objector, America was in some areas the worst of all possible
> places in 1917–18. Pressure to buy war bonds; scurrilous
> press treatment; bans on the use of the German language in
> schools, churches, and on the street; and economic and
> social ostracism marked the plight of Mennonites during the
> war.[14]

The Hutterites were the special targets of patriotic zealots, who treated them as enemy aliens. Their ministers were assaulted, sheep and cattle were stolen, and court actions were taken designed to absolutely exterminate the colonies in South Dakota.[15] The most torturous treatment, however, was assigned to individual pacifists, and one historian believes that "the darkest chapter in the entire story of the treatment received by the conscientious objectors is that of the four Hutterian Mennonites: Joseph Hofer, Michael Hofer, David Hofer, and Jacob Wipf."[16] So severely were they beaten, starved, and manhandled, first at Alcatraz and then at Leavenworth, that two of them died of the consequences.

The Hutterites had appealed to President Wilson for "liberty to live according to the dictates of our conscience," while committing themselves to be "loyal to our God-ordained government and to serve our country in ways which do not interfere with our religious convictions."[17] But in spite of their appeal and the provisions of the law, they bore the brunt of the special wrath of the American people whose blatant nationalism was so rudely insulted by the Hutterite insistence on a sovereignty higher than the nation-state. In their hour of need, the Hutterites remembered the arrangement made with the Canadian government in 1899.

The Mennonites also remembered that scores of families had successfully resettled on the Canadian prairies at the turn of the century. So they, like the Hutterites, turned their eyes northward.[18] The first Mennonites, only three of them, had left Minnesota for Canada immediately after the declaration of war. Further movement at that time was discouraged by the President's order of one-year imprisonment for anyone caught leaving the country to escape conscription.[19]

Early in 1918, the Hon. J. A. Calder, Canadian Minister of Immigration and Colonization, assured the Hutterites that the military exemption provisions granted them by an 1899 Order-in-Council at the time of their first settlement in Canada would be honoured.[20] Immediately 17 of the 18 colonies in South Dakota proceeded to purchase land, five of them in Manitoba and others in Alberta. By October the colonies had paid out one million dollars in cash for land and about 1,000 Hutterites had already resettled.[21] Of the estimated 350 Mennonites who had arrived in Canada by that time,[22] a fair number had come to relatives and acquaintances who had previously settled in the prairie provinces. These groups included complete family units from Kansas, Minnesota, Nebraska and Oklahoma settling at such places as Carnduff, Hepburn and Rosthern in Saskatchewan and at Morden in Manitoba, where they founded the Herold Mennonite Church. Some single men found a temporary new home at the Mennonite boarding schools at Gretna and Rosthern, partly because they had been helped in their border crossing and resettlement by the schools' leaders, H. H. Ewert and David Toews. These movements received little public attention.

Among those finding their way to Rosthern were the Rev. Jacob Klaassen and his family from Clinton, Oklahoma. A brother-in-law of David Toews, Klaassen had been on the same trek to Asiatic Russia and in the same immigration to Kansas in the 1880s. After marrying Toews' sister, the daughter of Bishop Jacob Toews, in Newton, Kansas, he had taken up a homestead in Oklahoma in 1895. By 1917 he had several sons of military age, and his concern was not only the military law but also the fact that Mennonites were not united on that question — at least this was his conclusion at the conference session in Kansas. "There was much talk," he wrote in his memoirs," about how we ought to remain faithful and loyal to our country, but not how we ought to be loyal to our confession of faith."[23]

Klaassen sadly agreed with Jacob and Martin, his oldest sons, that they should attempt to gain secret entry into Canada. If they were successful, the family would follow. The boys made their way to Hydro, Montana, where there was a Mennonite settlement and after a few days they found an opportunity to get across the border. Martin was arrested by the Royal Canadian Mounted Police and jailed at Moose Jaw because his identification documents were inadequate. From there he was sent to the military base in Regina where David Toews secured his release.

His oldest two sons having been "granted freedom," Klaassen decided to sell his farm and effects and take the rest of his family to Canada. There were other families with similar concerns who wanted their sons to join the party. In order not "to arouse any suspicions" along the way they bought tickets in stages and travelled first to Wichita, then to Kansas City, and then to Emerson, a Manitoba border town, where they "acquired harvest worker tickets for one cent a mile." They crossed the border on August 19, 1918, and eventually made their way indirectly to Rosthern. A third son, Henry (later a church leader and widely known as H. T. Klaassen), who was also approaching military age, was apprehended en route. Before they could continue on from Winnipeg, he had to face the American consul who "quizzed him thoroughly," but then sent him on his way. "In order not to attract any undue attention in Rosthern," David Toews had suggested that the group step out in Hague, to be brought to Rosthern by car. Finally, it was done in that way.[24]

The mediators in the new Mennonite immigration were the same land agents and Canadian government representatives strategically placed in various American centres who a few years previously had played such an active role in the Canadian attempt to fill the prairies with suitable agriculturalists. It became a most frustrating role, because it changed from enthusiastic promotion of Canadian land and liberty to cautious interpretation, and finally to reluctant reporting of Canadian restriction.[25]

At least two completely new communities were formed by these immigrants from the United States, one near Grande Prairie in Alberta and the other at Vanderhoof in British Columbia. These two settlements were farther north and west than Mennonites had yet gone in Canada. Settling on lands adjacent to Bear Lake, northwest of Grande Prairie and west of present-day Clairmont, were Krimmer Mennonite Brethren families from Kansas. Their leader was a D. Z. Wiebe, a lay preacher with five sons of or near military age.[26] This new community built its own meeting-house in 1919 and reached a peak of 60 members before disintegration set in a decade later due to migrations back to the U.S., and affiliation with local evangelicals. Of all the Mennonites, the Krimmer had not only gone the farthest north but they also proceeded to relate most energetically to their neighbours. Among their early converts were the George Beliskys, who embraced the new-found faith so thoroughly that they not only insisted on immediate baptism but on its detail in the Krimmer Mennonite Brethren style, meaning immersion. Since it was December, the leaders had no alternative but to cut a hole in the ice of Bear Creek and to baptize the Beliskys in its icy waters.

In the process of evangelism, the Krimmer Mennonite Brethren were themselves changed, and later they followed the Beliskys into missionary work, ministry and evangelism in impressive numbers, eventually to lose their Mennonite identity altogether and to become quite respectable. In the early days of their arrival, however, they were the target of community scorn and suspicion. For a time they were even blamed for the death of six trappers in the Bear Lake area, whose murder remained un-

solved. In that experience of early community abuse, they
shared the lot of the Mennonite Brethren who were settling to
the west at Vanderhoof, in the British Columbia interior. There
had been very little settlement in the west coast province until
that time — Renata in the southern interior was the only community. What attracted the newcomers was the availability of
both lands and jobs in the isolated interior.[27] The construction of
a railway from near Vancouver to Prince George was providing
work opportunities and there was good acreage for sale in the
Nechako Valley near Vanderhoof.

The Vanderhoof people became quite alarmed, and so did the
rest of British Columbia. By August 31, 1918, the Vanderhoof
postmaster was advising the Premier of British Columbia that
his town had become "the headquarters of all Mennonites coming
from the United States." By the end of October "some 200," it
was said, had "brought all their possessions from the prairie
provinces and the United States and settled permanently."[28]
Soon the newcomers were identified with the Doukhobors and
as "descendants of gypsies." The Mennonites sent a delegation
of two to Victoria to clarify their status. P. H. Neufeld and
D. J. Dick found that many of their problems were due to
inadequate information on the part of government officials. After
explaining themselves, they had no difficulty getting their teachers certified, and in the end they were quite amazed that "people,
who cannot understand being without arms, have so much
consideration."[29] They concluded that everything would go well
if only Mennonites could live up to their faith. Mr. Dick said:

> The Mennonite question is really a great question.
> According to our confession of faith, we are peaceable, quiet,
> yielding, upright, living entirely according to God's Word,
> unarmed people in every way. But often the world points a
> finger at us and asks, are those also Mennonites? A
> Mennonite preacher once spoke to an official of the War.
> The preacher had just explained the defencelessness of the
> Mennonites, saying, "We are people that live according to
> the Word of God." Just then, unfortunately, a Mennonite
> man stumbled by, smoking and cursing. Said the official,
> "That man accused his neighbour before the courts. Is he
> also a Mennonite?"[30]

The task of informing the public was much larger, however,
than a single trip to Victoria, because the content of the British
Columbia press quickly spread eastward where it was joined to

similar uneasiness over the "invasion" of the Hutterites. Thus, the Canadian public, which like the press did not always differentiate between Doukhobors, Hutterites and Mennonites, was told that Mennonites were "flocking" into the north country. Moreover these German-speaking settlers had plans laid "to hog the best available land" in order "to force Canadian settlers out." As the "pacifists closed in" veterans of the war had no alternative but to take up "homesteads 40 miles from the railway."[31]

Soon headlines, news stories, letters, and editorials identified Mennonites as a most undesirable lot. The *Free Press* referred to Mennonites as "dirty shirkers . . . without doubt no asset to any country."[32] An editorial writer in *Saturday Night* found "little, if anything, to recommend them." Mennonites, it was said, were a colonized and communal tribe living and trading among themselves and "retaining undisturbed all their antiquated propensities, most of which are out of harmony with the customs and aspirations of their country."[33] The *Calgary Eye-Opener* reported "German Mennonite colonies [Hutterites] swarming over Alberta . . ." Two million Mennonites from the States were coming to Canada, the *Eye-Opener* said, buying up large blocks of land which "the returning soldier should have."[34] The *Ottawa Citizen* headlined charges of "draft-dodging on a wholesale scale."[35] And the *Free Press*, often a defender of Mennonites, now concluded that "no immigrant ought to be allowed to come to Canada in the future unless he is prepared to become a Canadian; and to see his children Canadianized."[36]

Other papers, the *Regina Leader* for instance, were more moderate. On the one hand, the *Leader*'s editors wanted every commitment made in the past to these people honoured, since "solemn treaties and binding engagements" were not "mere scraps of paper to be torn up at will." On the other hand, none of those old agreements should "be stretched one point beyond their original meaning" and in the future no further agreements should be made guaranteeing immunity from military service.[37]

A very few papers, like the *Hamilton Herald*, came out defending or at least clarifying the situation by making some important differentiations. Mennonites were "not communistic" and their numbers both in Canada and the U.S. were small; they were not a major threat. On the contrary, the Mennonites who had been in Ontario for generations were "among the most industrious, thrifty, and prosperous." The *Herald* then proceeded to interpret the Mennonite creed, which for the most part was "Orthodox Christian":

... they give a literal interpretation to several of Christ's injunctions, which most other Christians are content to regard as inapplicable to modern times and conditions. With the Quakers, the Mennonites believe in the doctrine of nonresistance and teach it.[38]

A majority of people in Canada, however, were completely ready to accept the exaggerated and prejudicial accounts rendered in the press, and not without their own good reasons. The recent influx of large numbers of immigrants from central and eastern Europe to western Canada had given rise to strong fears that there could be thousands of "enemy aliens" within Canada's borders.[39] Canadian suspicions were strengthened by the memory of Doukhobor protests, leading in 1907 to the seizure of their Saskatchewan lands, and of conservative Mennonites in Manitoba and Saskatchewan resisting not only the use of English in their private schools but also attendance at English-language public schools.

Public uneasiness, fears and misgivings were also nurtured by other events. The public school attendance acts, which were passed during the war to help anglicize and Canadianize the intransigent, were attended by much publicity, reminding Canadians of the problem in their midst.[40] The disfranchisement which came in 1917 and the exemptions from military service further inflamed the feelings about special privileges for apparently totally alien, if not enemy, people. There were also troubling inconsistencies about the Mennonites, which occasionally bubbled to the surface and which made conscientious objection seem little more than an escape from citizenship dues on the part of people who were really pro-German.[41] One 48-year-old enlistee with "nine children living and my wife very delicate," for instance, admitted enlisting "while drunk." Yet he wanted out because "I can kill no man."[42] Bishop David Toews, who signed many identity certificates, was sometimes accused of turning many good-for-nothings into pacifistic Mennonites.[43]

The problem of questionable ministerial practice came up especially with reference to Klaas Peters of Waldeck, Saskatchewan, a man of many roles and identities. A businessman and land agent, first in southern Manitoba and then in southern Saskatchewan (where he also established a hotel), he travelled far and wide in both Canada and the States and was more informed than most, and quite clever besides. Not surprisingly, the government had asked him to go to Russia in the 1890s to find more Mennonite immigrants. Thus, Peters, like Gerhard Ens of Rosthern, had much to do with bringing Mennonite immigrants from wherever he could get them to settle Saskatchewan. At one time he was a chronicler and he wrote the story of the Bergthaler church;[44] at another time, when convenient, he functioned as a minister.

Around 1900, while still in southern Manitoba, Peters had, like Gerhard Ens of Rosthern and others, become fascinated with the writings of the dissenting Lutheran theologian named Immanuel Swedenborg. Gradually, small Mennonite groups of Swedenborgian disciples were formed, and Klaas Peters as a Swedenborgian minister ordained in 1902 ended up leading one of these New Church of Jerusalem groups at Waldeck near Herbert. This ecclesiastical connection, his role as a justice of the peace, and his management of a hotel made his Mennonite identity quite questionable. But Mennonite leaders had allowed him to go with them to Ottawa because he knew his way around and he in turn had found the Mennonite connection useful when it came to keeping young men out of the war. Under police investigation for some time, his activities as an "alleged Mennonite minister" caught up with him in court after the war had ended and contributed further to the detriment of the public image of the Mennonites.[45]

The Mennonite cause was hurt even more by the positions taken by most other religious communities and their spokesmen in Canada. Even "alien" church leaders, like the bishop of the Ukrainian Catholic Church, had become quite zealous about the war effort. Having at first encouraged the faithful to support the Austrian-Hungarian cause, he soon reversed himself under pressure and became more zealous for the British side.[46] Others similarly went out of their way to prove their loyalty. The large Protestant denominations were apparently fully behind the war effort. The primate of the Church of England in Canada urged his people to support the active prosecution of the war.[47] And the general superintendent of the Methodist Church called upon all Methodists to ascend to "the height of sacrifice" and "catch the martyr spirit of true Christianity."[48] According to J. S. Woodsworth, a recruiting service of St. James Church, Montreal, on October 4, 1915, by-passed hearing a New Testament lesson to give ear to a series of church and community leaders who deliberately attempted "through a recital of the abominable acts

of the Germans to stir up the spirit of hatred and retaliation."
Woodsworth reported further:

> The climax was reached when the pastor in an impassioned
> appeal stated that if any young man could go and did not
> go he was neither a Christian nor a patriot. No! The climax
> was the announcement that recruiting sergeants were
> stationed at the door of the church and that any man of
> spirit — any lover of his country — any follower of
> Jesus — should make the decision then and there.[49]

It was not only reactionary preachers who presented arms, but
rather progressives in the fledgling Canadian social gospel movement who heralded the war as part of the great moral crusade
towards the building of the kingdom.[50] Given the crusading spirit
of the day, in which Canadianization and Christianization of
immigrants were seen as one, geared to preparing good citizens
ready to fight in British imperial wars, it is not strange to find
the main-line Anglo-Saxon churches speaking out in opposition
to the Mennonites.[51] The Presbyterians in a well-publicized action
said:

> Attention having been called to the uneasiness existing in
> some of the western provinces in consequence to the recent
> advent of large numbers of Mennonite settlers from the
> United States, the executive [of the Board of Home Missions
> and Social Service] express their disapproval of the policy
> of permitting large numbers of persons of foreign language
> and tradition to settle in contiguity so that the process of
> assimilation becomes unduly slow and the growth of the
> proper national spirit is retarded. They are strongly of the
> opinion that all persons entering the country as settlers
> should be prepared to undertake their fair share of all
> national burdens, including national defence, and the
> strongest discouragement should be given to the instituting
> of schools in which work is carried on in the German or
> other foreign language.[52]

There were, of course, other religious pacifists of varying degrees in Canada. The Catholics of Quebec had, for the most
part, opposed conscription. In Toronto W. Greenwood Brown,
of the Quaker organization, remained an opponent throughout
the war, and in Winnipeg the Rev. J. S. Woodsworth was saying
repeatedly that Christ was against war and that moral issues

could not be settled by force.[53] There was no coalition of all those pacifist forces, however. Mennonites at least, being not even joined to each other, were not connected to the Woodsworth cause, and their historic Upper Canada alliance with the Quakers had also been modified with the changing times and personalities.

The federal government found ways of appeasing public opinion. As we have seen, Mennonite preachers from the States had been prevented by immigration officials from entering Canada to conduct anti-war revival meetings. Also, the chief press censor had halted publication of German Mennonite papers and barred certain literature from Canadian circulation.[54] Furthermore, attempts were made to exclude the arriving immigrants from exemption privileges. At first it was explained that Canadian guarantees to pacifist groups applied only to those immigrant movements protected by special orders-in-council — those of 1873 for the Mennonites, 1899 for the Hutterites, and 1898 for the Doukhobors. Such explanations, at first unfounded, did become law with the limiting Order-in-Council of October 25, 1918.

Some agitators also sought a way out in the British-American conventions, which obligated one nation or empire to draft or to repatriate the draft-dodgers and deserters of the other. That plan also fell through because Canada could legally draft only British subjects and repatriation did not sit well with a government which had officially welcomed the immigrants. Finally, Canada agreed to have Americans registered at American consulates while intending to draft them, but the war's end cut the plan short.

All these efforts to pacify the agitators were not enough, not even after the end of the war. The return of the veterans fanned the flames that otherwise might have died out. Government ministers travelling west were besieged by petitions from all kinds of groups and individuals. The resolutions and telegrams to Ottawa of the veterans' groups and political organizations were widely publicized. The Great War Veterans Association was particularly adamant, and threatened to allow returned veterans to confront these new settlers who were getting the desirable lands. The Great War Next-of-Kin Association wanted Mennonites in Canada to be drafted and anglicized "and those outside kept there."[55]

The agitation of veterans' groups and citizens' clubs was inconsistent and paradoxical. The veterans, for instance, stressed their having fought against totalitarianism and for fundamental human rights; however, they had not fought for total freedom of conscience. The Orangemen had also forgotten their tradition, and S. F. Coffman was quick to catch this. He reminded Member of Parliament W. D. Euler of this fact:

> I noted that the Orange friends are not of the same faith as their honoured head Prince William of Orange who was among the first rulers to grant relief to the people of nonresistant faith and to the Mennonites who had their first organization in his country, under the leadership of Menno Simons, a Hollander. I understand why the Orange Society should oppose religious liberty for it is the very thing for which William contended.[56]

All of the public pressure finally reached Canada's lawmakers in a way which they could not resist, and, even though the war was over, the politicians followed through on the demands born in the patriotism of international conflict and nurtured by the war's aftermath. In the spring of 1919, Parliament was ready to amend the Immigration Act of 1910, and the Cabinet was in the mood to issue restrictive Orders-in-Council, which affected first the Mennonites, Hutterites and Doukhobors, and later the Negroes, Chinese and Japanese. At this point, the most "undesirable" people were the Mennonites. Parliamentarians waxed eloquent as they pled for maintaining "the purity of the stream of our immigration" by cutting off the indiscriminate flow of "undesirables."[57] As one M.P. put it:

> The War Veterans of Canada have taken a position against the immigration of Hutterites and Mennonites into western Canada . . . But apart from the returned soldiers, a number of Canadian clubs throughout western Canada have declared themselves against the entrance of these people into the Dominion. Now the Canadian clubs, as I know them, are supposed to represent a very high type of citizenship, they want to perpetuate the very best ideals of our citizenship, and if after mature consideration by men of all parties and of all creeds, the Canadian clubs in Winnipeg and elsewhere in the West declare that it is not in the interest of Canada that these people should be allowed to settle in this country, I think their views are worthy of the attention of this Committee.[58]

Most derogatory in his comments was John Wesley Edwards, a physician, Methodist and Liberal-Conservative Member of

Parliament for Frontenac. Edwards used the word "cattle" repeatedly in his April 30 speech to describe the undesirable class, conscientious objectors, namely Mennonites.[59] Mr. I. E. Pedlow (M.P. for Renfrew S.), who, as a Quaker and a pacifist, felt himself included in the cattle reference, objected strongly on the grounds that conscientious objectors were "devout and eminently respectable and loyal citizens."[60] Joining Pedlow as a defender of the Mennonites was Mr. W. D. Euler, M.P. for Waterloo, who described them as "absolutely loyal," and "true Canadian," and volunteered the view that "if all of the inhabitants of Canada were Mennonites, Canada would never be at war."[61] The Pedlows and Eulers were minority spokesmen, however, and on the following day the government issued the order-in-council which prohibited Mennonites, Hutterites and Doukhobors from entering Canada. The reason given was that they were deemed

> ... undesirable, owing to their peculiar customs, habits, modes of living, and methods of holding property, and because of their probable inability to become readily assimilated to assume the duties and responsibilities of Canadian citizenship within a reasonable time after entry.[62]

The new ruling made even temporary entry of preachers and other visitors difficult, at least until S.F. Coffman and David Toews had once more clarified the situation in Ottawa and that clarification had reached the immigration officers at the ports of entry. Bishop E. L. Frey of Ohio was once again turned back at Windsor, the third time since 1916. This time Coffman was anxious for some differentiation between various classes of Mennonites, because in his opinion no conditions *in Ontario* had led to the expulsion order. But this time "the law made no distinctions in classes of Mennonites."[63] None the less, Coffman worked on the matter and soon the Immigration Minister opened the door to Bishop Frey. Thereafter, some distinctions were made. Two Amish brothers from Oregon bought a parcel of land at Ryley, Alberta, and gained admittance as immigrants because the Immigration Minister's office concluded that Amish were distinct from Mennonites, and consequently "not barred by the Order-in-Council."[64] Others could not enter quite that easily. American mission workers being placed in Toronto and teachers coming to Rosthern all had to go through a good deal of red tape before they were admitted. David Toews had great difficulty securing the admittance of one C. K. Penner of Beatrice, Nebraska, to teach at the German-English Academy, not because of legal impediments but because of bureaucratic bungling. In exasperation Toews wrote in September 1921, "Are we criminals who are deserving such treatment?"[65]

When immigration officers were in any doubt about visiting Mennonites returning to the United States, they would ask for a deposit of money. On one occasion a party of 17 people from Mountain Lake, Minnesota, were held up at Emerson because they could not produce a deposit amounting to $50 per person. They were therefore detained until a sufficient amount could be wired from home. For the night the group had the option of going either to the hotel or to the jail. For economic reasons they chose the jail and survived the night with six quart pails of hot coffee and blankets provided by immigration officials. Additional money did not arrive on the following day, and so the officer accepted what they had, $275, and sent them on their way.[66]

The new immigration ruling had other implications which affected both Mennonites in Canada and those abroad. In Canada there were new and more determined pressures on the Mennonite private schools, particularly in Saskatchewan and Manitoba. The conservative Mennonite leaders became finally convinced that Canadian values were incompatible with their own, and that unless Canada would permit them to co-exist in freedom they would have to find another home. By mid-1919, a delegation was on its way to Latin America in search of a future for 6,000 Mennonites, who prepared in their hearts to leave Canada. Additional petitions such as the following to the provincial and federal governments, bore no fruit.

> We Mennonites, of the Reinland-Mennonite Church or the so-called Old Colony, who have immigrated into Canada, feel obligated to express our thanks to the kind and honorable Dominion government as well as to the provincial government for the truly benevolent protection and assistance which we have received; because of this we pray to God: "O Lord God, bless our king, the leaders of our land, and all the officials and executives in Canada as you have in the past, in that you directed your intents and desires so that we could exercise our religious rights, including the right to have our own schools under the protection of the government in joy and peace. Now give them wise hearts

and your Holy Spirit, that they may rule wisely in all
Canadian and British nations." Such similar prayers are
offered publicly every Sunday in all of our congregations
for the British government, under whose protection, thank
God, we are privileged to live. We have learned that the
possibility exists that a revision of the provincial school
acts will be presented to the legislative house. This revision
has the intention of revoking the privileges of having
our own independent schools, which the Mennonites have
enjoyed since the time of our immigrations . . . It has been
our tradition in our old home, Russia, that all our children
learned reading, writing, arithmetic, religion, industry, and
cleanliness, in such a manner as to meet the requirements
of the agricultural way of life to which we have belonged.[67]

At the same time, a delegation was being dispatched to North
America from Russia, where 110,000 Mennonites had also concluded that they and the new regime were incompatible. The
overthrow of the tsarist regime by the revolutionaries and the
seizure of power by the Bolsheviks in 1917 was followed by a
prolonged civil war which was fought in part on Mennonite soil
in the Ukraine. As the war front moved to and fro — some
villages of Chortitza and Molotschna changed control as many
as 23 times — the Mennonite paradise collapsed. Crops were
ruined, villages burned to the ground, institutions destroyed,
women and girls raped, horses and cattle stolen and many men
killed. At one point the Mennonites organized their own *Selbstschutz* or self-defence system to protect themselves against
the worst of the marauders, who were the followers of Nestor
Makhno, a former cowherd for wealthy Mennonites. That, however, was not the Mennonite way, and the action was regretted,
especially as the violence of the Selbstschutz was met with greater
violence by rebels and Red Army regulars. Besides, there was no
defence against venereal disease, typhus and the famine which
followed in the wake of social disorganization and crop destruction. The threat to physical survival was accompanied by the
Soviet decrees which were threats to the religious and cultural
survival of the Mennonites. The schools were placed completely
under state control and the churches were faced immediately by
anti-religious agitation and, in some instances, closure.[68]

Faced by the collapse of their paradise, Mennonites began to
flee their homes. Some, perhaps 100 families, followed the retreating German troops as early as 1918. Some were evacuated by the
retreating White Armies via Odessa and the Black Sea. Included

in this group were 62 men who had fought with the White Armies. As Red control tightened, hundreds, perhaps thousands, of others hoped to leave. Those Mennonites who had remained in Russia in the 1870s had multiplied and now numbered more than 100,000.

Where, when, and how to go became urgent questions. In December of 1919, a delegation of four called the *Studienkommission* (study commission) was chosen and sent abroad, first to seek relief and, second, to find a new home. They left Russia on January 1, 1920, and within a few months, the leaders of the delegation were seeking entry into Canada for themselves and for their co-religionists in Russia.[69]

Of course, in many ways it was not the right time for the Mennonites to be knocking on Canada's doors again. They had been barred from entering the country by the full force of the law, supported by public opinion. Simultaneously, even the conservative Mennonites who were already in the country were saying it was undesirable as a homeland. The separated people began to debate whether separation was the answer — or the obstacle — to their survival.

In other ways the time was propitious. A new leader on the Canadian scene, William Lyon Mackenzie King, had not forgotten the importance of the Mennonite people to his political success. His benevolence, coupled with the determination of the Mennonites, eventually succeeded in opening the Canadian door — and a new era in the history of the Canadian Mennonites.

FOOTNOTES

1. John Wesley Edwards, Liberal-Conservative Member of Parliament for Frontenac, in the House of Commons, *Commons Debates*, April 30, 1919, p. 1929.
2. "German Propaganda and Plots in the United States," *Canadian Annual Review* (1917), pp. 254–69; "German Organization in the United States," *Canadian Annual Review* (1916), pp. 221–27.
3. "Pacifists in the United States," *Canadian Annual Review* (1917), pp. 270–77; "US Alien Enemies and German Propaganda: Pacifists and the War," *Canadian Annual Review* (1918), pp. 253–61; "Pacifism in Canada," *Canadian Annual Review* (1916), pp. 445–46.
4. *Canada Gazette*, 1917.
5. PAC, *Chief Press Censor*, Record Group 6, E, Vol. 13, 116-c.5.

Letter of David Toews to Chief Press Censor, Col. E. J. Chambers, July 30, 1917.

6. *Ibid.*, Letter of B. G. Johnson, Yuma, Arizona, January 23, 1917. From this and other correspondence it appears that Johnson was an agent of the press censor.

7. *Ibid.*, Letter of Col. E. J. Chambers, Chief Press Censor, to John F. Foster, Consul-General for the United States, July 24, 1919.

8. "Censorship Notice," *Canada Gazette*, June 26, 1919, p. 30.

9. PAC, *Chief Press Censor*, Record Group 6, E, Vol. 138, 370-g-a-25 and 119-s-2.

10. Hon. J. A. Calder, Minister of Colonization and Immigration, in *Commons Debates*, May 19, 1919, p. 2570.

11. Allan Teichroew, "World War I and Mennonite Migrations," *Mennonite Quarterly Review*, XLV (July 1971), p. 246.

12. Guy F. Hershberger, *War, Peace and Nonresistance* (Scottdale, Pa.: Mennonite Publishing House, 1944), 113 ff.

13. Hershberger, *op. cit.*, p. 119.

14. Teichroew, *op. cit.*, pp. 221–28.

15. Victor Peters, *All Things Common: The Hutterian Way of Life* (Minneapolis: University of Minnesota Press, 1966), pp. 43–5.

16. Hershberger, *op. cit.*, p. 121.

17. David Hofer, Elias Walter, and Joseph Kleinsasser, "The Hutterite Brethren and War," *Gospel Herald*, X (August 9, 1917), pp. 354–55.

18. For additional treatment on experiences of Hutterites and Mennonites during the First World War, see John D. Unruh, "The Hutterites During World War I," *Mennonite Life*, XXIV (July 1969), pp. 130–37; Donald C. Holsinger, "Pressures Affecting the Mennonite German-Americans in Central Kansas During World War I" (Bethel College research paper, March 1970), 57 pp.; Jacob Klaassen, "Memories and Notations About My Life (1867–1948)," translated by Walter Klaassen, 41 pp. Also see: Leonard Gross, "Alternative to War: A Story Through Documents," *Gospel Herald*, LXVI (January 16, 1973), pp. 52–5, one of a series; Roy Buchanan, "A Time to Say 'No'," *Christian Living*, VII (September 1960), pp. 6–10, 34–5, first in a series of six; James C. Juhnke, "John Schrag Espionage Case," *Mennonite Life*, XXII (July 1967), pp. 121–22; James C. Juhnke, "The Agony of Civic Isolation: Mennonites in World War I," *Mennonite Life*, XXV (January 1970), pp. 27–33; Rufus M. Franz, "It Happened in Montana," *Mennonite Life*, VII (October 1952), pp. 181–84.

19. Teichroew, *op. cit.*, pp. 219–49.

20. A. M. Willms, "The Brethren Known as Hutterites," *The Canadian Journal of Economics and Political Science*, XXVI (August 1958), p. 392.

21. PAC, *Immigration Branch*, Record Group 76, I, Vol. 173, 58764,

2. Letter of Alexander Adams, Winnipeg, to J. A. Calder, Minister of Immigration and Colonization, October 19, 1918.

22. Frank H. Epp, *Mennonite Exodus: The Rescue and Resettlement of the Russian Mennonites Since the Communist Revolution* (Altona, Man.: D. W. Friesen & Sons, 1962), pp. 99–101.

23. Jacob Klaassen, "Memories and Notations About My Life," *op. cit.*, p. 29.

24. *Ibid.*, p. 34.

25. PAC, *Immigration Branch*, Record Group 76, 1, Vol. 173, 58764, 1 and 58764, 2. Notable among the Canadian Government Agency representatives were J. C. Koehn of Omaha and Mountain Lake, J. A. Cook of Kansas City, M. J. Johnstone, Watertown, South Dakota, and F. H. Harrison, Harrisburg, Pa.

26. Frank H. Epp, "The True North (2): The Church that Disappeared Whose Influence Lives On," *Mennonite Reporter*, IV (March 18, 1974), p. 11.

27. Teichroew, *op. cit.*, pp. 230–32.

28. PAC, *Immigration Branch*, Record Group 76, 1, Vol. 173, 58764, 2. Letter of J. W. Paterson, Postmaster, Vanderhoof, British Columbia, to John Oliver, Premier of British Columbia, August 31, 1918.

29. PAC, *Immigration Branch,* Record Group 76, 1, Vol. 173, 58764, 3. J. Dick article in *Our Visitor*, translated from *Unser Besucher*, XVIII (April 15, 1919), Mountain Lake, Minnesota.

30. *Ibid.*

31. "Mennonites are Flocking into North Country," *Vancouver World*, November 1, 1918.

32. "A Matter of Moment," and D. A. Ross, "Protest Against Mennonites," *Winnipeg Free Press*, September 4, 1918.

33. "Mennonite Presence Deeply Resented," *Saturday Night* (c. 1918–19).

34. "The Mennonite: The War Veteran," *Calgary Eye-Opener,* October 5, 1918.

35. "Western Furore Over Exemption of Mennonites: Charge That Situation is Permitting Draft-Dodging on Wholesale," *Ottawa Citizen*, September 25, 1918, p. 6.

36. "A Matter of Moment," *Free Press*, September 4, 1918.

37. "The Mennonites," *The Regina Leader*, September 25, 1918, p. 4.

38. "Mennonites and Others," *Hamilton Herald*, May 5, 1919.

39. J. A. Boudreau, "The Enemy Alien Problem in Canada, 1914–1921" (Ph. D. dissertation, University of California, 1965), 218 pp.

40. E. K. Francis, *In Search of Utopia: The Mennonites of Manitoba* (Altona, Man.: D. W. Friesen & Sons, 1955), pp. 161–86. See also J. A. Stevenson, "The Mennonite Problems in Canada," *The Nation*, CVII (November 9, 1918), pp. 551–52.

41. W. G. Smith, *A Study in Canadian Immigration* (Toronto: Ryerson Press, 1920), pp. 191–92.

42. PAC, *Army Headquarters Records*, Record Group 24, C.1, Vol. 115. Letter of Heinrich Klassen, Osler, to Department of Militia and Defence, June 2, 1916.

43. Epp, *Mennonite Exodus, op. cit.*, p. 97.

44. Klaas Peters, *Die Bergthaler Mennoniten und deren Auswanderung aus Russland und Einwanderung in Manitoba* (Hillsboro, Kans.: Mennonite Brethren Publishing House, n.d.), 45 pp.

45. PAC, *Army Headquarters Records*, Record Group 24, C.1, Vol. 115, 1918 Correspondence of Chief Inspector, Civil Section.

46. "The Alien Enemy Question of 1918," *Canadian Annual Review*, XXVIII (1919), pp. 578–81. See also Paul Yuzyk, *Ukrainian Canadians*.

47. "The Churches in the Election," *Canadian Annual Review* (1917), pp. 628–30.

48. *Ibid.* See also "Methodist Church in Relation to the War," *Hamilton Times*, October 17, 1918. See also J. M. Bliss, "The Methodist Church and World War I," *Canadian Historical Review*, XLIX (September 1968).

49. Kenneth McNaught, *A Prophet in Politics: A Biography of J. S. Woodsworth* (Toronto: University of Toronto Press, 1959), p. 70.

50. Richard Allen, *The Social Passion: Religion and Social Reform in Canada 1914–1928* (Toronto: University of Toronto Press, 1971), Chap. 3.

51. J. W. Grant, *The Church in the Canadian Era* (Toronto: McGraw-Hill Ryerson Limited, 1972), pp. 118–21; N. K. Clifford, "His Dominion: A Vision in Crisis," *Studies in Religion*, II (Spring 1973), pp. 315–26.

52. PAC, *Borden Papers*, M.G. 26, H, RLB 1167, 121140. Letter from Mrs. Elizabeth Longworth, President, Great War Next-of-Kin Association, to Robert L. Borden, September 22, 1918.

53. "Pacifism in Canada," *Canadian Annual Review* (1916), pp. 445–46.

54. Frank H. Epp, *I Would Like to Dodge the Draft-Dodger, But . . .* (Waterloo, Ont.: Conrad Press, 1970), pp. 11–12.

55. PAC, *Borden Papers*, M.G. 26, H, RLB 1167, 121120. Letter of Robert L. Borden to Michael Scott, Winnipeg, February 7, 1918.

56. CGC. SFC. Letter of S. F. Coffman to W. D. Euler, House of Commons, May 19, 1919.

57. Donald Sutherland, Liberal-Conservative M.P. for Oxford South in *Commons Debates*, April 30, 1919, p. 1912.

58. Major Daniel Lee Redman, Unionist M.P. for Calgary East, in *Commons Debates*, April 30, 1919, p. 1922; William Ashbury Buchanan, Liberal-Unionist M.P. for Lethbridge, in *Commons Debates*, April 30, 1919, p. 1914.

59. John Wesley Edwards, *loc. cit.*
60. Isaac Ellis Pedlow, Liberal M.P. for Renfrew South, in *Commons Debates*, April 30, 1919, p. 1930.
61. William D. Euler, Independent Liberal for Waterloo North, in *Commons Debates*, April 30, 1919, p. 1928.
62. PAC, *Order-in-Council*, Record Group 2, 1, 923, May 1, 1919, and 1204, June 9, 1919.
63. CGC. SFC. Letter of S. F. Coffman to M. C. Cressman, Kitchener, Ontario, October 11, 1919.
64. PAC, *Immigration Branch*, Record Group 76, 1, Vol. 174, 58764, 7. George J. Kanagy, Hubbard, Oregon, to Minister of Immigration, November 29, 1920, and reply, December 11, 1920.
65. *Ibid.*, David Toews to J. A. Calder, Minister of Immigration and Colonization, September 21, 1921.
66. PAC, *Immigration Branch*, Record Group 76, 1, Vol. 174, 58764, 8. Letter of T. J. Connell, Inspector, Emerson, to Thomas Galley, Commissioner, Winnipeg, June 30, 1922.
67. C. W. Redekop, *The Old Colony Mennonites: Dilemmas of Ethnic Minority Life* (Baltimore: Johns Hopkins Press, 1969), Appendix A.
68. John B. Toews, *Lost Fatherland: The Story of the Mennonite Emigration from Soviet Russia, 1921–1927* (Scottdale, Pa.: Herald Press, 1967), pp. 21–50.
69. Frank H. Epp, *Mennonite Exodus, op. cit.*, pp. 39–48.

Epilogue

THE END of this Canadian Mennonite history in 1920 bears some resemblance to the time of the movement's birth in Switzerland in 1525, to Upper Canada around 1800, and to Pennsylvania before that time. In all of these times and places, the experiences of the Anabaptist-Mennonites could not be described without reference to the state and their relations to it. Those relations were expressed in terms of "the separation of church and state," though not infrequently such separations were really confrontations. After all, the original meaning of separation was that the state did not have authority over the religious conscience, could not prescribe religious liturgy and ordinances, and should not conduct or supervise ecclesiastical organization and appointments.

For the Anabaptists, the doctrine of separation meant, among other things, the subordination of the state to God. Consequently they spoke of an allegiance to an authority higher than the state on some matters, though not counter to it on most matters, and in many everyday affairs actually quite complementary to it.

This higher authority was variously described as the Kingdom of God or the Lordship of Christ. Historically, the higher authority applied most critically to military service, to which the Mennonites objected. But it often extended also to the total value system of the outside society. The societal focus in Canada was the public school and its overt attempt to prepare children not for the advance of the Kingdom but for the undergirding of the Empire.

Since the Mennonites also respected and obeyed the rulers, their paradoxical position confronted them with a real dilemma. Somehow they had to reconcile their position, which normally emphasized obedience, with the occasional stance of critical resistance and determined disobedience. They learned that one way to resolve the dilemma was to isolate themselves geographically and to withdraw also socially and politically. As *die Stillen im Lande* (the quiet in the land), they learned, as it were, to mind their own business, seeking only to be industrious in their agriculture, self-sufficient in their communities, happy in their families, and devout in their religion. As far as they were concerned, the state could likewise go its own way, even engage in wars, without Mennonite protestation, as long as it didn't force them to join such adventures. In the isolation of the two spheres of life from each other, the separation of church and state began to take on new meanings. The confrontation element in the original separation was replaced by non-involvement, and the separation of church and state was largely redefined in those terms by the Mennonites. The confrontation which did remain was primarily the witness of an alternate society.

As has been amply illustrated in this history, there was, however, another experience of the "separate people" of which this epilogue must give account, namely that of the internal fragmentation. The temptation is great to simply write off their many divisions as by-products of Mennonite stubbornness and petty quarrelling among the leaders. Or, at best, as the inevitable consequence of political pressure, social harassment and many migrations and resettlements.

The roots of internal separation, however, lie much deeper and must be sought in the origins of the Reformation and Anabaptist movements themselves. The reactions against the size of the universal Roman church and against the pressures of the mighty Roman empire were general. Out of the Reformation came a host of separated protestantisms and new political entities. The independence-minded nobles on the edge of the empire welcomed the persecuted Anabaptists not only because of their entrepreneurial usefulness but also because of a certain spiritual commonness, the desire of both to disentangle themselves from the ecclesiastical and imperial monoliths.

The Anabaptists, however, added another factor to the equation of separation, namely their definition of the church as an intimate and sharing community of believers. The cosmic dimensions of the Kingdom of God did not escape them, but for them there could be no universal kingdom of righteousness — the Holy Roman Empire was ample proof of that — without a firm foundation in the hearts of true believers and without committed congregational communities. Such faithful nuclei were like the mustard seed and the yeast in the biblical parables, eventually destined to fill all the earth and leaven the whole lump of human society. They were, in short, prototypes of the coming Kingdom of God.

These communities could not exist without some authority and some discipline. The serious intent of the Anabaptists and the situation in which they found themselves required that the rules of their small congregations be spelled out rather clearly (with the passing of time, quite legalistically) and enforced rather consistently. Thus the stage was set for a kaleidoscopic Anabaptism whose many separate parts could only be multiplied by persecutions and immigrations on the one hand, and by internal differences of opinion, nurtured by personality clashes and leadership conflicts, on the other. Viewed more sympathetically, however, the fragmentations can be explained, at least in part, by repeated attempts, still motivated by the original impulse, to renew and redefine the small community through which God did his work in the world. And they further allowed the varieties of social and theological dynamics within the Mennonite fold to seek their own, while retaining those essentials which all Mennonites had in common.

Be that as it may, Mennonite identity and integrity did not particularly require complete ecclesiastical unity. Most Mennonites had never seen themselves in those terms. To be sure, not all were satisfied with fragmentation, and this is why every time of disjunction also gave birth to calls for unification. The result was the conference system, more precisely systems. Also in their ecumenical formations, only a plethora of possibilities could satisfy all the divergent Mennonite needs.

Thus the Mennonites began to choose several different directions for themselves as they faced their future. While some saw that future in terms of small, self-contained, unrelated communities and in withdrawal from society, others saw the need for accommodation and involvement. This latter position, however, also pointed in several directions. For some it meant total integration with society to the point of secularization; others sought only partial adjustments. For some it meant the conversion of outsiders, both at home and abroad, and their enrolment in Mennonite membership lists. For others it meant primarily a religious confrontation with both state and society, especially on the question of militarism. Again, for some accommodation meant a little bit of all of these in varying proportions.

After 1920 the Canadian Mennonite story provides ample expression for all of these options. History repeated itself in many ways. There were additional migrations from Russia to the Americas, from North America to South America, and from exposed communities to isolated areas within Canada. There were also additional differentiations between the conservatives and the progressives, between Mennonite culture and Anglo-Saxon culture, and not least of all, in another world war between pacifism and militarism. In all of these events during the ensuing decades, the question of separation, or the reaction to it, became more directly a question of survival. The pursuit of that theme, however, must be left to a second volume.

Chapter Bibliographies

CHAPTER I

Books

BAINTON, ROLAND. *The Reformation of the Sixteenth Century*. Boston: Beacon Press, 1952.

BAUMAN, CLARENCE. *Gewaltlosigkeit im Taeufertum*. Leiden, Germany: E. J. Brill, 1968.

BEHRENDS, ERNST. *Der Ketzerbischof*. Basel: Agape-Verlag, 1966.

BENDER, HAROLD S. *Conrad Grebel (1498–1526): Founder of the Swiss Brethren*. Goshen, Ind.: Mennonite Historical Society, 1950.

BLANKE, FRITZ. *Brothers in Christ*. Scottdale, Pa.: Herald Press, 1961.

BONNER, EDWIN B. *William Penn's "Holy Experiment": The Founding of Pennsylvania, 1681–1701*. New York: Temple University Publications, 1962.

BORNHAEUSER, CHRISTOPH. *Leben und Lehre Menno Simons: Ein Kampf um das Fundament des Glaubens (etwa 1496–1561)*. Tuebingen, W. Germany: Neukirchener Verlag, 1973.

BRAGHT, THIELEMAN J. VAN. *Martyrs' Mirror*. Scottdale, Pa.: Herald Press, 1950.

419

BRAITHWAITE, WILLIAM C. *The Second Period of Quakerism.* Cambridge: University Press, 1961.

CLASEN, CLAUS-PETER. *Anabaptism: A Social History, 1525–1618.* Ithaca: Cornell University Press, 1972.

DYCK, C. J., ed. *A Legacy of Faith.* Newton, Kans.: Faith and Life Press, 1962.

ESTEP, W. R. *The Anabaptist Story.* Nashville, Tenn.: Broadman Press, 1963.

FAST, H. *Der Linke Fluegel der Reformation.* Bremen: Schuenemann, 1962.

FRIEDMANN, ROBERT. *Mennonite Piety Throughout the Centuries.* Goshen, Ind.: The Mennonite Historical Society, 1949.

GISH, ARTHUR G. *The New Left and Christian Radicalism.* Grand Rapids, Mich.: Wm. B. Eerdmans, 1970.

GRATZ, DELBERT L. *Bernese Anabaptists.* Scottdale, Pa.: Herald Press, 1953.

HORST, IRVIN B. *Anabaptism and the English Reformation to 1558.* Nieuwkoop, Netherlands: B. de Graaf, 1966.

———. *A Bibliography of Menno Simons.* Nieuwkoop: B. de Graaf, 1962.

———. *Erasmus, the Anabaptists, and the Problem of Religious Unity.* Haarlem, Netherlands: Tjeenk, 1967.

———. *The Radical Brethren: Anabaptists in England.* Nieuwkoop, Netherlands: B. de Graaf, 1972.

HOSTETLER, JOHN A. *Amish Society.* Baltimore: Johns Hopkins University Press, 1963.

HULL, WILLIAM I. *William Penn and the Dutch-Quaker Migration to Pennsylvania.* Philadelphia: Patterson & White Company, 1935.

KEENEY, WILLIAM ECHARD. *The Development of Dutch Anabaptism Thought and Practice from 1539–1664.* Nieuwkoop, Netherlands: B. de Graaf, 1958.

KLAASSEN, WALTER. *Anabaptism: Neither Catholic Nor Protestant.* Waterloo, Ont.: Conrad Press, 1973.

KLASSEN, PETER JAMES. *The Economics of Anabaptism, 1525–1560.* New York: Humanities Press, 1964.

KRAHN, CORNELIUS. *Dutch Anabaptism.* The Hague: Martinus Nijhoff, 1968.

———. *Menno Simons.* Karlsruhe, Germany: Schneider Verlag, 1936.

LITTELL, FRANKLIN H. *The Anabaptist View of the Church: A Story of the Origin of Sectarian Protestantism.* Beacon Hill, Boston: Starr King Press, 1958.

PETERS, VICTOR. *All Things Common: The Hutterian Way of Life.* Minneapolis: University of Minnesota Press, 1965.

SEWEL, WILLIAM. *The History of the Rise, Increase, and Progress of the Christian People Called Quakers.* London: Darton and Harvey, 1934. 2 Volumes.

SMITH, C. HENRY. *The Mennonite Migration to Pennsylvania in the Eighteenth Century.* Norristown, Pa.: Norristown Press, 1929.

STAYER, JAMES M. *Anabaptists and the Sword.* Lawrence, Kans.: Coronado Press, 1972.

UNRUH, B. H. *Die Niederlaendischen-Niederdeutschen Hintergruende der Mennonitischen Ostwanderungen im 16. 18. und 19. Jahrhundert.* Karlsruhe, Germany: Karlsruhe-Rueppurr, 1955.

WALTON, ROBERT. *Zwingli's Theocracy.* Toronto: University of Toronto Press, 1967.

WENGER, JOHN C., ed. *Complete Writings of Menno Simons.* Scottdale, Pa.: Mennonite Publishing House, 1956.

―――. *Even Unto Death.* Richmond, Va.: John Knox Press, 1961.

WHALEN, WILLIAM J. *Separated Brethren: A Survey of Non-Catholic Christian Denominations.* Milwaukee: Bruce Publishing Company, 1958.

WILLIAMS, GEORGE H. *The Radical Reformation.* Philadelphia: Westminster Press, 1962.

WOLKAN, RUDOLF. *Die Lieder der Wiedertaeufer.* Nieuwkoop, Netherlands: B. de Graaf, 1965.

YODER, JOHN H. *Taeufertum und Reformation in der Schweiz.* Karlsruhe, Germany: Mennonitischer Geschichtsverein, 1962.

YODER, PAUL M., et al. *Four Hundred Years with Ausbund.* Scottdale, Pa.: Herald Press, 1964.

Articles

BENDER, HAROLD S. "The Anabaptist Vision." *Mennonite Quarterly Review*, XVIII (April 1944). Pp. 67–88.

―――. "The Historiography of the Anabaptists." *Mennonite Quarterly Review*, XXXI (April 1957). Pp. 88–104.

―――. "The Hymnology of the Anabaptists." *Mennonite Quarterly Review*, XXXI (January 1957). Pp. 5–10.

CROUS, ERNST. "Anabaptism, Pietism, Rationalism, and German Mennonites," in G. F. Hershberger, ed. *The Recovery of the Anabaptist Vision.* Scottdale, Pa.: Herald Press, 1962.

ESTEP, W. R., JR. "Were the Anabaptists Subversive? The Birth of a Counter Culture." *Mennonite Life*, XXI (January 1967). Pp. 14–18.

GASCHO, MILTON. "The Amish Division of 1693–1697 in Switzerland and Alsace." *Mennonite Quarterly Review*, XI (October 1937). Pp. 235–66.

GRATZ, D. "The Home of Jacob Ammann." *Mennonite Quarterly Review*, XXV (April 1951). Pp. 137–39.

HILLERBRAND, HANS J. "The Anabaptist View of the State." *Mennonite Quarterly Review*, XXXII (April 1958). Pp. 83–110.

KLAASSEN, WALTER. "The Nature of the Anabaptist Protest." *Mennonite Quarterly Review*, XLV (October 1971). Pp. 291–311.

KLASSEN, WILLIAM, H. POETTCKER, and WALTER KLAASSEN. "Anabaptist Interpretations of the Scriptures." *Mennonite Quarterly Review*, XL (April 1966).

KREIDER, R. "Anabaptism and Humanism: An Inquiry into the Relationship of Humanism to the Evangelical Anabaptists." *Mennonite Quarterly Review,* XXVI (April 1952). Pp. 123–41.

OYER, JOHN S. "Anabaptism in Central Germany: I. The Rise and Spread of the Movement." *Mennonite Quarterly Review*, XXXIV (October 1960). Pp. 219–48.

——. "Anabaptism in Central Germany: II. Faith and Life." *Mennonite Quarterly Review*, XXXV (January 1961). Pp. 5–37.

SMUCKER, DONOVAN E. "The Theological Basis for Christian Pacifism." *Mennonite Quarterly Review*, XXVII (July 1953). Pp. 163–86.

Miscellaneous

FRIESEN, ABRAHAM. "The Marxist Interpretation of the Reformation." Ph.D. dissertation. Stanford University, San Francisco, 1967. (microfilm)

SCHELBERT, LEO. "Swiss Migration to America: The Swiss Mennonites." Ph.D. dissertation. Columbia University, New York, 1966.

CHAPTER 2

Books

BEARSS, ASA. *Origin and History of the Tunker Church in Canada: As Gathered from Authentic and Reliable Souces.* Ridgeway, Ont.: M. V. Disher, 1918.

BELL, WINTHROP PICKARD. *The "Foreign Protestants" and the Settlement of Nova Scotia: A History of a Piece of Arrested British Colonial Policy in the Eighteenth Century.* Toronto: University of Toronto Press, 1961.

BENDER, W. J. *Non-Resistance in Colonial Pennsylvania.* Scottdale, Pa.: Herald Press, 1949.

BURKHOLDER, L. J. *A Brief History of the Mennonites in Ontario.* Markham, Ont.: Mennonite Conference of Ontario, 1935.

CANNIFF, W. M. *History of the Province of Ontario.* Toronto: A. H. Honey, 1872.

CARDINAL, HAROLD. *The Unjust Society: The Tragedy of Canada's Indians.* Edmonton: M. G. Hurtig Limited, 1969.

CLIMENHAGA, ARTHUR W. *History of the Brethren in Christ Church.* Nappanee, Ind.: Evangelical Publishing House, 1942.

COBER, GEORGE. *A Historical Sketch of the Brethren in Christ Known as Tunkers in Canada.* Gormley, Ont.: published by the author, 1953.

CRAIG, GERALD M. *Upper Canada: The Formative Years 1784–1841.* Toronto: McClelland and Stewart, 1963.

CUMMING, PETER A., and NEIL H. MICKINBERG, eds. *Native Rights in Canada,* 2nd ed. Toronto: The Indian-Eskimo Association of Canada in association with General Publishing Company Limited, 1972.

DAVIDSON, ROBERT L. D. *War Comes to Quaker Pennsylvania 1682–1756.* New York: Columbia University Press, 1957.

EBY, EZRA E. *A Biographical History of Waterloo Township: A History of the Early Settlers and their Descendants,* 2 vols. Berlin, Ont.: published by the author, 1895.

FUNK, CHRISTEL. *Ein Spiegel fuer Alle Menschen.* Reading, Pa.: Johann Ritter and Company, 1813.

GATES, FRANCIS LILLIAN. *Land Policies of Upper Canada.* Toronto: University of Toronto Press, 1968.

MACKINNON, IAN F. *Settlements and Churches in Nova Scotia, 1749–1776.* Montreal: Walker, 1930.

MACNUTT, W. S. *The Atlantic Provinces: The Emergence of Colonial Society, 1712–1857.* Toronto: McClelland and Stewart, 1965.

ROSENBERGER, JESSE LEONARD. *The Pennsylvania Germans: A Sketch of Their History and Life of the Mennonites and of Sidelights from the Rosenberger Family.* Chicago: University of Chicago Press, 1923.

ROTHERMUND, DIETER. *The Layman's Progress: Religious and Political Experience in Colonial Pennsylvania, 1740–1770.* Philadelphia: University of Pennsylvania Press, 1961.

SAUNDERS, EDWARD MANNING. *History of the Baptists of the Maritime Provinces.* Halifax: John Bergune, 1902.

UTTLEY, W. V. *The History of Kitchener, Ontario.* Kitchener: The Chronicle Press, 1937.

WALLACE, W. STEWART. *The United Empire Loyalists: A Chronicle of the Great Migration.* Toronto & Glasgow: Brook and Company, 1914.

WRIGHT, ESTHER CLARK. *The Loyalists of New Brunswick.* Fredericton: published by the author, 1955.

————. *The Petitcodiac: A Study of the New Brunswick River and of the People who Settled Along It.* Sackville: Tribune Press, 1945.

Articles

BENDER, WILBUR J. "Pacifism Among the Mennonites, Amish Mennonites, and Schwenkfelders of Pennsylvania to 1783." *Mennonite Quarterly Review,* I (July 1927). Pp. 23–40.

BRANT-SERO, J. O. "The Six Nations Indians in the Province of Ontario, Canada." *Wentworth Historical Society Transactions,* II (1899). Pp. 62–73.

BREITHAUPT, W. H. "First Settlements of Pennsylvania Mennonites in Upper Canada." *Christian Monitor,* XIX (1927). Pp. 180–83.

————. "The Germans." *Waterloo Historical Society,* XIV (1926). Pp. 220–25.

————. "The Settlement of Waterloo County." *Ontario Historical Society Papers and Records*, XXII (1925). Pp. 14–17.

————. "Some German Settlers of Waterloo County." *Waterloo Historical Society*, I (1913). Pp. 8–9.

————. "Waterloo County History." *Ontario Historical Society Papers and Records*, XVII (1919). Pp. 43–47.

BRICKER, IRWIN C. "The Trek of the Pennsylvanians to Canada in the Year 1805." *Waterloo Historical Society*, XXII (1934). Pp. 123–31.

BURKHOLDER, L. J. "The Early Mennonite Settlements in Ontario." *Mennonite Quarterly Review*, VIII (July 1934). Pp. 103–22.

CASSELMAN, A. C. "The Settlement of the Mennonites and Tunkers." *Canada and its Provinces*. Vol. XVII. Section IX. The Province of Ontario, 1914. Pp. 47–49.

COFFMAN, S. F. "The Adventure of Faith." *Waterloo Historical Society*, XIV (1926). Pp. 228–33.

CRUIKSHANK, E. A. "The Correspondence of Lieutenant Governor John Graves Simcoe." *Ontario Historical Society*. Toronto, 1923.

————. "The Reserve of the Six Nations on the Grand River and the Mennonite Purchase of Block No. 2." *Waterloo Historical Society*, XV (1927). Pp. 303–50.

DURNBAUGH, D. F. "Relationships of the Brethren with Mennonites and Quakers, 1708–1865." *Church History*, XXXV (March 1966). Pp. 35–59.

EBY, A. "Die Ansiedlung und Begruendung der Mennoniten Gemeinschaft in Canada." *Der Mennonitische Friedensbote*, XVI:2.

EPP, H. "From the Vistula to the Dnieper." *Mennonite Life*, VI (1951). Pp. 14–18.

"First Mennonite Settlement, Jordan, Ontario." *Mennonite Historical Bulletin*, XXIII (April 1962):1.

FRETZ, J. C. "Mennonites in Welland County, Ontario." *Mennonite Quarterly Review*, XXVII (January 1953). Pp. 55–75.

GRATZ, DELBERT L. "The Background of the Nineteenth Century Swiss Mennonite Immigrants." *Mennonite Life*, XI (April 1956). Pp. 61–64.

JOHNSTON, C. M. "Joseph Brant, The Grand River Lands and the Northwest Crisis." *Ontario History*, LV (1963). Pp. 267–82.

————. "An Outline of Early Settlement in the Grand River Valley." *Ontario History*, LVI (1962). Pp. 43–67.

KAISER, T. E. "Origins and Early Pennsylvania Dutch Settlements in Upper Canada." *Waterloo Historical Society*, XX (1932). Pp. 309–14.

LEHMANN, HEINZ. "Das Deutschtum in der Provinz Ontario." *Zur Geschichte des Deutschtums in Canada*. Stuttgart I (1931). Pp. 48–114.

MONTGOMERY, MALCOLM. "The Legal Status of the Six Nations Indians." *Ontario History*, LV (1963). Pp. 93–106.

MOSTELLER, J. D. "Baptists and Anabaptists." *The Chronicle*, XX (January 1957), pp. 3-27 and (July 1957), pp. 100–14.

"The Petition of John Troyer." *Ontario Historical Society Papers and Records*, XXIV (1927). Pp. 142–3.

QUIRING, H. "Die Auswanderung der Mennoniten aus Preussen, 1788–1870." *Mennonite Life*, VI (April 1951). Pp. 37–40.

RAYMOND, W. O. "Alexander McNutt and the Pre-Loyalist Settlements of Nova Scotia." *Royal Society of Canada*, 3rd Ser., Vols. IV, V, VI. 1910–12. Saint John, N.B., 1912.

REGEHR, T. D. "Land Ownership in Upper Canada, 1783–1796: A Background to the First Table of Fees." *Ontario History*, LV (1963). Pp. 35–48.

REMPEL, DAVID G. "From Danzig to Russia: The First Mennonite Migration." *Mennonite Life*, XXIV (January 1969). Pp. 8–28.

———. "The Mennonite Migration to New Russia, 1788–1870." *Mennonite Quarterly Review*, IX (April 1935). Pp. 71–91.

RICHTER, L. "Germans in Nova Scotia." *Dalhousie Review*, XV (January 1936). Pp. 425–34.

SEYFORT, A. G. "Migrations of Lancaster County Mennonites to Waterloo County, Ontario, Canada, from 1800 to 1825." *Papers and Addresses of the Lancaster Historical Society*, XXX (1926). Pp. 33–41.

SHERK, A. B. "The Pennsylvania Germans in Waterloo County." *Ontario Historical Society Papers and Records*, VII (1906).

STANLEY, G. F. G. "The Six Nations and the American Revolution." *Ontario History*, LVI (1964). Pp. 217–34.

Transcript of Original Deed for the German Company Tract, Waterloo Township. *Waterloo Historical Society*, IX (1919). Pp. 87–90.

WAMBOLD, I. A. "Early Mennonite Settlers in Canada." Published in the *Mennonite Year Book and Directory, 1920*. Scottdale, Pa.: Mennonite Publishing House, 1920. Pp. 8–10.

Miscellaneous

ALDERFEL, O. H. "The Mind of the Brethren in Christ: A Synthesis of Revivalism and the Church Conceived as Total Community." Ph.D. dissertation. Claremont Graduate School and University Centre, 1964.

CGC ARCHIVES. H. L. BURKHOLDER COLLECTION. "The Mennonite Church in York County, Ontario." 1933.

GREAT BRITAIN, TREATIES. *Indian Treaties and Surrenders from 1680 to 1890*. 2 vols. Ottawa, 1891.

HEINTZ, GLADYS ILEEN. "German Immigration into Upper Canada and Ontario from 1783 to the Present Day." M.A. thesis. Queen's University, Kingston, 1936.

LANGFORD, W. F. "Some Phases of Early Immigration to Upper Canada." M.A. thesis. Queen's University, Kingston, 1927.

The Loyalist Gazette. Dominion Council of United Empire Loyalists Association of Canada, Vol. I., Toronto, 1963.

PUBLIC ARCHIVES OF CANADA (PAC)

Records of the Deputy Superintendent of Indian Affairs. Record Group 10: Vol. 26, Folders for 1796–1797, 1798, 1801–1802, 1803–1804, 1805; Vol. 27, Folders for 1806–1807.

Records of the Executive Council of Upper Canada — Upper Canada State Papers. Record Group 1: Vol. 7, File No. 20, pp. 79–83 (1797); Vol. 68, File No. 26, pp. 143–46 (1798); Vol. 60, File No. 8, pp. 26–27 (1799); Vol. 12, File No. 6, p. 11 (1799), File No. 9, p. 19 (1799), File No. 14, pp. 26–28 (1800); Vol. 68, File No. 36, pp. 206–18 (1803); Vol. 32, File No. 40, pp. 108, 112–18 (1803); Vol. 7, File No. 12, pp. 31–64 (1804); Vol. 11, File No. 40, pp. 107–20 (1804); Vol. 7, File No. 25, pp. 92–101 (1805); Vol. 1, File No. 17, pp. 62–75 (1806); Vol. 79, File No. 76, pp. 20–23 (1806); Vol. 12, File No. 46, pp. 132–37 (1806); Vol. 58, File No. 49, pp. 100–01 (1807); Vol. 12, File No. 4, pp. 139–52 (1806), File No. 56, pp. 211-24 (1811).

REMPEL, D. G. "The Mennonite Colonies in New Russia, a Study of their Settlement and Economic Development from 1789–1914." Ph.D. dissertation. Stanford University, 1933.

SIDER, E. MORRIS. "History of the Brethren in Christ (Tunker) Church in Canada." M.A. thesis. University of Western Ontario, 1955.

CHAPTER 3

Books

Census of the Canadas: 1851–52. Quebec: John Lovell, 1853.

COOK, RAMSAY. *Canada: A Modern Study.* Toronto: Clarke, Irwin & Company, 1963.

DUNHAM, MABEL. *Grand River.* Toronto: McClelland & Stewart, 1945.

———. *The Trail of the Conestoga.* Toronto: Macmillan Company, 1945.

EBY, A. *Ansiedlung und Begruendung der Mennonitischen Gemeinshaft in Ontario.* Milford Square, Pa., 1872.

FRETZ, J. W. *The Mennonite in Ontario.* Waterloo, Ont.: Mennonite Historical Society of Ontario, 1967.

Gemeinschaftlicher Verein der Mennoniten zur Ersetzung von Brandschaden. Berlin, Ont.: Gedruckt in der Journal Office bei Rittenger und Motz, 1876.

GINGERICH, ORLAND. *The Amish of Canada.* Waterloo, Ont.: Conrad Press, 1972.

GLAZEBROOK, G. P. DE T. *Life in Ontario: A Social History.* Toronto: University of Toronto Press, 1968.

GOURLAY, ROBERT C. *Statistical Accounts of Upper Canada.* London: Simpkin & Marshall, 1822. 2 vols.

GUILLET, EDWIN C. *The Pioneer Farmer and Backwoodsman.* Toronto: Ontario Publishing Company, 1963. 2 vols.

HORST, SAMUEL. *Mennonites in the Confederacy.* Scottdale, Pa.: Herald Press, 1967.

Hundred Years of Progress in Waterloo County: Semi-Centennial Souvenir, 1856–1906. Waterloo, Ont.: The Chronicle Telegraph, 1906.

KLASSEN, PETER JAMES. *Mutual Aid Among the Mennonites: Doctrine and Practice.* Bluffton, Ohio: Association of Mennonite Mutual Aid Societies, 1963.

The Mennonite Mutual Fire Insurance Association of Canada. Berlin, Ont.: Office of the Daily News, 1881.

REAMAN, G. ELMORE. *The Trail of the Black Walnut.* Toronto: McClelland & Stewart, 1957.

SCHOTT, CARL. *Landnahme und Kolonization in Canada.* Kiel: Schmidt und Klaunig, 1936.

SHERK, MICHAEL GONDER. *Pen Pictures of Early Pioneer Life in Upper Canada, by a "Canuck" of the Fifth Generation.* Toronto: William Briggs, 1905.

SNYDER, MIRIAM H. *Hannes Schneider: Descendants and Times, 1532–1939.* Kitchener: Ont.: published by the author, 1937.

UTTLEY, W. V. *The History of Kitchener, Ontario.* Kitchener: The Chronicle Press, 1937.

WILSON, DOUGLAS J. *The Church Grows in Canada.* Toronto: Canadian Council of Churches, 1966.

WINK, ROBIN W. *The Blacks in Canada.* Montreal: McGill-Queen's University Press, 1971.

Articles

ALLEN, A. S. "Reminiscences of Early Waterloo." *Waterloo Historical Society,* XIII (1925). Pp. 139–43.

BAUMAN, H. M. "The Mennonite Settlements in Pennsylvania and Waterloo with Specific Reference to the Bauman Family." *Waterloo Historical Society,* X (1922). Pp. 225–45.

BERGEY, LORNE. "Founder of Preston Commemorated." *Waterloo Historical Society,* XLVIII (1960). Pp. 22–23.

———. "A History of Wilmot Township." *Waterloo Historical Society,* L (1962). Pp. 48–61.

———. "Wilmot Family Farms." *Waterloo Historical Society,* LI (1963). Pp. 70–73.

BREITHAUPT, W. H. "Early History of the County of Waterloo." *Waterloo Historical Society,* I (1913). Pp. 8–9.

———. "Early Settlements in Upper Canada." *Waterloo Historical Society,* XI (1923). Pp. 11–17.

BUHR, MARTIN. "Ontario Society Plans Centennial Pageant." *Mennonite Historical Bulletin,* XXVII (October 1966). Pp. 1–2.

DRIEDGER, JOHANNES. "Farming Among the Mennonites in West and

East Prussia 1534–1915." *Mennonite Quarterly Review*, XXXI (January 1957). Pp. 16–21.

DUNHAM, B. M. "Beginnings in Ontario." *Mennonite Life*, V (October 1950). Pp. 14–16.

———. "Some 'Plain' People of Canada." *The Canadian Magazine*, LXII (January 1924). Pp. 188–95.

———. "The Story of Conestoga." *Waterloo Historical Society*, XXXIII (1945). Pp. 16–23.

ERB, E. IRWIN. "Deed for First School Site in Waterloo County." *Waterloo Historical Society*, LIII (1965). Pp. 65–68.

FRANCIS, E. K. "Mennonite Commonwealth in Russia, 1789–1914: A Sociological Interpretation." *Mennonite Quarterly Review*, XXV (1951). Pp. 173–82, 200.

FRETZ, J. W. "Farming: Our Heritage." *Mennonite Life*, IV (April 1949). P. 3.

HAMILTON, O. "The Amish Settlement in the Township of Wilmot in the County of Waterloo." *Waterloo Historical Society*, XXXII (1944). Pp. 15–21.

JOHNSTON, M. A. "A Brief History of Elementary Education in the City of Waterloo." *Waterloo Historical Society*, LIII (1965). Pp. 56–66.

KALBFLEISCH, HERBERT K. "German or Canadian." *Waterloo Historical Society*, XL (1952). Pp. 18–29.

KLOTZ, OTTO. "Preston Reminiscences." *Waterloo Historical Society*, IX (1921). Pp. 171–82.

KRAHN, CORNELIUS. "Agriculture Among the Mennonites in Russia." *Mennonite Life*, X (January 1955). Pp. 14–20.

LANDIS, IRA D. "Mennonite Agriculture in Colonial Lancaster County, Pa.: The First Intensive Agriculture in America." *Mennonite Quarterly Review*, XIX (October 1945). Pp. 254–72.

MAGE, JULIUS, and ROBERT MURDIE. "The Mennonites of Waterloo County." *Canadian Geographical Journal*, LXXXI:1. Pp. 10–19.

MARTIN, AARON. "Courtship and Marriage Practices of Lancaster Mennonites." *Mennonite Life*, XVII (January 1962). Pp. 31–35.

"A Mennonite Legacy for Education Purposes in Waterloo." *Waterloo Historical Society*, LVIII (1970). P. 74.

MUNRO, ROSS. "The Snider Flour Mills, Waterloo." *Waterloo Historical Society*, XV (1927). Pp. 383–84.

NICOLAY, C. L. "Berlin, a German Settlement in Waterloo County, Ontario, Canada." *German American Annals,* V (1907). Pp. 105–21.

PEARCE, THOMAS. "School History, Waterloo County and Berlin," in Miriam Helen Snyder, *Hannes Schneider: Descendants and Times*. P. 211.

"Pioneer Map of Waterloo County." *Mennonite Community*, II (September 1948).

REMPEL, C. J. "The Waterloo Mennonites." *Mennonite Life*, XVII (July 1962). Pp. 106–8.

REMPEL, JOHN I. "Restoration and Reconstruction." *Waterloo Historical Society.* XLIX (1961). Pp. 10–14.

RICHARDS, J. H. "Lands and Policies: Attitudes and Controls in Alienation of Lands in Ontario During the First Century of Settlement." *Ontario History,* L (1958). Pp. 193–209.

SEYFERT, A. G. Excerpts from the address of Hon. A. G. Seyfert, representing the Lancaster County Historical Society at the dedication of the Mennonite Memorial, Waterloo County, Ontario, Canada, August 28, 1926. *Papers and Addresses of the Lancaster County Historical Society,* XXX (1926). Pp. 117–19.

SHERK, A. B. "The Pennsylvania Germans of Waterloo County." *Ontario Historical Society,* VII (1906). Pp. 98–109.

———. "The Pennsylvania-Germans in Canada." *The Pennsylvania German,* VIII (1907). Pp. 101–4.

———. "Recollections of Early Waterloo." *Waterloo Historical Society,* III (1914). Pp. 13–19.

SHOEMAKER, DOROTHY. "Dr. B. Mabel Dunham." *Waterloo Historical Society,* XLV (1957). Pp. 5–6.

SHUMWAY, GEORGE. *Conestoga Wagon.* Reviewed by Ira D. Landis in *Mennonite Historical Bulletin,* XXV (October 1964). Pp. 7–8.

SMITH, GEORGE. "The Amishman." *Ontario Historical Society,* XVII (1919). Pp. 40–42.

SNYDER, E. W. B. "Waterloo County Forests and Primitive Economics." *Waterloo Historical Society,* VI (1918). Pp. 14–36.

SPETZ, THEOBALD. "The Catholic Church in Waterloo County," in Miriam Helen Snyder, *Hannes Schneider: Descendants and Times.* P. 260.

SWARTZENTRUBER, D. "Education in Ontario." *Mennonite Life,* XVII (July 1962). Pp. 120–22.

Transcript of Original Deed for the German Company Tract, Waterloo Township. *Waterloo Historical Society,* VII (1919). Pp. 87–90.

TRESTAIN, W. G. "Mennonites Hospitable, Kindly; Stick Closely to Their Faith." *London Free Press.* September 9, 1938.

"The Waterloo County Pioneer's Memorial Tower." *Waterloo Historical Society,* XIV (1926). P. 185.

WEBER, ELDON D. "Waterloo Township German Company Tract." *Waterloo Historical Society,* LVIII (1970). P. 8.

WEBER, LORNE B. "The Trek of the Conestoga." *Waterloo Historical Society,* XL (1952). Pp. 13–17.

WELLS, CLAYTON W. "A Historical Sketch of the Town of Waterloo, Ontario." *Waterloo Historical Society,* XVI (1928). Pp. 22–67.

Miscellaneous

BURKHOLDER, L. J. *Papers.* CGC Archives.

GRAY, ELMA E. "Threads of Mennonite History." Unpublished manuscript, 1972 (CGC).

HUCK, MARILYN GLYNN. "Early Settlement in Waterloo County (Upper Canada)." M.A. dissertation. University of Toronto, 1963.

JORDAN VILLAGE MUSEUM SCRAPBOOK. Jordan, Ontario.

PUBLIC ARCHIVES OF CANADA (PAC)
Province of Upper Canada. *Journal of Legislative Assembly.*
Upper Canada and Canada. *Petitions for Land Grants and Leases,* Record Group 1, L3, Vol. 340. Petitions submitted to the Executive Council of Upper Canada and the United Province of Canada by applicants for land grants, 1791–1867.

WATTS, CLAYTON R. "Study of Mennonite Communities in Western Ontario." Ph.D. dissertation. George Washington University, Washington, D.C., 1942.

CHAPTER 4

Books

DORLAND, ARTHUR G. *A History of the Society of Friends (Quakers) in Canada.* Toronto: Macmillan Company, 1927.
———. *The Quakers in Canada.* Toronto: Ryerson Press, 1968.

EPP, FRANK H. *Mennonite Exodus: The Rescue and Resettlement of the Russian Mennonites Since the Communist Revolution.* Altona, Man.: D. W. Friesen & Sons, 1962.

FRASER, ALEXANDER. *Eighth Report of the Bureau of Archives.* Toronto: King's Printer, 1911.
———. *Twenty-Second Report of the Department of Public Records and Archives.* Toronto: Herbert H. Ball, 1934.

GERBRANDT, HENRY J. *Adventure in Faith.* Altona, Man.: D. W. Friesen & Sons, 1970.

HITSMAN, J. MACKAY. *The Incredible War of 1812.* Toronto: University of Toronto Press, 1965.

MOIR, JOHN S., ed. *Church and State in Canada 1627–1867: Basic Documents.* Toronto: McClelland & Stewart, 1967.

ONTARIO HISTORICAL SOCIETY. *Papers and Records,* Vol. XIII (1915). Toronto, 1915.

SANDERSON, J. E. *The First Century of Methodism in Canada, 1775–1839.* Toronto: William Briggs, 1908.

WILSON, ALAN. *The Clergy Reserves of Upper Canada.* Booklet No. 23. Ottawa: Canadian Historical Association, 1969.

WRIGHT, EDWARD. *Conscientious Objectors in the Civil War.* New York: A. S. Barnes & Company, 1961.

Articles

BARRIE, E. G. "History of the Militia in Waterloo County." *Waterloo Historical Society,* XIX and XX (1931–1932). Pp. 266–271.

BENDER, H. S. "Church and State in Mennonite History." *Mennonite Quarterly Review*, XIII (April 1939). Pp. 83–103.
———. "New Data for Ontario Mennonite History." *Mennonite Quarterly Review,* III (January 1929). Pp. 42–46.
———. "The Pacifism of the Sixteenth Century Anabaptists." *Mennonite Quarterly Review,* XXX (January 1956). Pp. 5–18.
BENDER, WILBUR J. "Pacifism Among the Mennonites, Amish Mennonites, and Schwenkfelder of Pennsylvania to 1783." *Mennonite Quarterly Review*, I (July 1927). Pp. 21–48.
Complete Text of Privilegium assized by Czar I printed in D. H. Epp, *Die Chortitzer Mennoniten.* Odessa, 1889.
GREEN, DAVID. "Waterloo County's Militia." *Waterloo Historical Society,* LIV (1966). Pp. 62–68.
HORSCH, JOHN. "An Historical Survey of the Position of the Mennonite Church on Nonresistance." *Mennonite Quarterly Review*, I (July 1927). Pp. 5–22.
"An Ontario Mennonite Petition." *Mennonite Historical Bulletin,* XXIII (October 1962). Pp. 6–7.
"The Opinions of the Primitive Christians on the Lawfulness of War." *Herald of Truth,* III (December 1866). P. 93.
"The Petition of John Troyer." *Ontario Historical Society Papers and Records,* XXIV. Pp. 142–43.
SHERK, A. B. "Early Militia Matters in Upper Canada, 1808–1842." *Ontario Historical Society Papers and Records,* XIII. Pp. 67–73.
SIDER, E. MORRIS. "Nonresistance in the Early Mennonite Brethren in Christ Church in Ontario." *Mennonite Quarterly Review,* XXXI (October 1957). Pp. 278–86.
STACEY, C. P. "The War of 1812 in Canadian History." *Ontario Historical Society Papers and Records,* L (1958). Pp. 153–59.

Miscellaneous

BRITISH STATUTES
PUBLIC ARCHIVES OF CANADA (PAC)
Province of Upper Canada, *Journal of Legislative Assembly.*
Upper Canada Sundries, Record Group 5, A1, Vol. 93. Letters, petitions, and reports received by the Civil Secretary from correspondents resident in North America, 1766–1840.

CHAPTER 5

Books

BAUMAN, SALOME. *One Hundred Fifty Years First Mennonite Church.* Kitchener, Ont.: First Mennonite Church, 1963.
Berlin. Celebration of Cityhood 1912. Issued by Authority of City of Berlin, Ontario. Issued in commemoration of its celebration of city-

hood, July 17, 1912. Berlin, Ont.: German Printing and Publishing Company, 1912.

Briefe an die Mennoniten Gemeinde in Ober Canada: Mit Einer Zugabe. Berlin, Ober Canada: printed by Heinrich Eby, 1936.

Census of the Canadas 1851–52. Quebec: John Lovell, 1853.

COLLINS, DON. *St. Agatha: 1867–1967.* n.p.: 1967.

Die Gemeinschaftliche Liedersammlung: Zum Allgemeinen Gebrauch des Wahren Gottesdienstes. Berlin, Ober Canada: H. W. Peterson, 1836.

EBY, BENJAMIN. *Fibel zu der Ersten Lese-Uebung von Benjamin Eby.* Berlin, Ober Canada, 1843.

———. *Kurzgefasste Kirchen-Geschichte und Glaubenslehre der Taufgesinnten-Christen oder Mennoniten.* Berlin, Ont.: published by the author, 1841.

———. *Neues Buchstabir und Lesebuch, Besonders Bearbeitet und Eingesichtet zum Gebrauch Deutscher Schule. Enthalten das A.B.C. und Vielerlei Buchstabir-und Leseuebung.* Berlin, Ont.: H. W. Peterson, 1839.

EBY, EZRA. *History of the Eby Family.* Berlin, Ont., 1889.

HARTZLER, J. S., and DANIEL KAUFFMAN. *Mennonite Church History.* Scottdale, Pa.: Mennonite Book and Tract Society, 1905.

KALBFLEISCH, HERBERT K. *The History of the Pioneer German Language Press of Ontario 1835–1918.* Toronto: University of Toronto Press, 1968.

Kleiner Katechismus, Oder Kurzgefasste Unterweisung aus der Heiligen Schrift in Fragen und Antworten zum Gebrauch fuer Kinder: Herausgegeben von der Mennoniten Gemeinde. Berlin, Ont.: printed by Heinrich Eby, 1844.

Kurzgefasste Kirchen Ordnung der Mennoniten oder Wehrlosen Christen in Canada. Verfasst von einem von der Gemeinde dazu Verordneten Komitee. Preston, Canada West: printed by Martin Rudolph, 1850.

RISSER, J. *Taufe der Mennoniten in Deutschland.* Berlin, Ont.: Heinrich Eby, 1845.

RITTENHOUSE, WILLIAM. *Vineland Cemetery: Historical Sketch, Trust Deed, and Rules and Regulations.* n.p.: n.d. (1922?).

SANDERSON, J. E. *The First Century of Methodism in Canada, 1775–1839.* Toronto: William Briggs, 1908.

SNYDER, MIRIAM H. *Hannes Schneider and His Wife Catharine Haus Schneider: Their Descendants and Times, 1534–1939.* Kitchener, Ont.: published by the author, 1937.

STOLZFUS, GRANT M. *Mennonites of the Ohio and Eastern Conferences.* Scottdale, Pa.: Herald Press, 1969.

WALSH, H. H. *The Christian Church in Canada.* Toronto: Ryerson Press, 1956.

WEAVER, M. B. *Mennonites of the Lancaster Conference.* Scottdale, Pa.: Mennonite Publishing House, 1931.

WENGER, J. C. *History of the Mennonites of the Franconia Conference.* Telford, Pa.: Franconia Mennonite Historical Society, 1937.

WITMER, LESLIE D. *Pioneer of Christendon of Waterloo County 1800–1967: History of the Hagey-Preston Mennonite Church.* n.p., 1967.

Articles

BAUMAN, SALOME. "First Mennonite Church 1813–1963." *Waterloo Historical Society,* LI (1963). Pp. 19–28.

BENDER, H. S. "Catechism." *Mennonite Encyclopedia,* I. Pp. 529–30.

———. "The Historical Background of Our Present Ministerial Office." *Gospel Herald,* XLII (October 25, 1949). Pp. 1051, 1061.

———. "New Data for Ontario Mennonite History." *Mennonite Quarterly Review,* III (January 1929). Pp. 42–46.

———. "The Office of Bishop in Anabaptist Mennonite History." *Mennonite Quarterly Review,* XXX (April 1956). Pp. 128–32.

BERGEY, LORNA. "Hagey Mennonite Church." *Waterloo Historical Society,* LVIII (1970). Pp. 33–34.

"Bishop Benjamin Eby, 1785–1853." *Mennonite Historical Bulletin,* XXII (January 1961). P. 1.

BREITHAUPT, W. H. "Waterloo County Newspaper." *Waterloo Historical Society Annual Report,* IX (1921). Pp. 152–59.

BURKHOLDER, OSCAR. "Bishop Benjamin Eby (1785–1853)." *Gospel Herald,* XXII (April 1929). Pp. 61–62.

CRESSMAN, J. BOYD. "Benjamin Eby, Founder of Kitchener and the Spirit of Progress." *Canadian-German Folklore, Pennsylvania Folklore Society,* I (1961). Pp. 130–33.

———. "Bishop Benjamin Eby." *Waterloo Historical Society,* XXIX (1941). Pp. 152–58.

———. "Eby, Benjamin." *Mennonite Encyclopedia,* II. Pp. 138–39.

———. "First Mennonite Church, Kitchener." *Mennonite Quarterly Review,* XIII (July 1939). Pp. 159–86.

DYCK, C. J. "The Role of Preaching in Anabaptist Tradition." *Mennonite Life,* XVIII (January 1962). Pp. 21–25.

EBY, EZRA E. "Bishop Benjamin Eby." *Mennonite Historical Bulletin,* XXIII (January 1962). Pp. 1–3.

EBY, MARTIN C. "Peter Eby." *Mennonite Encyclopedia,* II. Pp. 139–40.

GINGERICH, MARY ETTA. "Hagey Mennonite Church, Preston, Ontario." *Christian Monitor,* XXIV (February 1932). Pp. 48–50.

———. "Mennonite Leaders in North America: Benjamin Eby (1785–1853)." *Gospel Herald,* LVIII (March 2, 1965). P. 178.

GROFF, JACOB. "A Benjamin Eby Letter." *Mennonite Historical Bulletin,* XXVIII (October 1967). P. 4.

GROH, HERBERT. "Benjamin Eby." *Waterloo Historical Society,* XLVIII (1960). Pp. 16–18.

———. "Berliner Journal." *Waterloo Historical Society,* XLVII (1959). Pp. 62–69.

———. "A Long-Neglected Son of Waterloo County." *Waterloo Historical Society,* XLIX (1961). Pp. 32–34.

GROSS, JACOB. "Letter to Upper Canada." *Mennonite Historical Bulletin.* XXVII (October 1966). Pp. 2–3.

"Historical Plaque to be Unveiled in Kitchener." Press release, June 21, 1960. Issued by Department of Travel and Publicity re Benjamin Eby.

"History of the Blenheim Congregation." *Mennonite Historical Bulletin.* XXIX (January 1968). P. 6.

"Interesting Highlights of the Mennonite Settlement of Waterloo Township." n.d. (*c.* 1950), newspaper report.

KOCH, MRS. LESTER. "Biehn Mennonite Church." *Waterloo Historical Society,* LII (1964). Pp. 61–62.

KRAHN, CORNELIUS. "The Office of Elder in Anabaptist Mennonite History." *Mennonite Quarterly Review,* XXX (April 1956). Pp. 120–27.

LANDIS, IRA D. "Bishop Peter Eby of Pequea." *Mennonite Quarterly Review,* XIV (January 1940). Pp. 41–51.

———. "Peter Eby (1765–1834)." *Gospel Herald,* LV (February 16, 1965). P. 123.

"An Old Letter on Mennonite Aid." *Mennonite Historical Bulletin,* XXI (October 1960). P. 4.

"An Old Ontario Letter (Johannes Baer to Jacob Groff *et al.*)." *Mennonite Historical Bulletin,* XXVIII (October 1967). Pp. 4–5.

PEACHEY, PAUL. "Anabaptism and Church Organization." *Mennonite Quarterly Review,* XXX (July 1956). Pp. 213–38.

SNYDER, O. A. "The First Mennonite Sunday School." *Waterloo Historical Society,* LI (1963). Pp. 23–27.

Miscellaneous

Archives of the Mennonite Church (AMC).

Conference Resolutions, Ontario Mennonite Conference, 1847–1928 (CGC).

Conrad Grebel College Archives (CGC).

Documents on Mennonite Conference of Ontario (CGC).

GARLAND, MERVIN A. "The Religious and Moral Conditions in Upper Canada, 1815–1840." M.A. thesis, University of Western Ontario, 1927.

KALBFLEISCH, HERBERT CARL. "History of German Newspapers in Ontario." Ph.D. dissertation, University of Michigan, Ann Arbor, 1953.

PUBLIC ARCHIVES OF CANADA (PAC).

Upper Canada Sundries, Record Group 5, A1, Vols. 74 and 173. Letters, petitions and reports received by the Civil Secretary from correspondents resident in North America, 1766–1840.

UMBLE, R. H. "Mennonite Preaching, 1864–1944." Ph.D. dissertation, Northwestern University.

CHAPTER 6

Books

BURKHOLDER, H. D. *The Story of Our Conference and Churches.* North Newton, Kans.: Faith and Life Press, 1951.

CLARKE, S. D. *Church and Sect in Canada.* Toronto: University of Toronto Press, 1948.

CLIMENHAGA, A. W. *History of the Brethren in Christ Church.* Nappanee, Ind.: E. V. Publishing House, 1942.

CROSS, WHITNEY R. *The Burnt-Over District: The Social and Intellectual History of Enthusiastic Religion in Western New York, 1800–1850.* New York: Harper & Row, 1950.

The Doctrine and Discipline of the Mennonite Brethren in Christ. Berlin, Ont.: Mennonite Brethren in Christ Publication Society, 1888.

GATES, HELEN K. *Bless the Lord, O My Soul: A Biography of Bishop John Fretz Funk.* Scottdale, Pa.: Herald Press, 1964.

GINGERICH, MELVIN. *Mennonite Attire Through Four Centuries.* Breinigsville, Pa.: Pennsylvania German Society, 1970.

GRANT, JOHN W., ed. *The Churches and the Canadian Experience.* Toronto: Ryerson Press, 1963.

HIEBERT, CLARENCE. *The Holdeman People: The Church of God in Christ Mennonite, 1859–1969.* South Pasadena, Calif.: William Carey Library, 1973.

HOCH, DANIEL. *Hauptsinn Einer Predigt, Gehalten den 5. Juni, 1855 in Clinton, Canada West, von Prediger Lehman, York County.* Published by the author, 1855.

——. *Matters of Fact! By Rev. Daniel High, a Pastor of the Mennonite Church, or a Defence of His Views of the Gospel.* Translated from the German. St. Catharines, Ont.: E. S. Leavenworth Book and Job Printing Establishment, 1870.

HOLDEMANN, JOHN. *A History of the Church of God as it Existed from the Beginning, Whereby it May be Known, and How it was Propagated Until the Present Time.* Lancaster: John Baer's Sons, 1876.

HUFFMAN, JASPER ABRAHAM, ed. *History of the Mennonite Brethren in Christ Church.* New Carlisle, Ont.: Bethel Publishing Company, 1958.

KAUFMAN, EDMUND G. *The Development of the Missionary and Philanthropic Interest Among Mennonites of North America.* Berne, Ind.: The Mennonite Book Concern, 1931.

KRAHN, C., ed. *A Century of Witness: The General Conference Mennonite Church.* Newton, Kans.: Mennonite Publication Office, 1959.

KREHBIEL, H. P. *The History of the General Conference Mennonite Church of the Mennonites of North America.* Canton, Ohio: published by the author, 1898. 2 vols.

———. *Unsere Stellung zu den Geheimen Gesellschaften und Warum.* Berne, Ind.: Mennonite Book Concern, 1898.

MARTY, MARTIN E. *Righteous Empire: The History of Protestantism in America.* New York: Religious Book Club, 1971.

MEAD, SIDNEY E. *The Lively Experiment: The Shaping of Christianity in America.* New York: Harper & Row, 1963.

PANNABECKER, S. F. *Faith in Ferment: A History of the Central District Conference.* Newton, Kans.: Faith and Life Press, 1968.

SHETLER, SANFORD G. *Two Centuries of Struggle and Growth, 1873–1883.* Scottdale, Pa.: Herald Press, 1963.

STORMS, EVEREK RICHARD. *History of the United Missionary Church.* Elkhart, Ind.: Bethel Publishing Company, 1958.

———. *United Missionary Church Year Book.* Kitchener, Ont.: 1950.

UNRUH, A. H. *Die Geschichte der Mennoniten-Bruedergemeinde.* Hillsboro, Kans.: General Conference of the Mennonite Brethren Church of North America, 1955.

WEAVER, W. B. *History of the Central Conference Mennonite Church.* Danvers, Ill.: published by the author, 1926.

WENGER, J. C. *The Mennonites in Indiana and Michigan.* Scottdale, Pa.: Herald Press, 1961.

Articles

CRESSMAN, J. BOYD. "First Mennonite Church, Kitchener." *Mennonite Quarterly Review*, XIII (July 1939). Pp. 159–86.

EPP, H. H., and W. ULRICH. "Mennonite Conferences in Ontario." *Mennonite Life*, XVII (July 1962). Pp. 109–12.

ESHELMAN, WILMER J. "History of the Reformed Mennonite Church." *Lancaster County Historical Society*, XLIX (1945). Pp. 85–116.

FRIEDMANN, ROBERT. "Anabaptism and Pietism." *Mennonite Quarterly Review*, XIV (April 1940), pp. 90–128, and XIV (July 1940). Pp. 149–69.

"Funk, John Fretz." *Mennonite Encyclopedia*, II. Pp. 421–23.

HERSHEY, MARY JANE. "A Study of the Dress of the (Old) Mennonites in the Franconia Conference 1700–1953." *Pennsylvania Folklife*, IX (Summer 1958). Pp. 24–47.

HOCKER, E. W. "Montgomery County History: Schism Among the Mennonites." *Bulletin of the Historical Society of Montgomery County, Pennsylvania*, XII (Spring/Fall 1960). Pp. 115–18.

KAUFMAN, E. G. "The General Conference of the Mennonite Church of North America." *Mennonite Life*, II (July 1947). Pp. 37–43, 47.

OBERHOLTZER, JOHN H. "Letter of John H. Oberholtzer to Friends in Germany, 1849." *Mennonite Quarterly Review*, XI (April 1937). Pp. 156–62.

PANNABECKER, S. F. "John H. Oberholtzer and His Time: A Centennial Tribute 1847–1947." *Mennonite Life*, II (July 1947). Pp. 29–32.

REDEKOP, C. "The Sect From a New Perspective." *Mennonite Quarterly Review*, XXXIX (July 1965). Pp. 204–17.

UMBLE, JOHN. "The Background and Origin of the Ohio and Eastern Mennonite Conference." *Mennonite Quarterly Review*, XXXVIII (January 1964). Pp. 350–60.

UNRUH, I. "John Holdemann, Founder of the Church of God in Christ Mennonite: Portrait of a Prophet." *Mennonite Life*, XIV (July 1959). Pp. 123–24.

Miscellaneous

FUNK, JOHN F. *Papers*. (AMC).

HIEBERT, CLARENCE. "The Holdeman People: A Study of the Church of God in Christ Mennonite, 1858–1969." Ph.D. dissertation, Case Western Reserve University, 1971.

HOCH, DANIEL. *Papers*. (CGC).

Letters from Christian Gross, Jacob Moyer, Wiebe and others, dated around 1845. (AMC).

LOEB, ELSE F. "The Mennonite Church of America: An Analysis of a Dissenting Sect." M.A. thesis, New School for Social Work Research, New York, 1952.

PANNABECKER, SAMUEL F. "The Development of the General Conference of the Mennonite Church of North America in the American Environment." Ph.D. dissertation, Yale University, 1944.

OBERHOLTZER, JOHN H. *Papers*. (MSHL).

CHAPTER 7

Books

BARTSCH, F. *Unser Auszug Nach Mittelasien*. Winnipeg: Echo Verlag, 1948.

BEHRENDS, ERNEST. *Der Steppenhengst*. Bodensee: Hohenstaufen Verlag, 1969.

EHRT, A. *Das Mennonitentum in Russland von Seiner Einwanderung bis zur Gegenwart*. Langensalza: Beltz, 1932.

Eine Einfache Erklaerung und Einige Glaubenssaetze der Sogenannten Kleinen Gemeinde. Quakertown, Pa., 1901.

EPP, D. H. *Johann Cornies*. Rosthern, Sask.: Echo, 1946.

EPP, FRANK H. *Mennonite Exodus: The Rescue and Resettlement of the Russian Mennonites Since the Communist Revolution*. Altona, Man.: D. W. Friesen & Sons, 1962.

EPP, HEINRICH. *Heinrich Epp, Kirchenaeltester der Mennoniten Gemeinde zu Chortitza*. Leipzig: Pries, 1897.

FRANCIS, E. K. *In Search of Utopia*. Altona, Man.: D. W. Friesen & Sons, 1955.

FRIESEN, P. M. *Alt-Evangelische Mennonitische Bruederschaft in Russland (1789–1910)*. Halbstadt, Taurien: Raduga, 1911.

FROESE, L. *Paedagogisches Kultursystem der Mennonitischen Siedlungsgruppe in Russland*. Akron, Pa.: Mennonite Central Committee, 1950.

HARMS, J. F. *Geschichte der Mennoniten Bruedergemeinde*. Hillsboro, Kans.: Mennonite Brethren Publishing House, 1925.

ISAAC, FRANZ. *Die Molotschnaer Mennoniten*. Halbstadt, Taurien: Kommissionsverlag, 1908.

JANZEN, A. E. *Mennonite Brethren Distinctives*. Hillsboro, Kans.: Mennonite Brethren Publishing Houses, 1966.

KLAASSEN, M. *Geschichte der Wehrlosen Taufgesinnten Gemeinde von den Zeiten des Apostels bis auf der Gegenwart*. Koeppenthal: Vorstand der Mennoniten Gemeinde, 1873.

KLAUS, A. *Unsere Kolonien. Studien und Materialien zur Geschichte und Statistik der Auslaendischen Kolonization in Russland*. Odessa: Odessaer Zeitung, 1887.

KROEKER, A. *Pfarrer Eduard Wuest, der Grosze Erweckungsprediger in den Deutschen Kolonien Suedrusslands*. Hillsboro, Kans.: Central Publishing Company: Leipzig, 1903.

LOHRENZ, J. H. *The Mennonite Brethren Church*. Hillsboro, Kans.: Mennonite Brethren Publishing House, 1950.

PATERSON, JOHN. *The Book For Every Land*. London: John Snow, 1858.

PETERS, VICTOR. *All Things Common: The Hutterian Way of Life*. Minneapolis: University of Minnesota Press, 1966.

QUIRING, WALTER. *Als Ihre Zeit Erfuellet War: 150 Jahre Bewaehrung in Russland*. Saskatoon, Sask.: Modern Press, 1963.

REGIER, PETER. *Kurzgefasste Geschichte der Mennoniten-Bruedergemeinde*. Berne, Ind.: Light and Hope Publishing Company, 1901.

REIMER, P. J. B., ed. *The Sesquicentennial Jubilee: Evangelical Mennonite Conference*. Steinbach, Man.: Evangelical Mennonite Conference, 1962.

SMITH, C. HENRY. *The Coming of the Russian Mennonites*. Berne, Ind.: Mennonite Book Concern, 1927.

STUMPP, KARL. *Das Schrifttum Ueber das Deutschtum in Russland*. Tuebingen, Germany, 1971.

———. *The German Russians*. New York: Atlanticforum, 1967.

UNRUH, A. H. *Die Geschichte der Mennoniten-Bruedergemeinde*. Hillsboro, Kans.: General Conference of the Mennonite Brethren Church of North America, 1955.

WEDEL, C. H. *Abriss der Geschichte der Mennoniten*, Vol. III. Newton, Kans.: 1901.

Articles

ADRIAN, VICTOR. "Born of Anabaptism and Pietism." *Mennonite Brethren Herald*, March 26, 1965.

BENDER, H. S. "Kleine Gemeinde." *Mennonite Encyclopedia*, III. P. 197.

BRAUN, PETER. "The Educational System of the Mennonite Colonies in South Russia." *Mennonite Quarterly Review*, III (1929). Pp. 169–82.

EWERT, H. H. "Abschrift eines Briefes den Wm. Ewert als Deputierter der westpreussischen Gemeinden im Jahre 1873 an seine Familie geschrieben hat." *Der Mitarbeiter*, 22 (October 1929). Pp. 1–5.

FRIEDMANN, ROBERT. "The Devotional Literature of the Mennonites in Danzig and East Prussia to 1880." *Mennonite Quarterly Review*, XVIII (July 1944). Pp. 162–73.

GOERZ, H. "The Cultural Life Among the Mennonites of Russia." *Mennonite Life*, XXIV (July 1969). Pp. 99–100.

KRAHN, CORNELIUS. "Mennonite Community Life in Russia." *Mennonite Quarterly Review*, XVI (July 1942). Pp. 174–77.

————. "Some Social Attitudes of the Mennonites of Russia." *Mennonite Quarterly Review*, IX (October 1935). Pp. 165–77.

KREIDER, ROBERT. "The Anabaptist Conception of the Church in the Russian Environment." *Mennonite Quarterly Review*, XXV (January 1951). Pp. 17–33.

NEFF, CHRISTIAN. "Flemish Mennonites." *Mennonite Encyclopedia*, II. Pp. 337–40.

————. "Frisian Mennonites." *Mennonite Encyclopedia*, II .Pp. 413–14.

QUIRING, WALTER. "Johann Cornies." *Mennonite Encyclopedia*, I. Pp. 716–18.

REIMER, PETER J. B. "From Russia to Mexico: The Story of the Kleine Gemeinde." *Mennonite Life*, IV (October 1949). Pp. 28–32.

SUDERMANN, JACOB. "The Origin of Mennonite State Service in Russia, 1870–1880." *Mennonite Quarterly Review*, XVII (1943). Pp. 23–46.

TOEWS, A. P. "Bernhard Harder's Critique of the Baptists and Mennonite Brethren." *Mennonite Life*, XIV (October 1959). Pp. 179–81.

UNRUH, BENJAMIN H. "The Mennonites of Russia." *Mennonite Quarterly Review*, II (1937). Pp. 61–67.

Miscellaneous

BECKER, J. P. "Die Entstehung der Mennoniten Brueder-gemeinde." Unpublished manuscript in Bethel College Historical Library, Newton, Kansas.

BELK, FRED RICHARD. "The Great Trek of the Russian Mennonites to Central Asia, 1880–84." Ph.D. dissertation, Oklahoma State University, 1973.

BLOCK, J. D. "A Survey of the History of the Mennonite Brethren Church in North America." B.D. thesis, California Baptist Theological Seminary, 1954.

British and Foreign Bible Society Reports and Correspondence, London, England (BFBS).

Congregational Council for World Mission (formerly the London Missionary Society). Russian Correspondence (CCWM).

"Ein Schreiben von Klaas Reimer." Unpublished manuscript, n.d. (CGC).

EPP, D. H. "Die Chortitzer Mennoniten: Versuch Einer Darstellung der Entwicklung Derselben." Rosenthal, Chortitza, n.d.

FRIENDS HOUSE, LONDON. Archives of Various Quakers to Russia 1819–1865 (FHL).

KLASSEN, A. J. "The Roots and Development of Mennonite Brethren Theology to 1914." M.A. thesis, Wheaton College Graduate School, 1966.

REMPEL, DAVID G. "Mennonite Agriculture and Model Farming as Issues of Economic Study and Political Controversy, 1870–1917." Unpublished manuscript, 1973 (CGC).

————. "The Mennonite Colonies in New Russia: A Study of Their Settlement and Economic Development from 1789 to 1914." Ph.D. dissertation, Stanford University, 1933.

————. "The Mennonite Commonwealth in Russia, 1789–1919." Unpublished manuscript, 1973 (CGC).

TOEWS, J. A. "The History of the Mennonite Brethren Church." Unpublished manuscript, 1973.

TOEWS, JACOB JOHN. "The Cultural Background of the Mennonite Brethren Church." M.A. dissertation, University of Toronto, 1951.

WALL, A. A. "Die Kirchliche Entwicklung in Ruszland." Unpublished manuscript, n.d., in possession of its author.

CHAPTER 8

Books

BARTSCH, F. Unser Auszug nach Mittelasien. Winnipeg, Man.: Echo Verlag, 1948.

BOESE, J. A. The Prussian-Polish Mennonites Settling in South Dakota 1874 and Soon After. Freeman, S. Dakota: Pine Hill Press, 1967.

CLARKSON, JESSE D. A History of Russia. New York: Random House, 1969.

DAWSON, CARL ADDINGTON. Group Settlement: Ethnic Communities in Western Canada. Toronto: Macmillan Company, 1936.

FAST, G. In den Steppen Sibiriens. Rosthern, Sask.: Hesse, 1957.

FRANCIS, E. K. In Search of Utopia: The Mennonites in Manitoba. Altona, Man.: D. W. Friesen & Sons, 1955.

FRIESEN, P. M. Alt-Evangelische Bruederschaft in Russland, 1789–1940. Halbstadt, Taurien: Naduga, 1911.

HILDEBRAND, J. J. Aus der Vorgeschichte der Einwanderung der Mennoniten aus Russland nach Manitoba. Winnipeg, Man.: published by the author, 1949.

KRAHN, C., ed. *From the Steppes to the Prairies.* Newton, Kans.: Mennonite Publication Office, 1949.

MACDONALD, NORMAN. *Canada, Immigration and Colonization 1841–1903.* Aberdeen: Aberdeen University Press, 1966.

MEYNEN, EMIL. *Bibliographie des Deutschtums der Kolonialzeitlichen Einwanderung in Nordamerika.* Leipzig, 1937.

MILLER, E. M. *From the Fiery Stakes of Europe to the Federal Courts of America.* New York: Vantage, 1963.

REIMER, GUSTAV E., and G. R. GAEDDERT. *Exiled by the Czar: Cornelius Jansen and the Great Mennonite Migration, 1874.* Newton, Kans.: Mennonite Publication Office, 1956.

SHANTZ, JACOB YOST. *Narrative of a Journey to Manitoba, Together with an Abstract to the Dominions Lands Act, and an Extract from the Government Pamphlet on Manitoba.* Ottawa: Department of Agriculture, 1873.

SMITH, C. HENRY. *The Coming of the Russian Mennonites.* Berne, Ind.: Mennonite Book Concern, 1927.

SUDERMANN, LEONHARD. *Eine Deputationsreise von Russland nach America.* Elkhart, Ind.: Mennonitische Verlagshandlung, 1897.

UNGER, P. *Von Russlaendischen Steppen nach Amerikas Goldfeldern: Fuenf Jahre Irrfahrten.* Bad Homburg: Wiegand, 1921.

WIEBE, GERHARD. *Ursachen und Geschichte der Auswanderung der Mennoniten aus Russland nach Amerika.* Winnipeg, Man.: Druckerei der Nordwesten, 1900.

Articles

"An Immigration Deputation." *Manitoba Free Press*, November 30, 1872. P. 4.

"Arrival by Steamer International." *Manitoba Gazette*, June 25, 1873.

BAILES, KENDALL. "Peaceful Invasion from Russia, 1874 — Mennonite Migration to Kansas." *Tribune Magazine.* South Bend, Ind., September 3, 1961.

BENDER, H. S. "A Passenger List of Mennonite Immigrants from Russia in 1878." *Mennonite Quarterly Review*, XV (October 1941). Pp. 263–76.

BOWMAN, H. M. "Jacob Y. Shantz, Pioneer of Russian Mennonite Immigration to Manitoba." *Waterloo Historical Society Annual Report*, XII (1924). Pp. 85–100.

CORRELL, E., ed. "Congressional Debates on the Mennonite Immigration from Russia, 1873–1874." *Mennonite Quarterly Review*, XX (July 1946), pp. 178–221; (October 1946), pp. 255–75.

CORRELL, ERNST. "Mennonite Immigration into Manitoba: Sources and Documents, 1872, 1873, 1874." *Mennonite Quarterly Review*, XI (July 1937), pp. 196–227; (October 1937), pp. 267–83.

———. "President Grant and the Mennonite Immigration from

Russia." *Mennonite Quarterly Review*, IX (July 1935). Pp. 144–52.

———, ed. "Sources on the Mennonite Immigration from Russia in the 1870s." *Mennonite Quarterly Review*, XXIV (October 1950). Pp. 329–52.

"Die Mennoniten in Russland." *Herold der Wahrheit*, IX (August 1872). Pp. 121–22.

"Die Mennonitische Delegation von 1873 Kommt in Winnipeg an." *Steinbach Post*, June 8, 1949. P.2.

"Die Russischen Brueder." *Herold der Wahrheit*, IX (November 1872). P. 169.

"Dominion Lands Act." *Manitoba Free Press*, November 30, 1872. Pp. 1–2.

EWERT, B. "Auswanderungen und Ansiedlungen der Mennoniten." *Mennonitische Volkswarte*, Heft 3, 1935. P. 93 ff.

EWERT, WILHELM. "A Defence of the Ancient Mennonite Principle of Non-Resistance by a Leading Prussian Mennonite Elder in 1873." *Mennonite Quarterly Review*, XI (October 1937). Pp. 284–90.

FRANCIS, E. K. "Mennonite Commonwealth in Russia, 1789–1914: A Sociological Interpretation." *Mennonite Quarterly Review*, XXV (July 1951). Pp. 173–82, 200.

———. "The Russian Mennonites, from Religious to Ethnic Group." *American Journal of Sociology*, LIV (September 1948). Pp. 206–11.

"From the Archives . . . Interesting Mennonite History Recalled in Markham Paper." *Red River Valley Echo*, November 12, 1952. P. 2.

FUNK, JOHN F. "The Russian Emigration." *Herald of Truth*, June, 1874. P. 104.

———. "Two Conflicting Newspaper Reports." *Minneapolis Daily Pioneer*, July 17, 1873; *Winnipeg Standard*, n.d.

———. "Unsere Reise im Westen." *Herold der Wahrheit*, December, 1972. Pp. 184–86.

GINGERICH, MELVIN. "Jacob Y. Shantz, 1822–1909, Promoter of the Mennonite Settlements in Manitoba." *Mennonite Quarterly Review*, XXIV (July 1950). Pp. 230–47.

———. "John F. Funk's Trip to Manitoba in 1873." *Mennonite Quarterly Review*, XXXIV (April 1960). Pp. 147–52.

GINGERICH, OWEN. "Relations Between the Russian Mennonites and the Friends During the Nineteenth Century." *Mennonite Quarterly Review*, XXV (October 1951). Pp. 283–95.

"Half-Breed Attack on the Mennonite Deputation at White Horse Plains: Houses Hotel Surrounded: Troops Sent to Their Assistance: Mennonites Back Safe!!" *Manitoba Gazette*, July 2, 1873.

"International." *Manitoba Gazette*, July 17, 1873. P. 2.

KRAHN, CORNELIUS. "Mennonite Migrations as an Act of Protest." *Mennonite Life*, XXV (January 1970). Pp. 20–27.

———. "Some Letters of Bernhard Warkentin Pertaining to the Migration of 1873–1875." *Mennonite Quarterly Review*, XXIV (July 1950). Pp. 248–62.

KUHN, W. "Cultural Achievements of the Chortitza Mennonites." *Mennonite Life*, III (July 1948). Pp. 35–38.

LEIBBRANDT, GEORGE. "The Emigration of the German Mennonites from Russia to the United States and Canada in 1873–1900." *Mennonite Quarterly Review*, VI (October 1932), pp. 205-26; VII (January 1933), pp. 3–41.

LOHRENZ, G. "The Emigration of the German Mennonites from Russia to the United States and Canada, 1873–1880." *Mennonite Quarterly Review*, VII (January 1933). Pp. 5–41.

The Manitoban, August 15, 1874, for description of arriving Mennonites.

MANNHARDT, J. "Koennen und duerfen wir Mennoniten der von dem Staate gefarderten Wehrpflicht genuegen?" *Mennonitische Blaetter*, 19:6 (August 1972), pp. 41–43; 19:7 (September 1872), pp. 49–51.

"Mennonite Delegation Arrived in Winnipeg." *The Manitoban*, June 21, 1873.

"Mennonite Deputation." *Manitoba Gazette*, June 25, 1873.

"Mennonite Migration, 1874-1884." *Mennonite Life*, V (January 1950). P. 7.

"The Mennonites." *Herald of Truth*, July, 1872. Pp. 106–7.

"The Mennonites." *The Manitoban*, July 5, 1873.

"Mennonites Back Safe." *Manitoba Gazette*, July 2, 1873.

"The Mennonites in Russia." *Herald of Truth*, June, 1872. P. 88.

"The Mennonites: Trip to Riding Mountains." *The Manitoban*, July 5, 1873. P. 2.

NEUFELD, PETER L. "Colonel J. S. Dennis: Catalyst of Prairie Development." *The Western Producer*, April 12, 1973.

Report by J. Y. Shantz in *Manitoba Weekly Free Press*, August 21, 1875.

SCHMID, M. "Jacob Y. Shantz." *Canadian German Folklore, Pennsylvania Folklore-Society of Ontario*, I (1961). Pp. 126–29.

SCHMIDT, JOHN F. "Cornelius Janzen Collection." *Mennonite Historical Bulletin*, XXVII (July 1966). P. 6.

———. "When a People Migrate: Footnote to the Mennonite Migration of the 1870s." *Mennonite Quarterly Review*, XXXIII (April 1959). Pp. 152–55.

SEEGER, WILLIAM. "The Russian Mennonites." *St. Paul Press*, January 3, 1874.

SHANTZ, FREDERICK R. "The Shantz Family History." *Waterloo Historical Society*, XVIII (1930). Pp. 208–12.

SHANTZ, J. Y. "From Manitoba." *Herald of Truth*, August 1874, p. 137; November 1875, p. 169.

Miscellaneous

BELK, FRED RICHARD. "The Great Trek of the Russian Mennonites to Central Asia, 1880–84." Ph.D. dissertation, Oklahoma State University, 1973.

BETHEL COLLEGE HISTORICAL LIBRARY. Jacob Y. Shantz Papers. List of Mennonites who migrated from Russia to Manitoba.

BRITISH AND FOREIGN BIBLE SOCIETY ARCHIVES (BFBS). Russia Agents Books 125, 137, 142, 149.

The Diary of Jacob S. Waldner in the Archives of the Mennonite Church, Goshen.

HOUSE OF COMMONS DEBATES

PAC, Adam Shortt Papers, M.G. 30, D45, Vol. 57. Copies of historical documents compiled by Dr. Adam Shortt (1859–1931), economist and historian. Dr. Shortt made the Mennonite emigration from Russia of 1872–73 one of his subjects of research.

PAC, Department of Agriculture, General Correspondence of the Minister, Record Group 17, A1, Vol. 62. Departmental correspondence dealing with Mennonite immigration and commitment of land grants to Mennonites.

PAC, Immigration Branch, Halifax and Quebec Passenger Lists, Record Group 76, Passenger Lists 9–11 (microfilm C4528-C4530).

PAC, Privy Council Office, Orders-in-Council, Record Group 2. All reports or submissions of the Committee of the Privy Council which have received the Governor General's approval.

JANSEN, CORNELIUS. Papers in the J. F. Funk Collection in the Archives of the Mennonite Church.

MOORE, J. A. "Immigration of the Russian Mennonites as Reflected in and Influenced by the Herald of Truth, 1870–1880." M.A. thesis, Illinois State University, Normal, Illinois.

PUBLIC RECORD OFFICE, LONDON (PRO). Foreign Office Files 65/837, 842, 852, 856, 861, 888, 892, 181/510.

SHANTZ, J. Y. List of Mennonites who migrated from Russia to Manitoba. Kitchener, Ont.: no publisher, n.d.

UNRUH, A. J. "Great Grandfather's Diary." (Diary of Tobias A. Unruh, Montezuma, Kansas).

WEDEL, P. P. *Kurze Geschichte der aus Volhynien, Russland, nach Kansas Ausgewanderten Schweizer Mennoniten.* 1929 (CMBC)

WISMER, PHILIP. "A Record of Russian Mennonite Aid Committee for Lincoln County, Ontario, 1873–1880." Unpublished manuscript, n.d., 7pp. (CGC).

CHAPTER 9

Books

BARNEBY, W. HENRY. *Life and Labour in the Far, Far West.* London: Cassell & Company, 1884.

BENNETT, JOHN W. *Northern Plainsmen: Adaptive Strategy and Agrarian Life*. Chicago: Aldine Publishing Company, 1969.

Census of Canada. 1901.

CLARK, LOVELL. *The Manitoba School Question: Majority Rule or Minority Rights?* Toronto: Copp-Clark Publishing Company, 1968.

CREIGHTON, D. G., et al. *Minorities, Schools, and Politics*. Toronto: University of Toronto Press, 1969.

Das 60-Jaehrige Jubilaeum der Mennonitischen Ost-Reserve. Steinbach, Man.: Warte-Verlag, 1935.

FRANCIS, E. K. *In Search of Utopia: The Mennonites in Manitoba*. Altona, Man.: D. W. Friesen & Sons, 1955.

FRIESEN, W. *A Mennonite Community in the East Reserve — Its Origin and Growth*. Winnipeg: The Historical and Scientific Society of Manitoba, 1964.

FUNK, R. N. *Bruderthal 1873–1964: 90th Anniversary*. Hillsboro, Kans.: Bruderthal Mennonite Church, 1964.

GALBRAITH, J. F. *The Mennonites in Manitoba 1875–1900: A Review of their Coming, their Progress, and their Present Prosperity*. Morden, Man.: The Chronicle Press, 1900.

Gedenkfeier (75) der Mennonitischen Einwanderung in Manitoba, Canada. Steinbach, Man.: Festkomitee der Mennonitischen Ostreserve, 1949.

GERBRANDT, HENRY J. *Adventure in Faith*. Altona. Man.: D. W. Friesen & Sons, 1970.

GERING, J. J. *After Fifty Years: A Brief Discussion of the History and Activities of the Swiss-German Mennonites from Russia who Settled in South Dakota in 1874*. Marion, S. Dakota: Pine Hill Printer, 1924.

GRANT, JOHN WEBSTER. *The Church in the Canadian Era*. Toronto: McGraw-Hill Ryerson, 1972.

HAMILTON, G. *In the Beginning. The Exciting Story of Manitoba's Past Told in an Arresting and Unique Way*. Steinbach, Man.: Derksen Printers, 1966.

HAMM, H. H. *Sixty Years of Progress 1884–1944, The Rural Municipality of Rhineland*. Altona, Man., 1944.

MORTON, W. L. *Manitoba, A History*. Toronto: University of Toronto Press, 1967.

Mennonite Scrapbook, 1884–1904. Manitoba Archives.

MEYERS, ROBERT. *Spirit of the Post Road: A Story of Self-Help Communities*. Altona, Man.: Federation of Southern Manitoba Co-operatives, 1955.

MILTON, HENRY, ed. *The Speeches and Addresses of the Rt. Hon. Frederick Temple, Earl of Dufferin*. London, 1882.

NOVOKAMPUS. *Kanadische Mennoniten: Bunte Bilder aus den 50 Jaehrigen Siedlerleben zu Jubilaeumsjahr, 1924*. Winnipeg: Rundschau Publishing House, 1925.

PETERS, KLAAS. *Die Bergthaler Mennoniten*. Hillsboro, Kans.: Mennonite Brethren Publishing House, 1924.

SCHULTZ, FERDINAND P. *A History of the German Mennonites from Russia at Mountain Lake, Minnesota.* Minneapolis, Minn.: published by the author, 1939.

SMITH, HENRY C. *The Coming of the Russian Mennonites.* Berne, Ind.: Mennonite Book Concern, 1927.

Steinbach: Facts About Steinbach. An Industrial Survey of the Town of Steinbach, Bureau of Industrial Development, Department of Industry and Commerce, Province of Manitoba, 1954.

WARKENTIN, ABE. *Reflections on Our Heritage: A History of Steinbach and the R. M. of Hanover from 1874.* Steinbach, Man.: Derksen Printers, 1971.

Articles

BERRY, B. "Manitoba's Monied Mile." *Saturday Night,* August 2, 1952. Pp. 14, 39.

BROWN, FRANK. "History of Winkler." *Winkler Progress,* December 17, 1951, to May 30, 1952.

——. "Winkler, Manitoba." *Mennonite Life,* XI (July 1956). Pp. 120–25.

CLIFFORD, N. K. "His Dominion: A Vision in Crisis." *Studien Religion,* II (Spring 1973). Pp. 315–26.

CORRELL, ERNST, ed. "Canadian Agricultural Records on Mennonite Settlements, 1875–77." *Mennonite Quarterly Review,* XXI (January 1947). Pp. 34–46.

——. "The Mennonite Loan in the Canadian Parliament, 1875." *Mennonite Quarterly Review,* XX (October 1946). pp. 255–75.

——. "The Sociological and Economic Significance of the Mennonites as a Cultural Group in History." *Mennonite Quarterly Review,* XVI (July 1942). Pp. 161–66.

DERKSEN, EUGENE. "Steinbach: Cradle of the Mennonites in Western Canada." *Mennonite Life,* XII (April 1957). Pp. 72–83.

DUECK, J. R. "Aus den Pionierjahren der Mennonitischen Siedlung in Manitoba." *Mennonitische Volkswarte,* I, 4 (1935), pp. 137–42; I, 5, pp. 117–78.

EPP, P. P. "Aus Meinen Erinnerungen." *Steinbach Post,* August 1, 1934.

EWART, ALAN C. "The Municipal History of Manitoba." *History and Economics Series.* University of Toronto, 2 (1904).

EWERT, H. H. "Die Ansiedlung der Russischen Mennoniten in Manitoba." *Der Mitarbeiter,* November, 1924. P. 86.

FRANCIS, E. K. "A Bibliography on the Mennonites of Manitoba." *Mennonite Quarterly Review,* XXVII (July 1953). Pp. 238–48.

——. "The Manitoba Mennonite Farm House." *Mennonite Quarterly Review,* XXVIII (January 1954). Pp. 56–60.

——. "Mennonite Contributions to Canada's Middle West." *Mennonite Life,* IV (April 1949). Pp. 21–23, 41.

——. "Mennonite Institutions in Early Manitoba: A Study of Their Origins." *Agricultural History,* XXII (July 1948). Pp. 144–55.

FRETZ, J. WINFIELD. "Manitoba — A Mosaic of Mennonitism." *Mennonite Life*, XI (July 1956). Pp. 126–27.

FRIESEN, WILLIAM. "A Mennonite Community in the East Reserve: Its Origin and Growth." *Historical Essays on the Prairie Provinces*, D. Swainson, ed. Toronto: McClelland & Stewart, 1970.

FUNK, JOHN F. "Minnesota and Dakota, Their Adaptation as a Place of Settlement for the Russian Mennonites." *Herald of Truth*, X (February 1873). Pp. 17–28.

GINGERICH, MELVIN. "The Reactions of the Russian Mennonite Immigrants of the 1870s to the American Frontier." *Mennonite Quarterly Review*, XXXIV (April 1960). Pp. 137–46.

———. "Russian Mennonites React to Their New Environment." *Mennonite Life*, XV (October 1960). Pp. 175–80.

GREGORY, H. E. "Among Mennonites." Toronto *Globe*, August 30, 1890. P. 5.

HIND, E. CORA. "The Mennonites or the Heroes of a Flat Country." *Winnipeg Free Press*, April 1892.

HOEPPNER, J. N. "Early Days in Manitoba." *Mennonite Life*, VI (April 1951). Pp. 11–15.

KRAHN, CORNELIUS. "Commemoration Seventy-Five Years." *Mennonite Life*, IV (October 1949). P. 3 ff.

———. "From Bergthal to Manitoba." *Mennonite Life*, XII (April 1957). Pp. 84–85.

———. "From Russia to Meade." *Mennonite Life*, VI (July 1951). Pp. 18–19.

The Manitoban, August 15, 1874. Description of arriving Mennonites.

Markham Economist and Sun, October 30, 1952. Blodwen Davies quotes from notebook of Simeon Reesor who accompanied seven families to Manitoba in 1875.

"Mennonite Reserves [around Dufferin and Rat River]." *The Emigrant*, II (July 1, 1887). P. 20.

PETERS, J. B. "Die Ersten Pioniere aus Sued-Russland in Kanada." *Steinbach Post*, October 4, 1939.

REGIER, C. C. "Childhood Reminiscences of a Russian Mennonite Immigrant Mother 1859–1880." *Mennonite Quarterly Review*, XV (April 1941). Pp. 83–94.

REIMER, K. J. B. "Historical Sketches of Steinbach." *Carillon News*, January 4–May 2, 1952.

REIMER, P. J. B. "First Mennonite Settlers in Manitoba Come to Kleefeld-Steinbach, 1874." *Canadian Mennonite*, August 8, 1964.

REMPEL, J. J. "Die Ansiedlung auf der Ostreserve in Manitoba." *Der Bote*, October 1933.

REMPEL, W. "Die Mennoniten in Sued-Manitoba." *Bundesbote-Kalendar*, 1898. Pp. 36–41.

"Rosenort–Rosenhoff Settlements." *Red River Valley Echo*, July 2, 1958.

SHANTZ, J. Y. "From Manitoba." *Herald of Truth*, November 1875. P. 169.

"A Sketch of the Morden District." *Morden Chronicle,* March 11, 1897.

SMITH, ALLAN. "Metaphor and Nationality in North America." *Canadian Historical Review*, LI (September 1970). Pp. 247–75.

TANNER, HENRY. "The Mennonite Settlement" in *Successful Emigration to Canada.* Ottawa: Department of Agriculture, 1885. Pp. 11–12.

"The Vice-Regal Visit." *Manitoba Free Press*, August 23, 1877. Pp. 1–2.

WARKENTIN, JOHN. "The Development of Trading Centers in the Mennonite East Reserve of Manitoba." *The Shield*, No. 7 (1956). Pp. 24–29.

———. "Mennonite Agricultural Settlements of Southern Manitoba." *Geographical Review*, XLIX (July 1959). Pp. 342–68.

———. With photography by Eberhard Otto. "Time and Place in the Western Interior." *Artscanada*, August 1972. Pp. 20–37.

WARKENTIN, J. W. "Carving a Home out of Primeval Forest." *Mennonite Quarterly Review*, XXIV (April 1950). Pp. 142–48.

Winnipeg Free Press, August 21, 1877, before and after. Coverage of Lord Dufferin visit.

Miscellaneous

BERGEN, JOHN J. "An Historical Study of Education in the Municipality of Rhineland." M.Ed. dissertation, University of Manitoba, 1959.

———. "School District Reorganization in Rural Manitoba." Ph.D. dissertation, University of Alberta, 1967.

EWERT, B. "Mennonitische Ansiedlungen und Gemeinden in den Westlichen Provinzen in Canada." 1955 (CGC).

GOVERNMENT DOCUMENTS
House of Commons Debates
Journals of the House of Commons, 1875, 1877, 1886.

KORNELSON, G. E. *Diaries and Notebooks* in possession of G. G. Kornelson, Steinbach, Manitoba.

RISTUBEN, JOHN B. "Minnesota and the Competition for Immigrants." Ph.D. dissertation, University of Oklahoma, Norman, Oklahoma, 1964.

SHANTZ, M. B. "The Biography of Jacob Y. Shantz." Manuscript in possession of Waterloo Historical Society, Kitchener, Ontario.

SHIPLEY, HELEN B. "The Migration of Mennonites from Russia, 1873–1883, and Their Settlement in Kansas." M.A. dissertation, University of Minnesota, 1954.

WARKENTIN, JOHN H. "The Mennonite Settlement of Southern Manitoba." Ph.D. dissertation, University of Toronto, 1960.

WISMER, PHILIP. "A Record of Russian Mennonite Aid Committee for Lincoln County, Ontario, 1873–1880." Manuscript, n.d., 7 pp. (CGC).

CHAPTER 10

Books

BENDER, H. S. *Mennonite Sunday School Centennial.* Goshen, Ind., 1940.

————. *Two Centuries of American Mennonite Literature: A Bibliography of Mennonitica Americana, 1727–1928.* Goshen, Ind.: The Mennonite Historical Society, 1929.

BLUFFTON COLLEGE. *An Adventure in Faith, 1900–1950.* Berne, Ind.: Witness Press, 1950.

BURKHOLDER, L. J. *A Brief History of the Mennonites in Ontario.* Markham, Ont.: Mennonite Conference of Ontario, 1935.

CLARKE, S. D. *Church and Sect in Canada.* Toronto: University of Toronto Press, 1948.

COFFMAN, BARBARA F. *His Name was John: The Life and Story of an Early Mennonite Leader.* Scottdale, Pa.: Herald Press, 1964.

ESAU, H. T. *First Sixty Years of Mennonite Brethren Missions.* Hillsboro, Kans.: Mennonite Brethren Publishing House, 1954.

FRIEDMANN, ROBERT. *Mennonite Piety Through the Centuries.* Goshen, Ind.: Mennonite Historical Society, 1949.

FUNK, JOHN F. *The Mennonite Church and Her Accusers.* Elkhart, Ind.: Mennonite Publishing Company, 1878.

————. *Warfare, Its Evils, Our Duty: Addressed to the Mennonite Churches Throughout the United States, and All Others who Sincerely Seek and Love the Truth.* Markham, Ont.: printed at Economist Office, 1863.

GATES, HELEN KOLB. *Bless the Lord O My Soul: A Biography of Bishop John Fretz Funk 1835–1930.* Scottdale, Pa.: Herald Press, 1964.

GENERAL CONFERENCE BOARD OF PUBLICATIONS. *Twenty-Five Years with God in India.* Berne, Ind.: Mennonite Book Concern, 1929.

GINGERICH, MELVIN. *Mennonite Attire Through Four Centuries.* Breinigsville, Pa.: Pennsylvania German Society, 1970.

HARTZLER, JOHN E. *Education Among the Mennonites of America.* Danvers, Ill.: Central Mennonite Publication Board, 1925.

HARTZLER, J. S., and DANIEL KAUFFMAN. *Mennonite Church History.* Scottdale, Pa.: Mennonite Book and Tract Society, 1905.

HOSTETLER, JOHN A. *God Uses Ink.* Scottdale, Pa.: Herald Press, 1958.

————. *The Sociology of Mennonite Evangelism.* Scottdale, Pa.: Herald Press, 1954.

KAUFFMAN, DANIEL. *Fifty Years in the Mennonite Church.* Scottdale, Pa.: Mennonite Publishing House, 1941.

KAUFMAN, EDMUND GEORGE. *The Development of the Missionary and Philanthropic Interest Among the Mennonites of North America.* Berne, Ind.: Mennonite Book Concern, 1931.

———. *Mennonite Missionary Interest.* Berne, Ind.: Mennonite Book Concern, 1931.

KREHBIEL, H. P. *The History of the General Conference Mennonite Church of the Mennonites of North America.* 2 vols. Canton, Ohio: published by the author, 1898.

LEHMAN, M. C. *Our Mission Work in India.* Elkhart, Ind.: Mennonite Board of Missions and Charities, 1939.

LOUCKS, AARON. *John F. Funk: Pioneer Publisher and Mennonite Literature, 1835–1930.* N.p., n.d.

MEAD, SIDNEY S. *The Lively Experiment: The Shaping of Christianity in America.* New York: Harper & Row, 1963.

MILLER, MARY. *A Pillar of Cloud: The Story of Hesston College, 1909–1959.* Hesston, Kans.: Mennonite Board of Education, 1959.

REMPEL, G. S. *A Historical Sketch of the Churches of the Evangelical Mennonite Brethren, 1889–1939.* Rosthern, Sask.: Conference of the Evangelical Mennonite Brethren, 1939.

STEINER, M. S. *Pitfalls and Safeguards.* Elkhart, Ind.: 1899.

STORMS, EVEREK RICHARD. *History of the United Missionary Church.* Elkhart, Ind.: Bethel Publishing Company, 1958.

WEISBERGER, BERNARD A. *They Gathered at the River.* Boston, 1958.

WENGER, J. C. *The Mennonite Church in America.* Scottdale, Pa.: Herald Press, 1966.

Articles

BENDER, H. S. "What the Sunday School did for the Mennonite Church." *Christian Monitor,* XXXII (October 1940). Pp. 312–14.

CASSELS, M. "Mennonites Take the Bible Literally." Chicago *Daily News,* October, 1860.

"The English and German Herald." *Herald of Truth,* IX (January 1872). P. 8.

FRETZ, CLARENCE. "A History of Winter Bible Schools in the Mennonite Church." *Mennonite Quarterly Review,* XVI (April and June 1942). Pp. 51–87 and 178–95.

FUNK, JOHN F. "A Journey to New York and Canada." *Herald of Truth,* IX (May 1872). Pp. 73–74.

"A General Conference." *Herald of Truth,* IX (September 1872). P. 138.

GINGERICH, MELVIN. "Two Letters of John F. Funk." *Mennonite Historical Bulletin,* XXVI (April 1965). Pp. 5–6.

GINGERICH, M., and H. S. BENDER. "Mennonite Yearbooks and Almanacs." *Mennonite Quarterly Review,* XXIV (July 1950). Pp. 281–87.

"Great Meeting." *Kitchener Daily News,* Berlin, Ont. June 10, 1890.

HARTZLER, J. S. "John F. Funk." *Gospel Herald,* XXII (October 24, 1929). Pp. 619–20.

KAUFFMAN, DANIEL. "Forty-Eight Years in the Mennonite Church: The Rise of Evangelism." *Gospel Herald,* XXXI (July 21, 1938). P. 1 ff.

KOLB, AARON C. "John Fretz Funk, 1835–1930: An Appreciation." *Mennonite Quarterly Review*, VI (July 1932), pp. 144–55, and (October 1932), pp. 250–63.

KOLB, J. CLEMENS. "John Fretz Funk as Seen Through His Diary." *Gospel Herald*, XXIV (May 21, 1931). Pp. 170–71.

KREIDER, A. "Beginning of Theological Training Among the Mennonites: Wadsworth School." *Mennonite Life*, XIV (April 1959). Pp. 66–69.

LOUCKS, AARON. "John F. Funk, Pioneer Publisher of Mennonite Literature." *Christian Monitor*, XXII (March 1930). Pp. 82–83.

Mennonite Encyclopedia articles.

NAURAINE, TILLIE. "John F. Funk as we Remember Him." *Christian Living*, XI (June 1964). Pp. 12–13.

SCHNELL, KEMPES. "John Fretz Funk, 1835–1930, and the Mennonite Migration of 1873–75." *Mennonite Quarterly Review*, XXIV (July 1950). Pp. 199–229.

WENGER, J. C. "John F. Funk, 1835–1930." *Gospel Herald*, LVIII (June 15, 1965). Pp. 523–24.

———. "Mennonite Yearbooks." *Mennonite Quarterly Review*, XIV (January 1940). Pp. 59–63.

Miscellaneous

BENDER, H. S. "Nineteenth Century Protestant Revivalism and Its Effect on the Mennonite Church." Unpublished paper, n.d. (AMC).

Conference Journal of the Mennonite Brethren in Christ Church, 1905.

DEAN, WILLIAM WARD. "John F. Funk and the Mennonite Great Awakening." Ph.D. dissertation, University of Iowa, 1965.

FUNK, JOHN F. Collection (AMC).

FUNK, JOHN F. "Two Conflicting Newspaper Reports." Unpublished document in J. F. Collection, January 15, 1873 (CGC).

GROVE, LORNE. "Exodus from Mennonitism." Unpublished research paper, April 1, 1970 (CGC).

HARDER, M. S. "The Origin in Philosophy and Development of Education Among the Mennonites." Ph.D. dissestation, University of Southern California, 1949.

HERSHBERGER, G. F. "The Founding of the Mennonite Central Committee." Unpublished manuscript.

HOSTETTER, JOHN NORMAN. "Mission Education in a Changing Society: Brethren in Christ Mission Education in Southern Rhodesia, Africa, 1899–1959." Ed.D. dissertation, State University of New York at Buffalo, 1967.

MARTIN, JASON S. "John Fretz Funk, Mennonite Leader 1868 to 1900." Unpublished manuscript, Goshen, Ind., 1959 (AMC).

Mennonite Yearbook and Directory. Goshen, Ind. Published annually since 1905 except 1910–13.

Minutes. Mennonite Evangelization and Benevolent Board, 1899–1905. Elkhart, Ind.

PETERS, FRANK C. "The Coming of the Mennonite Brethren to the

United States and Their Efforts in Education." Th.D. dissertation, Central Baptist Theological Seminary, Kansas City, Kansas, 1957.

PETERS, G. W. "The Growth of Foreign Missions in the Mennonite Brethren Church." Ph.D. dissertation. Also Hillsboro, Kans.: Mennonite Brethren Publishing House, 1952.

SAWATZKY, RODNEY. "The Influence of Fundamentalism on Mennonite Nonresistance, 1908–1944." M.A. dissertation, University of Minnesota, 1973.

CHAPTER II

Books

BURKHOLDER, L. J. *A Brief History of the Mennonites in Ontario.* Markham, Ont.: Mennonite Conference of Ontario, 1935.

CLIMENHAGA, ARTHUR W. *History of the Brethren in Christ Church.* Nappanee, Ind.: Evangelical Publishing House, 1942.

GATES, HELEN KOLB. *Bless the Lord, O My Soul: A Biography of Bishop John Fretz Funk, 1835–1930.* Scottdale, Pa.: Herald Press, 1964.

GINGERICH, ORLAND. *The Amish of Canada.* Waterloo, Ont.: Conrad Press, 1972.

HORST, MARY ANN. *My Old Order Mennonite Heritage.* Kitchener, Ont.: Pennsylvania Dutch Craft Shop, 1970.

HOSTETLER, J. A. *Amish Society.* Baltimore: Johns Hopkins University Press, 1963.

———. *Annotated Bibliography of the Amish.* Scottdale, Pa.: Mennonite Publishing House, 1951.

———. *Educational Achievement and Life Styles in a Traditional Society: The Old Order Amish.* Washington, D.C.: Department of Health, Education, and Welfare, 1969.

MARTIN, ISAAC G. *The Story of Waterloo-Markham Mennonite Conference (CGC).*

SCHREIBER, WILLIAM I. *Our Amish Neighbours.* Chicago: University of Chicago Press, 1962.

SMITH, CLYDE. *The Amishman.* Toronto: William Briggs, 1912.

WARNER, JAMES, and DONALD M. DENLINGER. *The Gentle People.* New York: Grossman Publishers, 1969.

WENGER, J. C. *The Mennonite Church in America.* Scottdale, Pa.: Herald Press, 1966.

Articles

DE VISSER, JOHN. "St. Jacob's Pony Express." *Canadian Weekly,* March 28, 1964. Pp. 9–13.

FRANCIS, E. K. "Tradition and Progress Among the Mennonites in Manitoba." *Mennonite Quarterly Review,* XXIV (October 1950). Pp. 312–28.

FUNK, J. F. "Konferenz der Amischen Mennoniten." *Herold der Wahrheit*, IX (June 1872). P. 89.

GINGERICH, MELVIN. "A Note on the Diener-Versammlung of 1866." *Mennonite Historical Bulletin*, XXII (October 1961). P. 2.

JAFFRAY, W., GEORGE DAVIDSON, and J. KING "German Peace Festival 1871." *Waterloo Historical Society*, LIV (1966). Pp. 78–80.

KAUFFMAN, DANIEL. "48 Years in the Mennonite Church: The Rise of Evangelism." *Gospel Herald*, XXXI (July 21, 1938). P. 1 ff.

KOLB, A. C. "John Fretz Funk, 1835–1930: An Appreciation II." *Mennonite Quarterly Review*, VI (October 1932). Pp. 250–63.

LANDING, JAMES. "Geographic Models of Old Order Amish Settlements." *The Professional Geographer*, XXI (July 1969). Pp. 238–43.

Mennonite Encyclopedia articles.

MILLER, ALEX R. "The Old Order That Does Not Change." *Mennonite Historical Bulletin*, XXVII (October 1966). Pp. 4–6.

MILLER, LEVI. "The Amish Word for Today." *The Christian Century*, XC (January 17, 1973). Pp. 70–73.

WENGER, J. C. "Jacob Wisler and the Old Order Mennonite Schism of 1872." *Mennonite Quarterly Review*, XXXIII (April 1959), pp. 108–31; (July 1959), pp. 215–39.

Miscellaneous

DEAN, WILLIAM WARD. "John F. Funk and the Mennonite Great Awakening." Ph.D. dissertation, University of Iowa, 1965.

FREY, KENNETH. D. "Comparative Occupational Aspirations of Old Order Mennonite and Non-Old Order Mennonite Farm Youth." M.A. thesis, University of Guelph, 1971.

General Journal of the Mennonite Brethren in Christ. 1905.

MARTIN, MARY. "The Church of Christ and the Old Mennonites in Waterloo County." Unpublished manuscript, Conrad Grebel College, University of Waterloo, 1970 (CGC).

Mennonite Yearbook and Directory. 1906.

SCHRAG, MARTIN. "The Brethren in Christ Attitude Toward the World." Ph.D. dissertation, Temple University, 1967.

Semi-Annual Conference Minutes, Berlin, September 12, 1884.

WEITZEL, NINA, and SHARON MATHIES. "Education in the Old Order Mennonites of Waterloo County." Term paper, Conrad Grebel College, 1971.

CHAPTER 12

Books

BROWN, FRANK, ed. *Mennonite Brethren Church, Winkler, Manitoba, 1888–1963: A 75th Anniversary Publication.* Winkler, Man., 1963.

Burwalde School, Diamond Jubilee Yearbook, 1888–1948. Winkler, Man., n.d.

DYCK, ISAAK M. *Auswanderung der Reinlander Mennoniten Gemeinde von Canada Nach Mexico.* Cuahtemoc, Chihuahua, Mexico: Imprenta Colonial, 1970.

FRANCIS, E. K. *In Search of Utopia: The Mennonites in Manitoba.* Altona, Man.: D. W. Friesen & Sons, 1955.

FUNK, JOHN F. *The Mennonite Church and Her Accusers.* Elkhart, Ind.: Mennonite Publishing Company, 1878.

GERBRANDT, HENRY J. *Adventure in Faith.* Altona, Man.: D. W. Friesen & Sons, 1970.

HARDER, LELAND. *Steinbach and its Churches.* Elkhart, Ind.: Mennonite Biblical Seminary, 1970.

HOLDEMANN, J. *Ein Spiegel der Wahrheit.* Lancaster, Pa.: Baehr, 1878.

HOLDEMAN MENNONITE CHURCH. *Centennial History of the Holdeman Mennonite Church, 1851–1951.* Wakarus, Ind., 1951.

KREHBIEL, H. P. *The History of the General Conference Mennonite Church of the Mennonites of North America.* 2 vols. Canton, Ohio: published by the author, 1889.

Mennonite Brethren Fundamentals of Faith. Hillsboro, Kans.: Mennonite Brethren Publishing House, n.d.

PENNER, J. M. *Concise History of the Church of God.* Hillsboro, Kans.: 1951.

REDEKOP, CALVIN. *The Old Colony Mennonites: Dilemmas of Ethnic Minority Life.* Baltimore: Johns Hopkins University Press, 1969.

REIMER, P. J. B., ed. *The Sesquicentennial Jubilee: Evangelical Mennonite Conference 1812–1962.* Steinbach, Man.: Evangelical Mennonite Conference, 1962.

UNRUH, A. H. *Die Geschichte der Mennoniten-Bruedergemeinde.* Hillsboro, Kans.: General Conference of the Mennonite Brethren Church of North America, 1955.

WARKENTIN, ABE. *Reflections on our Heritage: A History of Steinbach and the R.M. of Hanover from 1874.* Steinbach, Man.: Derksen Printers, 1971.

WIEBE, GERHARD. *Ursachen und Geschichte der Auswanderung der Mennoniten aus Russland nach Amerika.* Winnipeg, Man.: Druckerei der Nordwesten, 1900.

Yearbook of the Church of God in Christ Mennonite, 1944.

Articles

CLASSEN, DANIEL J. "Meade — A Changed Community." *Mennonite Life,* VI (July 1951). Pp. 14–17.

EPP, FRANK H. "Bolivia." *Mennonite Reporter,* II (October 30, 1972).

FRANCIS, E. K. "Tradition and Progress Among the Mennonites in Manitoba." *Mennonite Quarterly Review,* XXIV (October 1950). Pp. 312–28.

HILDEBRAND, MENNO. "The Sommerfelder Mennonites of Manitoba." *The Canadian Mennonite*, XVIII (November 27, 1970). Pp. 6–7, 15–6.

KRAHN, CORNELIUS. "The Old Colony Mennonites." *Mennonite Weekly Review*, XXIX (January 1951–August 1952).

Mennonite Encyclopedia articles.

TOEWS, JOHANN B. "A Brief Account of the Origin of the Church of God in Christ (Mennonite) of Manitoba, Canada." *Mennonite Historical Bulletin*, IX, 4 (1948).

WENGER, H. D. "The Church of God in Christ." *Mennonite Life*, XIV (July 1959). Pp. 122–23.

Miscellaneous

BUHLER, ABRAM J. "Schriftmaessige Erwaegung ueber den Zustand unserer Gemeinde." Unpublished manuscript, 1878 in which Wilhelm Rempel was the scribe. (CGC).

DOERKSEN, J. G. "History of the Mennonite Brethren of Canada." M.A. dissertation, University of Manitoba, 1963.

EPP, FRANK H. "The Making and Unmaking of Inter-Mennonite Periodicals." Unpublished research paper, Bethel College, 1956.

HIEBERT, CLARENCE. "The Holdeman People; A Study of the Church of God in Christ Mennonite, 1858–1969." Ph.D. dissertation, Case Western Reserve University, 1971.

REDEKOP, C. "The Relation of Cultural Assimilation to Changes in the Value System of the Sect." Ph.D. dissertation, University of Chicago, 1959.

SCHMITT, P. "Die Sommerfelder Mennoniten." Unpublished manuscript, Goshen College Historical Library, 1953.

TOEWS, J. A. "History of the Mennonite Brethren Church." Unpublished manuscript, in possession of the author, 1973.

WALL, J. P. "Statistics of the Old Colony Mennonites from 1910." Microfilm, Bethel College Historical Library, n.d.

CHAPTER 13

Books

BLACK, NORMAN FERGUS. *History of Saskatchewan and the Old North West*. Regina: North West Historical Company, 1913.

BOWMAN, A. S. *Homestead Days and Early Settlement of the Waterloo District South West of Guernsey, Saskatchewan*. Rosthern, Sask., 1951.

BROWN, R. C. *Canada's National Policy, 1883–1900: A Study in Canadian-American Relations*. Princeton: University Press, 1964.

CANADA. *Dominion Census Reports*. 1901, 1911, 1921.

DAWSON, CARL ADDINGTON. *Group Settlement: Ethnic Communities in Western Canada.* Toronto: Macmillan Company, 1936.

DAWSON, C. A., and E. R. YOUNG. *Pioneering in the Prairie Provinces: The Social Side of the Settlement Process.* Toronto: Macmillan Company, 1940.

Echoes of the First-All-Mennonite Convention in America. Hillsboro, Kans., 1913.

ENGLAND, ROBERT. *The Central European Immigrant in Canada.* Toronto: Macmillan Company, 1929.

EPP, FRANK H. *Mennonite Exodus: The Rescue and Resettlement of the Russian Mennonites Since the Communist Revolution.* Altona, Man.: D. W. Friesen & Sons, 1962.

GALBRAITH, J. F. *The Mennonites in Manitoba, 1874–1900: A Review of their Coming, their Progress, and their Present Prosperity.* Morden, Man.: The Chronicle Press, 1900.

GIBBON, JOHN MURRAY. *Canadian Mosaic.* Toronto: McClelland & Stewart, 1938.

HALLMAN, E. S. *The Hallman-Clemens Genealogy With a Family's Reminiscence.* Tuleta, Kans.: E. S. Hallman Family, n.d.

HAWKES, JOHN. *The Story of Saskatchewan and its People.* Regina: J. S. Clarke Company, 1924.

HEALY, DAVID. *U.S. Expansionism: The Imperialist Urge in the 1890s.* Madison: University of Wisconsin Press, 1970.

HEDGES, JAMES B. *Building the Canadian West, the Land and Colonization Policies of the Canadian Pacific Railway.* New York: Macmillan Company, 1939.

KANADISCHE MENNONITEN. *Bunte Bilder aus dem 50. Jaehrigen Siedlerleben zum Jubilaeumsjahr 1924, von Novokampus.* Winnipeg: Rundschau Publishing House, 1925.

MORTON, A. S. *History of Prairie Settlement.* Toronto: Macmillan Company, 1938.

PETERS, VICTOR. *All Things Common: The Hutterian Way of Life.* Minneapolis: University of Minnesota Press, 1966.

REMPEL, J. G. *Die Rosenorter Gemeinde in Saskatchewan: In Wort und Bild.* Rosthern, Sask.: D. H. Epp, 1950.

———. *Fuenfzig Jahre Konferenz-Bestrebungen, 1902–1952.* Steinbach, Man.: Derksen Printers, 1952.

SIMONS, MENNO. *Complete Writings of Menno Simons.* Scottdale, Pa.: Mennonite Publishing House, 1956.

STORMS, EVEREK RICHARD. *History of the United Missionary Church.* Elkhart, Ind.: Bethel Publishing Company, 1958.

SWALM, NOAH. *History of the United Missionary Church: Canadian Northwest Distribution, 1894–1962.* N.p., 1965.

UNRUH, A. H. *Die Geschichte der Mennoniten-Bruedergemeinde.* Hillsboro, Kans.: General Conference of the Mennonite Brethren Church of North America, 1955.

WENGER, J. C. (ed.). *Complete Writings of Menno Simons.* Scottdale, Pa.: Mennonite Publishing House, 1956.

WRIGHT, J. F. C. *Saskatchewan: The History of a Province*. Toronto: McClelland & Stewart, 1955.

Yearbook of the Northern District Conference of the Mennonite Brethren Church for the Year 1911.

Articles

ALLARD, WILLIAM A. "The Hutterites: Plain People of the West." *National Geographic*, CXXXVIII (July 1970). Pp. 98–125.

BARGEN, PETER F. "The Coming of the Mennonites to Alberta." *Mennonite Life*, XI (April 1956). Pp. 83–7.

———. "Mennonite Land Settlement Policies." *Mennonite Life*, XV (October 1960). Pp. 187–90.

———. "Four Mennonite Migrations Bring Settlers to Alberta." *The Canadian Mennonite*, II (July 1, 1955). Pp. 5–10.

BEYERS, N. E. "The All-Mennonite Convention." *Mennonite Life*, III (July 1948). Pp. 7–8, 10.

BURKHOLDER, ADELINE. "Recollections of Fifty Years: The Salem Congregation, 1910–1960." *Mennonite Historical Bulletin*, XXII (April 1961). P. 3.

DRIEDGER, LEO. "Hague-Osler Settlement." *Mennonite Life*, XIII (January 1958). Pp. 13–17.

———. "Louis Riel and the Mennonite Invasion." *The Canadian Mennonite*, XVIII (August 28, 1970). P. 6.

———. "Saskatchewan Old Colony Mennonites." *Mennonite Life*, XIII (April 1958). Pp. 63–66.

DYKE, GEORGE. "I Remember Gerhard Ens." *The Canadian Mennonite*, XV (June 13, 1967). P. 44.

FRANK, OLIVER. "Editorial." *Edmonton Bulletin*, October 24, 1898. P. 2.

EPP, PETER G. "At the Molotschnaya — A Visit, 1890." *Mennonite Life*, XXIV (October 1969). Pp. 151–55.

HEINRICHS, MARGARET. "Hague in Saskatchewan." *Mennonite Life*, XIII (January 1958). Pp. 18–19.

HERSHBERGER, GUY F. "Maintaining the Mennonite Rural Community." *Mennonite Quarterly Review*, XIV (October 1940). Pp. 214–33.

KLAASSEN, H. T. "Eine Kirche Entsteht auf der Westlichen Prairie." *Der Bote*, XLVI (July 29, 1969–August 19, 1969).

Mennonite Encyclopedia articles.

"Mennonite Migration to Alberta." *Star Phoenix*, July, 1949 and September 11, 1952.

"Mennonites." *Methodist Magazine*, June 1900. P. 508.

"The Mennonites, Picturesque Tillers of the Soil." *Niagara Falls Journal*, March 1892.

MUSSER, MARTIN D. "Correspondence: Guernsey, Saskatchewan." *Gospel Herald*, VI (August 14, 1913). P. 313.

PANABAKER, D. N. "Extending Our Frontiers in Canada's West." *Waterloo Historical Society*, 1934. Pp. 132–35.

REGIER, (FRAU) P. "Ueber die Entstehung der Rosenorter Gemeinde." *Christlicher Bundesbote*, November 10, 1931.

Saskatoon Star-Phoenix, article on Gerhard Ens, XLV, January 2, 1947. P. 3.

"Statistik der Mennoniten-Gemeinde." *Der Mitarbeiter*, VII (February 1913). P. 37.

TOEWS, D. "Mennonites of Canada." *Mennonite Quarterly Review*, XI (January 1937). Pp. 83–91.

WEBER, M. "The Part Played by Immigrants from Waterloo County to the Didsbury, Alberta Settlement, 1894." *Waterloo Historical Society*, XXXVIII (1950). Pp. 13–21.

ZADO, HELEN. "The Western Mennonites." *Maclean's Magazine*, June 1931. Pp. 23, 32, 61.

Miscellaneous

BARGEN, PETER FRANK. "The Mennonites of Alberta." M.A. thesis, University of British Columbia, 1953.

DRIEDGER, LEO. "A Sect in a Modern Society: A Case Study: The Old Colony Mennonites of Saskatchewan." M.A. thesis, University of Chicago, 1955.

GOVERNMENT DOCUMENTS

PAC. Department of Interior, Dominion Lands Branch, Record Group 15, Vols. 232 and 233. Subject files containing letters addressed to various officials of the department, together with departmental memorandum and other relevant documents.

PAC. Department of Interior, Immigration Branch, Central Registry Series, Record Group 76, Vol. 173, 174, 175 & 176. Volumes entitled "Mennonites" and "Hutterites" relating to immigration matters.

PAC. Privy Council Office, Orders-in-Council, Record Group 2, 1.

Revised Statutes of Canada, Militia Act c. 41, Sect. 21, Sub-Sect. 3.

HIEBERT, CLARENCE. "The Holdeman People: A Study of the Church of God in Christ Mennonite, 1858–1969." Ph.D. dissertation, Case Western Reserve University, 1971.

KEMBALL, WALTER A. "Group Settlement in the Canadian West (The Mennonites)." M.A. thesis, McGill University, n.d.

REGEHR, THEODORE DAVID. "The Canadian Northern Railway: Agent of National Growth, 1896–1911." Ph.D. dissertation, University of Alberta, 1967.

SAWATZKY, ARON. "The Mennonites of Alberta and their Assimilation." M.A. thesis, University of Alberta, 1964.

WARKENTIN, JOHN H. "The Mennonite Settlement of Southern Manitoba." Ph.D. dissertation, University of Toronto, 1960.

YOUNG, MARY M. "The Mennonites of Tofield." Ph.D. dissertation, University of Alberta, 1972.

CHAPTER 14

Books

ANDERSON, J. T. M. *The Education of the New-Canadian.* Toronto: J. M. Dent & Sons, 1918.

CREIGHTON, D. G., et al. *Minorities, Schools and Politics.* Toronto: University of Toronto Press, 1969.

DYCK, ISAAK M. *Auswanderung der Reinland Mennoniten Gemeinde von Canada nach Mexico.* Cuahtemoc, Chihuahua, Mexico: Imprenta Colonial, 1970.

EPP, FRANK H. *Mennonite Exodus: The Rescue and Resettlement of the Russian Mennonites Since the Communist Revolution.* Altona, Man.: D. W. Friesen & Sons, 1962.

EWERT, HEINRICH H. *The Mennonites.* Winnipeg: General Conference of Mennonites in Canada, 1932.

FISHMAN, JOSHUA A., et al. *Language Loyalty in the United States: The Maintenance and Perpetuation of Non-English Mother Tongues by American and Religious Groups.* The Hague: Mouton & Company, 1966.

FRANCIS, E. K. *In Search of Utopia: The Mennonites in Manitoba.* Altona, Man.: D. W. Friesen & Sons, 1955.

GERBRANDT, HENRY J. *Adventure in Faith.* Altona, Man.: D. W. Friesen & Sons, 1970.

HARTZLER, JOHN E. *Education Among the Mennonites of America.* Danvers, Ill.: Central Mennonite Publication Board, 1925.

JANZEN, J. H. *David Toews: A Biographical Sketch.* Waterloo, Ont.: 1939.

KLASSEN, A. J. *The Bible School Story: Fifty Years of Mennonite Brethren Bible Schools.* Winnipeg: Mennonite Brethren Bible College, 1963.

MCGREGOR, F. A. *The Fall and Rise of Mackenzie King: 1911–1919.* Toronto: Macmillan Company of Canada, 1962.

NEWCOMBE, CHARLES K. *Special Report on Bi-Lingual Schools in Manitoba.* Department of Education, February 1, 1916.

PETERS, G. H. *Blumen am Wegrand.* Gretna, Man.: published by the author, n.d.

Plan Zur Foerderung des Religionsunterrichtes in den Volksschulen Innerhalb der Mennonitischen Ansiedlunge Manitobas. Gretna, Man.: n.d.

PRESTON, RICHARD A. *Canada and "Imperial Defense": A Study of the Origins of the British Commonwealth's Defense Organization, 1867–1919.* Durham, N.C.: Duke University Press, 1973.

REDEKOP, CALVIN. *The Old Colony Mennonites: Dilemmas of Ethnic Minority Life.* Baltimore: Johns Hopkins University Press, 1969.

SCHAEFER, P. J. *Heinrich H. Ewert: Lehrer, Erzieher, und Prediger der Mennoniten.* Gretna, Man.: Mennonite Youth Organization, 1945.

———. *Woher? Wohin? Mennoniten.* Altona, Man.: D. W. Friesen & Sons, 1946. 4 vols.

SISSONS, C. B. *Bi-Lingual Schools in Canada.* Toronto: J. M. Dent & Sons, 1917.

STANLEY, GEORGE F. G. *Canada's Soldiers: The Military History of an Unmilitary People.* Toronto: Macmillan Company of Canada, 1960.

STORMS, E. R. *History of the United Missionary Church.* Elkhart, Ind.: Bethel Publishing Company, 1958.

WEIR, G. M. *The Separate School Question in Canada.* Toronto: Ryerson Press, 1934.

WIEBE, GERHARD. *Ursachen und Geschichte der Auswanderung der Mennoniten aus Russland nach Amerika.* Winnipeg: Druckerei der Nordwesten, 1900.

Articles

"Agreement with Federal Government Stands in Way of Province Abolishing Bilingualism." *Winnipeg Tribune*, February 9, 1916.

BERGEN, ELIZABETH. "Rhodes Scholar from Gretna." *Red River Valley Echo,* January 10, 1973 (quoted from *Manitoba Free Press,* August 30, 1912).

"Bi-Lingualism and Compulsory Education in Manitoba." *Canadian Annual Review*, 1916. Pp. 670–87.

"The Bi-Lingual Schools of Manitoba." *Manitoba Free Press*, XL (February 4, 5, 6, 7, 8, 10, 11, 12, 1913). Series of 8 articles.

Der Mitarbeiter articles.

"A Description of the First Reaction of the Conservative Mennonites to the Appointment of a Mennonite School Inspector as Given by Novokampus" in *Kanadische Mennoniten — Zum Jubilaeumsjahr.* Winnipeg: Rundschau Publishing House, 1924.

"Education in Manitoba During 1916." *Canadian Annual Review*, 1916. Pp. 684–87.

EWERT, H. H. "Mennoniten in Manitoba." *Bundesbote-Kalendar*, 1903. Pp. 31–35.

FRANCIS, E. K. "The Mennonite School Problem in Manitoba." *Mennonite Quarterly Review*, XXVII (July 1953). Pp. 204–37.

———. "Tradition and Progress Among the Mennonites in Manitoba." *Mennonite Quarterly Review.* XXIV (October 1950). Pp. 312–28.

GOERZ, H. "Wenn in des Lebens Angst und Not," in *Gedichte.* Winnipeg: published by the author, n.d.

HAYWARD, VICTORIA. "Mennonites in Manitoba." *Canadian Magazine*, LVIII (November 1921). Pp. 63–70.

"Judges of King's Bench Clash on Bilingualism." *Winnipeg Tribune*, February 6, 1916.

LOEWEN, GERHAND. "Gebet" in *Feldblumen*. Steinbach, Man.: Arnold Dyck, 1946.

MCKEGNEY, PATRICIA. "The German Schools in Waterloo County, 1851–1913." *Waterloo Historical Society*, LVIII (1970). Pp. 54–56.

Mennonite Encyclopedia articles.

"Mennonites and Excommunication." *The Regina Leader*, January 20, 1909. P. 4.

"The Mennonites of Manitoba." *Free Press News Bulletin*, XXXVIII (November 26, 1910). Pp. 44.

PETERS, G. H. "Der Werdegang der Mennonitischen Lehranstalt zu Gretna, Manitoba." *Warte-Jahrbuch*, I (1943). Pp. 20–26.

REMPEL, D. G. "The Mennonite Commonwealth in Russia: A Sketch of its Founding and Endurance, 1789–1919." *Mennonite Quarterly Review*, XLVII (October 1973). Pp. 259–308.

SCHAEFER, P. J. "Der Neubau der Gretnaer Gemeinschaftsschule." *Warte-Jahrbuch*, II (1944). Pp. 15–17.

———. "Heinrich H. Ewert — Educator of Kansas and Manitoba." *Mennonite Life*, III (October 1948). Pp. 18–23.

STAEBLER, H. L. "Mackenzie King." *Waterloo Historical Society*, XXXVIII (1950). Pp. 10–13.

THORNTON, R. S. (Minister of Education). "Bi-Lingual Schools." Address in the Legislature, Winnipeg, January 12, 1916.

Miscellaneous

BERGEN, JOHN J. "An Historical Study of Education in the Municipality of Rhineland." M.Ed. thesis, University of Manitoba, 1959.

BURKHOLDER, L. J. *Papers* (CGC).

EPP, FRANK H. "The History of Rosthern Junior College." Unpublished manuscript, 1970.

FRIESEN, A. "The Relation of the Various Manitoba Mennonite Groups Toward Each Other During the School Crisis of 1916–1919." M.A. thesis, University of Manitoba, 1959.

FRIESEN, ISAAC I. "The Mennonites of Western Canada with Special Reference to Education." M.Ed. thesis, University of Saskatchewan, 1934.

KLASSEN, PETER G. "A History of Mennonite Education in Canada, 1786–1960." Ph.D. dissertation, University of Toronto, 1970.

————. "A History of Mennonite Education in Manitoba." M.Ed. thesis, University of Manitoba, 1958.

Manitoba: Report of the Department of Education, 1891.

PUBLIC ARCHIVES OF CANADA

PAC. Department of Interior, Immigration Branch, Central Registry Series, Record Group 76, 1, Vols. 173, 174, 175, & 176.

PAC. Privy Council Office, Dormants, Record Group 2, 3, Vol. 155. Memorandum, Correspondence, Petitions, etc., submitted which did not result in the production of an Order-in-Council.

PAC. Robert L. Borden Papers, M.G. 26, H, RLB 1167 (C-342). A subject file entitled "Mennonites" in the Borden Papers containing all references to as well as letters from and to Mennonites in years 1916–18 (105 entries).

PAC. Wilfrid Laurier Papers, M.G. 26, G, 1a, Vol. 668 (C-900). Correspondence and other related materials for 1911.

PAC. W. L. Mackenzie King Papers, M.G. 26, J, 1, Vols. 12 & 17. Correspondence together with enclosures and replies of the Prime Minister.

SASKATCHEWAN ARCHIVES BOARD (SAB) documents and papers.

THIELMAN, GEORGE GERHARD. "The Canadian Mennonites: A Study of an Ethnic Group in Relation to the State and Community with Emphasis on Factors Contributing to Success or Failure of its Adjustment to Canadian Ways of Living." Ph.D. dissertation, Western Reserve University, 1955.

WILLOWS, ANDREW. "A History of the Mennonites, Particularly in Manitoba." M.A. thesis, University of Manitoba, 1924.

CHAPTER 15

Books

BAINTON, R. H. *Christian Attitudes Toward War and Peace.* Nashville, Tenn.: Abingdon Press, 1960.

DETWEILER, RICHARD. *Mennonite Statements on Peace, 1915–1966.* Scottdale, Pa.: Herald Press, 1968.

DYCK, ISAAK M. *Auswanderung der Reinlander Mennoniten Gemeinde von Canada nach Mexico.* Cuahtemoc, Chihuahua, Mexico: Imprenta Colonial, 1970.

EPP, FRANK H. *Mennonite Exodus: The Rescue and Resettlement of the Russian Mennonites Since the Communist Revolution.* Altona, Man.: D. W. Friesen & Sons, 1962.

EWERT, BENJAMIN. *Wichtige Dokumente Betreffs der Wehrfreiheit der Mennoniten in Kanada.* Gretna, Man.: 1917.

GOERZ, A. *Ein Beitrag zur Geschichte des Forsteidienstes der Mennoniten in Russland.* Gross Tokmak, Russia: Lenzmann, 1907.

GRODZINS, NORTON. *The Loyal and the Disloyal: Social Boundaries of*

Patriotism and Treason. Chicago: University of Chicago Press, 1956.

HARTZLER, J. S. *Mennonites in the World War or Nonresistance Under Test.* Scottdale, Pa.: Mennonite Publishing House, 1921.

HERSCHBERGER, GUY F. *War, Peace, and Nonresistance.* Scottdale, Pa.: Mennonite Publishing House, 1944.

KNISS, LLOYD A. *I Couldn't Fight: The Story of a C.O. in World War I.* Scottdale, Pa.: Herald Press, 1971.

LEATHERMAN, NOAH. *Diary Kept by Noah L. Leatherman While in Camp During World War I.* Linden, Alta.: Aaron L. Toews, 1951.

MORRIS, PHILIP H. *The Canadian Patriotic Fund: Records of Its Activities.* N.p., n.d.

NECKAR, HEILBORN A. *Die Mennoniten-Gemeinden in Russland waehrend der Kriegsund Revolutions Jahre, 1914 bis 1920.* Kommissions Verlag der Mennonitischen Fluechtingsfuersorge, 1921.

PETERSON, H. C. *Opponents of War, 1917–1918.* Madison: University of Wisconsin Press, 1957.

SWALM, E. J. *Nonresistance under Test: Experiences of the C.O.'s in World Wars I and II.* Nappanee, Ind.: Evangelical Publishing House, 1949.

VARIOUS AUTHORITIES. *Canada and the Great World War.* 6 vols. Vol. II, *Days of Preparation.* Toronto: United Publisher of Canada, c. 1918.

WRIGHT, J. F. C. *Saskatchewan: The History of a Province.* Toronto: McClelland & Stewart, 1955.

Articles

"The Alien Enemy Question of 1918." *Canadian Annual Review* (1919). Pp. 578–81.

"Aliens and Alien Enemy Influence in Canada." *Canadian Annual Review* (1917). Pp. 434–39.

"Anti-Recruiting Revivalists are Deported to US." *Windsor Record,* November 16, 1917.

"Attitudes of Canadian Churches in the War." *Canadian Annual Review* (1917). Pp. 410–17.

BAHNMANN, N. W. "Der Ausgang des Prozesses gegen den Lehrdienst der Altkolonier Gemeinde bei Hague, Sask." *Der Mitarbeiter,* XI (November 1916). P. 3.

"Bestaetigung der gegebenen Versicherung in Angelegenheit der Wehrfrage." *Der Mitarbeiter,* XI (January 1917). Pp. 6–7.

"Canadian War Notes of 1916." *Canadian Annual Review* (1916). Pp. 444–47.

"Carnegie on War." *Christian Monitor,* III (March 1911). P. 93.

"The Catholic Church in Quebec and the War." *Canadian Annual Review* (1917). Pp. 502–9.

"The Churches and the War in 1916." *Canadian Annual Review* (1916). Pp. 434–37.

"The Churches of Canada and the War." *Canadian Annual Review* (1916). Pp. 338–65.

DAVIES, BLODWEN. "From Militia Tax to Relief." *Mennonite Life*, V (October 1950). Pp. 27–28.

"Die Denkschrift welche die Mennoniten des Kanadischen Regierung am 8. Januar ueberreicht haben." *Der Mitarbeiter*, XI (January 1917). Pp. 4–6.

"Disapprove of Mennonite Law." *Regina Leader*, September 26, 1917. P. 1.

"Ein Bittgesuch der Mennoniten von Ontario an die Kanadische Regierung." *Der Mitarbeiter*, XII (November 1917). Pp. 1–2.

ENNS, GERHARD. "Waterloo North and Conscription, 1917." *Waterloo Historical Society*, LI (1963). Pp. 60–69.

EWERT, BENJAMIN. "Bemuehungen zur Sicherung der Wehrfreiheit fuer unsere ungetauften Juenglinge." *Der Mitarbeiter*, XII (June 1918). Pp. 3–7.

——. "Die Mennoniten und die Wehrfrage." *Der Mitarbeiter*, XI (January 1917). Pp. 1–4.

——. "Predigerzusammenkunft in Altona, Manitoba." *Der Mitarbeiter*, XII (June 1918). P. 7.

GRIMM, GEORGE S. "War Not in Harmony with Christian Civilization." *Gospel Herald*, V (February 20, 1913). Pp. 738–39.

——. "What is War?" *Gospel Herald*, III (March 16, 1911). P. 790.

GROSS, LEONARD. "Alternatives to War: A Story Through Documents." *Gospel Herald*, LXVI (January 16, 1973). Pp. 52–55.

HEICK, W. H. "The Lutherans of Waterloo County During World War I." *Waterloo Historical Society*, L (1962). Pp. 23–32.

HERSHEBERGER, GUY F. "Is Alternative Service Desirable and Possible?" *Mennonite Quarterly Review*, IX (January 1935). Pp. 20–35.

HORSCH, JOHN. "A Popular Objection to Nonresistance." *Gospel Herald*, V (March 27, 1913). Pp. 819–20.

KRAHN, CORNELIUS. "Public Service in Russia." *The Mennonite*, LVIII (June 22, 1943). P. 2.

"The Mennonites." *The Regina Leader*, September 25, 1918. P. 4.

"Mennonites and Others." *Hamilton Herald*, May 5, 1919.

"Mennonites Free of Military Duty." *Steinbach Post*, February 7, 1917, quoting a dispatch from the Toronto *Mail and Empire*.

"The Mennonites: The War Veteran." *Calgary Eye-Opener*, October 5, 1918.

"Methodist Church in Relation to the War." *Hamilton Times*, October 17, 1918.

NORRIS, PAUL. "The Mennonites in Western Canada." *The Winnipeg Telegram*, September 21, 1918.

O'DONOVAN, P. "Exemptions from Military Service." *Saturday Night*, May 6, 1939.

OESCH, W. W. "The Possibility of World Peace." *Christian Monitor*, III (August 1911). Pp. 245–46.

"Pacifism in Canada." *Canadian Annual Review* (1916). Pp. 445–46.

"Pacifists in the United States: Peace Organization and the War." *Canadian Annual Review* (1917). Pp. 270–77.

"Peace Movements in America." *American Studies*, XIII (Spring 1972). P. 210.

PETERS, FRANK H. "Non-combatant Service Then and Now." *Mennonite Life*, X (January 1955). Pp. 31–35.

POWELL, W. I. "Nonresistance." *Gospel Herald*, VI (May 29, 1913). Pp. 130, 131, 133.

"A Proper Stand on the Mennonite Question." *Saturday Night*, October 19, 1918.

"Rather Die Than Slay, So Mennonites Will Not Fight." *Toronto Daily Star*, November 25, 1916.

RESSLER, J. A. "What the Bible Teaches." *Gospel Herald*, V (May 9, 1912). P. 82.

SMITH, C. HENRY. "The Forces that Make for Peace." Part III, *Christian Monitor*, II (May 1910). Pp. 532–33.

SUDERMANN, JACOB. "The Origin of Mennonite State Service in Russia, 1870–1880." *Mennonite Quarterly Review*, XVII (January 1943). Pp. 23–46.

TOEWS, JOHN B. "The Russian Mennonites and the Military Question, 1921–1927." *Mennonite Quarterly Review*, XLIII (April 1969). Pp. 153–68.

"Visit of Governor General." *Berlin Daily Telegraph*, May 9, 1914. P. 1.

"War Problems of Saskatchewan, Legislative Session." *Canadian Annual Review* (1917). Pp. 630–37.

"Western Furore Over Exemption of Mennonites." *Ottawa Citizen*, September 25, 1918. P. 6.

WITMER, JOHN. "A World War I Conscientious Objector." *Mennonite Historical Bulletin*, XXIV (October 1963). Pp. 3–4.

Miscellaneous

BEARINGER, NOAH M. *Papers*. CGC.

BOUDREAU, JOSEPH A. "The Enemy Alien Problems in Canada, 1914–1921." Ph.D. dissertation, University of California, 1965.

British Statutes

COFFMAN, S. F. *Papers*. CGC.

Court Martial of Allen B. Christophel. Hist. Mss. 1-319. AMC.

EPP, FRANK H. "The Story of Rosthern Junior College." Unpublished manuscript, 1970.

EWERT, BENJAMIN. *Papers*. CMBC.

Minutes of the Executive Committee of the Mennonite Conference of Ontario, August 4, 1917.

PUBLIC ARCHIVES OF CANADA (PAC)
Adam Shortt Papers, M.G. 30, D. 45, Vol. 57.
Department of Interior, Immigration Branch, Record Group 76, 1, Vols. 173, 174, 175, & 176.
Department of Labour, Lacelle Files, Record Group 27, Vol. 132, 601 (Justice Adamson File). Article by P. C. Locke, describing his involvement in convincing the Mennonites of southern Manitoba to register in the national inventory of 1916.
Privy Council Office, Orders-in-Council, Record Group 2, 1.
Robert L. Borden Papers, M.G. 26, H, RLB 1167 and RLB 1414.
W. L. Mackenzie King Papers, M.G. 26, J, 1.
SAWATSKY, RODNEY JAMES. "The Influence of Fundamentalism on Mennonite Nonresistance 1908–1944." M.A. thesis, University of Minnesota, 1973.
Statutes of Canada.

CHAPTER 16

Books

ALLEN, RICHARD. *The Social Passion: Religion and Social Reform in Canada 1914–1928*. Toronto: University of Toronto Press, 1971.
Canada Gazette, 1917.
EPP, FRANK H., ed. *I Would Like to Dodge the Draft-Dodger, But . . .* Waterloo, Ont.: Conrad Press, 1970.
———. *Mennonite Exodus: The Rescue and Resettlement of the Russian Mennonites Since the Communist Revolution*. Altona, Man.: D. W. Friesen & Sons, 1962.
FRANCIS, E. K. *In Search of Utopia: The Mennonites in Manitoba*. Altona, Man.: D. W. Friesen & Sons, 1955.
GRANT, J. W. *The Church in the Canadian Era*. Toronto: McGraw-Hill Ryerson Limited, 1972.
GROSS, PAUL S. *The Hutterite Way*. Saskatoon, Sask.: Freeman Publishing Company, 1965.
HERSHBERGER, GUY F. *War, Peace, and Nonresistance*. Scottdale, Pa.: Mennonite Publishing House, 1944.
HIEBERT, P. C. *Feeding the Hungry*. Scottdale, Pa.: Mennonite Central Committee, 1929.
HOFER, D. M. *Die Hungersnot in Russland*. Chicago: Krimmer Mennonite Brethren Publishing House, 1924.
HOFER, P. *The Hutterian Brethren and Their Beliefs*. Starbuck, Man.: Hutterian Brethren of Manitoba, 1955.
HORSCH, JOHN. *The Hutterian Brethren, 1528–1931: A Story of Martyrdom and Loyalty*. Goshen, Ind.: Mennonite Historical Society, 1931.
HOSTETLER, J. A. *Hutterite Life*. Scottdale, Pa.: Herald Press, 1965.
———. *The Hutterites in North America*. New York: Holt, 1967.

MCNAUGHT, KENNETH. *A Prophet in Politics: A Biography of J. S. Woodsworth.* Toronto: University of Toronto Press, 1959.

PETERS, G. A. *Die Hungersnot in den Mennonitischen Kolonien.* Scottdale, Pa.: Herald Press, 1932.

PETERS, KLAAS. *Die Bergthaler Mennoniten.* Hillsboro, Kans.: Mennonite Brethren Publishing House, 1924.

PETERS, VICTOR. *All Things Common: The Hutterian Way of Life.* Minneapolis: University of Minnesota Press, 1966.

REDEKOP, CALVIN W. *The Old Colony Mennonites: Dilemmas of Ethnic Minority Life.* Baltimore: Johns Hopkins University Press, 1969.

RILEY, M. P. *The Hutterite Brethren: An Annotated Bibliography with Special Reference to South Dakota Hutterite Colonies.* Brookings, S. Da.: University of South Dakota, 1965.

SMITH, W. G. *A Study in Canadian Immigration.* Toronto: Ryerson Press, 1920.

SPRUNGER, LEITH L., JAMES C. JUHNKE, and JOHN D. WALTNER. *Voices Against War.* North Newton, Kans.: Bethel College, 1973.

TOEWS, JOHN B. *Lost Fatherland: The Story of the Mennonite Emigration from Soviet Russia, 1921–1927.* Scottdale, Pa.: Herald Press, 1967.

YODER, SANFORD C. *For Conscience Sake: A Study of Mennonite Migrations Resulting from the World War.* Scottdale, Pa.: Herald Press, 1945.

Articles

BLISS, J. M. "The Methodist Church and World War I." *Canadian Historical Review*, XLIX (September 1968).

"Canadian Labour and the War: Alien Problems." *Canadian Annual Review* (1916). Pp. 430–33.

"Censorship Notice." *Canada Gazette*, June 26, 1919, P. 30.

DICK, D. J. Article in *Our Visitor,* translated from *Unser Besucher,* Mountain Lake, Minnesota XVIII (April 15, 1919), PAC. RG. 76-F58764-V3.

"Educational Conditions in Manitoba." *Canadian Annual Review* (1920). Pp. 138–249.

"Educational Conditions in Manitoba During 1919." *Canadian Annual Review* (1919). Pp. 548-53.

EPP, FRANK H. "The True North: The Church that Disappeared, Whose Influence Lives On." *Mennonite Reporter*, IV (March 18, 1974). P. 11. One of a series of articles on subject.

EPP, J. P. "The Mennonite Selbstschutz in the Ukraine: An Eye Witness Account." *Mennonite Life*, XXVI (July 1971). Pp. 138–42.

EWERT, H. H. "Die Behandlung der Eingezogenen Mennonitischen Juenglinge in den Ruestungslagern der Vereinigten Staaten." *Der Mitarbeiter*, XII (November 1917). Pp. 2–3.

FRETZ, A. J. "The Exodus to Canada." *Waterloo Historical Society*, XVII (1929). Pp. 133–35.

"German Organizations in the United States." *Canadian Annual Review* (1916). Pp. 220–27.

"German Propaganda and Plots in the United States." *Canadian Annual Review* (1917). Pp. 255–79.

"German Propaganda: U.S. Aliens and Pacifists." *Canadian Annual Review* (1918). Pp. 252–61.

HOFER, DAVID, WALTER ELIAS, and JOSEPH KLEINSASSER. "The Hutterite Brethren and War." *Gospel Herald*, X (August 9, 1917), Pp. 354–55.

HOFER, H. M. "Paul Tschetter's Diary." *Mennonite Quarterly Review*, V (April 1931), pp. 112–27, and (July 1931), pp. 198–219.

JUHNKE, JAMES C. "The Agony of Civic Isolation: Mennonites in World War I." *Mennonite Life*, XXV (January 1970). Pp. 27–33.

———. "CO's and Chemical Warfare in the First World War." *Mennonite Historical Bulletin*, XXX (October 1969). P. 4.

———. "John Schrag Espionage Case." *Mennonite Life*, XXII (July 1967). Pp. 121–22.

KLASSEN, CORNELIUS F. "The Mennonites in Russia, 1917–1928." *Mennonite Quarterly Review*, VI (April 1932). Pp. 69–80.

"Mennonites May Flee to Canada to Escape Army." *Daily Oklahoman*, Oklahoma City, June 9, 1918.

"Pacifism in Canada." *Canadian Annual Review* (1916). Pp. 445–46.

SCHMIDT, JOHN F. "Probing the Impact of World War I Experience." *Mennonite Life*, XXV (December 1971). Pp. 161–62.

SCHULTZ, HAROLD J. "Search for Utopia: The Exodus of Russian Mennonites to Canada, 1917–1927." *Journal of Church and State*, XI (1969). Pp. 487–512.

TEICHROEW, ALLEN. "World War I and the Mennonite Migration to Canada to Avoid the Draft." *Mennonite Quarterly Review*, XLV (July 1971). Pp. 219–49.

THIELMAN, GEORGE G. "The Mennonite Selbstschutz in the Ukraine During the Revolution." *The New Review: A Journal of East European History*, X (March 1970). Pp. 50–60.

TOEWS, JOHN B. "The Origins and Activities of the Mennonite Selbstschutz in the Ukraine, 1918–1919." *Mennonite Quarterly Review*, XLVI (January 1972). Pp. 5–40.

UNRUH, JOHN D. "The Hutterites During World War I." *Mennonite Life*, XXIII (July 1969). Pp. 130–37.

"US Alien Enemies and German Propaganda: Pacifists and the War." *Canadian Annual Review* (1918). Pp. 253–61.

WILLMS, A. M. "The Brethren Known as Hutterites." *The Canadian Journal of Economics and Political Science*, XXIV (August 1958). P. 392.

Miscellaneous

BOLDT, EDWARD P. "The Hutterites of Alberta." M.A. thesis, University of Alberta.

BOUDREAU, J. A. "The Enemy Alien Problem in Canada, 1914–1921." Ph.D. dissertation, University of California, 1965.

COFFMAN, S. F. *Papers*. CGC.

Commons Debates.

FRIESEN, ABRAHAM. "Emigration in Mennonite History with Special Reference to the Conservative Mennonite Emigration from Canada to Mexico and South America After World War One." M.A. thesis, University of Manitoba, 1962.

FRIESEN, LYLE. "The Russian Mennonite Selbstschutz in its Historical Perspective." Conrad Grebel College research paper, 1973.

HARDER, D. "Von Canada Nach Mexico." Manuscript Microfilm in Bethel College Historical Library, North Newton, Kans.

HOLSINGER, DONALD C. "Pressures Affecting the Mennonite German-Americans in Central Kansas During World War I." A Bethel College research paper, 1970.

KLAASSEN, JACOB. "Memories and Notations About My Life: 1867–1948." Translated by his grandson, Walter Klaassen, 1964.

MENNONITE RESEARCH FOUNDATION. Conscientious Objectors in World War I. Box 1-5, V-7-19. AMC.

PUBLIC ARCHIVES OF CANADA (PAC)
Department of Interior, Immigration Branch, Record Group 76, 1, Vols. 173, 174, 175, & 176.
Department of National Defence, Army Headquarters Records, Record Group 24, C. 1, Vol. 115.
Department of the Secretary of State, Chief Press Censor — Correspondence, Record Group 6, E, Vol. 13 & 138. The first organization ever established to enforce censorship restrictions in Canada. These records contain information on subversive elements in the country, public opinion and war propaganda.
Privy Council Office, *Orders-in-Council*, Record Group 2, 1.
Robert L. Borden Papers, M.G. 26, H, RLB, 1167.

REMPEL, RON. "Attitudes of the Mennonite Conscientious Objector in World War I Army Camps." Goshen College research paper, 1968.

TIECHROEW, ALLEN. "Accommodation and Escape: The Mennonite Response to World War I." Bethel College research paper, 1969.

YODER, SANFORD C. "Mennonite Migrations Resulting from Conscientious Rejection of World War Demands." S.T.D. dissertation, Gordon Divinity School, Wenham, Mass., 1939.

Libraries and Archives

Mennonite Archives and Historical Libraries

Bethel College Historical Library and Archives, North Newton, Kansas (BCHL).

Contains one of the largest collections of Mennonitica in North America. Useful especially for this study are documents relating to immigration in the 1870s, more particularly the Jacob Y. Shantz papers.

Canadian Mennonite Bible College Library, 600 Shaftesbury Blvd. Winnipeg 29, Manitoba (CMBC).

For this study the Benjamin Ewert Collection was of special significance. Most valuable also is the College's "Bibliography of Anabaptist-Mennonite Historical Works," compiled by Victor D. Kliewer.

Conrad Grebel College and Archives, University of Waterloo, Waterloo, Ontario (CGC).

A 19-page archives inventory summarizes this most valuable source for Ontario Mennonite history. Of special value are the David Bergey, L. J. Burkholder, S. F. Coffman, Christian Eby, J. C. Fretz, and Daniel Hoch Collections. Also available here is the "Bibliography: Mennonite Imprints in Ontario: A Preliminary Checklist," compiled by Victor G. Wiebe.

Goshen College Mennonite Historical Library and Archives of the Mennonite Church, Goshen, Indiana (AMC).
> One of the largest collections of Mennonitica in North America. Of special important for this study was the John F. Funk Collection.

Menno Simons Historical Library/Archives, Eastern Mennonite College, Harrisonburg, Virginia (MSHL).
> The John H. Oberholtzer documents.

Public Libraries and Archives

All the provincial, and some regional, libraries and archives contain Mennonite listings, but for the period of this book, the following were most helpful.

Department of Public Records and Archives, Queen's Park, Toronto, Ontario.
> Useful materials here are the Mennonite references in the Campbell (Sir Alexander), Cartwright, Young (James), and Blodwen Davies papers, as well as several miscellaneous items. The *Journals of the Legislative Assembly* were a source for the first half of the nineteenth century.

Kitchener Public Library Reference Department, Kitchener, Ontario.
> Useful particularly for its newspapers, clipping files, and the collection of the Waterloo Historical Society.

Provincial Library of Manitoba, Winnipeg, Manitoba.
> Of special value are the historical scrapbooks on Mennonites.

Saskatchewan Archives Board, University of Saskatchewan, Regina and Saskatoon.
> Most useful sources, in addition to several miscellaneous items, are the Ministerial Papers of Charles Avery Dunning; the 1908 Minutes of Evidence, Commission of Inquiry re practices of Old Colony Mennonite Church; and the Latta Papers.

Public Archives of Canada (PAC)

Improved indexing and more intensive searching has uncovered some Mennonite sources for the first time. The following document collections were useful for this study.

Executive Council, State Papers, Upper Canada, R.G. 1, E3, Vol. 7.
> Petitions, correspondence, reports, and other documents submitted in support of matter brought to the consideration of the Executive Council of Upper Canada, 1791–1841.

Department of Agriculture, General Correspondence of the Minister, R.G. 17, A1, Vol. 62. Department correspondence dealing with Mennonite immigration and commitment of land grants to Mennonites.

Department of Indian Affairs, Deputy Superintendent General's Office, Correspondence, R.G. 10, A2, Vols. 26 and 27. Letters received by the Deputy Superintendent General and by other officials of the Indian Department, together with various office records, 1789–1830.

Department of the Interior, R.G. 15, B-1(a), Vol. 292 #917620(1) and Vol. 293 #917620(2). Correspondence relating to Swift Current Reserve; Box 1124 #270476. Correspondence relating to Hague-Osler Reserve.

Department of the Interior, Dominion Lands Branch, R.G. 15, Vols. 232 and 233. Subject files containing letters addressed to various officials of the department, together with departmental memorandum and other relevant documents.

Department of the Interior, Immigration Branch, Central Registry Series, R.G. 76, I, Vols. 173, 174, 175, and 176. Volumes entitled "Mennonites and Hutterites" relating to immigration matters.

Department of Labour, Lacelle Files, R.G. 27, Vols. 132, 601(Justice Adamson file). Article by P. C. Locke, describing his involvement in convincing the Mennonites of southern Manitoba to register in the national inventory of 1916.

Department of National Defence, Army Headquarters Records, R.G. 24, C. 1, Vol. 115.

Department of the Secretary of State, Chief Press Censor — Correspondence, R.G. 6, Vols. 13 and 128. The first organization ever established to enforce censorship restrictions in Canada. These records contain information on subversive elements in the country, public opinion, and war propaganda.

Immigration Branch, Halifax and Quebec Passenger Lists, R.G. 76, Passenger Lists #9-11 (Microfilm C4528–C4530). Also available CGC, CMBC, and MCHL.

Robert L. Borden Papers, M.G. 26, H, RLB 1167 (C-342). A subject file entitled "Mennonites" in the Borden Papers containing all references to as well as letters from and to Mennonites in years 1916–18 (105 entries).

W. L. Mackenzie King Papers, M.G. 26, J, 1, Vols. 12 and 17. Correspondence, together with enclosures and replies of the Prime Minister.

Wilfrid Laurier Papers, M.G. 26, G, 1a, Vol. 668 (C-900). Correspondence and other related materials for 1911.

Adam Shortt Papers, M.G. 30, D45, Vol. 57. Copies of historical documents compiled by Dr. Adam Shortt (1859–1931), economist and historian. Dr. Shortt made the Mennonite emigration from Russia of 1872–3 one of his subjects of research.

Privy Council Office, Orders-in-Council, R.G. 2. All reports or submissions of the Committee of the Privy Council which have received the Governor General's approval.

Privy Council Office, Dormants, R.G. 2, 3, Vol. 155. Memorandum, Correspondence, Petitions, etc., submitted which did not result in the production of an Order-in-Council.

Province of Upper Canada, *Journal of Legislative Assembly*.

Upper Canada and Canada, Petitions for Land Grants and Leases, R.G. 1, L3, Vol. 340. Petitions submitted to the Executive Council of Upper Canada and the United Province of Canada by applicants for land grants, 1791–1867.

Upper Canada Sundries, R.G. 5, A1, Vols. 74, 93, and 173. Letters, Petitions, and Reports received by the Civil Secretary from correspondents resident in North America, 1766–1840.

Miscellaneous

British and Foreign Bible Society Archives (BFBS). Russia Agent Books 125, 137, 142, 149.

Congregational Council for World Mission (formally the London Missionary Society). Russian Correspondence (CCWM).

Friends House London. Archives of various Quakers to Russia, 1819–1865 (FHL).

Public Record Office, London (PRO). Foreign Office Files 65/842, 837, 852, 856, 861, 888, 892, 181/510. Correspondence of the Foreign Office with Mennonites in Russia and the Government of Canada.

Index